News from Afar

*Ezra Pound and Some
Contemporary British Poetries*

News from Afar

Ezra Pound and Some Contemporary British Poetries

edited by
Richard Parker

Shearsman Books

Published in the United Kingdom in 2014 by
Shearsman Books Ltd
50 Westons Hill Drive
Emersons Green
BRISTOL
BS16 7DF

Shearsman Books Ltd Registered Office
30–31 St. James Place, Mangotsfield, Bristol BS16 9JB
(this address not for correspondence)

ISBN 978-1-84861-364-5
First Edition

Cover
'Here's your fucking light, Shithead: Marie Curie runs towards Ezra
Pound with a flask of light' (oil on canvas) by Allen Fisher,
reproduced by permission of the artist.

CONTENTS

News from Afar

Richard Parker

"Here's Your Fucking Light Shithead": Ezra Pound and Contemporary British Poetry

"This country is really supposed to be on the eve of a xtzbk49ht
(parts of this letter in cypher)"
Canto XXXI

This volume brings together some of the most gifted voices in contemporary British poetry to discuss the importance of Ezra Pound to their work and the work of other British poets and authors. Many of these writers, like Pound, write poetry in which formal innovation is a necessary concomitant to intellectual innovation; they are poets that in less testing times might have been termed the avant-garde. I concentrate on this cadre unapologetically and in the belief that if Pound is to have a legacy in Britain it must involve such practices, though Pound's influence extends beyond the *avantist* ghetto. This collection is preceded by *Sons of Ezra: British Poets and Ezra Pound*, a volume edited by James McGonigal and Michael Alexander that features essays about the importance of Pound to Edwin Morgan, Donald Davie, Charles Tomlinson, Gael Turnbull, Robert Crawford, William Cookson, Roy Fisher and Douglas Dunn as well as, at a somewhat further heft from Pound studies, Hugh MacDiarmid and Robert Graves. In his contribution Crawford, an insightful and central critic of modernism, sums up the position of many poets writing nearer to what might be termed the poetic mainstream, refusing point-blank to engage with Pound as a political poet: "As regards politics, Pound was a vicious nincompoop" (178). Many of today's non-mainstream political poets might well agree that Pound was vicious, and perhaps most vicious in his criticism, in which he introduced a vital, clarifying, encouraging viciousness. This is just the viciousness that Keston Sutherland diagnoses in the first piece of this book—and it cannot be disassociated from his politics. To think of him as a nincompoop, political or otherwise, is to forego much that he achieved in his prose criticism; the essays on Imagism, "How to Read" and his other great contributions to the modernist aesthetic. Pound's vicious invective would be a crucial building block in the foundations of modernism, as well as being a contributing factor to the direction of his political involvements in the 1930s. Crawford further elaborates on difference between the "Sons of Ezra" and the poets discussed in this collection, imagining a fantastic version of Pound: "I wish he had written with more deft, gentle humour, and striven less to infernalize all his enemies" (178); a Pound-lite, suited to Faber's current list or the poems pages of the *London Review of Books* is what Crawford would have, a character of little appeal to the urgently experimental strands of British poetry in which I am interested and one who will not be found in this volume.

In his essay on Andrew Crozier's Poundian inheritance Alexander Howard usefully sets up such resistance in British poetry to Pound – or Pound's avant-gardism – as a product of the Movement, a group of poets who instigated a wholesale anti-modernist realignment of taste in Britain around the mid-twentieth-century which Howard calls a "conservative and distinctly parochial redefinition of literary taste" (112). The line of succession from Pound to the contemporary British poets in this volume is not, then, through the Movement, not the British "Sons of Ezra", but, for the most part, via a bridging generation of American poets – prominent among whom are those collected in Donald Allen's *The New American Poetry*. The New American Poets took up the baton of experimental Poundianism where their British *confrères* refused it – and these essays repeatedly argue that the mid-century U.S. poets are of greater interest to the British writers addressed here than the British poets of the period. All of *The New American Poetry*'s most important figures had complex and fruitful relationships with Pound as readers, and many of them, including Charles Olson, Robert Duncan and Allen Ginsberg, had significant personal exchanges with him. Olson met, "saved"[1] and, in turn, despised Pound at St. Elizabeths; Duncan reinvented the Poundian inheritance as synthetic Romantic Baroque; Ginsberg met Pound in Venice and miraculously extracted his famous late retraction of his abiding anti-Semitism, that "stupid suburban prejudice" (Reck 57), there. Olson's Projectivist undertaking is certainly Poundian in its group-forming intent, as well as in many *points de repère* in its formal ambitions, while both Olson's and Duncan's "open fields" are self-consciously Poundian. Ginsberg less frequently recalls the Pound of *The Cantos*, but that vein of muscular interaction with traditional forms that characterises Pound's early verse, and which introduces his distinctive modernism under the guise of the studied hard work of the poet-artisan, is repeated by Ginsberg, who exercises an interest in adapting traditional forms from within an unusual subjectivity that runs counter to the reactionary parochialism of the Movement.

While formal innovations are accepted and fundamental to both Projectivist poetics and Beat Poetry, alongside Pound's critical perspicacity and even his epistolary style – the modernist's politics and political praxis are most certainly not acceptable. Pound is a poet – in Duncan's, Olson's and Ginsberg's versions of him – whose selective abilities are suspect. For the endlessly eclectic Duncan, Pound was a poet who cannot chose and who, implicitly, mis-chose his political allegiances at the time of the century's greatest conflagration. Olson's disappointment with Pound follows a similar route, with an initially energising interaction at St. Elizabeths coming to frustrate Olson, pushing the younger poet towards a realignment of the primacy of mind over body that he perceived in Pound and therefore onto the Projectivist verse of *The Maximus Poems*.[2] Ginsberg neutralises Pound's threat, writing that

> anyone with any sense can see it as a humour, in that sense part of the drama – you manifest the process of thoughts – make a model of the consciousness and anti-Semitism is your fuck-up like not liking Buddhists but it's part of the model as it proceeds – and the great accomplishment was to make a working model of your mind – I mean nobody cares if it's Ezra Pound's mind – it is a *mind*, like all our minds, and that's never been done before – so you made a working model all along, with all the dramatic imperfections, fuck-ups – anyone with sense can always see the crazy part and see the perfect clear lucid perception-language-ground. (*Composed on the Tongue* 8-9)

At this point we reach the departing point with the British Poundians contained in this volume with the New American Poets. In contradiction to Ginsberg – at least for those deciding on the extent of Pound's treason, and for Pound himself, and anyone wishing to read him seriously – the matter of whose "mind" or "fuck-up" we see modelled in *The Cantos* actually *is* of some import; to suggest it is as interchangeable as the great singular Beat-Romantic self/consumer is to write off Pound's project rather violently.

Through the 1950s and '60s this American reading that posits an Ezra Pound who, in spite of his manifest importance as formal innovator and literary critic, fails to make the political choices that seem elementary to the liberal consensus of the period, remains dominant. For Olson, Duncan, Ginsberg and others, the trick was to present a Pound whose political sensibilities could be dismissed in their entirety: to ignore him as a political writer while adopting his formal and critical inventions from within something approaching a vacuum. Elizabeth Bishop produced the nadir of this tendency with "Visits to St. Elizabeths" (1950); which builds to the following list:

This is the soldier home from the war.
These are the years and the walls and the door
that shut on a boy that pats the floor

to see if the world is round or flat.
This is a Jew in a newspaper hat
that dances carefully down the ward,
walking the plank of a coffin board
with the crazy sailor
that shows his watch
that tells the time
of the wretched man
that lies in the house of Bedlam. (*Poems, Prose, and Letters* 127)

Bishop's accretive method reduces Pound, through its child-like con-
struction and pat thumbnails of his ward-mates, to a madman. It thereby
offers a far less threatening poet than a Pound unchained, sane *and* fascist.
The double meaning of "lies", thickens the image – either Pound "lies in
the house of Bedlam" in that he has been incarcerated there, or he has lied
in order to get there an evade his just punishment for treason. This position
does not just state that Pound's political beliefs were wrong, but insists his
whole method of political understanding and communication – his entire
output as a political poet, and, thus, *The Cantos* – can be dismissed as an
aberration, something both mad and/or bad and separate from Pound's
formal innovations.

In spite of their continued championing of Pound after Britain had
abandoned him, the New American Poets were, then, centrally ambivalent
about Pound – and the difference in attitude towards Pound between today's
British avant-gardists and their American forebears is important. As Gavin
Selerie writes, "[g]iven the prevailing conservatism of British poetry, Pound's
articulation of what is valuable in the tradition and his model of a re-formed
poetics still resonated in a later era" (216) going on to state that "Olson and
Ginsberg negotiated a way through the negative features of Pound's ideology,
and these manoeuvres fed into the experimental British scene from the
late 1950s on." (216) It is unarguable that while the New American Poets'
strategy of neutralising Pound's ideological inheritance did indeed ease the
passage of the poet's legacy to later generations, it is in part the *reinstatement*
of Pound's approach to the political that is of primary importance to many
of the poets under discussion in this volume. J.H. Prynne's position does
not go much further than Crawford's in this regard, suggesting that Pound's
"overall grasp of political thought in any complexion was close to infantile"
(Prynne/Sutherland 206). Prynne's poetics, however, would offer routes into
a far more involved Poundianism, as we shall see.

If we wish to identify a British Poundian poetry of more relevance than
that of the "Sons of Ezra" we must reclaim Pound as an avant-gardist, and, in

contrast to the New American Poets, it is perhaps time that serious readers of Pound, and serious writers using his example in their work, must also reclaim him as a political poet. Robert Hampson points us towards this realisation in his essay on Eric Mottram, writing that reading Pound, as studied in the Mottram manner, "forced a confrontation with the relationship between poetry and politics (that in Yeats or Eliot was obfuscated or side-stepped)" (90). Selerie also implies a similar engagement in his essay, while younger, post-Poundian and post-Prynnian, writers such as Danny Hayward and Laura Kilbride foreground the utility of Pound as a political poet – a marked development from the "confrontation" Hampson and Selerie describe.

This double reclamation is what marks out this collection and contemporary British thinking on Pound: all of them in one manner or another adapt formal innovations broached by Pound, and the most successful ones, I would argue, make use of Pound's example as a political poet as well. Which isn't to suggest that anti-Semitism, fascism or even Social Credit and Gesellite economics are aspirations of today's political poets. Many of the poets discussed here tend to be more implacably opposed to the politics of the right than the liberal consensus that damned Pound at the time of the Bollingen prize; and their alignment is representative of a general tendency in Britain's experimental poetry scene. In fact, Pound's return to Britain comes at a time when much of the period's poetry is shaped by a concern with the oppressive and liberatory powers of language as displayed in the poetry of Prynne and those that have followed him, a lineage that descends to Prynne from Pound via Olson and Ed Dorn, as Ryan Dobran and Joshua Kotin demonstrate. These poets recognise the immense persuasive force of Pound's poetic-political rhetoric, and the underlying connection between this aspect of his thought and his technical innovations and critical aperçus. Pound here is an American Augustan, a poet for whom the question of how to address political concerns in a public poetry is central.

The central Pound for such poets is exactly the Pound that neither the New American Poets nor Crawford (nor, perhaps, even Prynne) can stomach – a man apoplectically sacrificing his judgement upon the altar of his rage. In his piece "In Memory of Your Occult Convolutions" Sutherland captures the essence of this Pound with an extended collage of Poundian invective. This is a Popian Pound, pursuing a combined political/aesthetic/moral criticism that Duncan and Ginsberg optimistically hope might be useful shorn of its anger – hoping that the anger distorts elements in the poetry that are recoverable if we extract them. Sutherland proves, however, the centrality of this mode – exactly that desire to "infernalize all his enemies" – to Pound's political, critical and aesthetic senses. Elsewhere Sutherland has written that

Nietzsche's philosophy [...] is so intensely dependent on its pageant of idiots that it couldn't exist for a single untimely moment without them. [...] [T]he same is true for Pound's poetry and essays, which everywhere project, mock and vilify the halfwit incapable of being bucked up by beauty, hearing the subtle measure of Pound's verse, or correctly despising Carlo Dolci, as the perennial "Mr. Buggins" cannot.[3] (*Stupefaction* 5)

The Cantos and Pound's criticism become a modern *Dunciad* and *Peri Bathous* respectively. The objects of Pound's rage and the rage itself are shown to be at the heart of Pound's project; invective *is* Pound's poetry, and as such is unavoidable for a Poundian poetics. To dismiss Pound's politics as "fuck up" is to dismiss all of Pound.

Danny Hayward's "Or Storming the Shopping Centre: Poetry, Competition, Pound, *Quid*" places this connection in the context of a generation and of the specific political anxieties of that generation. The Pound and Wyndham Lewis of *BLAST*, a signal moment in early-twentieth-century infernalizing, are shown to predict *Ira Quid*, a publication which is the expression of the indignation of a poetic generation, as well as being a conscious infernalization every bit as violent as *BLAST*. Sean Pryor's essay "Some Thoughts on Refrigeration" develops this concern to connect Sutherland's *The Stats on Infinity* (2010) to Pound's *Homage to Sextus Propertius* (1919). Pryor maintains the centrality of contemporary political consideration in both pieces, and proceeds to demonstrate that connection through a powerful close reading.

Laura Kilbride demonstrates a similar utility in Pound's invective for the radical leftist poet Anna Mendelssohn; a poet for whom an interest in Pound might seem unlikely. As Kilbride's essay demonstrates, however, an ear for Pound's invective does not obviate the need to criticise Pound, as Mendelssohn does fulsomely, often in a mode clearly derived from Pound. This rebarbative reaction to Pound in Poundian terms is a feature of many of the poets addressed here; Allen Fisher's poem "Atkins Stomp" (first published in *Brixton Fractals* in 1985 – and contextualised here by Juha Virtanen), which co-opts Pound's language of transcendence in terms of the far-right politics of the 1980s, captures some of this, as does his painting, "Here's your fucking light, Shithead: Marie Curie runs towards Ezra Pound with a flask of light" (1988), which is reproduced on the cover of this volume and depicts an enraged Marie Curie pursuing an aged Pound in a Cold War/Thatcherite waste land. Mendelssohn and Ian Sinclair also emerge from this scene, as do many of the poetries described by Hampson and Selerie. While

David Vichnar primarily connects Pound to Sinclair through a shared, historiographical interest in psycho-geography, it is also clear that Sinclair's Pound is one connected with the political topography of 1980s London. Gareth Farmer's essay on Veronica Forrest-Thomson's Pound adds another approach to this nexus, with a careful reading of Forrest-Thomson's testing of the Poundian rhetorical programme within a recognisably Prynnian method.

§

Just as McGonigal and Alexander stretched their conception of the contemporary to allow Graves and MacDiarmid into *Sons of Ezra*, the conception of the "contemporary" held in this volume is flexible enough to accommodate the deceased, such as Forest-Thomson and Mendelssohn, and more than forty years of poetic history. I would suggest that the contemporary moment of critical appreciation of Pound that we are currently experiencing began in the 1960s, with the contributions of Donald Davie, crucially present at the University of Essex from 1964 till 1968 (his key work on Pound, *Ezra Pound: Poet as Sculptor*, appearing in 1964), and Eric Mottram, a leading propagator of Poundian critical sense and poetics at King's College London from 1960 until 1990. Though Davie is the better-known poet, his Movement stylings are some way from Pound, and would seem to fall into the anti-camp delineated by Howard. His contribution to *Sons of Ezra* reveals this clearly; he admits that "the Poundian practices I defended for in theory, I could not make work in practice" (*Modernist Essays* 229), going on to quote from his poem "Mickiewicz in England", written "conspicuously, if not very inventively, in one of the styles of Pound's *Cantos*." (229) A brief quote will serve to show Davie's failure to approximate a persuasive Poundian voice:

> Did Belloc baulk, did Pound protest
> When Saintsbury found Sienkiewicz unlicked?
> Who quoted Kochanowski, and to cap
> What Latin tag? Who cared
> That he was salvaged from Cyrillic script,
> The Ronsard of Czarnólas? (230)

The iambic tendency, the rolling syntax and the readily traceable argument from statement to statement, all mitigate against Davie having any profound understanding of either Pound's prosody or argument – a supposition which is entirely dismissed, however, by Davie's ground-breaking analysis of the mechanics of Pound's verse in *Poet as Sculptor* – a work cited as paramount in both Hampson's and Selerie's accounts of British Poundian poetics.[4] Davie's simultaneous understanding and misunderstanding of Pound shall remain mysterious, and though his contribution to Pound studies endures, his was not the voice to pass on Pound's poetics.

As Hampson demonstrates, Mottram produced more satisfactory poetry in the Poundian vein than Davie, and the length and inter-connectedness of his time in London allowed him a thoroughgoing influence on the generation of critics and poets that passed through his seminars at King's College London, as well as those he encountered at the numerous events he organised showcasing new poetry elsewhere in the city. Hampson makes it clear that it is Mottram's intervention, as an evangelical Poundian also committed to the continuing project of new poetry, that marks the beginning of "now" in contemporary Poundian poetry in Britain, and this volume therefore includes both Hampson's memoir and Amy Evans' retrieval of a symptomatic essay by Mottram on Pound from the archive at King's, with the intention that they should serve as keystones for this volume's argument about Poundian poetics in Britain today.

Selerie's essay extends the narrative from Mottram's circle to suggest some of the variousness with which Pound's precepts have been taken up and reacted against in London over recent decades. Like Hampson's piece, with which Selerie occasionally disagrees, this paper is a valuable contribution to the historiography of Pound in British poetry and should likewise be considered one of the keystones of this collection.

§

Of the poets addressed in this book it is Geoffrey Hill that comes closest to the dualism regarding Pound of the New American Poets. In *Scenes from Comus* (2005) we find:

> Nothing is unforgettable but guilt.
> Guilt of the moment to be made eternal.
> Reading immortal literature's a curse.

> Beatrice in *The Changeling* makes me sweat
> even more than Faustus' Helen, let alone
> Marlowe's off-stage blasphemous fun with words

> or Pound's last words to silence. Well,
> let well alone. The gadgetry of nice
> determinism mákes, breáks, comedians.

All the better if you go mad like Pound
(*grillo*, a grasshopper; *grido*, a cry from the fields).
The grief of comedy | you have to laugh. (66)

We all know that Pound wasn't mad, even Bishop, with that lie/lie pun, acknowledges the convenience of denoting him as such; we all know that that pose was a fiction as functional as the New Americans' discarding of the Poundian invective. The myth of Pound's late silence was also a convenience, convenient to Pound and a family wishing to avoid further scandal; and, conveniently for Ginsberg, a deep, ponderous silence can be tantamount to an apostasy. Perhaps we might forgive Hill his claim for Pound's madness in the context of his late sequences, all of which are written primarily in the confessional mode: it is really Hill that is mad here. In fact, Hill's version of Pound's mad silence isn't quite the exculpatory silence Ginsberg enjoys. Rather, it is a silence in the face of the great works of Hill's predecessors, Thomas Middleton, William Rowley and Christopher Marlowe, great tragedians, for whom Pound is relevant for his own apparently tragic life; his late silence equivalent to the silence at the conclusion of *Hamlet*. That Pound was in any way a tragic figure is of course a reformulation of the New Critical dualism (it was of course the fascist/anti-Semitic tragic flaw that was to blame, not anything more central to Pound's aesthetic sensibility) – but at least it's a more complex reduction than Bishop's.

Besides, as Mark Scroggins demonstrates, Hill's connection of Pound to Ruskin is revelatory and shows a profound understanding of Pound's aesthetic sense that is of great use. In fact, Sutherland's insistence that it is necessary to Pound's aesthetic project that the poet "vilify the halfwit incapable of being bucked up by beauty" (*Stupefaction* 5) sounds like a militant version of the Ruskinian aestheticism that Hill insists upon.[5] But that he couches it in a rhetoric some of the way towards the British mainstream, Hill is very much in agreement with Sutherland and Mendelssohn.

Tony Lopez, a quite different poet from Hill, should perhaps be grouped with Hill here, as another poet that employs Pound's historical sense, or, more accurately, his historiographical sense. Lopez, however, describes a technique that is elaborated out of Pound's fragmentary, innovative late poetics that is quite removed from Hill. Whereas Hill's primary poetic lifting from Pound is the same synthetic Anglo-Saxonism that Michael Alexander picks up and runs with in his Pound-inflected Anglo-Saxon translations (the reader might compare Alexander's *The Earliest English Poems* [1966] and *Beowulf* [1973] with Hill's *Mercian Hymns* [1971]), Lopez, like Iain Sinclair, uses an extrapolated modernism that goes beyond the limits of Pound's experimentalism to address cultural and historiographical concerns that are intimately connected with Pound's project.

§

This volume collects a series of translations in self-consciously Poundian styles, as well as an essay on Poundian / Zukofskian traductory practice. Pound's achievements as a translator are more frequently emulated by the poets in and around the British mainstream than the rest of his work; Christopher Logue, David Harsent, Seamus Heaney and Alice Oswald are all his "sons" in this respect, openly accepting the influence of his example and producing works that reproduce some of the cadences he uses in some of his translations. Michael Alexander's Anglo-Saxon translations for Penguin must be considered among the central vehicles of distribution for one of these kinds of Poundian translation. *Cathay* (1915) and "The Seafarer" (1911), rather than *The Cantos*, are the points of reference here, texts which, through their innovations, would prove medial to the project of *The Cantos*, and which safely pre-date the vicious nincompoopism of the 1930s while also eliding the particular contextual references that colour even much of his early work. *Cathay* introduces a manner of translation that is timeless and, in some senses, neutral – something close to a translatorese readily applicable to all styles and ages; Eliot's quip that "Pound is the inventor of Chinese poetry for our time" (*Selected Poems* xvi) is not entirely complimentary; Lewis calls this innovation Pound's "translation racket" (*Pound/Lewis* 234).

Eliot was the inventor of Pound having been the inventor of Chinese poetry in English for our time, and Harry Gilonis must be the inventor of the Poundian translation racket for the contemporary moment. Harry Gilonis and Robert Sheppard both attempt refurbishments of Pound's far-Eastern translations here, with Gilonis retranslating poems from *Cathay* in a manner that sounds little like its recent imitators, and Sheppard translating Li Shang-yin in a style that is again far from the sonorities of Pound's Fenollosa period. In "How to Read" Pound writes that "Before I die I hope to see a few of the best Chinese works printed bilingually, in the form that Mori and Ariga prepared certain texts for Fenollosa, a "crib", the picture of each letter accompanied by a full explanation." (*Literary Essays* 39) Both of these sets of translations are deeply indebted to the Poundian processes suggested here. While neither reproduce the ideograms, they both attempt to mime the act of deciphering such ideograms in all their non-English complexity. In that respect their translations can be read as something like the "cribs" that Pound valorises, in all their partialness and fragmentariness.

Alex Pestell's essay on Michael Kindellan and Reitha Pattison also looks at a translation practice that is doubly Poundian, highlighting a procedure derived from Louis Zukofsky's (itself complicatedly Poundian) homophonic technique to approach the work of Bertran de Born, a key figure in Pound's early engagement with the poetry of the troubadours.

Tim Atkins' "Happiness" is the final piece in the book and presents a unique blend of essay, meditation and poetry. Atkins is a translator in and out of the Poundian tradition, his extensive translations of Petrarch, which have appeared in a number of volumes, feature a welter of post-Poundian free-translation techniques. The piece here announces itself as "a Translation of the 10 Buddhist Ox-Herding Poems", material that Pound would have been unlikely to translate, though Atkins makes implicit use of and explicit reference to Pound's traductory practices throughout. It offers an account of Atkins' passionate reading of Pound; a Pound defused not through Bishop's condescension or Ginsberg's wishful thinking, but by an insistence upon and proving of (in both senses) the great love that lies at the heart of Pound's craggy project. As Atkins concludes, partly in defiance of Pound but also in affirmation, "happiness is the only economy" (322).

§

The Cantos is the defining political poem of its era and thus any poets of whatever political persuasion attempting to write a public verse in English must inevitably encounter it. This volume displays a variety of uses to which Pound has been put by British poets writing in the contemporary moment that runs from Mottram to Now. It is in the fields of political writing, historiography and translation that Pound is most useful for these poets, and in which his experiments have been extrapolated away from his work to the furthest extent. To be a practicing Poundian today is to be outside of Pound's purview in terms of his signature tones, techniques and politics; yet it is necessary to have passed along Poundian paths to have arrived at such a point.

Notes

[1] In a note that Pound made at the time of Olson's visits to St. Elizabeths Pound insists that "Olson saved my life". A facsimile letter containing this statement is printed in Julien Cornell's *The Trial of Ezra Pound* (71).

[2] See Olson's memoir "GrandPa, GoodBye", collected in *Charles Olson and Ezra Pound: An Encounter at St. Elizabeths*.

3 See Pound's *ABC of Reading* (26) for a gloss on "Mr. Buggins".

4 Davie was Ph.D. supervisor to and, later, colleague of J.H. Prynne. Prynne, in his turn, via important personal correspondences with Olson, Dorn and other American poets, opened an important line of communication between Cambridge and the American avant-garde. Ryan Dobran notes Davie's acknowledgement of Prynne's collaborative assistance in a footnote to his paper in this collection, noting about the book's chapter on Cavalcanti that "[s]ome pages of Chapter VI derive immediately from conversations with J.H. Prynne" (*Poet as Sculptor* vi).

5 "Pound / was a Ruskinian, so it works out, so it // fits and sits fair to being plausible; / which is our métier." (*Without Title* 52)

Works Cited

Alexander, Michael. *Beowulf.* London: Penguin, 1973.

——. *The Earliest English Poems.* London: Penguin, 1966.

Alexander, Michael and James McGonigal (eds.). *Sons of Ezra: British Poets and Ezra Pound.* Amsterdam: Rodopi, 1995.

Bishop, Elizabeth. *Poems, Prose, and Letters.* New York, NY: Library of America, 2008.

Cornell, Julien. *The Trial of Ezra Pound.* London: Faber, 1966.

Davie, Donald. *Ezra Pound: Poet as Sculptor.* London: Routledge & Kegan Paul, 1964.

——. *Modernist Essays: Yeats, Pound, Eliot.* Manchester: Carcanet Press, 2004.

Fisher, Allen. *Brixton Fractals.* London: Aloes Books, 1985.

Ginsberg, Allen (ed. Donald Allen). *Composed on the Tongue.* Bolinas: Grey Fox, 1980.

Hill, Geoffrey. *Mercian Hymns.* London: André Deutsch, 1971.

—— . *Scenes from Comus.* London: Penguin, 2005.

—— . *Without Title.* London: Penguin, 2006.

Olson, Charles (ed. Catherine Seelye). *Charles Olson and Ezra Pound: An Encounter at St. Elizabeths.* New York, NY: Pentagon House, 1975.

—— . (ed. George F. Butterick). *The Maximus Poems.* Berkeley, CA: University of California Press, 1984.

Pound, Ezra. *ABC of Reading.* London, Faber: 1951.

——. (ed. T.S. Eliot). *Literary Essays.* New York, NY: New Directions, 1968.

——. (ed. Richard Sieburth). *Poems & Translations.* New York, NY: Library of America, 2003.

—— . (ed. T.S. Eliot). *Selected Poems.* London: Faber, 1948.

—— . *The Cantos.* New York, NY: New Directions, 1995.

Pound, Ezra and Wyndham Lewis (ed. Timothy Materer). *Pound/Lewis: The Letters of Ezra Pound and Wyndham Lewis.* New York, NY: New Directions, 1985.

Prynne, J.H. and Keston Sutherland. "Introduction to Prynne's Poems in Chinese". *The Cambridge Quarterly*, Volume 41, Number 1, March 2012.

Reck, Michael. "A Conversation between Ezra Pound and Allen Ginsberg", *Evergreen Review*, June 1968.

Sutherland, Keston. *Stupefaction.* Calcutta: Seagull Books, 2011.

——. *The Stats on Infinity.* Brighton: Crater Press, 2010.

Keston Sutherland

In Memory of Your Occult Convolutions

Low-brow reader, it shall be you; those who try to make a bog, a marasmus, a great putridity in place of a sane and active ebullience, from sheer simian and pig-like stupidity; half-knowing and half-thinking critics with one barrel of sawdust to each half-bunch of grapes; out-weariers of Apollo continuing in Martian generalities, it shall be you; all those with minds still hovering above their testicles; less determinate sorts of people who comprise the periphery; the diluters whose produce is of low intensity, some flabbier variant, some diffuseness in the wake of the valid; those who add but some slight personal flavour, some minor variant of a mode, without affecting the main course of the story; those who at their faintest do not exist, it shall be you; the starters of crazes whose wave of fashion flows over writing for a few centuries or a few decades, only then to subside, leaving things as they were, it shall be you; the communicators of known maladies, specimens for the good physician or neuropsychiatric aristocrat; those who prolong the use of demoded terminology; those who continue dangling in mid-chaos emitting the most imbecile estimates that vitiate their whole lifetime's production; those who acquire what is acquirable without having the root, it shall be you; conflaters of poetry with "lofty and flowery language", it shall be you; those who cannot follow the method of annihilating imbecility employed by Voltaire, Bayle, and Lorenzo Valla, it shall be you; the floribund; those who lick off the page in rapid, half-attentive skim-over; the half-civilized and barbarous and those who never have shed barbarism it shall be you; shaggy and uncouth marginalians it shall be you; those who are wholly muddled with accessories; those who cannot spot the best painting or who are absorbed in idle consternation at the defects of the tertiary painter; she who, content with her ignorance, simply admits that her particular mind is of less importance than her kidneys or her automobile, it shall be you; those who are blind to some part of the spectrum; those who are clumsy at languages; those who use vague general terms; those who ascribe ridiculous values to works of secondary intensity; those who neglect to omit all study of monistic totemism and voodoo; those who treat the ostrich and the polar bear in the same fashion, universalists undeterred by the precisions of zoology it shall be you; those who falsify their reports as to the nature of man, as also to their own natures, as also to the nature of their ideals of this, that or the other it shall be you; those who have nothing within them differing from the contents of apes; those who, rather than liking beauty, covet or make do with slither, sentimentalizing about beauty, and telling people that beauty is the proper and respectable thing; those who seek the kind of art they don't like, who read the classics because they are told to, who aspire to good taste but do not have it, who sham before a work of art; those who wish to be slobbered over by people with less brains than they have it shall be you; the vulgus, genus aegrum or grovelling; shareholders in the Marconi company; those who do not detest quackery; those of defective hearing; the sloppy, inaccurate and negligent; denizens of the fog and outer darkness it shall be you; the unserious who are the commoner brand it shall be you; those who obfuscate the lines of demarcation it shall be you; those of insufficient intelligence to tell whether or not a person is in good health and who cannot spot the lurking disease beneath the appearance of vigour it shall be you; those who endeavour conscientiously to be great but are not great it shall be you; those who do not exercise perfect control, or who control only a thing that has in it no energy it shall be you; the mystificateurs it shall be you; whoever skimps paper or screws about like Tacitus to get his thought crowded into the least possible space it shall be you; he who will never communicate with the greatest possible despatch; those who do not develop beyond the yeowl and the bark into the dance and the music, but keep up their yeowling and barking; those whose acorn does not yield an oak; the admirers of Shelley's Sensitive Plant; those whose lamentations jiggle to the same tune as A little peach in the orchard grew and who do not recover to write the fifth act of the Cenci, it shall be you; very good marksmen who however cannot shoot from a horse it shall be you; those who poetize more or less, between the ages of seventeen and twenty-three; those who do not have much mind or personality to be moved; those who go in for elaboration and complication rather than swiftness and violence; the gorgers on flummery and fustian; contemporary versifiers with their pests and abominations it shall be you; those who lack technique because they do not do the thing they set out to do, who take three pages to say nothing; those who have never seen a work of art because they are apt to want to buy the rare at one price and sell it at another; those who do not acknowledge that their art, like the art of dancing in armour, is out of date and out of fashion; those who do not write a poetry that can be carried as a communication between intelligent men; those who do not know what one means by great art, for they do not know that one means by great art something more or less proportionate to one's experience, it shall be you; those who make the grand abnegation, who refuse to say what they think, if they do think, and who quote accepted opinion, and who are vermin, treacherous to the past, it shall be you; those who sell defective thermometers to hospitals; those who are replicas of the editor of the *Atlantic*

Monthly; the affable, suave and moderate, all of them incapable of any twinge of conscience on account of any form of mental cowardice or any falsification of reports whatsoever; those who sin against the well-being of the nation's mind; those of so humble a mind as to profess incomprehension of the criminality of lacking intellectual interests, it shall be you; those whose personal vanity in reportage remains unabolished; doctors who try to tell you that the fever temperature of patients from Chicago is always lower than that of sufferers from the same kind of fever in Singapore, it shall be you; the magazine blokes; the local practitioner who disdains to make use of known prophylactics; those distinguished by mental laziness, lack of curiosity and the desire to be undisturbed, whose habit it nonetheless is to be very busy along habitual lines it shall be you; those whose erasers are in disorder; those whose abstraction has spread like tuberculosis; those who are just lumps of dead clay clogging up the system since they do not wish to distinguish the branches from the twigs it shall be you; those who transmit knowledge by general statement without knowledge of particulars; those who fill the student's mind with a great mass of prejudice and error; assistants in the successive dilutions; the hurried and usually incompetent; the dispersers and waterers down; those who contrived to allow the idea of liberty to degenerate into mere irresponsibility and the right to be just as pifflingly idiotic as the laziest sub-human, and whose exercise of almost "any and every" activity has been utterly regardless of its effect on the commonweal, it shall be you; displayers of appalling, blameless simplicity; those who, because they do not direct the will toward the light, do not concurrently slough off laziness and prejudice; those whose demand for the facts is not inexorable, it shall be you; the human deadwood still clogging the system; the saboteurs and suppressors of the searchers for Truth, adjuncts to the pillar of infamy; those who do not abandon a false idea as soon as they are made aware of its falsity, or a mis-statement of fact as soon as it is corrected; the treasonable and dastardly who may yet well be charming on the surface but whose fundamental perversion is damnable, it shall be you; those who are chosen for their sycophantic talents and not for their intellectual acumen or their desire to enliven; those who consider anything not from the 1890s as bumptious silliness; the pretenders who prosper by preventing contemporary ideas from penetrating the Carnegie library until they have gathered a decade's mildew or two decades' mildew; those who let printed inaccuracy pass unreproved; those who do not correct their errors gladly; those who are ignorant and who therefore have no criteria, it shall be you; those who say for the one-thousand-one-hundred-and-eleventh time that poetry is made to entertain; those whose statements are made to curry favour with those who sit at fat sterile tables, or are made in ignorance which is charlatanry when it goes out to vend itself as sacred and impeccable knowledge; those who like to be flattered into believing that the lordliest of the arts was created for their amusement; you, ut credo, a few buckets of water tied up in a complicated fig leaf, whose minds are circumvolved about you like soap-bubbles reflecting sundry patches of the macrocosmos, our author dotes forever on yourselves.

Amy Evans

"So I think a beginning has been made": Ezra Pound, Robert Duncan and Eric Mottram —Introduction to an annotated essay

Ezra Pound in the Eric Mottram Archive

Eric Mottram's papers are held in the Eric Mottram Collection at King's College London, where Mottram lectured from 1960 until 1990. The poet Bill Griffiths assembled and catalogued its contents. The full catalogue, completed in 1999, is available to the public on the College website (King's College London, "Archive Catalogues"). The archived material includes several boxes of unpublished academic conference papers and teaching notes. Mottram's Pound looms large in these unpublished notes, papers and essays. Pound is one of the dominant figures around whom Mottram based his teaching courses, which were rare at the time for their concentration on the critical reading of contemporary American poetry and prose.[1] These ground-breaking courses constituted the beginning of American Studies in the UK and are remembered fondly by students, several of who are, in turn, now lecturers specialising in poetry. Mottram organised his classes so as to explore categories such as "The City", "The Thirties" and "The Epic". He delivered versions of the essays that resulted from research in these areas as conference papers at various stages of their composition. Not all of the completed essays have been published. For example, whereas Mottram's work on epic led to an essay on Pound entitled "Pound, Whitman and the American epic transmission", which appeared in the volume *Pound in Multiple Perspective* in 1993, both of the major pieces grouped within work on "The City" remain unpublished (216-244). The two manuscripts, "Documents of city perception in America since 1945" and what appears to be a predecessor of this, "The city: Pound, Brown, Fuller", each open with Pound as the point of departure from which Mottram argues encyclopaedic investigations of poets and political and cultural thinkers.

In addition to Mottram's teaching material and academic papers, he compiled what is today one of the largest collections of twentieth-century small-press poetry publications in the UK. As a result, his archive is a rich resource of small-press poetry magazines relevant to the history of contemporary poetry, some of which are not available at larger research libraries such as the British Library. Copies of Mottram's own poetry collections and manuscripts lie among the archive's holdings. These demonstrate a creative outpouring as prolific as the scholarship with which it is evidently in dialogue. Pound features as an ever-present influence in Mottram's poetry. Several of the poems make this debt explicit by beginning with either epigraphs taken from the American poet or dedications offered to him, as in "Elegy 1: Wonders of Nature", which is dedicated to Pound and Kerouac.[3] In the collection *The Legal Poems,*[2] Mottram's embrace of Pound as a poetic forefather is particularly evident: the poem "Thirtysecond Legal" opens with an epigraph from Pound's Canto 92, "and their filth now observes mere dynamic". Pages later, "Thirtyfifth Legal" not only again begins with Pound in the epigraph, but also comprises a collage of Pound's poetry, as recorded in Mottram's own marginalia to a typescript of the poem. Epigraphs and dedications are not unusual in Mottram's poetry, espousing his ideas of international poetic community. Nevertheless, admirers of his at times difficult poetry, such as William Rowe, find distinctly Poundian engagements and shared sources in the creative work.[4] In this way, Mottram's volumes of poetry, which number in excess of thirty publications, are as much testimony to his engagement with Pound as are the manuscript essays and teaching notes. Uncovering the scholarly manuscript material and the now insufficiently well-known poetry together fully yields Mottram's Pound and the Pound whom younger British poets inherited from him. At the same time, among the critical work that has already appeared in print, discoveries – or rather, rediscoveries – remain necessary.

Beyond the Archive

Mottram's six published essays on Pound[5] include one that is of particular interest when exploring the impact of his scholarship and teaching on the legacy of Pound and American modernist poetry for twentieth and twenty-first century Anglo-American poetry. The essay, "Pound, Olson and *The Secret of the Golden Flower*"[6], is reproduced in this volume (pages 55-87) with new critical annotations. It originally appeared in 1972 in *Chapman* magazine, which was based in Edinburgh and edited variously throughout its history by George Hardie, Walter Perrie and Joy Hendry. Together, they produced 110 issues of poetry, short fiction, essays and reviews between 1969 and 2010. Due to its length, Mottram's essay was divided into two large sections in the same issue. A typographical slip in the title, "POUND, OLSEN [sic] and THE SECRET OF THE GOLDEN FLOWER", suggests the unfamiliarity of members of a then emergent Poundian lineage to some sections of the contemporary UK poetry readership, and in turn further highlights the valuable contribution of Mottram's research in promoting such work. The issue in which the essay featured was a special edition, "The Chinese Issue". Mottram's piece appeared alongside a review of his own *Rexroth Reader*, published the same year, and a review of Rexroth's two volumes of translations, *One Hundred Poems from the Chinese* and *One Hundred More Poems from the Chinese*.[7] The first part of Mottram's essay appears between these reviews and "Two Poems in [sic] War by Tu Fu" translated by Koef Nielsen. The second part constitutes the last item in the journal, following "Two Chinese Love Poems by John Scott". The issue featured several Chinese poems in translation, including "Seven New Translations from Li Ch'ing Chao" by Rexroth and Ling Chung, and a two-page piece by Dick Russell entitled "Pound, Fenollosa and the Ideogram".

The essay included the following abstract:

> *The Secret of the Golden Flower* is a Chinese yogic text of considerable philosophic importance. This article (which forms a chapter of a new book on which Mottram is currently working) examines the use made of the thought enshrined in this text by two major poets. (20)

Mottram's letters to the American poet Robert Duncan indicate that he envisaged the essay as the basis of a volume on Olson, referring to it in 1974 as "the first of the three pieces which so far appear in print of what I hope to be a book on Olson".[8] He clarified his plans as follows:

> The idea is to have a set of essays in themselves discrete and assembled around the idea of Olson: to be called the pawl post – which he uses in a *Maximus* poem – the post around which is bound wire for chain, navally, to hold a winch or cable-dispenser from running out. (134)

He makes clear that the work to create such a monograph lies in his reading of Olson within the Poundian tradition as outlined in the *Chapman* essay. It is reasonable to assume that he would have opened the intended study with its reappearance. Mottram did not go on to publish the essay in a book; nor did he publish his essays on Olson as a single volume. It is for this reason that its republication is worthwhile: the essay is no longer easily accessible, available via scarce editions of the magazine such as the copy held in the Eric Mottram Collection. In addition, the contents of the essay deserve tidying and annotation. Mottram's wide spectrum of contemporary and historical references can no longer be assumed, and his citational practice was to footnote sparingly and, indeed, sometimes erratically. Primarily, however, the essay demands further attention because its argument stands out amid the numerous lectures and essays that Mottram opens with statements of Pound's importance for his maps of poetry, society, philosophy and contemporary politics. It is conspicuous for the fact that, while Mottram's argument is as dense and wide-ranging as in his unpublished work on Pound, throughout this out-of-print essay Mottram remains focused on Pound, and on Olson in relation to Pound.

COMPOSITION

At the time of writing "Pound, Olson and *The Secret of the Golden Flower*", Mottram was working at King's College London, where he was lecturing in English and American Literature, and editing *Poetry Review* at the Poetry Society. He completed the essay in his first year as Editor, having been appointed while teaching at Kent State University in the USA and returning to the UK to organise the first issue. By the time the essay appeared in *Chapman*, Mottram's controversial editorship, which ran from 1971 to 1977, was entering its second year. The period known as the "poetry wars", and documented in a book-length study by Mottram's MA student, Peter Barry, had begun.[9] It is against a background of, and in debate with, these infamous hostilities between the *avant-garde* and poetic establishment that Mottram sought to increase scholarly and public awareness of American poetics, via both the research that he presented in his *Chapman* essay and his activities as Editor. The divisions dominated his editorship. Robert Vas Dias, Mottram's colleague at the Poetry Society, remembers him as a figure whose "eclectic and international"[10] interests provoked discontent as a consequence of both his publication of innovative poetries and his inclusion of more mainstream poets' work. Under his editorship, *Poetry Review* featured the work of such major *avant-garde* poets as John Ashbery, Basil Bunting, Roy Fisher, Ian Hamilton Finlay, Barbara Guest, Lee Harwood, Denise Levertov, Barry MacSweeney, Christopher Middleton, George Oppen and Gary Snyder. It also published more mainstream poets such as James Berry, Kevin Crossley-Holland, Elaine Feinstein, Michael Hamburger, George MacBeth, F.T. Prince, Peter Redgrove, Penelope Shuttle, Ken Smith and D.M. Thomas. More than four decades later, the period's disputes and Mottram's position in relation to them remain foremost subjects of UK-based poets' discussions, forming an influential and still relatively unmapped recent history of today's UK poetry scene.

Mottram considered his primary task as Editor to be the education of a UK readership in the Poundian tradition. In a letter to Duncan in September 1971, he lamented, "The Poetry Society receives hundreds of mss weekly and they are astonishing in their ignorance and laziness – very few of the aspirants have any sense of what has happened to poetry and science since 1900: the English ignorance of Pound, Williams, Zukofsky, Olson and, of course, Duncan, is abysmal." (Evans and Zamir, eds., 41) The wider reading public similarly disappointed him with what he often experienced as their steadfast intolerance of the poetry that he sought to promote. He received public criticism of his approach in the *Times Literary Supplement* and encountered additional obstacles in production due to complaints regarding content. Mottram gave lively accounts of both events to Duncan in the same letter of 1971:

> Dear Robert Duncan,
>
> First, to apologise, without exactly making futile excuses, for this long delay in replying to your encouraging and fertilising letter – and the fine contribution of poems. Let me say immediately that there have been times when I thought I'd give up this *Poetry Review* editing. [...] The *TLS* attacked my incipient editorship with fears that what they believe are my notorious avant-garde (they still use the term) and Black Mountain-barbaric tastes (they used the term "barbarisms") – but said, with aristocratic graciousness that "it will be fun to watch" – which at least, I suppose, has the amusement of being characteristically voyeuristic. Then I had trouble with the word "shit" in one of the poems – the printers objected: this became the opportunity for rumours to be spread that I was having serious trouble getting the whole thing out, and the printers' delays didn't help scotch that one. The *Times* gossip columnist phoned around – including me – trying to get newsworthy dope on it all: and failed to find any, which made him more irate… The whole thing was time-wasting and boring in the extreme, but had to be gone through with.[11]

Nevertheless, Mottram believed that with his editorial guidance, particularly his promotion of contemporary poets influenced by Pound, *Poetry Review* would prove a vehicle for real change. In the letter of 1971, he expresses a sense of achievement despite these considerable difficulties: "[t]he good part is that many people are looking forward to the first issue of the new regime, that young poets are responding to what they take as a[n] opportunity, and that bookshops who would never have stocked the PR earlier have ordered fairly well" (42). He reassures Duncan regarding Duncan's own contribution to the issue that "the printer finally made a very decent job of the typography, so you will not, I think, be irritated here" (42). He then takes pleasure recounting to Duncan that it also contains work by Michael McClure, Muriel Rukeyser, Gilbert Sorrentino, Gael Turnbull, Jeff Nuttall, Stuart Montgomery, Paul Evans, Bill Butler, Roy Fisher, dom sylvester houédard "and three young unknowns: Val Warner, Richard Miller and Allen Fisher" (42). He continues with an outline of the Winter issue, which includes Snyder, Ashbery, Feinstein, Tom Pickard, Bob Cobbing and Harry Guest "for a start – and others which I am deciding on now" (42), before summarising the wealth of contemporary poets detailed with the words "So I think a beginning has been made" (42). The *Chapman* essay constitutes a significant portion of Mottram's critical writing on Pound that shared this overarching goal to create a "beginning" for the reading of a new kind of poetry in the UK. He considered an important part of this starting point to be the creation of a fresh critical landscape for contemporary poetry that was itself inclusive of the contemporary in poetry and its relation to a tradition.

In addition to Mottram's lecturing and editing, he wrote the essay within a particularly productive period for his own research and organization of poetry readings. Shortly prior to its composition, he completed the book *Allen Ginsberg in the Sixties* (which was published the same year as the essay) and an article on Denise Levertov and others for the newly-launched *Parnassus: Poetry in Review*.[12] After writing the essay on Pound and Olson, he began the book *Paul Bowles: Staticity & Terror* and an article, "1924-1951: politics and form in Zukofsky", for the magazine *Maps*.[13] He was also constructing his "Confidence in America" teaching course. Another letter to Duncan at the time reflects that, despite feeling the loss of readings run by Paul Selby and held at the Better Books shop, he felt positive about the London poetry scene due to the *Poetry Information* series that he had started with Cobbing at the Institute of Contemporary Arts in London and what he considered to be improvements in the poetry readings programme at the Poetry Society (Evans and Zamir, eds., 94).

CREATIVE AND CRITICAL CONTEXTS WITHIN MOTTRAM'S WORK

In its comparative argument regarding Pound and Olson, the essay can be read alongside Mottram's unpublished poem, "Pound – Olson – Order".[14] It can also be placed together with a better-known essay among his published, critical works, as a fuller exploration of what he touches on in the essay "Pound, Merleau-Ponty and the Phenomenology of Poetry".[15] In this essay, which was published ten years later than the *Chapman* piece, he writes:

> In Canto 85 Pound meditates on the ideogram of total process, both substantive and objective – that concern with process which infuses Monty-Pearleau, Whitehead, Charles Olson and the post-Olson poets including Robert Kelly and the ethnopoetic figures in *Alcheringa*, New Series Vol 2. No. 2 – a record of the first international symposium of ethno-poetics in 1975:
>
> > But if you will follow this process
> > not a lot of signs, but the one sign
> >   etcetera
> >   plus always   Techne. . . .[16]

While at this point Mottram briefly compares the ideogrammatic content of the *Cantos* with process philosophy and poetics, in "Pound, Olson and *The Secret of the Golden Flower*", he extensively analyses Pound's engagement with "yogic" (more specifically, Taoist) thought and its relevance for younger poets such as Olson. In both essays, he is clear in his determination to read Pound's attention to ancient Chinese texts within what he receives as a secular twentieth-century philosophical tradition. In the *Chapman* essay, he continually removes or limits the most overtly religious assertions of the spiritual tradition that he discusses. He does so even while arguing for the importance of Pound and Olson's most unavoidably esoteric and occultist interests and exploring poems that are consequently among their most seriously engaged with religious philosophy. Furthermore, this focus on a yogic text accounts for the fact that in "Pound, Merleau-Ponty and the Phenomenology of Poetry", Mottram's distinctively political message is discernible to a greater extent than it is in his *Chapman* essay. All of Mottram's criticism is resolutely activist in its preoccupations and the two essays constitute companion pieces in this regard. Reading Pound against Merleau-Ponty, Mottram adopts the more explicitly socialist terms characteristic of most of his work in order to return to the same issues that guide the earlier comparison of Pound and Olson:

> Peace within process, for Pound, depended on the benevolent despot's ability to maintain stability, the pivot of the total process. He prefers Yong Tching to Locke or Milton in Canto 61; Mussolini

correctly cut back bureaucracy to create stable centralism. But, of course, such views were commonplace in the interwar years; strong leaders were to solve government rather than democracy or socialism. Heroes in the *Cantos* are exactly the heroes of the masses and their rulers – kings, emperors and the quasi-republican replicas. Divine right has to be transferred to "heroic vitalism". Pound's typical monism is a longing for subsumption in the One. His yearning for peace, within his warrior combativeness and constant intervention, is a ground base [sic] in the *Cantos*. [...] His discovery of Adams' *Law of Civilization and Decay* in the 1940s, with its structuring of history by cycles from an economic point of view, confirmed his more intuitive reading of rise and fall in cultures. The *Cantos* is an eminently practical work.

Pound's particularity of information continuously worked towards a poem demonstrating a refusal of what Merleau-Ponty also rejected as "high altitude thinking" (and both Rilke and Wittgenstein show a repeated understanding of the necessity to criticize any kind of supervisory vision in which the totalitarian authority is rooted), particularly that version which reduces "hinge and anchorage" to personal anarchism, a kind of enfeebling relativism. Clearly Pound found it hard to reconcile despotism with a refusal of what Wittgenstein termed the urge to the *übersichlich* stance. But dogmatic doctrine is relegated in both men, whatever their engagement in political action, Left or Right. (Mottram, 123-124)

CORRESPONDENCES: A TRANSNATIONAL CONTEXT

Mottram refers directly to the *Chapman* essay in a letter to Duncan soon after its publication in 1972 before sending him a copy in 1974. His doing so gestures towards an important transnational context for its argument, one that moves further still beyond both the archive and Mottram's published critical *œuvre*. In his letter, he presents the essay as a significant part of a particularly productive period of his life for his scholarly and creative writing. Mottram mentions the survival of this work during a demanding time in his life and employment. He begins by mentioning his poetry, before making Duncan aware of his new essay:

My own work has been ok in spite of the house-search and the removals: my poems in *The He Expression* are due from Aloes Press [sic; Books], and *Points of Honour* from Turret again. *Beau Fleuve* will also do a book in Buffalo. *Chapman* published a long piece on Olson, Pound and the Golden Flower, [. . .][17]

The letter colourfully reveals how, as both critic and editor, Mottram's engagement with a poetic tradition shaped by Pound is always part of an exchange between America and the contemporary scene in the UK. His invitations of established American poets such as Duncan to contribute to *Poetry Review* form one part of this dialogue. The correspondence further demonstrates and sustains this interdependent relationship. Duncan depended upon Mottram to be more informed about the UK's contemporary poetry and literary criticism, as well as censorship and obscenity trials, miners' strikes and the North-East poetry scene in all their affinities with Duncan's own concerns in Cold War America.

Duncan undoubtedly found the British academic all the more valuable a poet comrade for the recent loss of his life-long correspondent, Levertov. Duncan and Levertov's friendship eventually ruptured due to their escalating disagreements regarding Levertov's poems about the Vietnam War and, more generally, the duties of the protest poet in times of political crisis. Duncan describes how corresponding with Mottram provided a support while he was preparing critical work on Levertov: "I'd used writing to you to bring up matters I have to work out – an uncomfortable task – in critique of Denise's poems...]" (Evans and Zamir, eds., 53). Indeed, in many ways, Mottram provided the American poet with a replacement interlocutor with whom he could think through his most pressing concerns relating to poetry and politics. In the section of the correspondence that is contemporaneous with Mottram's Pound essay, he follows his announcement of its publication with a personal update that assumes and affirms an intimacy between the two poets' writing and a shared sense of purpose. He begins with an account of his recent publications, including a detailed account of the one he describes as "most important to me": "one on Bob Cobbing, placing his work as sound-text concretist in the perspective of that international scene" (95). This is followed by an account of a number of American literature projects:

My little Ginsberg book is out at last – and looks like being the first in a small series of books on English and American poets who need introducing to us all, at a serious rather than a journalistic level. Meanwhile I work at a piece on Zukofsky's political action in his poetry (for *Maps*), and another on Paul Bowles. (95)

He concludes with details of work that more directly addresses Duncan and his interests:

> This year's lectures on American literature I want to make around the theme of confidence – I start with Thoreau, Melville and Whitman, Henry Miller and Jack Kerouac: to examine the nature of confidence in self, the state, nature, the cosmos as it changes in your culture – the kind of appositions you make in "Passages" impress me here immensely and I shall use them in the second term: that is what I'm trying to get to. I wrote an article for *Parnassus* (at Herbert Leibowitz's request) recently – it is partly a criticism of Levertov's latest book, *To Stay Alive*, she will not like it, I'm afraid, since I criticize her strongly for her assumption that her shift from liberalism to what she calls a revolutionary position is relevant – to a European and a socialist, the astonishment is that she took so long and now boasts of it. It seems an affront to all those who sacrificed for revolutionary action in this century. [...] (95-96)

Duncan responds to such updates and to Mottram's more intensely discursive letters on poetry, philosophy and politics as an instructive part of a shared life of transnational contemporary poetry. He eagerly begins a second part of one reply "Back to our to-be-continued tale of the drama of poetics, fictions, and imperatives in our own time." (111)

It is of note that two of the essays by Olson with which Mottram constructs his comparative reading of Olson and Pound, *Against Wisdom as Such* and *Causal Mythology*, are those in which Olson is in direct dialogue with Duncan. Indeed, in the former, Olson quotes Duncan concerning the writing of Confucius, to whom Mottram devotes much of his argument in "Pound, Olson and *The Secret of the Golden Flower*". As a result, when considering the importance of Mottram's Pound for the next generation of poets, the *Chapman* essay can be triangulated with Mottram's two lengthy essays on Duncan. Far less well-known than his essays on Pound, both of these essays were published in Mottram's lifetime: "Heroic Survival through Ecstatic Forms: Robert Duncan's *Roots and Branches*", which featured in a book of essays edited by Robert Bertholf in the USA in 1979, *Scales of the Marvelous,* and "Robert Duncan: The Possibilities of an Adequate History and of a Poetics of Event", which appeared in 1988 in *Talus*, the small-press magazine that Mottram co-founded and co-edited based at King's College London.[18]

Mottram's correspondence with Duncan further informs this triangulated approach to the essay on Pound, recording his reading of both

Olson (and the Poundian poetics that Olson represents for Mottram) and the younger poet Duncan. The correspondence comprises an exchange of lengthy letters on poetics and politics between 1971 and 1979 and again in 1986. Griffiths discovered what he considered to be the uniquely extensive correspondence among Mottram's papers during his cataloguing of the archive and suggested it to Shamoon Zamir for publication as an important dialogue on contemporary poetry and politics. A former student of Mottram's, Zamir was one of the founding members of a department at King's College London dedicated to American Studies and to the teaching of poetry in the Poundian tradition. The resultant volume of letters was one of the last publications to emerge from the department before its closure in 2010 (followed by the continuation of its post-graduate programmes within an Institute of North American Studies). At the time of the *Chapman* essay's appearance, this new conversation in letters with a major American poet and fellow socialist was gaining momentum, having begun when Mottram wrote to Duncan in order to invite a submission for his first issue of *Poetry Review* in the Autumn of 1971. Mottram warmly refers to the letters that follow as "dissertation-letter[s]" (106) after Duncan apologises for a particularly lengthy reply (97). On Mottram's part, the debate that they contain functions as a continuation of much of the essay's explorations. For example, Duncan's discussion of a Promethean poetics takes up much of Mottram's argument in the essay regarding Olson and the poet's role in society (122-123). Indeed, the generally lively and affectionate, often very humourous exchange arguably reaches its peak regarding Olson, catalysed by Duncan reading Mottram's essays "Charles Olson's Apollonius of Tyana" and "Performance: Charles Olson's Rebirth Between Power and Love"[19] and declaring "How you open my mind where it had determined to be closed!" (122-123). Mottram's letters articulate his concerns that Olson encapsulates the risk of authoritarian power as well as the socialist potential of a figure who, on the one hand, is problematically upheld by "tribal" admirers as a visionary bard and, on the other, offers a politically powerful poetry (121-146). Annotations provided to the essay as it appears here include Mottram and Duncan's shared readings of Olson in the line of Poundian poetry.

Pound himself is a key co-ordinate for the correspondence between the two poets. Indeed, Mottram encouraged Duncan's involvement in *Poetry Review* in large part due to the latter's participation in a Poundian poetic tradition in his poetry, criticism and teaching. Duncan devotes much of *The H.D. Book*, an extensive study of modernism and its poetic legacy, to reading Pound and evaluating Pound's impact as a personal influence.[20] Mottram painstakingly collated the several published sections of this work during its lengthy composition by xeroxing serialisations as they appeared in journals between 1966 and 1988.[21] He subsequently created the UK's only near-complete copy of the volume available to the public. Duncan's text remained unpublished until as recently as 2011. As a result, for many years, Mottram's copy, kept in small blue binders in his archive, itself constituted a key resource for contemporary poets' access to and understanding of Pound and the modernist tradition. Mottram followed Duncan's teaching of Pound and his contemporaries just as closely. On occasions when he was unable to be in the States, he made arrangements for tape recordings of Duncan's lectures to be made and posted to him. One such lecture was "Pound, Eliot and HD: The Cult of the Gods in American Poetry", which Duncan delivered at Kent State University in October 1972.[22] These and other cassette tapes form a substantial part of the archive. The holdings related to Duncan are rich with details of the extent to which Mottram traced the interconnections of Pound and contemporary poetry, and illustrate how he believed Duncan's work to be as firmly rooted within the Poundian tradition as Olson's. Unsurprisingly, Duncan features prominently in his writing on Pound. For example, Mottram's unpublished essay on Pound, "Documents of city perception in America since 1945", moves from its focus in the opening two pages on the older American poet directly to Duncan by means of a handwritten insertion that quotes Duncan's "Dante Études". Later in the essay, Mottram refers to "The Multiversity," "Orders" and "The Soldiers" from Duncan's *Passages* sequence in *Bending the Bow*. Similarly, it is clear that when reading Duncan's essays and poetry, he was mindful of Pound: a page of his xeroxed copy of Duncan's "Man's Fulfilment in Order and Strife", which appeared in *Caterpillar* in 1969, is annotated with the note "NB Pound". He remarked in a letter to Duncan that the line "Poetry! Would Poetry have sustained us?" (*Ground Work* 40) from "Santa Cruz Propositions" importantly intersected with his critical work at the time on D.A. Levy and Amiri Baraka (then LeRoi Jones) as well as Pound's "Religion, oh, just another of those numerous failures resulting from an attempt to popularize art".[23]

POETRY AND THE "PRIESTLY"

The letters between Mottram and Duncan give full voice to the sympathies and tensions in Mottram's essay between what he presents as complex and atheistic occult teachings, in the form of the yogic text that he places at his argument's centre, and his socialist priorities. Similarly, the *Chapman* essay brings to the fore several of the major concerns of the letters and, ultimately, gives voice to what becomes the major difference between the two correspondents. Their mutual reflections on the nature of authority eventually developed into an, if not strained, certainly, on Mottram's part, directly challenging interchange regarding the role of faith and faith-based ritual in a poet's writing, tradition and reception. Mottram queries Duncan's unwillingness to re-examine his commitment to what Duncan's major essay celebrates in its title as "The Truth and Life of Myth" (1968).[24] The debate is worth quoting at length for its relevance to Mottram's essay, especially since the letters are not widely known.

Discussion of the "priestly" in poetry is prominent from the beginning of the correspondence. In his second letter to Duncan, Mottram praises Duncan's poetry for being "News that stays news: add risk that stays risk. It's the risk that is the sparking gap for the reader-participant. And stops the poet being a priest—the kind of poet who is valuable resist[s] disciples and beaten paths of content." (Evans and Zamir, eds., 43) Their debate on this matter gains momentum two years later when Mottram writes to Duncan in March 1973 politely criticising Duncan's former close ally Spicer for being a poet who "confuses the main issue of secular art by playing with dictatorial inspiration" (104). He moves to Duncan's own work with the following:

> A poem reveals us to ourselves when we make it: everywhere your work and your writing on your work proclaims that glorious secularity, which is one of the major reasons we respect it—and why Paul Evans and I were worried by the apparent Platonism in certain parts of *Opening of the Field*, you may recall! Your distinction between revelation and persuasion is crucial, since the godly poet is in charge of the persuasive revealers – that is, a faked fusion. It comes back, then, to something we spoke of before in our letters – the need to read myth without urging a return to the tribal and the shaman: to have an historical sense of the past cultures which actually produced the myths. [...] Again and again it turns on what kind of authority is accepted or bowed to enforcedly; the sense of the body's autonomous power and beauty; the way the word "nature" is used as alibi for action; the place of the man-made, created, in the nonmade cosmos. Your poetry has meant for many of [us] that kind of garden where the nonauthoritarian power is received – what Goodman used to call "natural power", the authentic magic of the artist's formants [sic], the artist not as a magian ally with some out-there system. Which is where I become sceptical of Castaneda's admirers – especially over here – I keep returning them to Frances Yates and E.M. Butler and the magus in European and

Mediterranean culture – not from chauvinism but from necessity not to ape Indian tribalism, or any other. (104-105)

Duncan responds within a week in strong agreement:

> # I think I am with you 100% in regard to the question of "Authority". Whatever reality I sense in God, in angels, in demonic invisibles, in the Unconkshuss [sic], in the Intellect, in the people (and being a creative imagination in all my entertaining of such entities, their reality has always the dubious character of the imagined), even where I might give them ultimate actuality, I would give them no inroad but rather the fiercer resistance to any claim to authority. Outside that is of the authority that the matter the artist is drawing from and re-creating has, which is the authority of materials. That is, I do find myself studying out the truth of some matter: the truth of all this God and angel and authority business in the leavings of Man. But I'll stand with H.G. Wells' noble resolve: if HE does exist, I will resist his claims OVER me. (108)

However, the dialogue eventually leads Mottram to express his concerns about Duncan's work more openly, writing in May 1973:

> I think now, in consideration of your last letters, that what perturbs me is that, in "authority", there is always an historical structure derived from a culture, and so many of the cultures we blandly take our authorities from (an objection to Jung for me) (and to Joseph Campbell) were and are authoritarian – they conserve and promote the authoritarian character, either in submissive or dominant condition (the ghastly twin spectre of destructive erotic need – what Burroughs calls evil: the condition of total need, or addiction – but I have gone into all that in my book on him). So that we are back in our objections to "tribal", in so far as it initiates into being nothing but a transmitter – again, this is where I part from Spicer's dictated messages, and feel nearer James Koller's "Messages" in that beautiful *Curriculum of the Soul* pamphlet of his. We have to, it seems to me, keep the action of discovering what has gone so wrong in the West, culminating in our time, completely historical and anthropological, resisting any opportunity to reduce cultures to common denominators, at least for the time being, since these are always authoritarian selections under the desire of the reducer. The

artist playing with Freudian or Jungian reduction is less safe, for instance, than with Lévi-Strauss' reduction (at least in him there is a knowledge of the "bricoleur"). As you say: "the leavings of Man". But are we really to descend into them in order to recover "images"? Where you wrote in *Caesar's Gate* – "Images and the language of dreams are not, Freud tells us, to arouse us but to keep us asleep" – I wrote marginally: "but only when we are asleep already". Living is not sleeping only, after all: with your H.G. Wells' resistance we have to place what I find my students attached to with tenacity – Pascal's wager, which I find timid and they find liberal and skeptically tolerant. *Caesar's Gate* is a fine metamorphosis of old self into the "total reading" – that's the phrase I do so like in your book. That and "'responsibility'", but then you've always borne witness to that, which is the centre of our respect. Thinking about conceptual art and poetry lately, and its invasions of New York and Bolinas, and its place here in the Fluxshoe group and one or two other people, their safety in the reconceived is so strikingly opposite to your own risks in the Field: your ill-kept garden which so struck me as the useful conception when I first read you. That is the point of release from that other authority – "Duncan" as he has become: the penalty, I suppose, of having worked so consistently to shape experience in the Field – but let it be said that a *recognizable* body of work is part of the necessity called *ethos* (Aristotle's word for character, I mean). But I do recall that A. says a man has no *ethos* till he is dead – and the death by fixed *ethos* before actual death is what a poet has to resist. A toast, then, to your rebirth in 1983. (117-118)

Mottram continues by re-calibrating Duncan's reply with the same crucial and motivating distinction upon which he depends in his *Chapman* essay for his exploration of the importance of yogic thought for Pound's poetry. He confronts Duncan about what he supposes to be an evasive shift of his own word "belief" to Duncan's term "imagination":

What I meant by *belief*, which you countered with *imagine* was: belief is the length of time and the tenacity with which the findings of imagination are maintained. How long do you hold discovery – in this case of the Devil? And in this case too, of the Devil in the context of "his" permanence in cultural history? (That the Devil might be woman is there in Burroughs and yourself maybe). Your term, "superstition" may be something of the order of *belief* in this sense – is what I was trying clumsily to say. Belief therefore is political and just at that point which nearly interested me the most in *Caesar's Gate* – where you place against Lorca's "line of outrage", his sense of sexual pollution, and his need to purge it, your own fine sense of the puritan purge being the centre of all purgations and the Nazi action in particular in your time, and in mine. Like: "The Maypole of Merrymount" and the burning clean of the pograms. Puritans as perverts – we've had our share here (I'm thinking of my own involvements in the trials of *Last Exit to Brooklyn* and the Unicorn Bookshop in Brighton, in the Sixties): they image invasions from devil-populated space beyond their bodies, and set about establishing cleansing stations. So that that "line" you draw with Lorca, between the passionate abandonment to Eros and the rejection of "sexual speculators and pollutors", is the most difficult of all to understand: it is the centre of what could possibly be meant by the obscene. (120)

Mottram then develops this reading further by drawing on LeRoi Jones and Paul Goodman:

Let me put with it – I'm not attempting anything else, since there's no solution – certainly no "final solution" – LeRoi Jones' *The System of Dante's Hell*, where his process is exactly that area you speak of in *Caesar's Gate*, and – taking the clue from the "line" – Paul Goodman's *Drawing the Line*: where he writes – "Once his judgement is freed, then with regard to such 'crimes' the libertarian must act as he should in every case whatsoever: if something seems true to his nature, important and necessary for himself and his fellows at the present moment, let him do it with more good will and joy. Let him avoid the coercive consequences with natural prudence, not by frustration and timid denial of what is the case; for our acts of liberty are our strongest propaganda". So he sets up the idea of a non-coercive community based on "natural authority" – or authority which [is] particular and useful for one thing and does not seek nor is allowed to be totalitarian. (120-121)

He concludes his argument by rejecting the "tribal" and asserting the role of the socialist and ecologically aware poet:

Like Galileo in Brecht's play – "Unhappy is the land that needs a hero". Goodman: "The separation of personal and political and of moral and legal is a sign that to be coerced has become second nature....Power over nature is not the only condition of happiness." And right at the end of the chapter I'm suggesting: "social initiation" not habitual satisfactions or substitutes (state-permitted) for them. That is: the tribal doesn't initiate, it repeats, the grid goes on and on. The purgation-state is tribal in this sense: it needs the linearity of utter reductive continuity. Back to your exact sense of Marx's Europe-haunting spectre being not his working class but "interference" – can I take interference as the non-coercive and initiative? That the socialist poet *invents* forms and anticipates that his life will be spent entertaining interference. To redefine authority as continual invention: but that still, I do see, leaves what to do with that "leavings" business. I don't really know whether I want any of the "leavings" as such unless they are Monteverdi, Beethoven, Stravinsky, Constable, Marvell – OK, you list them too! Art is not reductive tribal leavings. That seems to me the core of *Caesar's Gate* – the wastes Alexander feared are deeply involved in the whole idea of conquest which your "empire" of poetry images suggest to me. I'm thinking of where Lynn White (in Shepard [sic] and McKinley's *The Subversive Science*) says: ("The Historical Roots of Our Ecological Crisis") – "By destroying pagan animism, Christianity made it possible to exploit nature in a mood of indifference to the feelings of natural objects." And: "Both our present science and our present technology are so tinctured with orthodox Christian arrogance toward nature that no solution for our ecologic crisis can be expected from them alone. Since the root of our troubles are so largely religious, the remedy must also be essentially religious, whether we call it that or not. We must rethink and refeel our nature and destiny." (121-122)

In this way, Mottram offers an increasingly directive reading of Duncan's poetry to the poet himself, recapitulating for a period of over a year the very same poetics that his essay on Pound and Olson celebrates. It is in one of his most pointed assertions to Duncan that Mottram refers explicitly to yogic teachings: "But clearly, the yogic self-regulation is here with you all right; now for the sociality context" (107).

Duncan's attentive replies to Mottram do not appease the British Professor regarding the presence of what he perceives to be religion (rather than myth) in a socially responsible poetry and Duncan's own poetic practice in this regard. In letters to the British poet and painter Allen Fisher two years later in 1976[25], Mottram gives further voice to his dissatisfaction with

Duncan's position, as a poet writing in the Poundian tradition, concerning the correlation of prophecy and poetry. The discussion about, rather than to, Duncan is informed by Mottram's direct correspondence with the American poet. As he directs his questions about Duncan to Fisher, the letter demonstrates Mottram's participation in a community of poets together with whom he persistently and actively interrogated the work of the major American poets of his age on what he considered to be the most urgent questions of a Poundian contemporary poetics. In a letter written in early 1976 (the exact date of which is obscured in Mottram's copy), he reiterates his unease about the spiritual content of Duncan's poetry in relation to systems of power:

> I was thinking we ought to ask if Duncan's Return of the Gods is possible even as an *idea* of any value. In his introduction to Radin's *The Trickster*, Stanley Diamond quotes a Maori native-court testimony: "Gods do not die" / "You are mistaken... Gods do die unless there are *tohungas* (priests) to keep them alive". So is Duncan saying that the Return of the Gods can be promoted without the aid of intervention or agency? Or is the priest-shaman-druid business a *necessary* way of re-proposing gods? In any case, "gods" needs careful definition if it is not to be authoritarian necessity under priests and kings. Quite apart from whether the believer in the Return is speaking of the return of Deity "out there" or the return of the idea invented by men which is called Deity. The hermeneutics of the thing must be clear from the start here – which is precisely where I find so much hypocrisy in this whole shaman-druid business. It looks to me as if the poets want power at any cost. (n.p.)

In the preceding letter, dated 31 January 1976, Mottram is unequivocal in his secular approach to the Taoist tradition with which he frames his *Chapman* essay's argument concerning Pound and Olson. He begins the letter by differentiating the teaching of the *I Ching (The Book of Changes)* from systems that he condemns as "priestly":

> Re Druidics and Poetic Action from a Distance (*Necropathia*): which are part of the same mania: and we had better throw in Egyptianisms. It is a matter of what "prophetic" may mean, not too ambitiously. Vertical analysis and an understanding out of it that suggests direction – yes – Dante's direction of the will. But Druids are priests, agents, powermen, coercers, the Establishment, a closed

cult for Celts. Action at a Distance is the dream of power: end of Mailer's *An American Dream*, everywhere in Pynchon, dreams of power by nutty poets – no more than sticking pins in an effigy? The serious part may be this – and I went a little way into this in the *I[nternational] T[imes]* article ["New time and space structures" (1969)] some time ago – fields of energy which a slight alteration in may serve to warp into radical metamorphosis – the basis of the *I Ching* for instance. But that is not a priestly divinatory system, as far as I know. Gods and devils are action from a distance: and Druids indulged in human sacrifice. Celts were headhunters. (n.p.)

Mottram insists that this stance concerning the spiritual in poetry and society constitutes for him a necessarily political position. In the letter written in January, he continues:

Current occultisms and Druidisms and shamanisms are power ploys of poets wanting action at a distance. A hidden politics which smacks of anything but trying to discover what socialism might mean as a beneficial, democratic society. There's no society in Castaneda at all. O[ccultism], D[ruidism], and S[hamanism] are laboratories with white-coated acolytes tending the sacred flame of the sacrificial altar. Poetry of this area is loaded with the dreck or refuse of past ages, old clogging consciousness, round and round, as per *Finnegans Wake* –
    We need to examine the dramaturgy of power in operation *in any field*. The idea that poetic power is exempt leads directly to o-d-s. (n.p.)

What follows is a manifesto-like list of aims and methods such as "a. aim: the demystification of power: *not* Sinclair, Kelly, Grossinger, etc., or o[ccultism]-d[ruidism]-s[hamanism]. Fascisms thrive on the perpetuating of the mystification of power: secret rites, *The Balcony*, secret societies, occult havens, covens" and "b. aim – to expose the dramaturgy of all power situations – [...]". He signs off this detailed blueprint of poetic activism with the words, "These are just notes towards: we'd better think seriously about this, since poets we respect somewhat move now towards [...] political-religious flunkeyism. Yours, Eric". (n.p.)

A Living Tradition

Mottram's interaction with Duncan is the closest that he came to a direct dialogue with, and close befriending of, the poetic tradition that he traced from Pound through Olson. Unlike Olson and Pound, Duncan is an American poet with whom Mottram was able to connect in person, meeting him for the first time in London in 1968. The poets Jeff Hilson and Iain Sinclair recount how Mottram would entertain the members of his many at-home reading groups by pointing out where Duncan had sat on his sofa, during subsequent visits to his Guernsey Road flat in South London.[26] Zamir remembers how, during several such sessions, students worked their way through cassette tapes of Duncan's entire *Passages* sequence while it was being written and performed across America.[27] Mottram recorded these reading groups in his almost illegibly small handwriting in his diaries, together with the impact that British weather occasionally had on attendance.

Mottram reminds Duncan of his absent-presence in London in a letter written in 1986, after a pause of several years in the correspondence:

> It does seem a long time since you were here or I was in San Francisco, having our wonderful conversations – I often recall your image, sitting on my sofa under the window, reading a poem or talking to me. Recalled with happiness. But I have your voice on tape, and I often teach your poetry and other writings here. Duncan is never forgotten in my life. But enough of all that: this letter is primarily just to register my deep thanks for *Ground Work*. [...] It is quite simply, for me, a wonderful access to that sense of vocation – elevated and central – which we are in terrible danger of losing in the welter of mass living, entertainment-values and peace as preparation for conflict, as conflict itself indeed, an endless futility. It's your sense of a dedicated life of learning and poetics – under Hermes, in fact – that is so salutary. And the belief in the necessity of finding forms which include and maintain. (Evans and Zamir, eds., 148-149)

In this re-affirmation of friendship and shared poetics, Mottram's resolve to formulate a new understanding of the function of "belief" in poetry and politics remains in the foreground. He is, however, careful to translate the mythic into the contemporary via ideas of research, pedagogy and tradition as he continues: "I love your sense of pride in vocational ability and the tempering of that justified approbation with the knowledge of other work, other times, and therefore the humility of how poetry is so much partly what used to be more frequently called the Muse – the unpredictable genetrix" (149).

Mottram's efforts to encourage British contemporary poets to pursue comprehensive "knowledge of other work, other times", and to gain inspiration from a living – and live – American tradition, also involved organising readings and conferences in association with the Polytechnic of Central London. Mottram helped to coin the term "British Poetry Revival" in his essay for one such conference.[28] Today's prominent scholars of Modernism, such as Maggie Humm, Emeritus Professor of Cultural Studies at the University of East London, credit these events with providing the sole opportunity at the time for readers of poetry in London, and in the rest of the UK, to hear several major American poets perform their work.[29] In this way, Mottram enabled others who, like him, were based in the UK, to experience American poetry as directly as possible. The present-day students of those who attended such historical events are well aware of Mottram's expertise in Beat poetics and his authorship of the first book-length study of William Burroughs, *The Algebra of Need*.[30] By contrast, several of his essays on Pound-influenced "open field" poetics are much less widely available to them, including those on Duncan. Mottram's creative engagement with a Poundian tradition in his own poetry is also less recognised, even by those who closely identify their writing with one or all of the several parts of the current UK scene upon which his actions had a formative influence. Why Mottram's poetry is less widely known than that of other British Poetry Revivalists, whose writing he promoted, remains the important subject of another essay altogether. Work to begin re-publishing his poetry is under way.[31]

Reading Mottram reading Pound provides a necessary foundation to understanding contemporary British, and particularly London-based, poetry's relationship to Pound. Only the briefest outlines of numerous contexts for the essay have been offered here: informative frameworks within which the essay can be approached include the archive, manuscript and published works, correspondences, biographical and anecdotal contexts, British literary history and emergent interest in studies of the transnational. Finally, an important acknowledgement must be added to any work that retrieves Mottram from the archive and out-of-print magazines in the twenty-first century. To the contemporary reader, these several contexts, and the triangulation of Mottram's engagement with Duncan with his essay on Pound further highlight Mottram's almost exclusively all-male canon and successors from among his students. Working closely with both the correspondence and essays, it is notable that when Mottram cites Duncan, and even when he quotes material in which Duncan himself makes repeated reference to significant women writers, he often actively removes the female voice. The essay "Pound, Olson and *The Secret of the Golden Flower*" is conspicuously bereft of female poets and cultural thinkers. The predominantly male canon in which it participates remains problematic and has its own difficult legacy. There are important exceptions, such as Levertov's grateful note to Mottram, held in his archived papers, for his later, more positive response to her poetry, his engagement with the writing of Frances Yates and E.M. Butler, and his inclusion of Geraldine Monk, Wendy Mulford and Denise Riley in the King's Readings series. Additionally, former students such as Robert Hampson convey that a more positive aspect of the apparent gender imbalance of Mottram's dedication to particular students and poets was his support for Northern, working-class male students within a Higher Education institution that catered for a predominantly female, "middle- and upper-middle-class", and occasionally *débutante*, cohort of Literature students.[32] Indeed, Monk's favourable accounts of Mottram's interest in her poetry (in which he was encouraged by both Cobbing and Ken Edwards) include his extending similar assistance to both working-class men and women outside of his own seminar groups: "he gave me a reference to get into university which was invaluable because I didn't have enough qualifications at the time".[33] The task of considering Mottram's reading of women's poetry is complicated further still by Monk's sense that few women poets aligned themselves with sections of the British poetry scene focused on innovative practice: "there weren't many women around writing the sort of [poetry] that Eric would have liked".[34] The function of both gender and class in British poets' reception of, and inclusion in, Mottram's Poundian tradition requires further critical attention.

The challenges and difficulties of Mottram's specific approach to ensuring the health of contemporary innovative and politically aware poetry are numerous. Nevertheless, much is lost if Mottram's scholarship and teaching are omitted from the history of contemporary poetry's engagement with Pound. Awareness of its impact is subsequently distorted as part of the more general gap in criticism and teaching that exists concerning the British Poetry Revival, its relationship with an Anglo-American modernist tradition and its influence on today's British poetry. The Ezra Pound familiar to the UK's contemporary poets is a Pound inherited in large part from Mottram's prolific writing. Furthermore, it was often through Mottram's preoccupation with Pound that readers learned of contemporary American poetry and its history. It is also due to his influence that many British poets writing after

Pound participated in small press poetry in both the UK and US, and that a British readership was encouraged to acknowledge the significance of American and British independent poetry presses for literary criticism and wider society.

Mottram's last letter to Duncan draws to its close with the words "Our British poetry scene – the unofficial one – thrives and thrives – against grim odds. And I have a book of poems out this month...."[35] By reading "Pound, Olson and *The Secret of the Golden Flower*" and Mottram's correspondence with Duncan as companions to one another, Mottram's Pound, and the relationship of this Pound to contemporary poetry, emerge more fully. So too do his aspirations for a British poetry that no longer remains in "ignorance" of the Poundian tradition, and is able to enjoy a creative dialogue with – and significantly contribute to – its line as transmitted by poets in the younger generation such as Olson and Duncan. The letters illuminate his indefatigable endeavours to educate and enthuse others about contemporary American poetry and, in a pre-internet age, to achieve this by facilitating direct experience of it in print, in tape recordings and at poetry readings. The essay belongs to his busiest and most productive period within this lifelong project as a scholar, teacher, editor and poet. As a result of such work, British academics and poets are able to engage with Poundian poetics, and with Anglo-American poetic traditions in general, with a confidence, self-awareness and humour characteristic of many of the most widely read and well-loved poems currently being written in the UK:

> I am open field I am
> right there & king, King's
> College.
> Like of king of experimental College,
> 1492,
> yet not too serious
> hey I am only searching for a genuine line
> maybe more
>
> — — — — — — — — — — — — —
>
> (Hilson, 40)

EDITORIAL NOTE

I have supplied all endnotes and citations in the essay that follows. Mottram's 61 original footnotes are incorporated within these critical annotations. In cases where it is helpful to know from which edition Mottram is working, I have provided his original citations. Where direction to more recent editions of the texts cited is useful, I have modernised bibliographical details. I have added page numbers for primary quotations and endeavoured to verify, correct or clarify those that Mottram provided.

The symbols §§§ indicate the break in the essay as it featured in Chapman magazine. Generally, the indentation of paragraphs and quotations has been standardised.

Numbers preceded by the letter "M" refer to translations from *Mathews' Chinese-English Dictionary.* (Shanghai: China Inland Mission and Presbyterian Mission Press, 1931; Revised American Edition, Cambridge, MA: Harvard University Press, 1943). I am indebted to Harry Gilonis for advice in the final editorial stages regarding Chinese lexicography and for the generous loan of his *C.E.D.* The initials "[HG]" in relevant endnotes indicate where his expertise was a guide. All ideograms included have been identified and provided with his assistance.

Mottram's prose presents an editor with several challenges. I made a decision regarding his writing style to preserve its conversational liveliness and idiosyncrasies, even where editorial adjustments ordinarily would be expedient. As a result, in most cases, I have avoided the method of "silent" correction and alteration of sentences. Instead, with the exception of a handful of instances, I have indicated even minor amendments of grammar and syntax within editorial brackets in the text. In this way, I treat the essay itself as an original manuscript of the history of contemporary poetry. The exception to this method concerns Mottram's occasional practice of dividing a quotation into separate parts with a colon for argumentative emphasis. In these cases, I have removed colons and additional speech marks in order to provide the quotation in uninterrupted form.

I have "silently" amended a large proportion of Mottram's quotations of primary material. Again, my aim in so doing is to preserve the argumentative flow of Mottram's prose style unimpeded by further endnotes. Mottram's compositional method was not uncommon to the period of the 1970s. He wrote his voluminous notes and essays from memory by hand or at the typewriter without the aid of primary texts for immediate reference. This process inevitably leads to occasionally misremembered words and uncited quotations. Furthermore, Mottram recalled certain prose quotations as poetry and lineated accordingly. Alternatively, he presented excerpts of poetry in the original essay as if they were prose. I have carried out most of these corrections without the distraction of editorial notation. Where significant repair to the quotation has been necessary, I have indicated such in the relevant endnote.

Printed with the permission of the Eric Mottram papers, King's College London Archives. © King's College London.

NOTES

[1] See Clive Bush, "'This Uncertain Content of an Obscure Enterprise of Form': Eric Mottram, America and Cultural Studies," in *A permanent etcetera: Cross-cultural perspectives on Post-War America,* ed. A. Robert Lee (London and Boulder, CO: Pluto Press, 1993) 145-168.

[2] "Elegy 1 (for Pound and Kerouac)" and "Elegy 2 (for Paul Blackburn)" were published in Eric Mottram, *Two Elegies* (Hayes: Poet and Peasant Books, 1974).

[3] Eric Mottram, *The Legal Poems: 29 December 1980-30 May 1981* (Colne, Lancashire: Arrowspire, 1986).

[4] Discussion with William Rowe at Writers Forum, New Series, London, 17 March 2012.

[5] For an overview of Mottram's published essays on Pound, see Robert Hampson "Eric Mottram and Ezra Pound: There is no substitute for a life-time" in this volume [pp.87-109]

[6] Eric Mottram, "POUND, OLSEN [sic] and THE SECRET OF THE GOLDEN FLOWER", Chapman 2.2 (1972) 20-31 and 55-64.

[7] See Eric Mottram, ed., *The Rexroth Reader* (London: Jonathan Cape Ltd, 1972); Kenneth Rexroth, *One Hundred Poems from the Chinese* 2nd ed. (New York, NY: New Directions, 1971, 1st ed., 1956); Kenneth Rexroth, *One Hundred More Poems from the Chinese: Love and the Turning Year* (New York, NY: New Directions, 1970).

[8] Amy Evans and Shamoon Zamir, eds., *The Unruly Garden: Robert Duncan and Eric Mottram, Letters and Essays* (Oxford and New York, NY: Peter Lang, 2007) 134. The further two essays to which Mottram refers are "Charles Olson's Apollonius of Tyana," *Sixpack* 3/4 (1973): 31-42; and "Performance: Charles Olson's Rebirth Between Power and Love," *Sixpack* 6 (Winter 1973/74): 95-114.

[9] See Peter Barry, *Poetry Wars: British Poetry of the 1970s and the Battle of Earls Court* (Cambridge: Salt Publishing, 2006).

[10] Discussions with Robert Vas Dias in London, 7 July 2013 and 3 January 2014.

[11] Mottram to Duncan, 30 September 1971, *The Unruly Garden,* Evans and Zamir, eds., 41-42. In a letter to the Chairman of the Poetry Society, 25 September 1971, Mottram names the columnist "as a certain Trewin who signs himself PHS. Having heard about the delay in publication and concern about the word 'shit' in one of the poems, he has phoned around information apparently leaked by a member of the Arts Council." See Eric Mottram Collection, King's College London, Mottram 4/3/1-11, 1970-1975. In this and subsequent quotations, Mottram's ellipses appear without brackets, and editorial ellipses are contained in square brackets.

[12] See Eric Mottram, *Allen Ginsberg in the Sixties* (Brighton & Seattle: Unicorn Bookshop, 1972); "The Limits of self-regard: Hall, Kizer, Levertov, Wakosi," *Parnassus* 1 (1972): 14-25.

[13] See Eric Mottram, *Paul Bowles: Staticity & Terror* (London: Aloes Books, 1976); "1924-1951: Politics and Form in Zukofsky," *Maps* 5 (1973): 76-103.

[14] See Eric Mottram Collection, King's College London, Mottram 9/19/8-13, 1969-1991. For Mottram's published poems, see King's College London, "A Checklist of his Published Poems," College Archives <http://www.kingscollections.org/catalogues/kclca/collection/m/10mo70-1/1mo70-a2>

[15] See Eric Mottram, "Pound, Merleau-Ponty and the Phenomenology of Poetry," *Ezra Pound: Tactics for Reading*, Ian Bell ed., (London: Vision Press, 1982) 121-147.

[16] Mottram, "Pound, Merleau-Ponty and the Phenomenology of Poetry" 123.

[17] Evans and Zamir, eds., 94. Mottram did not publish a book entitled *Points of Honour*, nor did he bring out a book of poems with Beau Fleuve. For his earlier collection with Turret Books, see Eric Mottram, *Shelter Island & The Remaining World* (London: Turret Books, 1971, as Tall Turret 1).

[18] Eric Mottram, "Heroic Survival through Ecstatic Forms: Robert Duncan's *Roots and Branches*," Robert Bertholf and Ian Reid, eds., *Scales of the Marvelous* (New York, NY: New Directions, 1979) 116-142; "Robert Duncan: The Possibilities of an Adequate History and of a Poetics of Event," *Talus* 3 (London, 1988): 118-148. Both essays are reproduced and annotated in the volume of the Duncan-Mottram correspondence. See Evans and Zamir, eds., 153-203 and 205-243.

[19] See n.8.

[20] Robert Duncan, *The H.D. Book* ed. Michael Boughn and Victor Coleman (Berkeley and Los Angeles, CA: University of California Press, 2011).

[21] Prior to this publication, sections appeared in the following journals and small press magazines: *Aion, Coyote's Journal, Caterpillar, Chicago Review, Credences, H.D. Newsletter, Ironwood, Montemora, Origin, Sagetrieb, Southern Review, Stony Brook Poetics Journal* and *Sumac*.

[22] See Amy Evans and Shamoon Zamir, eds., "'Between Revelation and Persuasion': Eric Mottram and Robert Duncan, A Compilation," *Jacket* 34 (October 2007).

[23] Evans and Zamir, eds., *The Unruly Garden* 47-48. The quotation from Pound is taken from an undated letter to his fiancée, Mary Moore, cited in Humphrey Carpenter, *A Serious Character* (New York, NY: Delta, 1988) 77.

[24] Duncan's long essay was first published in a limited edition *The Truth & Life of Myth: An Essay in Essential Autobiography* (New York, NY: House of Books, 1968) and again in *Fictive Certainties: Essays by Robert Duncan* (New York, NY: New Directions, 1979) 1-59. It is included in the recent *Collected Essays and Other Prose* ed. James Maynard (New York, NY: New Directions, 2014).

[25] Reproduced in Evans and Zamir, eds., "Between Revelation and Persuasion".

[26] Discussion with Jeff Hilson at *Blue Bus* reading, London, 19 November 2012.

[27] Discussions with Shamoon Zamir in the Eric Mottram Collection, King's College London Archive, September 2006 to December 2007.

[28] See Eric Mottram, "British Poetry Revival, 1960-1974," *Modern British Poetry Conference* (London: Polytechnic of Central London, 197) 86-117.

[29] Discussion with Maggie Humm at the 24th International Ezra Pound Conference at the Institute for English Studies, University of London, 7-9 July 2011, 8 July 2011.

[30] Eric Mottram, *William Burroughs: the Algebra of Need*, Beau Fleuve series no.2 (Buffalo, NY: Intrepid Press, 1971)

[31] Eric Mottram, *The Legal Poems* ed. Amy Evans with a Critical Introduction by William Rowe is forthcoming in 2015.

[32] Discussion with Robert Hampson at the School of English Research Seminar, University of Kent, 20 November 2013; Hampson, email to author, 9 January 2014; discussion with Thomas Evans, London, 10 July 2008.

[33] Geraldine Monk, email to the author, 14 January 2014.

[34] Geraldine Monk, email to the author, 15 January 2014.

[35] Evans and Zamir, eds., 149. The book of poems to which Mottram refers is *The Legal Poems*. See n.3.

Works Cited

Barry, Peter. *Poetry Wars: British Poetry of the 1970s and the Battle of Earls Court.* Cambridge: Salt Publishing, 2006.

Bush, Clive. "'*This Uncertain Content of an Obscure Enterprise of Form': Eric Mottram, America and Cultural Studies.*" *A Permanent Etcetera: Cross-Cultural Perspectives on Post-War America.* Ed. A. Robert Lee. London and Boulder, CO: Pluto Press, 1993. 145-168.

Carpenter, Humphrey. *A Serious Character.* New York, NY: Delta, 1988.

Duncan, Robert. *The H.D. Book.* Ed. Michael Boughn and Victor Coleman. Berkeley and Los Angeles, CA: University of California Press, 2011.

——. *Collected Essays and Other Prose.* Ed. James Maynard. New York, NY: New Directions, 2014.

——. *Fictive Certainties: Essays by Robert Duncan.* New York, NY: New Directions, 1979.

——. *The Truth & Life of Myth: An Essay in Essential Autobiography.* New York, NY: House of Books, 1968.

Evans, Amy, and Shamoon Zamir, eds. "'Between Revelation and Persuasion': Eric Mottram and Robert Duncan, A Compilation." *Jacket* 34 (October 2007): n.p.

——, eds. *The Unruly Garden: Robert Duncan and Eric Mottram, Letters and Essays.* Oxford and New York: Peter Lang, 2007.

Hampson, Robert. "Eric Mottram and Ezra Pound: 'There is no substitute for a lifetime.'"[this volume]

King's College London. "A Checklist of his Published Poems." Compiled by Valerie Soar. *College Archives.* Web. 15 Jan 2012.<http://www.kingscollections.org/catalogues/kclca/collection/m10mo70-1/1mo70-a2>

——. "MOTTRAM, Professor Eric Noel William (1924-1995)." *Archive Catalogues.* Nov 1999. Web. 15 Jan 2012. <http://www.kingscollections.org/catalogues/kclca/collection/m/10mo70-1/>

Mottram, Eric. *Allen Ginsberg in the Sixties.* Brighton & Seattle, WA: Unicorn Bookshop, 1972.

——. "British Poetry Revival, 1960-1974." *Modern British Poetry Conference.* London: Polytechnic of Central London, 197. 86-117.

——. "Charles Olson's Apollonius of Tyana." *Sixpack* 3/4 (1973): 31-42.

——. "Heroic Survival through Ecstatic Forms: Robert Duncan's *Roots and Branches*." *The Unruly Garden: Robert Duncan and Eric Mottram, Letters and Essays*. Ed. Amy Evans and Shamoon Zamir. Oxford and New York, NY: Peter Lang, 2007. 153-203.

——. *The Legal Poems: 29 December 1980-30 May 1981*. Colne, Lancashire: Arrowspire, 1986.

——. "The Limits of self-regard: Hall, Kizer, Levertov, Wakosi." *Parnassus* 1 (1972): 14-25.

——. *Paul Bowles: Staticity & Terror*. London: Aloes Books, 1976.

——. "Performance: Charles Olson's Rebirth Between Power and Love." *Sixpack* 6 (Winter 1973/74): 95-114.

——. "Pound, Merleau-Ponty and the Phenomenology of Poetry." *Ezra Pound: Tactics for Reading*. Ed. Ian Bell. London: Vision Press, 1982. 121-147.

——. "POUND, OLSEN [sic] and THE SECRET OF THE GOLDEN FLOWER." *Chapman* 2.2 (1972): 20-31 and 55-64.

——, ed. *The Rexroth Reader*. London: Jonathan Cape Ltd, 1972.

——. "Robert Duncan: The Possibilities of an Adequate History and of a Poetics of Event." *The Unruly Garden: Robert Duncan and Eric Mottram, Letters and Essays*. Ed. Amy Evans and Shamoon Zamir. Oxford and New York: Peter Lang, 2007. 205-243.

——. *Shelter Island & The Remaining World*. London: Turret Books, 1971.

——. *Two Elegies*. Hayes: Poet and Peasant Books, 1974.

——. *William Burroughs: the Algebra of Need*. Beau Fleuve Series 2. Buffalo: Intrepid Press, 1971.

——. "1924-1951: Politics and Form in Zukofsky." *Maps* 5 (1973): 76-103.

Rexroth, Kenneth. *One Hundred Poems from the Chinese*. 1956. New York, NY: New Directions, 1971.

——. *One Hundred More Poems from the Chinese: Love and the Turning Year*. New York, NY: New Directions, 1970.

Wilhelm, Richard, trans. *The Secret of the Golden Flower: A Chinese Book of Life*, Trans. from the German by Cary F. Baynes. Foreword and Appendix by C.G. Jung. Rev. ed. New York, NY: Harcourt, Brace, 1962.

Eric Mottram

Pound, Olson and *The Secret of the Golden Flower* [1]

Edited and Annotated by Amy Evans

Both Ezra Pound and Charles Olson place themselves within an onward going process of informational and emotional discovery whose form is the Work, in the alchemical sense, of their lifetimes: the *Cantos* and *Maximus Poems* primarily.[2] Part of the process is directed towards the discovery of what forces, unexplored or to be recovered or renewed, the body may hold as the field of Psyche and Eros. Their work is visionary in this sense, since it is a process of continuous growth and the invention of forms, whose informational parameters open out into a vision of a way of life. This Way is indeed like that of the alchemists in that the transformations of the basic propositions of geology and the transformations of the self proceed as parts of that situation of total energy we experience as the ecology of the universe. Comprehensive understanding of the historical environment and of the psychic and erotic body are the Way. As Cary F. Baynes observes in her introduction to *The Secret of the Golden Flower*,[3] the cosmic principle, *hsing* [性 pinyin *xìng*: nature, disposition, spirit, temper; sex. M. 2771] co-ordinated with *ming*, [命 pinyin *mìng*: fate, destiny; life. M. 4537] is at once essence of human nature,[4] body as human nature, cosmic principle, and (since *hsing* is related to *hsui*[5] [{*hui*}]) consciousness, the object of yoga. It is that sense, embodied in the ideograms, of the coherence of energy, and access to it, which Pound and Olson make for in their epic poetic processes. But what is not included, and, to judge only from printed resources, does not seem to appeal, is in fact the yogic method itself, the techniques of reverting energy from the body back into the body – "backward-flowing energy" – which Chinese and Tantric yoga have in common. The *Golden Flower* is not only, as C.G. Jung says in his foreword to the translation, a Taoist text of Chinese yoga but also "an alchemical tract," similar to such documents in medieval alchemy, "the connecting link between Gnosis and the processes of the collective unconscious" (*Secret* xiv).

Pound was acquainted with the work of Gurdjieff, although he did not become, as A.R. Orage, Pound's early supporter, did, a convert at the Château Prieuré.[6] Nor did he become as influenced by Gurdjieff as Buckminster Fuller apparently was:

> The invisible reality's integrities are infinitely reliable. It can only be comprehended by metaphysical mind, guided by bearings toward something sensed as truth. Only metaphysical mind can communicate...[7]

Neither Olson nor Pound seems to have been concerned with meditational processes of change in the psyche-eros which may reunite the Body through those transformed "states of consciousness" described in C. Daly King's book of that title, itself a neurological study written within the Gurdjieffian orbit and through the instruction of Orage.[8] Early in his career, Pound referred tersely to the "incommodities of ascetic yoga".[9] The principles involved seem to be similar to the two poets' preoccupations:

> The unification of the two elements via meditation is the principle upon which the work is based. The unconscious must be inseminated by the consciousness being immersed in it. In this way the unconscious is activated and thus, together with an enriched consciousness, enters upon a supra-personal mental level in the form of a spiritual rebirth. This rebirth then leads first to a progressing inner differentiation of the conscious state into autonomous thought structures. However, the conclusion of the meditation leads of necessity to the wiping out of all differences in the final integrated life, which is free of opposites.[10]

Rebirth into a condition free of opposites is central to Pound and Olson, and in both poets is focussed through the Chinese "Way," but not through meditation. In "The Ring of" and "An Ode on Nativity" (first printed in 1953 and 1952, respectively, and written earlier),[11] Olson articulates the theme of birth taking place between the elements within and without the human body – "the genital/ wave"[12] and "that which unborn form you are the content of, which you/ alone can make to shine".[13] In the *Reading at Berkeley* in 1965,[14] after reading these two poems, he speaks of how life, the earth and the universe move through them into the fourth term, "ourselves, any one of us",[15] a form of proprioception – "the word comes from *proprius*, proper to yourself".[16] Pound and Olson are concerned with an essentially occidental fusion of the praxis of eros and the praxis of knowledge of the world. It is as if the inner condition is brought about without "backward-flowing". Olson acknowledged his relationship with Blake's condition of freedom from opposites, in which contraries are related in a coherence rather than remaining antagonistic. Pound centres on the total light process, the *ming* ideogram of the sun and moon together [明 pinyin *ming*: bright, clear, intelligent; light, brilliant; to understand. M. 4534][17] everywhere in the *Cantos*, as an immersion of consciousness in the unconscious. Olson's sense of this immersion comes through, for instance, in certain scenes of Timothy Leary's *High Priest*[18] in which he collides with Arthur Koestler – the characteristic clash of a man willing to yield to whatever the psyche-eros contains and the man for whom ordinary consciousness has become, to a pathological degree a life-line from which he could never happily release himself. The "mushroom ritual" needed Olson, "guide and friend to our work"[19]: "...his wit, his intellect, his noble stature, his wise animal energy. He was striving for redemption but it will take him all his time."[20] Even before the ritual, Olson had his Zen confrontation with Koestler:

> I brought A.K. up to Olson. The giant poet turned, looked down at the small figure of the novelist, and beamed out of his jolly eyes that really were animal's eyes, except that animal's eyes are always serious, while his always laughed and turned into human eyes.
> Olson was holding a toy pistol in his hand.
> Arthur Koestler's eyes went up, up, up to look at Olson and then dropped quickly to the pistol. He paled and pulled back. Then he stood face-to-face with what he feared.
> Olson roared out genial greetings.[21]

The rest of Leary's account is vague, at least as far as Olson is concerned – his "gestural games with a sofa cushion," his "Mohawk Sachem Funny chiefness," his "bridges of silence" – and one reference to "the great tribal love feast with the Dionysius from Gloucester".[22] But, again judging from Olson's written work, he was drawn neither to Gurdjieff nor to psilocybin for the birth of consciousness, although Gerard Malanga reports him saying: "If you do treat the sacred drugs sacredly you discover that they really yield what everybody else finds. God does, love does, life does, they do. The problem is not the quality."[23]

Pound's man of enlightenment is the man in whom the total light process – the sun and moon together as the light of the crystal of *virtu* in the *Pisan Cantos*, for example – is a slowly achieved experience, a lifetime of accurately inheriting the traditions of Demeter-Kore, Eleusis and Montségur – the Mediterranean extension of the oriental process of becoming conscious: "Let us speak of the osmosis of persons" (Canto 29). His translation of the *Analects* of Confucius mentions the *I Ching* but he does not appear to have investigated its significance, as he knew the Chinese Master had: "He said: If many years were added to me, I would give fifty to the study of *The Book of the Changes*, and might thereby manage to avoid great mistakes."[24] But he does use the key term from the *Book of the Changes, chen* or *tchen* [貞 pinyin *zhēn*: to inquire by divination; lucky; the lower half of the diagrams of the *Book of Changes*; upright, correct; pure, virtuous, chaste. M. 346]: "He said: The proper man has a shell and a direction (*chen*)."[25] Pound notes that this is more than the Greek *ataraxis* – "the insensitivity, ability to 'take it'['']"[26]: or in the OED definition, "freedom from disturbance of mind or passion".[27] It is not passive stoicism but active direction and it is present vitally in Cantos LXXXV, LXXXVI, LXXXIX, and XCVII, used as the word for going somewhere, being on the way, rather than either stoic insensitivity of passive epicureanism.

Olson, too, is concerned with the active, alchemical metamorphoses of energy, a direction in which Taoism developed: Lu Yen's movement, of which the book of the Golden Elixir of Life – the *Golden Flower* – the *T'ai I Chin Hua Tsung Chih*, is part, takes the form of a return to Lao-Tse's *Tao Te Ching*: "The alchemistic signs became symbols of psychological processes" (*Secret* 6). Olson refers to this in "Against Wisdom as Such" (1954)[28] where he criticizes the *I Ching* as a form of sectarian or falsely "separable" wisdom, separated from the man: "wisdom, like style, is the man" (*Collected* 261), and it is not a matter of signs and symbols in secret: "wisdom itself, or at least the cultivation of energy-states *per se*, thrives on secrecy, on sect, and – at exactly the time we are in – finds its pleasure in conspiracy ("*épater tout le monde*"). (261) This is to be checked with "the morphology of forms which is everywhere and every thing"[29]:

> [The poet] is not free to be a part of, or to be any, sect;…there are no symbols to him, there are only his own composed forms, and each one solely the issue of the time of the moment of its creation, not any ultimate except what he in his heat and that instant in its solidity yield. That the poet cannot afford to traffick [sic] in any other "sign" than his one, his self, the man or woman he is. Otherwise God does rush in. And art is washed away, turned into that second force, religion.[30] (261-262)

This is the core of "An Ode on Nativity," the central care [sic] from which that poetic and historical action moves outwards. A secular "way" is here derived from the Anglo-Saxon *wise* – wise as way [sic] of being or acting. Olson recognizes that, in spite of fashionable dispensations drawn from "the East," there is information to be properly gained:

> I believe that the traditional order of water to fire to light – that is, as of the sectaries, as well as the Ionian physicists, that except

a man be born of water and of the spirit, he cannot enter into the kingdom of God – has to be re-taken. Light was the sign of the triumph of love and spirit before electronics. And we are after. So, fire… (*Collected* 262)[31]

Olson cuts through alchemic and gnostic [sic] to: "all but heat, is symbolic… reductive" (263), and asks Robert Duncan, to whom the essay is addressed, "if it wasn't his own experience that a poem is the issue of two factors, (1) heat, and (2) time" (263). And then he refers directly to Wilhelm's *Golden Flower* materials: "How plastic, cries Wilhelm, is the thought of "water" as seed-substance in the *T'ai I Chin Hua Tsung Chih*. And time is, in the hands of, the poet" (*Collected* 263). The flow for Olson here is time and not "backward-flowing" energy. There is an almost perceptible resistance to the yogic and alchemic definitions of energy transformations of the *Golden Flower* here – especially since they are what Wilhelm's seed-substance eventually refer[s] to. Both Olson, by inference, and Duncan (directly – in *The H.D. Book* II, 4/5)[32] criticize Pound's total light process as centre of enlightenment. Olson concludes: "A song is heat. There may be light, but light and beauty is not the *state* of: the state is the grip of (and it is not feverish, is very cool, is – the eyes are – how did they get that way?" (*Collected* 264)

But both Olson and Pound are concerned with that rebirth or birth which appears in the *Golden Flower* as "circulation of the light" and the creation of a divine seed – kernel; in the *Golden Flower* the process is an initiation or re-enaction of Creation in the Self – an act in which the theogony ideas in Olson, and also in Duncan, are deeply involved. The great Chinese book not only contains Taoism and Mahayana Buddhism (in its shifts from the world toward *nirvana*[)], but Confucianism "in the form which is based on the *I Ching*"[33] (*Secret* 8). The eight basic trigrams are symbols of inner processes.

The book, then, appears as a coherence from various sources concerned with enlightenment instanced as the circulation or articulation of light, the common image of life-energy in both Asian and Eastern Mediterranean cultures (and perhaps, if James Churchward is to be believed, dating back to Mu[34]): the light of the eye, the light of sun and moon, the birth of light from water and fire in the earth-body. It is these classic formants which Olson so beautifully projects in 'An Ode on Nativity'. But the hesitance and resistance are clear:

HOW — AS. *hu* — PROCESS (is "to move") — METHOD IS (*meta hodos*, the way after: TAO)[35]

and

         (I Ching-
             ness)

       sorts
   accidence
     (anything goes or
     all *is* interesting Or
     nothing is[36]

Wilhelm summarizes the materials which Chinese and Mediterranean (Christian is too narrow a term – but Olson's vestigial Catholicism may have coloured his thinking in this area more than this essay investigates) hold in common: "Man is spiritually reborn of water and fire, to which must be added 'thought-earth' (spirit), as womb or tilled field… 'Except a man be born of water and of the spirit, he cannot enter into the kingdom of God…'" (*Secret* 8) and "…the boy within ourselves (the *puer aeternus*, the Christ, who must be born in us and who, in another way, is the bride-groom of the soul)…." (9). The passage Olson uses in "Against Wisdom as Such" appears between these quotations. *Kuang*, the character for light [光 pinyin *guāng*: light; favour; brightness; honour; to illumine. M. 3583] can be written so as to signify *Chin Hua* [*Chin* 金 pinyin *jīn*: gold; precious; metal; money. M. 1057. *Hua* 花 pinyin *huā*: flowers, blossoms; to spend {money, time}. Substituted for No. 2217, its original form used in ancient times: flowers; flowery, variegated; glory, splendour. M. 2212], the Golden Flower, and, Wilhelm adds, this was indeed a sign invented for secrecy but "in a time of persecution"[37] (*Secret* 9). Olson should have regarded this context more carefully, to qualify his criticism of the forms of wisdom, especially since, in his own time and place, it has been unwise for many men to be open in their expression of wisdom. But in *Maximus IV* he ends "MAXIMUS FROM DOGTOWN – II" with an ideogram of energy formed from carbon, coal, diamond, love and ocean as black diamond throne of creative force, transposing light into the earth's dark energy: "Carbon Ocean," "the Diamond (Coal)," "the soft/ (Coal) LOVE" (*Maximus* 180). It is the geological and alchemical image of love – love placed within the ecology of the Earth's interactive changes:

    Heart to be turned to Black
    Stone   the Black Chrysanthemum
    is the Throne of Creation   Ocean

                    is the Black Gold Flower
                         (*Maximus* 180)

Olson here transposes Jung's stress on monogenesis in alchemy and the Wilhelm statements on the reactive agents of rebirth. The immediate reference is to a passage in *Psychology and Alchemy* where Jung writes of "...a curious 'sport of nature' that the chief chemical constituent of the physical organism is carbon, which is characterized by four valencies; also it is well known that the diamond is a carbon crystal. Carbon is black – coal, graphite – but the diamond is 'purest water'"[38] (218). The "phenomenon of four" is not "a poetic conceit" but "a spontaneous production of the objective psyche["][39] (218): in this way "psyche" coalesces with "body" – or in Jung's words on the following page: self and spirit may be said to "erupt" ["irrupts"] into space-time at this "creative point"[40] (220). Olson augments the relationships in the following poem of *Maximus IV*, "Maximus,/ to himself,/ as of 'Phoenicians',," (181) which concluded by moving out from "The SWASTIKA// broken up" (181) to "the padma/ is what was there BEFORE/ one was".[41] (181) His image for eternal process or "what ALL/ issues from" (181) ends the poem:

> ...The GOLD

> flower All the heavens,
> a few miles up — and even with the sun out —
> is BLACK   (181)

What the astronauts experience is fused back into geology, oriental philo-sophy and the knowledge of origins in ecology. The link with Pound is that in Chapter Five of *The Spirit of Romance* he had concluded that the myths of Psyche and Eros like all myths arose from the body's mechanism and "our kinship to the vital universe" (92):

> We have about us the universe of fluid force, and below us the germinal universe of wood alive, of stone alive. Man is – the sensitive physical part of him – a mechanism, for the purpose of our further discussion a mechanism rather like an electric appliance, switches, wires, etc. Chemically speaking, he is *ut credo*, a few buckets of water, tied up in a complicated sort of fig-leaf. (92)

and

> It is an ancient hypothesis that the little cosmos "corresponds" to the greater, that man has in him both "sun" and "moon". (94)

Sex is related therefore to the two paths from this premise – the
ascetic and the chivalric, contemplation and action: "as we see in
the realm of fluid force, one sort of vibration produces at different
intensities, heat and light". It is this set of functions which Pound
incorporates in the *Cantos* with Mediterranean and Chinese
definitions of the whole man (the figure Olson takes from Blake's
four-fold man).

A basis for both Pound and Olson is contained, then, in the Chinese idea
of man as part of the universal process, participating in all cosmic events,
"inwardly as well as outwardly interwoven with them" (*Secret* 11). Tao or the
Way – a term Olson uses centrally in his work[42] – governs nature and human
nature. Wilhelm's summary will make the references for Olson obvious:

> The character for Tao in its original form consists of a head, which
> probably must be interpreted as 'beginning', and then the character
> for 'going' in its dual form in which it also means 'track', and
> underneath, the character for 'standing still', which is omitted in the
> later way of writing. The original meaning, then, is that of a 'track
> which, though fixed itself, leads from a beginning directly to the
> goal'. The fundamental idea is that Tao, though itself motionless, is
> the means of all movement and gives it law...Lao-Tse has used this
> word, though in the metaphysical sense, as the final world principle,
> which antedates realization and is not yet divided by the drawing
> apart of the opposites on which emergence into reality depends.[43]
> (*Secret* 11)

Pound's use of the Chinese is, of course, more Confucian. His "unwobbling
pivot" is related to the undivided *T'ai-chi* – the "great ridge-pole, the supreme
ultimate," a form of the Tao, from which the light *yang* and the dark or
shadowy *yin* develop. The *Cantos* fuse this into a light and dark relationship
drawn from the Eleusinian tradition, both profoundly erotic and chthonic.
As Wilhelm says, the monad divides also into *hsing*, human nature, and *ming*,
life. *Hsing* [性] is heart or mind plus origin or being born – *hsin* [心 pinyin
xīn: the heart; the moral nature, the mind, the affections; intention. M. 2735]
plus *sheng* [生 pinyin *shēng*: to produce; to bring forth; to beget; to be born;
life, living. M. 5738]. *Hsing* is "a transcendental, supra-conscious condition"
– Pound interprets this largely through Mencius' definition as "eternal idea".
He uses *ming* centrally as "the measure of vital energy at one's disposal...
closely related to eros". *Ming* and *eros* are both, in Wilhelm's terms, "supra-

individual" (*Secret* 13) – this is Olson's sense of "limits" which man adapts but cannot change, a working out of the Buddhist *karma*:

> ...Limits
> are what any of us
> are inside of   ("LETTER 5," *Maximus* 21)

Wilhelm also characterizes the *yin* principle as *anima*, body process which sinks into earth at death. *Animus* or *yang* rises and flows into "the common reservoir of life" (*Secret* 14) – an idea strongly placed in William Carlos Williams' dialectic of ascent and descent, as well as being central to Olson's "An Ode on Nativity" processes: "the downward-flowing life-process, is the one in which the two souls enter into relations as the intellectual and animal factors" (*Secret* 15). Mrs Baynes adds that yoga meditation is a technique "whereby the natural flow of energy can be reversed, and the energy made to rise to the higher centres, where it becomes spirit".[44] This is described in neurological detail in C. Daly King; and it is the goal of Olson's "Ode," except that Olson seems not to use the system of yoga in any way. As in the practice of tantra, the body is not isolated behind its skin, but functions as part of all energy – "The GOLD// flower" (*Maximus* 181):

> The Golden Flower alone, which grows out of inner detachment from all entanglement with things, is eternal. A man who reaches this stage transposes his ego; he is no longer limited to the monad, but penetrates the magic circle of the polar duality of all phenomena and returns to the undivided One, the Tao. In Taoism, on the other hand, the goal is to preserve in a transfigured form the idea of the person, the "traces" left by experience. That is the light which, with life, returns to itself and which is symbolized in our text by the Golden Flower.[45] (*Secret* 17)

The use of *I Ching* trigrams in the text is also relevant to Pound and Olson. *Chen*, thunder, is arousing, life which "breaks out of the depths of the earth," "the beginning of all movement" (17). *Yin*, sun, is "the streaming of the reality-energies into the form of the idea" (17) – or realized energy, the form of energy. The fire of *Li* is a lucidity which "dwells in the eyes, forms the protecting circle, and brings about rebirth" (18). *K'un*, earth, embodies "the energies of the earth" (18) which gives form to the seed. *K'an*, water, is the abysmal, "the origin of eros" (13); the moon to *Li*'s sun. The marriage of sun and moon produces, here as in Greek myths of the conjunctive birth of energy in form, the child or the new man.[46] These ideas and images of the process appear throughout the poetry of Olson and Pound, to an extent which would be too great to enumerate here. The initial section of the text itself seems to have been a primary *locus* for Olson, but it also suggests ways in which a number of mid-century poets, and other writers, have moved towards this articulation of the field of process or ecology. It begins:

> Master Lu-tsu said, That which exists through itself is called the Way (Tao). Tao has neither name nor shape. It is the one essence [*Hsing*, otherwise translated as 'human nature' (C. F. B.)], the one primal spirit. Essence and life cannot be seen. They are contained in the light of heaven. The light of heaven cannot be seen. It is contained in the two eyes....
>
> The Golden Flower is the light. What colour has the Light? One uses the Golden Flower as a symbol. It is the true energy of the transcendent great One.[47] (*Secret* 21)

A later commentary[48] adds: "But even if man lives in the energy (vital breath, *prana*) he does not see the energy (vital breath), just as fishes live in water but do not see the water." (*Secret* 21) Therefore we must grasp and guard this "circulation of the light and the maintaining of the centre" (22). The text then reads: "The work on the circulation of the light depends entirely on the backward-flowing movement, so that the thoughts [(the place of heavenly consciousness, the heavenly heart)] are gathered together. The heavenly heart lies between sun and moon (i.e. between the two eyes)"(22).[49] From the *Book of the Yellow Castle* it is cited that this centre for Buddhists is "the terrace of living" (22), and for Taoists "the ancestral land, or the yellow castle, or the dark pass, or the space of former heaven" (22):

> ...Heaven is not the wide blue sky but the place where corporeality is begotten in the house of the Creative. If one keeps this up for a long time there develops quite naturally, in addition to the body, yet another spirit-body.
>
> The Golden Flower is the Elixir of Life (*Chin-tan*; literally, golden ball, golden pill). All changes of spiritual consciousness depend upon the heart.[50] (23)

The search for adequate articulation of the elixir has had an energetic lease since 1940: in fact it is the centre of the "counter-culture" of the second half of this century. Norman Mailer places it there in 1957 in his essay "The White Negro"[51], and the effects of Wilhelm Reich's desire to establish orgone energy and the bion are yet to be as penetrative as they will be. Even Marshall

McLuhan's predominantly theocratic electronic incarnation of divine energy is articulated as an ecology of immersion drawn from the *Golden Flower*: "One thing about which fish know exactly nothing is water, since they have no anti-environment which would enable them to perceive the element they live in"[52] and "Media effects are environments as imperceptible as water to a fish, subliminal for the most part."[53] The point McLuhan necessarily misses is that the *Golden Flower* provided techniques which do not restrain a man within some theological prison of – in his case – Roman Catholic dogma and cosmic hierarchy. More significantly, it is Pound who grasps that the total light process images can fuse Hellenic and Chinese articulations of energy, and, like Pound, Olson well understands the text's concern with the eyes – for instance, in the "Ode". The centering of energy is a major focus for Pound, and also, through what she learned from Olson and John Cage at Black Mountain College, and from her own practice of the art of pottery, for M. C. Richards.[54] Perhaps, too Pound's terrace of Dioce in the exemplary City[55] may have been affected by the text's "terrace of living".

§ § §

But that transformation of energy by yogic practice central to the description of the achieved consciousness in C. Daly King is replaced in Pound and Olson by the poetic process, which continually moves by parataxis and collage towards a state of ecstatic, sometimes euphorically synchronistic, apprehension of oneness with the whole ecological basic process. Certain frustrations in both poets – especially Pound's statement in Canto 116 about lifting the Crystal Ball and the failure of coherence – refer to an absence of final "take off" or transformation of consciousness into the transcendental. Olson's drug experiences may have been directed towards this end, and there are indications in the *Reading at Berkeley* that he was concerned to arouse the "spirit-body," the *Golden Flower*, as the ultimate condition of Oneness: "This is the dream of my life".[56] But this opening section of the text, besides being present everywhere in his work, especially in the *Letters for Origin*, is directly used in his definition of methodology as "the process by which form is accomplished to the degree that is deeper than technique," as a will to form, as the initiation or bringing into being of forms. In the *Letters for Origin* it is:

(1)   to have a path
(2)   and that such a path is only accomplishable by the habitual practice of orderliness and regularity in *action*[57]

But this does not mean the co-ordinations and transcendence of yoga – as defined, for instance, at the beginning of Mircea Eliade's *Yoga: Immortality and Freedom* (1969),[58] Olson believes in action in the world as the Way. He refers to a "stage where man is free of dream," where he is "utterly clear, limpid, in the sense that he has so possessed his own 'form', so knows the structure of himself (in the face of all forms) that he works from that alone". He is the man of genius a man of true consciousness, the "exceptional man" ("The Gate and The Center," 1951),[59] the man who in the form of Apollonius of Tyana (in Olson's work of 1952)[60] remains silent for five years and descends into a place of "the light of the mind" to regain his alert form – "an alert man": "a middle term, as it were, between gods and men."[61] In 1965, in a letter to Jack Clarke, this had become:

> Knowing is simply
> purifying oneself to be tuned in
> _____ to
> *play*   (the music.[62]

In *Apollonius*, it takes the form of that process of *recognition* which is the profoundly democratic, non-secretive centre of Olson's work and life: a dance of recognition, an experience of recognition. Whereas this is "spiritual" in Augustine, in Apollonius the "conflagration of myself" remains bodily:

> St. Augustine said of his experience of recognition, "It was a conflagration of myself," but with Apollonius the terms stay physical in another way, and in that way are neither light nor fire – with him it is a burning, surely, but with nothing consumed, on the contrary, it is as the action of the sun on us and on things, increase is the issue, more growth, more life, more life, leaves, men.[63] (*Selected* 151).

But Apollonius' "personal rite" of separating himself daily from others – three times "to pay his respects, those times, to the sun, to source" – derives from his visit to India. Olson does not go into this rite but simply says: "What Apollonius found there was what he knew: that here was a will which asserted itself inward, a sort of will the West had lost the law of, and so, only turned it outward" (*Selected* 149). When he was asked what he saw in India, he replied: "men possessed of nothing but what all possess". The dance which follows does use apparently some of the movements and *mudra*s of yogic dance, so that Olson is aware, at least, that the essential coherence of body is a skill from training, an achievement and not *simple* a recognition. Apollonius dances "the only full vision capable of delivering man from his split" (149), "a dance of recognition" (151), "recognition of the daemonial nature in anything, including ourselves, and only these guileless paths five health" (152).

In *Causal Mythology* the four-fold man – Blake's Son of Man ideal – is the possible product of recognition not of the yogic dance but of the accurate analytical separation of Earth, Image of the World, History or City, and Spirit of the World. The united and reborn man appears under the epigraph, italicized in the text: *"that which exists through itself is what is called meaning"* (*Causal* 2). There is no acknowledgement of the *Golden Flower*'s opening sentence, from which the causal basis is drawn,[64] either by Olson or by his editor. Olson's aim is to place us firmly in the world (the case or basic proposition, in Wittgenstein's sense) rather than to offer transcendence. The derivation from the *Golden Flower* is, arbitrarily, used to designate the Earth as a One; the poem is then given as the result of the operation "to find the term that stands for what we have known that's there"[65] (*Causal* 36) and of which "everyone has their own recognitions... something that the word 'myth' used to mean"[66] (*Causal* 37). One of his examples in the essay is his poem "The Song of Ullikummi" because it concerns the myth of a figure for both genetic and morphological principles, and for political action, since he stands against the gods and "the bosses". The four-fold man who will found Jerusalem, the realization of the "human universe" as *polis* is related to another tradition than the Chinese: "in the Tarot deck it's the *El Mundo*, card XXI is *anima mundi*"[67] (*Causal* 35). It is the poet, though, who creates the picture of the universe, the *Imago Mundi*, not the yogic sages. Olson is careful, however, to balance the action: "I don't think you can get your recognitions by going out. I think they come by going – from within"[68] (*Causal* 37). This is more nearly Pound's 1911 idea of a union of ascetic and chivalric[69] to produce the man who combines sun and moon.

For Olson, then, the Black Flower of primal energy is a statement of the possible vision in *Maximus IV* but not a condition for the poet. It is, rather, another mythological source for his *Imago Mundi* and perhaps it exemplified Jung's comment on the opening passages of the *Golden Flower* and its translation problems: "It is characteristic of the Western mind that it has no concept for Tao. The Chinese character is made up of the character for 'head', and that for 'going'. Wilhelm translates Tao by *Sinn* (Meaning). Others translate it as 'way', 'providence', or even as 'God' as the Jesuits do" (*Secret* 97). Olson gives it as "meaning," following Wilhelm, and uses it as a way of ridding himself of Platonic apparatus – allegory, metaphor and symbol, as contorting ways of referring to "something behind" in the cosmos. From "The Ring Of" and "An Ode on Nativity" onwards he is concerned to elucidate Eros – what the *Golden Flower* calls "seed-water" –

logos ("spirit-fire"), and "thought-earth" (*Secret* 26), the middle dwelling place of intuition,[70] as methods of the creative – "the circulation of the light" (51). Where Pound is fascinated by "the radiance of light" and the Mediterranean culture which extends Eleusis into Provence and into the possibility of revival in his own time, Olson's field is the human universe and the city in a context which draws in pre-Grecian cultures. The immediate *logos* of Gloucester is a concrete locality placed in the world as the poet's home in a way Pound has never had a home. In this, Olson is a major figure in the movement towards an ecological poetry, which includes both Robert Duncan and Gary Snyder. Snyder, in particular, places his poetic action firmly within ecology, using both the transformations of the eros-psyche through Zen and the ecological myths of the American Indians for his purpose. The passage in the *Golden Flower* of special relevance here occurs in the third section of the *T'ai I Chin Hua Tsung Chih*:

> The light is not in the body alone, nor is it only outside the body. Mountains and rivers and the great earth are lit by sun and moon; all that is this light. Therefore it is not only within the body. Understanding and clarity, perception and enlightenment, and all movements (of the spirit) are likewise this light; therefore it is not just something outside the body. The light-flower of heaven and earth fills all the thousand spaces. But also the light-flower of the individual body passes through heaven and covers the earth. Therefore, as soon as the light is circulating, heaven and earth, mountains and rivers, are all circulating with it at the same time. To concentrate the seed-flower of the human body above in the eyes, that is the great key of the human body.[71] (*Secret* 33)

The process of centring is parallel to and not identical with the actions of M.C. Richards and Olson:

> Keeping the thoughts on the space between the two eyes allows the light to penetrate. Thereupon, the spirit crystallizes and enters the centre in the midst of conditions. The centre in the midst of conditions is the lower Elixir-field, the place of energy (solar plexus). (38)

Although Olson placed D.H. Lawrence's works on the fantastic unconscious in his bibliography of work to be done,[72] the nearest in the poetry to this kind of material in the *Golden Flower* occurs in a late poem, finally not put in the last *Maximus* book but which he read at the Vancouver Conference in 1963 as part of it. The poem begins "the southeast wind blows over/ Dogtown".[73] It presents "the goddess of all things" rising from "infolding Dogtown" [{sic} "wide-enfolding/ Dogtown"]; her spilled eggs (begot with the coiling great serpent) hatch out as "all which is living, the sun, the moon, the planets, the stars/ the earth with its mountains and rivers/ Dogtown and all living things".

The difference between the achievement of poetry and the action of the *Golden Flower* is clear:

> Since heart and breath are mutually dependent, the circulation of the light must be united with the rhythm of breathing. For this, light of the ear is above all necessary. There is a light of the eye and a light of the ear. The light of the eye is the united light of the sun and moon outside. The light of the ear is the united seed of sun and moon within. The seed is thus the light in crystallized form. Both have the same origin and are different only in name. Therefore, understanding (ear) and clarity (eye) are one and the same effective light. (*Secret* 40)

The yoga of the *Golden Flower* transforms the body's life. Poetry cannot have that ambition, and perhaps it is the absence of metamorphosis in the body which Pound specifies in Canto 116 – the crystal ball is not lifted and the pain in the poem is an overwhelming desire not to *write about* metamorphosis but to experience it without or beyond verbal statement. In George Oppen's terms:

> Clarity
>
> In the sense of *transparence*,
> I don't mean that much can be explained.
>
> Clarity in the sense of silence.[74]

At least Pound and Olson avoid that "distraction" which haunted T.S. Eliot in his *Four Quartets* and for which the *Golden Flower* provides a method of transformation into active energy. "To become conscious of distraction is the mechanism by which to do away with distraction". (*Secret* 42) Indolence and lethargy are eliminated by a technique of inward looking which is "the vision of the seed and the light of the sun and moon," a vision which obviates puritan and Freudian repression, and both Eliot's and Roethke's fatal frustrations of sex, perception and religious urge. The *Golden Flower* way of release is similar to the Zen-learned bases of John Cage's work:[75]

> If one can attain purposelessness through purpose, then the thing has been grasped. Now one can let oneself go, detached and without confusion, in an independent way.... If, when there is quiet, the spirit has continuously and uninterruptedly a sense of great joy as if intoxicated or freshly bathed, it is a sign that the light-principle is harmonious in the whole body; then the Golden Flower begins to bud....the body of the heart opens itself to clarity. It is a sign that the Golden Flower is opening.[76] (*Secret* 49)

Cage's music as *purposeful purposelessness* finally transcended itself and became the onward-going sounds of what is called silence. The paradisal goal of The Poetry of Pound and Olson (and, although not discussed here, of Duncan and William Carlos Williams) is to make a work which exemplifies living in the world detached from competition and being part of the process of eros, rather than the hell of the inter-war period of the *Cantos*, the divorce and division of *Paterson*, and the "pejorocracy" of the *Maximus Poems*. The transcendentalism here has little beyond common language to do with conventional mysticism. The body is to be the crucible for a restorative alchemy. The process of metamorphosis is the Way and can be imaged through water, fire and light processes. Olson's *Ode* is impregnated with an action which in the Wilhelm text appears as a Seventeenth- and Eighteenth-Century commentary on the *Golden Flower*:

> This magical spell [for the journey] states that the secret wonder of the Way is how something develops out of nothing. In that spirit and energy unite in crystallized form, there appears, in the course of time, in the midst of the emptiness of nothing, a point of the true fire. During this time the more quiet the spirit becomes, the brighter is the fire. The brightness of the fire is compared with the sun's heat in the sixth month. Because the blazing fire causes the water of the Abysmal to vaporize, the steam is heated, and when it has passed the boiling point it mounts upward like flying snow. It is meant by this that one may see snow fly in the sixth month. But because the water is vaporized by the fire, the true energy is awakened; yet when the dark is at rest, the light begins to move; it is like the state of midnight. Therefore adepts call this time the time of the living midnight. At this time one works at the energy with the purpose of making it flow backward and rise, and flow down

to fall like the upward spinning of the sun-wheel. Therefore it is said: 'At the third watch the sun's disk sends out blinding rays'. The rotation method makes use of breathing to blow on the fire of the gates of life; in this way one succeeds in bringing the true energy to its original place.[77] (*Secret* 60-61)

The elixir or state of the Golden Flower is brought about when the fire and the water change to spirit: "the golden colour is white, and therefore white snow is used as a symbol" (62). Energy is not dispersed but conserved and changed. The change is ecologically conceived: "A man who holds to the way of conservation all through life may reach the stage of the Golden Flower, which then frees the ego from the conflict of the opposites, and it again becomes part of the Tao, the undivided, great One" (65). Olson always sought germinal eros in the ecology of history and in particular location. His "man of achievement" in *The Special View of History*[78] is the man who lives, as the *Golden Flower* suggests, within the order of nature. The spirit of the teaching of Maximus of Tyre, a prototype of Olson's own poetic *persona*, opposes the spirit of dominion and conquest embodied in the man of power. The *Golden Flower* says:

> When these two paths (the functioning and the controlling) can be brought into unbroken connection, then all energy-paths are joined. The deer sleeps with his nose on his tail in order to close his controlling energy-path. The crane and the tortoise close their functioning-paths. Hence these three animals become at least a thousand years old. How much further can a man go! A man who carries on the cultivation of the Tao, who sets in motion the circulation in conformity with the law, in order to let consciousness and life circulate, need not fear that he is not lengthening his life and is not completing his path.[79] (*Secret* 74)

In such a passage, Olson and Snyder may both find a presence, the former in his sense of discovering law — the methodology of cultivation, and the latter in his sense of the immediate, almost totemic relationship with animals. Their aim is common: to complete human energy within the body and into other parts of the basic proposition, to avoid false separations, boundary and stasis. Snyder's use of Buddhist texts and Olson's acknowledgement of the Tao and usage of the *Golden Flower* are part of their understanding of the interior politics needed in our time: a sense of the limits of human nature in the human universe, and a sense of freedom from opposites (the Hindu *nirdvanda* which Jung cites in his commentary).

So ego is to be limited – away from both caesarism and passive submission – by a self-regulating system. But where Snyder knows meditation, Olson seems to have been less inclined to bring into focus deliberate techniques for changing consciousness – at least in his writings, whatever he may have practiced privately. But he is aware of the *Golden Flower* as Jung describes it – a mandala blossom growing from darkness and developing light at its summit, a centering whose yoga is the making of the poet as a performance which leads "back to an inner, sacred domain [which is the source and goal of the soul and] which contains the unity of life and consciousness"[80] (*Secret* 103). There is no concern for the androgyne, the archetype of the union of sexes, prominent theoretically in Jung's *Symbols of Transformation, Psychology and Alchemy* and *Mysterium Coniunctionis*, and less theoretically in the writings of Norman O. Brown.[81] That "acute state consciousness" which yoga works for is hardly Olson's forefront concern, although it seems to haunt his career. For Olson the Way is secular, unmysterious and based on practical eros: "It is with EROS that mythology is concerned. Which amounts to saying that as a psyche man is only an order comparable to kosmos when he or she is in love."[82] Olson is – to use Duncan's phrase for his own work – "a maker of a way"[83] rather than a yogic revealer of the Way. Like Apollonius, Olson – and a number of American writers in the disastrous mid-twentieth-century of their country – has "spun the spiritual threads from Europe back to Asia, perhaps to remotest India".[84] But his usage of ancient materials is his own; it is for the *Maximus Poems*, even if towards the end of his life there is evidence that he once again turned to *The Secret of the Golden Flower*.[85]

The living example of the American paradigm remains Ezra Pound. As early as Canto 23 Montségur exemplified dogma rigidifying love's body and its cultural rites. In *The Spirit of Romance* he wrote: "Provençal song is never wholly disjunct from the pagan rites of May Day" (*Spirit* 90) – with a footnote that "the lady" of Tuscan poetry "assumed all the properties of the Alchemist's stone" (90 n.2). He was attracted deeply to "a cult stricter, or more subtle, than that of the celibate ascetics, a cult for the purgation of the soul by a refinement of, and lordship over, the senses" (90) and what an unnamed mystic speaks of as "the intellect as standing in the same relation to the soul as do the senses to the mind" (91). But the poet's function is to develop a more complex knowledge than yogic asceticism affords – to actively discover and engage in the *paideuma*. Pound saw the lady of the troubadours as "a sort of *mantram*" (97) for *amor* or eros, and everywhere in the *Cantos* light gathering gold to itself in darkness is the imaged process of substantiating and surviving energy in a time of disaster. Montségur is the seminal city, the mound, the temple, the sacred mountain, the Celestial City, the *mons veneris* of the Earth. But the key to Paradise is not the changes of the *Golden Flower* but woman, eros, the Mediterranean mysteries. Love is the perception of form; art defines the form; *tan*,[86] the ideogram for dawn [旦 pinyin *dàn*. M. 6037], signifies the return of the gods as the forms of the eternal states of the human. The rites in the temple of Na-khi in Canto 110 are devoted to this process of love-art-*tan*, but of what the rites of purification for the self are, or what takes place in the temple, Pound is tacit. The *Cantos* concern the temporal and historical terms for the vertical rites, and it is exactly this decision that Eliade sees as the western as distinct from the oriental preoccupation, in his book on yoga.[87] In Canto 111 the metamorphic transcendence has taken place:

> Soul melts into air,
> > anima into aura,
> > > Serenitas.
>
> > > > (*Cantos* 803)

– and the following reference to gold reflects back to the alchemic-psychological *aura*, as so often in the *Cantos*. *Thrones* had given keys to the rites for gaining Paradise, but awareness of possible visionary condition is not the condition itself. In *Section: Rock-Drill* the poet cries out "Not yet!/ Do not awaken",[88] as if deeply troubled by the potentiality of revelation, as well as concerned for the proper timing of its rites, both Eleusinian and at the Na-khi's mountain, Seng-ge ga-mu.[89] But the yellow iris of Canto 111 refers to a figure in a Noh play:[90] it is not in the *Golden Flower*. According to sources cited by Mircea Eliade in *Shamanism: Archaic Techniques of Ecstasy* (rev. ed. 1964)[91] it is the *llü-bu* (probably a woman in ancient times) who practiced the healing rites of the Na-khi. This shaman is chosen in the psychopathic crisis of a dance to the temple divinity; during the rite of *²Mùan ¹bpö*, Canto 112, prayers are offered to Earth and to the juniper tree, the Cosmic Tree rising at the World's Centre to support the universe. The multiplicity of demons made the shaman necessary (the Na-khi conceptions are close to those of the *Tibetan Book of the Dead*). But Pound is not a shaman,[92] nor does his society include this function. In Canto 110 old daemonic evil still threatens; loss of vision is threatened by division, separations and opposites, and hints at the suicidal are given through the "wind of darkness," the power of chaos: "Lux enim – versus the tempest" (*Cantos* 801). Resistance to body transformation came early to Pound. In his essay "Remy de Gourmont: A Distinction," body-soul dualism is refused but the erotics are firmly static: "...the brain itself, is, in origin and development, only a sort of great clot of genital fluid held in suspense or reserve".[93] It is exactly that clot which the *Golden Flower* seeks to circulate. Pound clings to the personally held experience of love and friendship as a raft against the world of his times. It is there most movingly in a passage which may well derive from the *I Ching*'s "what is truly yours and is honestly won cannot be taken from you":

> What thou lovest well is thy true heritage
> What thou lov'st well shall not be reft from thee
>
> (*Cantos* 81.541)

Notes

[1] "POUND, OLSEN [sic] and the SECRET OF THE GOLDEN FLOWER," *Chapman* 2.2 (1972) 20-31 and 55-64.

[2] Ezra Pound, *The Cantos* (New York, NY: New Directions, 1996); Charles Olson, *The Maximus Poems,* ed. George F. Butterick (Berkeley and Los Angeles, CA: University of California Press, 1984). Subsequent quotations from these works are cited in the text, abbreviated as *Cantos* and *Maximus* respectively.

[3] Richard Wilhelm, trans. *The Secret of the Golden Flower: A Chinese Book of Life*, trans. from the German by Cary F. Baynes, Foreword and Appendix by C.G. Jung, rev. ed. (New York, NY: Harcourt, Brace, 1962) xi. Mottram abbreviates the title to *Golden Flower* hereafter. Originally published as part of Routledge's International Library of Psychology, a series of over 200 volumes published between 1910 and 1965, reprinted in 1999. The series included volumes by Sigmund Freud, Jean Piaget, Otto Rank, James Hillman, Erich Fromm, Karen Horney, Susan Issacs and W.H.R. Rivers. The advertisement for the reprint stated:

> The series not only traces the evolution of thinking on such key areas as child psychology, education, the emotions, perception and religion, but also includes titles on subjects which were subsequently discarded by modern mainstream psychology, such as telepathy, clairvoyance, palmreading and eugenics. (n.p.)

Subsequent quotations from this work are cited in the text, abbreviated as *Secret*.

[4] On the matter of translation, *hsing* ("nature". M. 2771) does not uncomplicatedly mean, as Mottram quotes here, "human nature". See editorial brackets p.55. Mottram takes his translation from *Secret*. Wilhelm defines *hsing* as "human nature," as does Baynes in an editorial footnote. See *Secret* xi (quoted below) and 21. n.1. Mottram's opening argument of this essay regarding *hsing, ming* and *hui* lead him to discuss "human nature". In this, he is again led by Wilhelm's own argument. The fifth German edition and subsequent English translations of *Secret* include material from another Chinese text, *Hui Ming Ching* (*The Book of Consciousness and Life*), and "an introductory note by Salome Wilhelm containing a brief but important comment by her husband on the *Hui Ming Ching*" (xi). For discussion of these key terms, their relation to one another and alterations in their translation, see Baynes' Translator's Preface to the 1962 revised edition, in which she outlines that Wilhelm's son Helmut introduced the translation of *hsing* as "human nature":

> Revision has brought about some radical changes in terminology in this edition. On the advice of Helmut Wilhelm, *hsing*, which was translated

as "essence" (*Wesen*), has been changed to "essence of human nature," or, briefly, "human nature". *Hsing*, very often co-ordinated with *ming*, life, like the latter, is a cosmic principle. It is, of course, startling to the Western reader to think of human nature in those terms, but the idea is fundamental to Chinese philosophy. A third world principle, *hui*, has importance in the new edition because of the *Hui Ming Ching*. *Hui*, consciousness, is related to *hsing*, human nature, but is not identical with it. A link in common is that both are opposites of *ming*, life, but they are separate concepts in Chinese thought. (*Secret* xi)

⁵ Probably a typographical error. Possible contenders for a relevant definition of *hui* are "[c]lever, intellectual, wise. Quick-witted" (M. 2333) and "[t]o understand, acquired ability [sic]" (M. 2345, sense "b"). [HG] Given Mottram's adherence to the Wilhelm-Baynes translation in this essay, it can be assumed that he intends *hui*. He echoes Wilhelm and Baynes' interpretation of *hui* as "consciousness". He also takes the relation of *hsing* to *hui* from their translation and the "radical changes in terminology" of the 1962 revised edition. See *Secret* xi. For quotation from Baynes' Translator's Preface regarding this matter, the significance of *hui* in the first English edition, and Mottram's definition of *hsing* as "human nature" throughout this essay (which he also takes from Wilhelm and Baynes), see n.4.

⁶ See Noel Stock, *The Life of Ezra Pound* (London: Routledge and Paul, 1970) 253.

⁷ R. Buckminster Fuller, Introduction to *Expanded Cinema* by Gene Youngblood (New York, NY: Dutton, 1970) 26.

⁸ C. Daly King, *The States of Human Consciousness* (New Hyde Park, NY: University Books, Inc., 1963) 100-101.

⁹ Pound, *The Spirit of Romance* rev. ed. (New York, NY: New Directions, 2005) 91. Subsequent quotations from this work are cited in the text, abbreviated as *Spirit*. For the edition from which Mottram is working, see rev. ed. (Norfolk, CT: J. Laughlin, 1952).

¹⁰ Quotation has been amended by the editor in keeping with the original text. Salome Wilhelm, Foreword to *The Secret of the Golden Flower* by Richard Willhelm xvi.

¹¹ Charles Olson, "The Ring Of," written in October 1951, *In Cold Hell, In Thicket* (Palma de Mallorca: Divers Press, 1953); "An Ode on Nativity," written in December 1951, appeared in *Montevallo Review* 1/3 (Spring 1952) and was reprinted the following year in *In Cold Hell, In Thicket*.

¹² Lineation replaced by editor. Mottram quotes from the first verse of "The Ring Of," which reads as follows:

> it was the west wind caught her up, as
> she rose
> from the genital
> wave, and bore her from the delicate
> foam, home
> to her isle

See *The Collected Poems of Charles Olson: Excluding the Maximus Poems*, ed. George F. Butterick (Berkeley and Los Angeles, CA: University of California Press, Reprint 1997) 243. Subsequent citations from this text are abbreviated as *Collected*.

[13] Lineation replaced by editor. Mottram quotes section III of "An Ode on Nativity":

> Any season, in this fresh time
> is off & on to that degree that any of us miss
> the vision, lose the instant and decision, the close
> which can be nothing more and no thing else
> than that which unborn form you are the content of, which you
> alone can make to shine, throw that like light
> even where the mud was and now there is a surface
> ducks, at least, can walk on. And I
> have company
> in the night (*Collected* 248)

[14] Olson read at Berkeley at the Poetry Conference 23 July 1965. The now legendary event is documented in *Reading at Berkeley*, transcript by Zoe Brown (Salinas, CA: Coyote Press, 1966). Mottram refers to the date of the reading itself. The title that Mottram gives is that of the published transcription of the reading that was made available the following year, from which he is working. The publication circulated in reproduced typescript form with an index. For Mottram's essay on the reading see "Performance: Charles Olson's Rebirth Between Power and Love," *Sixpack* 6 (winter 1973/74): 95-114. The essay's concluding paragraph is available in *The Unruly Garden: Robert Duncan and Eric Mottram, Letters and Essays*, eds. Amy Evans and Shamoon Zamir (Oxford and New York, NY: Peter Lang, 2007) 122 n.185. For Robert Duncan's enthusiastic response to it in correspondence with Mottram, see 122-130. For quotation from his letter, see footnote 61.

[15] Brown, *Reading at Berkeley* 16.

[16] Brown 32.

[17] Note that this character 明, *míng* is different to the character 命, *mìng* (fate, destiny; life M. 4537) which Mottram refers to in the opening of this essay, and it is pronounced differently. [HG] For Pound on the former, see 'The Great Digest,' *Confucius: The Great Digest, The Unwobbling Pivot, The Analects*, translation and commentary by Ezra Pound (New York, NY: New Directions, 1969) 20.

[18] Timothy Leary, *High Priest* (New York, NY: College Notes & Texts, 1968) 143.

[19] Leary 143. The paragraph reads:

> To put on a good mushroom ritual, I had wired up to Charles Olson, our father who art in Gloucester. The giant Olson, genial guru, father of modern poetry… Unfortunately it is a habit, a vice of his, always to speak his mind, as indeed Goethe did in his better moments. A few years previous he had retired to a rocky promontory overlooking the harbor whence he served as guide and friend to our work. Olson dominates any gathering with his size…

It continues by leading in to the text that Mottram cites in his next quotation.

[20] Leary 143. Leary's paragraph then concludes: "He was the person, surely, to introduce Arthur Koestler to the open-brain and its ecstatic possibilities."

[21] Leary 147. Quotation has been amended by the editor in keeping with the original text.

[22] Leary 148.

23 Words omitted by Mottram have been replaced by the editor in keeping with the original text. Charles Olson interviewed by Gerard Malanga, "The Art of Poetry No. 12," *The Paris Review* 49 (Summer 1970): 191. This interview is available as part of *The Paris Review* online archive, "Charles Olson, The Art of Poetry No. 12," *The Paris Review*, Web, 10 January 2012 <http://www.theparisreview.org/interviews/4134/the-art-of-poetry-no-12-charles-olson>. In a footnote at this point in the essay, Mottram also directs readers to Olson's *Causal Mythology* and quotes him as follows: "due to Allen [Ginsberg] I was brought into that early mushroom experience". See *Causal Mythology* (San Francisco, CA: Four Seasons Foundation, distributed by City Lights Books, 1969) 15. The essay is a lecture that Olson delivered at Berkeley in 1965. Subsequent quotations from this work are cited in the text, abbreviated as *Causal*.

24 Ezra Pound, *Confucius* 221.

25 Pound, Confucius 268. The quotation continues: "He does not merely stick to a belief." [AE] Pound interprets the upper part of the ideogram for *chen* as "shell" and the lower, "direction". To do so, he depends upon arguably dubious visual etymology, reading *chen* [貞 pinyin *zhēn*: to inquire by divination; lucky. M. 346] as the upper half of the Chinese word for change [易 *i*, pinyin *yì*: to change. M. 2592 sense "c"]. Combined with *ching* [經 pinyin *jīng*: classic book. M. 1123], it denotes the famous book of divination *The Book of Changes* or *I Ching*. Pound is correct in so far as the etymology of *chen* is combinatorial, involving a character meaning "shell" [貝 *p'ei*, pinyin *bèi*: cowries, shells, formerly used as currency; thus – valuables, precious. M. 5005]. However, the other component is in fact *pu* [卜 pinyin *bǔ*: to divine; to foretell. M. 5378], not, as Pound sees it, a schematic representation of directed motion. For that latter concept, see Ernest Fenollosa, edited by Ezra Pound, *The Chinese Written Character as a Medium for Poetry* (San Francisco, CA: City Lights Books 1964) 8-9. The character *p'ei*, "shell," occurs several times in the *Cantos*. [HG]

26 Pound, *Confucius* 268. For translation of the word *chen*, Mottram refers to Pound's note, embedded in the text of *The Analects* Book Sixteen, XXXVI. The note is reproduced here in full: "This *chen* is a key word, technical, from the 'Changes' it [sic] is more than the ataraxia of stoics, the insensitivity, ability to 'take it.' It implies going somewhere. The Confucian will find most terms of Greek philosophy and most Greek aphorisms lacking in some essential; they have three parts of a necessary four, or four parts where five are needed, nice car, no carburetor, gearshift lacking."

27 "Ataraxy:…Freedom from disturbance of mind or passion; stoical indifference," J.A.H. Murray et al, *The Oxford English Dictionary*, Vol. 1., 2nd ed. (Oxford: Oxford University Press, 1989) 742.

28 Olson's essay "Against Wisdom As Such" first appeared in *Black Mountain Review* 1 (Spring 1954): 35-39. He wrote it in response to Duncan's "Pages From a Notebook," *The Artist's View* 5 (July 1953): n.p.. See Robert Duncan, *A Selected Prose*, ed. Robert J. Bertholf (New York, NY: New Directions, 1995) 13-23; Robert Duncan, *Collected Essays and Other Prose* ed. James Maynard (New York, NY: New Directions, 2014); Charles Olson, *Collected Prose*, eds. Donald Allen and Benjamin Friedlander (Berkeley and Los Angeles, CA: University of California Press, 1997) 260-64. Subsequent quotations from this work are cited in the text, abbreviated as *Collected*. Duncan quotes from the same sections that Mottram goes on to quote in this essay when he refers to "Against Wisdom as Such" in *The H.D. Book* eds. Michael Boughn and Victor Coleman (Berkeley and Los Angeles, CA: University of California Press, 2011) 569.

[29] Quotation is not from "Against Wisdom as Such". See Duncan, "Rites of participation," which constitutes Part I, Chapter 6 of *The H.D. Book* 153-199. In it Duncan writes: "The very form of man has no longer the isolation of a superior paradigm but is involved in its morphology in the cooperative design of all living things, in the life of everything, everywhere" (153). The essay first appeared in two parts in *Caterpillar* 1 (October 1967): 6-29 and *Caterpillar* 2 (January 1968): 124-54 before appearing as a whole in Duncan, *A Selected Prose* 97-137.

[30] Mottram's editorial brackets and ellipsis.

[31] Words from the original text have been inserted at the end of the quotation by the editor. Olson's ellipsis.

[32] See "Book 2: Nights and Days," Chapters 4 and 5 in *The H.D. Book* 313-402.

[33] The paragraph from which Mottram quotes reads as follows:

> An unprejudiced reading will, however, disclose the fact that these two sources, Taoism and Buddhism, do not suffice to cover the whole range of thought: Confucianism in the form which is based on the *I Ching* is also introduced. The eight basic trigrams (*Pa Kua*) of the *I Ching* are brought into various passages of our text as symbols for certain inner processes, and further on we shall try to explain the influence resulting from this use of the symbols. For the rest, since Confucianism has a broad common base with Taoism, the union of these two schools of thought did not bring about a loss in coherence. (*Secret* 8).

[34] Mottram refers to "James Churchwarden"; properly Colonel James Churchward (1851-1936). See Churchward, *The Sacred Symbols of Mu* (New York, NY: Ives Washburn, 1933; Albuquerque, NM: Brotherhood of Life Inc., 1988) and Charles Olson, *Mayan Letters* ed. and with a preface by Robert Creeley (Bañalbufar, Mallorca: Divers Press, 1953; London: Jonathan Cape, 1968) 91. Mu is the name of a hypothetical, vanished continent in the Pacific Ocean. The name originates from the first attempted translation of the longest of the remaining Maya codices, the Madrid Codex, by the archaeologist Augustus le Plongeon. He linked Mu with Atlantis and made claims, later dismissed as erroneous, for its role in the founding of Egyptian culture. Churchward claimed that proof of the existence of Mu as the centre of civilisation lay in symbols from across the world in which he identifies common themes of birds, the relation of the Earth and the sky, and in particular the Sun. For the first of his books on this subject, see *The Lost Continent of Mu, the Motherland of Man* (New York, NY: W.E. Rudge, 1926).

[35] *A Bibliography on America for Ed Dorn* (San Francisco, CA: Four Seasons Foundation, 1964) 9. Reprinted in *Additional Prose: A Biblio-graphy on America, Proprioception & Other Notes & Essays* ed. George F. Butterick (San Francisco, CA: Four Seasons Foundation, 1974). See *Collected* 297-310.

[36] Olson, *Proprioception* (San Francisco, CA: Four Seasons Foundation, distributed by City Lights Books, 1965) 5. See *Collected* 186.

[37] Wilhelm writes:

> ...It is worth mentioning that the expression 'Golden Flower' (*Chin Hua*), in an esoteric connection, includes the word 'light'. If one writes the two characters one above the other, so that they touch, the lower part

of the upper character and the upper part of the lower character make the character for 'light' (*kuang*). Obviously this secret sign was invented in a time of persecution, when a veil of deep secrecy was necessary to the further promulgation of the doctrine. That was in turn the reason the teaching always remained limited to secret circles. Even to-day, however, its membership is greater than appears from the outside. (*Secret* 9)

The characters referred to are as follows: *Chin* 金, gold, *Hua* 花, flower and *Kuang* 光, light. (See editorial brackets, p.60). Note that Wilhelm's claim, to which Mottram refers, regarding the sign's invention and hidden "esoteric connection," depends upon an exaggeration of the Chinese characters via orthographical accident. To consider this, see M. 2212 and M. 1057. [HG and AE]

[38] Quotation has been amended by the editor in keeping with the original text. Mottram is working from C.G. *Jung Psychology and Alchemy*, trans. R.F.C. Hull (New York, NY and London: Routledge & Kegan Paul, 1953) 209. See C.G. Jung, *Psychology and Alchemy: The Collected Works of C.G. Jung Vol. 12*, Bollingen Series 20, ed. Sir Herbert Edward Read, Michael Fordham and Gerhard Adler, trans. R.F.C. Hull, 2nd ed. (London: Routledge & Kegan Paul, 1968) 218. Subsequent quotations from this work are cited parenthetically, abbreviated as *Collected*. For Olson's interest in Jung's Foreword to *Secret* and for further consideration of the importance of Jung's work for the *Maximus* project, see also Charles Stein, *The Secret of the Black Chrysanthemum: Poetic Cosmology of Charles Olson and His Use of the Writings of C.G. Jung* (Barrytown, NY: Station Hill Press, 1978). The text contains a facsimile and transcription of Olson's "Secret of the Black Chrysanthemum."

[39] Jung's text reads as follows:

…but the diamond is purest water. To draw such an analogy would be a lamentable piece of intellectual bad taste were the phenomenon of four merely a poetic conceit on the part of the conscious mind and not a spontaneous product of the objective psyche. Even if we supposed that dreams could be influenced to nay appreciable extent by auto-suggestion – in which case it would naturally be more a matter of their meaning than of their form – it would still have to be proved that the conscious mind of the dreamer had made a serious effort to impress the idea of the quaternity of the unconscious." *Collected Vol 12* 218.

[40] Jung's next page of text falls after two pages of illustrations and reads as follows:

And a spiritualistic interpretation might retort that this "self" is nothing but "spirit," which animates both soul and body and irrupts into time and space at that creative point. I purposely refrain from all such physical and metaphysical speculations and content myself with establishing the empirical facts, and this seems to me infinitely more important for the advance of human knowledge than running after fashionable intellectual crazes or jumped-up "religious" creeds.

To the best of my experience we are dealing here with very important "nuclear processes" in the objective psyche – "images of the goal," as it were, which the psychic process, being goal-directed, apparently sets up on its own accord, without any external stimulus. *Collected Vol 12* 220-221.

[41] These two quotations represent one continuous part of the poem.

[42] Mottram directs readers in particular to Olson, *Letters for Origin*, 1950-1956, ed. Albert Glover (London: Cape Goliard Press, 1969. Reprinted New York, NY: Grossman 1970), 106-107.

[43] *Tao* 道 pinyin *dào*: a road; a way; a path; from which comes the idea of *The Way*; the Truth; a doctrine; a principle; reason. M. 6136. The sentence that Mottram omits and indicates with an ellipsis reads as follows: "Heavenly paths are those along which the constellations move; the path of man is the way along which he must travel."

Mottram footnotes his quotation with the following statement: "Olson uses Blake, as we have seen, for the rejection of opposites for 'contraries', and this seems in many ways to be a more useful method of handling the division".

See William Blake, *The Marriage of Heaven and Hell* in *The Complete Poetry and Prose of William Blake*, ed. David V. Erdman rev. ed. 1982 and foreword 2008 (Berkeley and Los Angeles, CA: University of California Press 1965, 1981 rev. ed. 1982 and foreword 2008) pl. 3, 34. Blake writes:

> Without Contraries is no progression. Attraction and Repulsion, Reason and Energy, Love and Hate, are necessary to Human existence.

[44] Mottram quotes from Baynes' editorial footnote. See *Secret* 15, n.1.

[45] Words from original text have been re-inserted. The words replaced where Mottram employs ellipses are as follows: "In Taoism, on the other hand, the goal is to preserve in a transfigured form the idea of the person, the 'traces' left by experience. That is…".

[46] In a footnote at this point in the essay, Mottram directs readers to Jung's *Mysterium Coniunctionis* (1955-6). See C.G. Jung, *Mysterium Coniunctionis: An Inquiry into the Separation and Synthesis of Psychic Opposites in Alchemy. The Collected Works of C.G. Jung Vol. 14*, Bollingen series 20, ed. Sir Herbert Edward Read, Michael Fordham and Gerhard Adler, trans. R.F.C. Hull, (London: Taylor and Francis 1963. 2nd ed. London: Routledge & Kegan Paul, 1970).

[47] Quotation has been amended by the editor in keeping with the original text. Mottram's original editorial brackets contained part of Baynes' footnote from *Secret*, inserted above in full. Mottram's ellipsis. Paragraph indentation and words have been re-inserted ("The Golden Flower is the light. What colour has the Light? One uses…"). An elided paragraph has not been replaced. Butterick comments on Olson's marked up copy of *The Secret of the Golden Flower* at this section: "…rather than the source, the text is probably the confirmation of an experience" (512, n.III.18). Note that Butterick's (and for his purposes, Olson's) edition of *Secret* differs extensively in punctuation and translator's word choice when compared to the edition from which Mottram is working, particularly in terms of the use of the term "Way," Mottram's focus in this essay. For example, in the edition to which Butterick refers, "the Way" appears as "Meaning," "primal" is "primordial," "shape" is "force," "symbol" is "image," and so on.

[48] Quotation is from the next paragraph of *Secret* 21.

[49] Square brackets contains words from the original text, replaced by the editor where Mottram employs ellipses.

[50] As provided in editorial brackets at pp.32 and 46: *chin* 金 pinyin *jīn*: gold; precious; metal; money (M. 1057) and *tan* 丹 pinyin *dān*: a pill; a decoction that confers immortality. (M.6026). The latter character also means "red" or "cinnabar," an ore of

mercury. Mercury was thought by early Taoists to confer immortality, although it is in fact lethally toxic. [HG]

[51] Norman Mailer, "The White Negro: Superficial Reflections on the Hipster," *Dissent* 4.3 (1957). Reprinted with criticism and Mailer's responses in *The White Negro: Superficial Reflections on the Hipster* (San Francisco, CA: City Lights Books, 1957). Now available as part of the *Dissent* online archive, "The White Negro (Fall, 1957)," *Dissent* 20 June 2007, web, 15 January 2012 <http://www.dissentmagazine.org/online_articles/the-white-negro-fall-1957>.

[52] Quotation has been amended by the editor in keeping with the original text. Marshall McLuhan, *War and Peace in the Global Village* (New York, NY: Bantam Books, 1968) 175.

[53] Marshall McLuhan and Harley Parker, *Counterblast* (Toronto: McClelland & Stewart, 1969) 22. McLuhan's own magazine version appeared in 1954. Parker created the layout and design for later editions. A republication of the original 1954 text, on the occasion of the McLuhan centenary, is available from Gingko Press (Hamburg) in a hardcover limited edition facsimile of the original, with an Introduction by McLuhan's biographer Terrence Gordon and an Afterword by Elena Lamberti.

[54] Quotation has been amended by the editor in keeping with the original text. See Mary Caroline Richards, *Centering in Pottery, Poetry, and the Person* (Middletown, CT: Wesleyan University Press, 1964).

[55] See the opening lines of Pound's *Pisan Cantos*, which include the following: "To build the city of Dioce whose terraces are the colour of stars" (*Cantos* 74.445). See also *Cantos* 80.530. For discussion of Pound's notes regarding Dioce and its inclusion or absence in different versions of the poem, see Lawrence Rainey, *A Poem Containing History: Textual Studies in The Cantos*, (Ann Arbor, MI: University of Michigan Press, 1997) 201.

[56] Olson, *Reading At Berkeley* 22.

[57] Olson, *Letters for Origin* 107.

[58] First published in French: *Le Yoga: immortalité et liberté* (Paris: Librairie Payot, 1954). See *Yoga: Immortality and Freedom*, trans. W.R. Trask, Bollingen Series 41 (Princeton, NJ: Princeton University Press, 1969).

[59] See *Collected* 172. Text reads "the EXCEPTIONAL man, the 'hero'". As Donald Allen and Benjamin Friedlander explain regarding "The Gate and the Center":

> Developed into an essay on the basis of two letters to Robert Creeley (of 27 July and 4 August 1950); published in the inaugural issue of Cid Corman's magazine *Origin*, Spring 1951; reprinted in HU [*Human Universe and Other Essays*, ed. Donald Allen (Berkeley and Los Angeles, CA: University of California Press, 1965)]. Donald Allen and Benjamin Friedlander outline the origins of "The Gate and the Center" as follows: "From Frances Boldereff Olson's interest in archaic history received new stimulus. She sent him Samuel Noah Kramer's translations of Sumerian poetic texts in May of 1949, and in the summer of 1950, after meeting Edith Porada, the book on cylinder seals quoted in the essay." (*Collected* 412, n.168.)

[60] *Apollonius of Tyana: A Dance, with Some Words, for Two Actors* (Black Mountain, NC: Black Mountain College, 1951). Reprinted in 1966 as part of the *Selected Writings of*

Charles Olson series (see next endnote). For Mottram's essay on Apollonius, see "Charles Olson's *Apollonius of Tyana*," *Sixpack* 3/4 (1973): 31-42. In a letter to Mottram 23 January 1974 Duncan praises both this essay and Mottram's "Performance: Charles Olson's Rebirth Between Power and Love," *Sixpack* 6 (Winter 1973/74): 95-114. Duncan discusses himself and Olson in relation to the figures of Prometheus and Zeus:

> That curious exchange of configurations between mine in which (Prometheus) (Titan) (pre-fire man) or (pre-control or pre-secret man) 'steals' the secret, i.e. the use of fire from Zeus (no father of Prometheus, who in all accounts is of an earlier order) (but portrayd [sic] by me as the 'Fire-Source.'
>
> and Olson's in which he wld – again put off the father – Zeus Olympian he always was AGIN [sic]; and in 'I never knew I was Promethean' 'until now' claim again the titanic (in Whiteheadian terms – the primordial) nature of the instant.

See Evans and Zamir, eds., 122-123. See also Olson, *Causal* 2. Olson opens the essay with a page-long statement by Duncan in which derivation from the older, and rapidly disappearing, generation is presented as Promethean robbery. Olson responds by means of introducing his lecture as follows: "You know I'm very obliged to get rid of that rap for being Zeus. I never knew I was Prometheus until now. It's a fine thing – I've been a father figure too long. [Laughter]."

For details of Olson's Berkeley reading, see endnote 14. For Apollonius in Pound's *Cantos*, see *Cantos* 91, 92, 93, 94 and 101.

[61] Mottram is working from *Selected Writings of Charles Olson* ed. Robert Creeley (New York, NY: New Directions, 1966) 142. Subsequent quotations from this work are cited in the text, abbreviated as *Selected*.

[62] Mottram provides a footnote directing readers to *The Magazine of Further Studies* 6 (Buffalo, NY: The Institute of Further Studies, Fall 1969): n.p.. This final issue of the magazine, which was published between 1965 and 1969, opened with Olson's piece. His writing also featured in issues 3, 4 and 5. Mottram discusses the same quotation in his essay "Robert Duncan: The Possibilities of an Adequate History and of a Poetics of Event" (Evans and Zamir, eds., 230). He compares Olson's lines with Duncan's untitled, two-page entry in the same issue of the magazine, in which the latter outlines seven "kinds of form and their associations with ideas of the universe" (n.p.). Mottram asks "What would an anarchist poetics be, then, as an organizing process of the language of de-centred, anarchist life?" before summarizing Duncan's list of categories, and arguing "[h]ow near this is to Olson's belief" in the relationship of form and knowledge, the poet as creator, and the poet's relationship to the universe. See Evans and Zamir, eds., 229-230.

[63] Words from the primary text preceding "the terms" have been re-inserted by the editor.

[64] Olson's words, quoted by Mottram, echo the opening sentence of *The Secret of the Golden Flower* (21). Butterick records that Olson's copy of *Secret* is marked on this page and discusses its influence on Olson's image of light ("Imbued/ with the light"). See *A Guide to The Maximus Poems* 512 n.III.18. For quotation from this note, see endnote 47. Olson envisages these particular words of Wilhelm's translation important enough to act as an epigraph to his lecture. He explains:

> The thing that I would like to do instead of what sounds like a subject, like Causal Mythology, is actually to talk four things [sic]:

> The Earth
> The Image of the World
> The History or City
> and   The Spirit of the World

> and do those four things under an epigraph which would be:

> *that which exists through itself is what is called meaning.* (2)

[65] Note that this quotation refers to a statement of Robert Duncan's and not Olson's. For large sections, the text of *Causal Mythology* takes the form of a dialogue between the two poets.

[66] Charles Olson. The text reads in full: "And believe you me I know everyone has their own recognitions, which Duncan knows so well too. This is one of the exciting things about something that the word 'myth' used to mean." (*Causal* 37)

[67] Olson's statement is in reply to a question concerning representation of the feminine: Richard Duerden asks "Could you give a different shot at that anima mundi as woman, did you say?" Olson responds: "Yeah, I just meant the rather classic figure which I... well, for example in the Tarot deck it's the El Mundo, card XXI is anima mundi... She's the Virgin...she's the whole works. She's it" (35). Olson's ellipses. The question refers to Olson's earlier words: "...I'd like finally to end with the spirit of the world, which I have never been able to see as other than the figure of woman as she is such in the very phrase *anima mundi...*" (32). Butterick directs readers of "Anima/ Mundi" in *Maximus* to Jung, *Psychology and Alchemy*, figures 8 and 91. See *A Guide to The Maximus Poems* 295, n.II.36. These figures are as follows: figure 8 demonstrates "The *anima mundi*, guide of mankind, herself guided by God" depicted in an engraving by J.T. de Bry, from Fludd, *Utriusque cosmi maioris scilicet et minoris metaphysica* (1617-1621) and figure 91 illustrates *"Anima Mundi,"* titled "Anima Mercury" within the figure itself, taken from Thurneisser zum Thurn, *Quinta essentia* (1574). See Jung, *Psychology and Alchemy* 47 and 189.

[68] Quotation has been amended by the editor in keeping with the original text.

[69] 1911: the date of publication of *The Spirit of Romance*, which Mottram mentions throughout the essay. See in particular "Psychology and the Troubadours," in which Pound states:

> [t]here are at least two paths – I do not say that they lead to the same place – the one ascetic, the other for want of a better term "chivalric." In the first the monk or whoever he may be, develops, at infinite trouble and expense, the secondary pole within himself, produces his charged surface which registers the beauties, celestial or otherwise, by "contemplation." In the second, which I must say seems more in accord with "mens sana in corpore sano" the charged surface is produced between the predominant natural poles of two human mechanisms. (*Spirit* 94)

[70] The section of text to which Mottram refers reads as follows:

> Spirit-fire is the light (logos). Thought-earth is the heavenly heart of the middle dwelling (intuition). Spirit-fire is used for effecting, thought-earth for substance, and seed-water for the foundation. Ordinary men make their bodies through thoughts. The body is not only the seven-foot-tall outer body. In the body is the anima. The anima, having produced consciousness, adheres to it... (*Secret* 26)

[71] Quotation has been heavily amended by the editor in keeping with the original text.

[72] See D.H. Lawrence, *Fantasia of the Unconscious and Psychoanalysis and the Unconscious* (Harmondsworth: Penguin, 1971): see also Olson, *A Bibliography on America for Ed Dorn*, to which Mottram probably refers and from which he quotes on p.9.

[73] See "the southeast wind blows over / Dogtown...," *OLSON: The Journal of the Charles Olson Archives* 9 (Spring 1978) 50. The poem to which Mottram refers features within a selection of several poems from the same period that Olson did not include in *Maximus*. See "Maximus Poems, 1959-1963" 3-74 and editor's notes provided by Butterick 75-86. The relevant opening lines of the poem are as follows:

> the southeast wind blows over
> Dogtown rain-bearing wind well-watered wide-enfolding
> Dogtown
> now the Goddess of All Things rises
> from Chaos and turning like a dizzy top
> ...

The editorial note to the poem reads:

> Handwritten manuscript along with xeroxed copy made by poet found among *Maximus IV, V, VI* materials. It was read at Vancouver, 14 Aug. 1963, immediately following "Dogtown the dog town..." (*Maximus II* 18) from 15 Nov. 1960, so that it may have been written that early although another version – or at least its opening portion – was found in a notepad containing "On Schedule Ahead," dated "before Feb 14th 1962." At some point Olson apparently lost track of the date, because a note on the original reads: "placement abt right? note Dec 3rd, 1962." It was, in any case, abandoned from *Maximus IV, V, VI*. The xeroxed original additionally indicates the poem was intended for that volume, but it was left out of the manuscript sent Jeremy Prynne for typing in 1964, so that Olson had excluded it from the series before then.
>
> The poem draws upon what Robert Graves calls the pre-Hellenic or 'Pelasgian' creation myth, as recounted in his *Greek Myths I* 27-28.

[74] Mottram's italics. He is working from Section 22 of George Oppen, *Of Being Numerous* (New York, NY: New Directions, 1968). See Oppen, *New Collected Poems*, ed. Michael Davidson (New York, NY: New Directions, 2002) 175.

[75] Mottram directs readers in a footnote to John Cage's *Silence*. See Cage, *Silence: Lectures and Writings*, (Middletown, CT: Wesleyan University Press, 1961).

[76] Mottram's quotation covers a large section of the original text that comprises several paragraphs and a titled section break. His use of ellipses to achieve this has not been altered.

[77] Mottram's editorial brackets, in which he quotes from the previous sentence in *Secret*: "This section mentions first Yii [sic] Ch'ing's magical spell for the far journey." (60)

[78] *The Special View of History*, ed. Ann Charters (Berkeley, CA: Oyez, 1970). This is a series of lectures at Black Mountain College that Olson delivered during May 1956. The lectures were previously included in *Human Universe and Other Essays* ed. Donald Allen (Berkeley, CA: University of California Press, 1965).

[79] Wilhelm's parenthesis. Mottram's editorial brackets, possibly typographical errors, have been replaced.

[80] Editorial brackets, replacing words from the original text where Mottram employs ellipses.

[81] At this point in the essay, Mottram provides a footnote listing the following works by Norman O. Brown: *Life Against Death: The Psychoanalytic Meaning of History* (Middletown, CT: Wesleyan University Press, 1959) and *Love's Body* (New York, NY: Random House, 1966). See also C.G. Jung, *Symbols of Transformation. The Collected Works of C.G. Jung Vol 5*. Bollingen Series 20. Ed. Sir Herbert Edward Read, Michael Fordham and Gerhard Adler. Trans. R.F.C. Hull (1952, a revision of *Psychology of the Unconscious*, 1911-12. 2nd ed. London: Routledge & Kegan Paul, 1967); see n.38 and n.46.

[82] Olson, *The Special View of History* 54.

[83] Robert Duncan, *Derivations: Selected Poems, 1950-1956* (London: Fulcrum Press, 1968) 130. In "Source," Duncan writes: "I work at language as a spring of water works at the rock, to find a course, and so, blindly. In this I am not a maker of things, but, if maker, a maker of a way. For the way is itself." Mottram quotes more extensively from this work by Duncan and discusses it at length in his essay "Robert Duncan: The Possibilities of an Adequate History and of a Poetics of Event" (1988). The essay was originally available in the British small press magazine that Mottram co-founded and co-edited, *Talus* 3 (1988): 118-148. It is reproduced and annotated in the Duncan-Mottram correspondence. See Evans and Zamir, eds., 211. The volume also includes Mottram's earlier and better-known essay on Duncan, "Heroic Survival through Ecstatic Forms: Robert Duncan's *Roots and Branches*," which originally featured in *Scales of the Marvelous*, eds. Robert Bertholf and Ian Reid (New York, NY: New Directions, 1979) 116-142.

[84] C.G. Jung, "Appendix in Memory of Richard Wilhelm," *Secret* 147. Note that Mottram's comparison of Olson with Apollonius also echoes Jung's praise of Wilhelm in the Appendix:

> …We have to-day a Gnostic movement in the anonymous masses which exactly corresponds psychologically with the Gnostic movement nineteen hundred years ago. Then, as to-day, solitary wanderers like the great Apollonius spun the spiritual threads from Europe back to Asia, perhaps to remotest India.
>
> Looked at from such a historical perspective, I see Wilhelm in the guise of one of those great Gnostic intermediaries who brought the cultural heritage of Asia Minor into contact with the Hellenic spirit, and thereby caused a new world to rise out of the ruins of the Roman Empire. Then, as now, the continent of the spirit was inundated, leaving only single peaks projecting like islands from the limitless flood. Then, as now, all sorts of devious paths beckoned the mind and the wheat of false prophets flourished. (*Secret* 146-147)

[85] For example, see Olson's final text, "The Secret of the Black Chrysanthemum," *OLSON: The Journal of the Charles Olson Archives* 3 (Spring 1975): 64-92. Though unavailable to Mottram in this publication at the time of writing, he is clearly aware of the poem, written by Olson while in Manchester Memorial Hospital, Connecticut, in 1970. The opening lines read as follows:

The Secret of the Golden Flower ---- The Secret of the Black Chrysanthemum

                                   Everything issues from, & nothing is
                                              anything but itself
                                              measured so,
are both <u>alchemical</u> dictations   no mine was a dictation, Lu Tung Pin's
a careful complete   [are not therefore
& completing both I have not
written or made the dictation to my self   [yet presently seems the same
                                    Cosmos   spiritual teaching as
              Garden   Al Paradis ...   (64)

At the beginning of his editorial notes to the poem, Butterick states that the title and much of the poem's content are based upon *The Secret of the Golden Flower*. Butterick reminds readers that "chrysanthemum, in its original Greek means 'golden flower'" and gives direction to words of the same poem that Mottram cites earlier in this essay, "MAXIMUS, FROM DOGTOWN – II," written by Olson a decade before "The Secret of the Black Chrysanthemum": "the Black Chrysanthemum... is the Black Gold Flower". See also endnote 38

[86] M. 6037. See *Cantos* 486, 496, 574, 635, 695, 697, 699, 743. Compare Pound's symbol for temple, <u>*hieron*</u>: in *Cantos* 699 and 741. [HG]

[87] Eliade, *Yoga* xvi-xix.

[88] Ezra Pound, *Section: Rock-Drill* (London: Faber and Faber, 1955). See *Cantos* 93.629.

[89] On the Na-Khi and Pound, see Emily Mitchell Wallace, "'Why not spirits?' – 'the universe is alive': Ezra Pound, Joseph Rock, the Na Khi, and Plotinus," in *Ezra Pound & China*, ed. Zhaoming Qian (Ann Arbor, MI: University of Michigan Press, 2003) 213-77; and references cited therein. As a corrective, see also Chapter 10 of Zhaoming Qian, *Ezra Pound's Chinese Friends: Stories in Letters* (New York, NY: Oxford University Press, 2008). [HG]

[90] The play to which Mottram refers is *Kakitsubata*. It takes its title from the word for a Japanese species of the iris flower. See Ezra Pound and Ernest Fenollosa, *The Classic Noh Theater of Japan* (New York, NY: New Directions, 1959) 122-130. See also Fenollosa, *"Noh" or Accomplishment: a Study of the Classical Stage of Japan* (London: Macmillan, 1916).

[91] First published in French: Mircea Eliade, *Le Chamanisme et les techniques archaiques de l'extase* (Paris: Librairie Payot, 1951). The edition to which Mottram refers is Mircea Eliade, *Shamanism: Archaic Techniques of Ecstasy* trans. W.R. Trask, Bollingen Series 76 (1964; reprint 1974).

[92] For Mottram's ongoing exchange with Duncan regarding the poet as shaman, belief and poetic "tribalism," particularly in relation to Olson, see Evans and Zamir, eds., 55, 60, 81-82 and 105.

[93] "Postscript to *The Natural Philosophy of Love* by Remy de Gourmont," *Pavannes and Divagations* trans. and with a postscript by Ezra Pound (New York, NY: Boni and Liveright, 1922. Reprinted New York, NY: New Directions, 1958) 203. For "Remy de Gourmont: A Distinction," see Section III of Part One, "Instigations of Ezra Pound: Together with an Essay on the Chinese Written Character (1920)," *Literary Essays of*

Ezra Pound ed. T.S. Eliot (New York, NY: New Directions, 1954) 339-358. See also Richard Sieburth, *Instigations: Ezra Pound and Remy de Gourmont* (Cambridge, MA: Harvard University Press, 1978).

Robert Hampson

ERIC MOTTRAM AND EZRA POUND: "THERE IS NO SUBSTITUTE FOR A LIFE-TIME."

SOME REMINISCENCES

When I was interviewed for an undergraduate place at King's College, London, early in 1967 by Patrick Yarker, I was told about a "bright young man" King's had recently appointed. (Eric Mottram had been appointed as Lecturer in American Literature in 1961 and was 42 at the time of the interview.) Eric was to prove a stimulating teacher, bursting with energy and information: among other things, he introduced us to a range of recent counter-cultural thinking from Buckminster Fuller, Marshall McLuhan and Situationism to Wilhelm Reich and the importance of good sex. I remember his second-year lectures on American Literature (on Faulkner and Pynchon, in particular) and his third-year revision seminars on Donne and Milton, but I don't remember him teaching me explicitly about Pound. Nevertheless, through Eric's teaching, I absorbed elements of a Poundian approach to poetry, thinking of poetic forms as containers of energy and information. He had taught Donne as a poet energised by the fear and excitement of having a familiar framework of knowledge ruptured by new information – and *Paradise Lost* as an attempt to contain new knowledge within a Christian paradigm, which made sense of many of Milton's anachronistic epic similes.

Besides his passionate commitment to radical thought and the intellectual life, what Eric also brought to his teaching was a readiness to cross disciplinary boundaries (before we knew there were boundaries there to be crossed) and an openness to a range of cultures. Although we didn't think of him as a World War II veteran, his war-service in the navy had taken him from the North Sea, the Arctic Circle and Murmansk to the Indian Ocean, Thailand and the rivers of Burma; he had subsequently travelled in Japan, the Philippines, and Vietnam; and he had taught for some years in Switzerland, Singapore and Holland before his arrival at King's.[2] This, no doubt, was related to his love of Pound: as Clive Bush recalls, Eric liked, in Pound, "the big cultural field, the depth of historical culture, the internationalism, the use of different languages… the devotion to the Provençal, the Italian, the Chinese".[3]

My return from a Commonwealth Scholarship to Toronto University in 1971 to begin doctoral research at King's coincided with the start of Eric's editorship of the *Poetry Review*. The next decade included not only events at the Poetry Society, but also the "Modern British Poetry Conference" (1974), the "Poetry of the Americas Conference" (1975) and the "Conference on British Poetry" (1977) which Eric co-organised at the Polytechnic of Central London as well as various colloquia on contemporary US poetry at the Institute of United States Studies, where Eric co-directed and taught on the MA. The first PCL conference, a manifestation of what Eric called the British Poetry Revival, featured 15 poets including Basil Bunting and Hugh MacDiarmid, who affirmed the continuity with earlier modernism.[4] I remember seeing Eric, Bob Cobbing and Jeff Nuttall standing together in conversation at one point during the conference and thinking of them as the centres of three distinct sub-groups within the "London School" of experimental poetry.

The second PCL conference came with a conference essay by Eric, "The Entrance to the Americas: Poetry, Ecology, Translation", which began with the assertion that "Dada, Surrealist, Projective Verse, the Pound and Williams ideogrammatic forms and concrete / soundtext poetry structures are international" before moving through Noam Chomsky, Claude Lévi-Strauss and Jerome Rothenberg to explore "primitivism" and to foreground translation as "the means of moving between cultures". That opening assertion reflects what I took from Eric as the matrix of modern and contemporary poetry; while the focus on translation explicitly picked up on Denise Levertov's notion of "the artist as translator", in the sense of "the translation of experience... putting the receiver in the place of the event" and led, among other things, into an extended account of the magazines *El Corno Emplumado* (1962-69) and *Io* (1965-74) to demonstrate the democratic role of translation: "What to the conventional and fearful appeared to be an elitist erudition was in fact a profoundly democratic invitation to exciting and necessary knowledge".[5]

The third conference, another manifestation of the British Poetry Revival, featured some twenty-two poets, from Elaine Feinstein to Bill Griffiths. The conference booklet concluded with a long essay by Eric on "Inheritance Landscape Location: Data for British Poetry 1977", which began with the assertion that a poet "works at the intersection of his time and his place": "the poem emerges from complex location which includes the poet's understanding of his cultural inheritance, his urban or country experience, the work he does for a livelihood, his regional and political affiliations, and his incorporation or refusal of other cultural resources than those of his immediate nation" (Mottram, 1977, 85). The essay then considers the work of the various contributors to the conference in relation to this set of propositions before discussing more generally the relation between poetry, mental maps and the perceptual environment. This part of the essay is clearly influenced by Charles Olson – Eric quotes from "The Distances" and cites Olson's "Human Universe" and "Causal Mythology" essays – but he concludes with Pound's phrase that not only "gave the coherence of the *Cantos*" but also "could include major work in this century by both British and American poets": namely, "the building of the City, that whole tradition".[6] Iain Sinclair began his reading at the conference with a psychogeographic engagement with the lecture room in which the conference took place, but most of us were already aware of at least one ghost haunting the location. In January 1909 Pound had begun a series of lectures at what was then the Regent Street Polytechnic; he was re-employed for a second series of lectures starting in October 1909, which became his first critical book, *The Spirit of Romance*.

This decade also marked my period of closest collaboration with two other King's graduates, Peter Barry and Ken Edwards.[7] It was during this period that we co-edited *Alembic* and developed our own mental mappings of contemporary British and US poetry. By the end of the decade I had derived, largely from Eric, a sense of the importance of Pound as *fons et origo* for modernist poetics.[8] There was the mythical originating moment in 1912 in the teashop in Kensington (or the British Museum tearoom), when Pound "corrected" HD's poem "Hermes of the Ways" and founded Imagisme. More importantly, there were the sacred texts of Imagisme; the need to "break the pentameter"; notions of the impersonal and the "objective"; and the ideogrammatic method as a form of "*condensare*", one of the poetic procedures for rendering complexity. *The ABC of Reading*, Pound's *Literary Essays* and his engagement with Fenollosa's work on the Chinese written character provided further guidance. Pound's definition of the epic as a poem including history fitted well with my earlier interest in Virgil, Dante and Milton, but the conception of the long poem as a research project and the emphasis on formal experiment were Poundian practices that reached us through Eric.[9] Otherwise, reading of Pound was dominated by Hugh Kenner's *The Pound Era* and was further mediated through engagement with William Carlos Williams and Charles Olson. Pound's explicit attachment to fascism was also important: it forced a confrontation with the relationship between poetry and politics (that in Yeats or Eliot was obfuscated or side-stepped). Here again Olson was an important figure, but Eric too embodied an attempt to derive a method of "democratic composition" from a man who sought totalitarian order.[10]

LIGHT OVER LIGHT:[11]

Eric published six essays either on Pound or giving prominence to Pound. The earliest of these was "Pound, Olson and the Secret of the Golden Flower", published in the "Chinese Issue" of *Chapman* (Edinburgh) in the summer of 1972.[12] The essay begins by asserting that both Pound and Olson placed themselves "within an onward going process of informational and emotional discovery whose form is the Work, in the alchemical sense of their lifetimes" (20). Part of the process is "the discovery of what forces, unexplored or to be recovered or renewed, the body may hold as the field of Psyche and Eros" (20); the other part is "that situation of total energy we experience as the ecology of the universe" (20). Out of this comes, for the poet, "a process of continuous growth and the invention of forms, whose informational parameters open out into a vision of a way of life" (20). The essay engages with *The Secret of the Golden Flower*, a Taoist text of Chinese yoga, a translation of which was published with an Introduction by Jung.[13] Eric's essay considers Pound and Olson in this context and works towards an opposition between Pound's sense of failing to reach transcendence in the *Cantos* and Olson's effort "to place us firmly in the world" (56): "For Olson, the Way is secular, unmysterious, and based on practical eros" (62).

The second piece was an extended essay on "Sixties American Poetry, Poetics and Poetic Movements" in Marcus Cunliffe's monumental *Sphere History of Literature in the English Language*.[14] The essay begins with "cubist and Dadaist dislocations and re-assemblages" as a "resource in innovative literature from the 1920s" before citing William Carlos Williams, Pound and Zukofsky and their use of US speech cadences as basic measures (271). It is Pound, however, who dominates the early part of the essay: his editing of Ernest Fenellosa's work as *The Chinese Written Character as a Medium for Poetry*, which revealed the "possibilities of new spatial organization in poetry" from 1908; his 1915 essay "Imagisme and England" on lyric poetry where melody moves into speech; and his transmitting of "Laforgue's interplay of animate and inanimate, and his syllabic forms" into US currency (272). Eric would have had in mind here work such as Pound's "Our Tetrarchal Précieuse", based on Laforgue's "Salomé", which was first published in the *Little Review* and collected in *Pavanes and Divisions* (1918). As David Moody observes, Pound "wanted to administer Laforgue to America as "a purge and a critic" (Moody, 336).

Although the essay is nominally about "Sixties American poetry", it reaches the sixties after a long, tightly-written account of modernist and anti-modernist counterforces from the start of the century. Thus, after working through surrealists, conceptualists and Southern Agrarians, Eric picks out

89

Pound's *Active Anthology* (1933) as a "fairly representative summary of major writing in the early 1930s" (276), before alighting on the "peaks" of that period: "the continuously inventive forms of Williams' *Patterson*... the ideograms and lyrics of Pound's *Cantos*, and the nervous argumentative journals of Zukofsky's *A*" (277). These three are presented as the "masters" for the "New American poetry", but it is also clear which is pre-eminent for Eric. The *Cantos* "were not only a compendium of poetic resources but demonstrated the ability to compose an epic poetry which placed the active self within a wide range of defining information" (278). They also evolved "a syntax which was not bound to the traditional sentence" (282). The *Cantos*, accordingly, provided the model for the long poem during the period 1950-1970 – for major works such as Olson's *Maximus* and Duncan's *Bending the Bow*. Indeed, "as late as 1969, Pound's *Drafts & Fragments of Cantos CX-CXVII* showed how this great onward-going work remained the central act of poetry" (279).

However, Eric's interest in Pound, Williams and Zukofsky is not just a matter of "fine craftsmanship", but also because they "speak urgently of society" (277). In Pound's case, the *Cantos* address "the main interests of major American poets of a younger generation": "the renewal of a city, the renewal of mythology, the destruction of a degenerate economic system, the placing of the Southeast Asian conflict within the historical conduct of America and the West, and the possibility of strategies of survival without being overwhelmed by the defeats of compromise" (279). As a result, Eric claims, with the publication of *Drafts*, "More than ever the *Cantos* could be seen as the measure, both in their poetics and their information, for the committed American poet" (279).

The essay offers a reading of the *Drafts* in terms of "scorn for materialistic greed" combined with Pound's "remorse at his own behaviour and a search for personal charity" that seeks to align them with "the 1960s Movement" (279). It asserts, apparently against the grain of Pound's earlier support for Mussolini and Confucius, that "Civilisation "without tyranny" had always been Pound's criterion" (279). Eric is on firmer ground when he then presents Olson as building on Pound's "structure of continuous and overlapping ideograms" (281) and developing Pound's notion of *melopoeia*. He is on firmer ground still when he presents Olson and Duncan, poets "in the immediate tradition of Pound", as "radical" in their "opposition to official America" and "erudite in the Miltonic sense" (293) through the amount of information in the work of both.

In his next essay, "Pound, Merleau-Ponty and the Phenomenology of Poetry", published in Ian Bell's *Ezra Pound: Tactics for Reading* (1982), Eric returns to *Drafts* and the issue of Pound's politics. The essay begins with "the writer's responsibility in the twentieth century: his active commitment in its social determinations" (121). It approaches Pound through Merleau-Ponty's response to "the urgencies of contemporary catastrophic life" (123), an involvement in the French Resistance in combat against Nazi Occupation, which turned his thoughts to "the dynamic interchange of perception and history" (122). This is implicitly compared with Pound's support for Mussolini, while Merleau-Ponty's post-war disillusion with socialism implicitly echoes Pound's post-war despair at the failure of his very different political dream. An early reference to "Capitalism, Fascism and Communism" as "the three major totalitarian systems" (122) underwrites these implied equivalences. The essay then turns to the similarities between the philosopher and the poet in order to tease out an "essentially phenomenological position" that is increasingly apparent as Pound's epic poem "moves towards Canto 90" (122). Thus both men explore "how to confront history and nature as they simultaneously envelop us and are under our control" (122), and Pound's "particularity of information" is compared to Merleau-Ponty's refusal of "high-altitude thinking" (124). Merleau-Ponty's statement that we "must bring forth an order" in things "not inherent in them" leads to a reading of the start of Canto XCI as presenting just such "a vision and knowledge, the elements of Pound's highly mobile phenomenology, in an image of perception and form" (124). The essay then argues that this phenomenology has been present throughout the *Cantos*.

First the essay turns to anthropology as "a primary phenomenological method by which to ascertain bases" (127). It juxtaposes Merleau-Ponty's essay "From Mauss to Lévi-Strauss" (and "the configurations of the perceptual field" through various totalities called structures) to Pound's engagement with "European, Chinese, African, as well as American cultures" (127). This exploration of different "ethnographical examples of the human praxis" (129) make for a deepening of our "insertion in being" (129). Then, after explaining Pound's idea of the "complex" as "a form of latent energy provoked by experience, operating in memory" (130), Eric compares this to Merleau-Ponty's account of the gaze in his essay "Eye and Mind" ("its present mission was to erect from this motion [through time] the ever-absent unity starting from multiplicity", 133) and to Gerard Manley Hopkins' concept of inscape (135).[15] Here the essay confronts again Pound's sense of failure expressed in his late *Cantos* ("I cannot make it cohere", CXVI). First, it asserts that Cantos XC and CXI "maintained a physical sense of interface with the universe through the phenomenology of perception" (139). Then it argues that "coherence, in the terms proposed by the *Cantos* themselves," is precisely "the mobility of the poem's perceptions" (141). Finally, the essay argues that, in the late *Cantos*, Pound resumes "the accoutrements of the gods, spirit, crystal and that renaissance region of belief" as a fiction "and edges these into a certain understanding of physics" but, inevitably, falls short of the absolute at which it aims. Eric concludes: "the final cantos express his irritation with that as if it were a failure. But it is no more failure than is *The Education of Henry Adams*" (143).

The fourth essay, "'Man Under Fortune': Bases for Ezra Pound's Poetry", published in Herbie Butterfield's *Modern American Poetry* (1984), offers a reading of the *Cantos* in order to explore "Pound's decision to retrace and possibly regain the bases of a viable culture" (77). After noting Pound's discriminations of the components of poetry as *melopoeia* (words "charged… with some musical property"), *phanopoeia* ("casting of images upon the visual imagination") and *logopoeia* ("the dance of the intellect among words"), the essay begins with an examination of Pound's belief in "ultimate and absolute rhythm".[16] In an earlier essay, "A Retrospect", Pound had famously advised poets to "score by the musical phrase rather than metronomic rigidities" (*Literary Essays*, 3). This means, Mottram's essay argues, that rhythm is, simultaneously, "interpretative" and the "'inner form' in poetic design": it extends "throughout the connotative and denotative meanings and the strongly visual lay-out of the pages", which Pound derived from the Chinese ideogram and Olson elaborated in his "Projective Verse" essay. In Pound's practice, this becomes "a spatial effect in poetry derived from music" (81): a move from "monolinear verbal rhythm" to working "in musical structure", which Pound dates to 1910.[17] As Basil Bunting put it, in the statement from his obituary for Pound with which Eric's essay concludes: "If you will read the *Cantos* aloud and listen, … you will find, especially in the later *Cantos*, a surge of music that is its own meaning".[18]

This essay also addresses some of the "gaps and lacks" in the *Cantos* – such as Pound's ignorance of science and neglect of technology, an area of particular interest to Eric. Above all, it offers Eric's most direct engagement with Pound's politics. After noting Pound's address in the *Cantos* to "law, the morality of money … and the nature of supreme leaders" (83), he attempts to contextualise the last of these by describing Pound as growing up "in a century haunted by the theory and presence of dominant leaders as saviours" (84). He then describes Pound's "search for instances – in Renaissance Italy, ancient China and the early American republic – of governmental control through enlightened if dictatorial leadership from Confucian emperors to Mussolini" (84). So far the implicit distinction between "tyranny" and enlightened dictatorship sounds like an anticipation of the late-century discourse of US foreign policy with its distinction between totalitarian dictators (the enemy) and "authoritarian leaders" (our allies). Against this search for dominant leaders, however, the essay sets Pound's abiding interest in Dionysus, "the figure of chthonic and cosmic energies which are never under total control" (84). From his first appearance in Canto XI, when he is captured by sailors planning to sell him into slavery, the type of "money criminals" for subsequent cantos, he reappears throughout the *Cantos* in a variety of forms: Zagreus, Bacchus, Lycaeus, Iacchus, Bromios, and Pan (84-5). Through these re-appearances, the essay suggests, the *Cantos* explores how "Dionysian erotics *may* be diverted from the tyrannies of war, economics and politics" (85), and, by this means, the *Cantos* becomes "a major twentieth-century work exploring the inflections of social control and erotic, a-moral forces" (84).

However, the essay also registers Pound's own severe limitation. After suggesting that he dreamed that "out of Bacchic energy must be produced the totalitarian man of laws without totalitarian tyranny" (86), and that he mistook the totalitarian control of Fascism for the centred man of Confucianism (89), it confronts directly the virulent anti-semitism that simultaneously overwhelms and articulates Pound's address to economic matters: his exploration of money, credit, and circulation, and his support of producers against bankers. The essay concludes with a roll-call of Poundian shortcomings: his failure to grasp that "any form of sovereignty" implies "hierarchy and therefore loss through dominance and subordination" (90); his failure to attend to "those nineteenth-century American writers who investigated threats to the democratic from the authoritarian" (91); and his failure to pay sufficient attention to "the open-endedness of Whitman" (91).

The fifth essay, "Ezra Pound in his Time" was published in Jacqueline Kaye's *Ezra Pound and America* (1992). Most of the essays in this volume were originally papers at the 1989 "Pound and America" conference at the University of Essex: Eric's essay was a version of a paper he had given at the 1981 Pound Conference there. It follows on directly from Eric's earlier essay on Pound, Merleau-Ponty and phenomenology, but seems written as a response to Charles Bernstein's criticism of "the theory of fragments whereby poetry became a grab bag of favourite items – packed neatly together with the glue of self-conscious and self-consciously epic composition".[19] Against this, Eric asserts a reading of the *Cantos* as "a horizontal phenomenological spread into which a vertical set of 'heroic vitalism' instances had been urgently inserted" (93).[20]

As in the earlier essay, Eric attempts to address Pound's Fascism by first situating Pound in a pre-war context and by then aligning the *Cantos* with the phenomenological project: the *Cantos* were written "in a time when *totality*... had been shifted into *totalitarian*", an "arrogance of unity" which "denied problems of phenomenological relativity" (95). By foregrounding the *Pisan Cantos* and *Drafts and Fragments*, Eric focuses on the failure of

Pound's fascist ambitions, and the *Cantos* turns into "a remarkable discourse on the insertion of the self in the world" (97). By reading Pound through Merleau-Ponty, the failure of the totalitarian project becomes the necessary "disclosure of an incomplete world" (97). In addition, Eric presents Pound's *Cantos* as enacting what Merleau-Ponty calls "primordial historicity" – the return of "thinking from above" to "the soil of the sensible": the *Cantos* take "a responsible stand within the world of experience", grounded in the interdependence of seer and seen, that becomes "the action of processual poetry" as, in Merleau-Ponty's words, "agile and improvisatory thought" grounded upon things (98). Finally, Eric links Williams, Zukofsky, Olson and Duncan in this poetic tradition of lived philosophy where every phenomenon is "an exposition of knowledge in the process of manifesting itself" (106).

What is at stake in the essay is not simply an enjoyment of (and fascination with) Pound's poetry, but also (*contra* Bernstein) a defence of the American processual poem grounded in a poetics "both disruptive and combinatory", based on "the unmapped act of composition and reading" (96), and taking place within the experienced space of the human body and its multiple extensions in the world. In contrast to Eliot's "already complete and comprehended world", Eric repeats Merleau-Ponty's assertion that "the only pre-existent logos is the world itself" and "no explanatory hypothesis is clearer than the act by which we take up this unfinished world in an effort to complete and conceive it"(103). This provides the basis for a life-work, a new *paideuma*, "the active making and mediating of a world or culture through the self" (107), undertaken within "an intercontextualised set of contemporaneous relations" and with a recognition of incomplete totality.[21]

The last essay Eric published on Pound, "Pound, Whitman and the American Epic Transmission" in Andrew Gibson's *Pound in Multiple Perspective* (1993), was, appropriately enough, addressed to the American epic. The essay considers the American epic from the nationalist epics, Timothy Dwight's *Greenfield Hill* (1794) and Joel Barlow's *The Vision of Columbus* (1798) and *Columbiad* (1807), a "self-conscious effort to transplant Virgilian state epic into the Republic" (223), through to Allen Ginsberg's *The Fall of America* and Ed Dorn's *Slinger*. Whitman figures as Pound's major precursor and as the turning point in this narrative of transmission: an epic poet who confronts the "fraud culture" of commerce (227) and works for "the renewal of America" (226). The essay begins with the problems inherent to the attempt to write a "poem including history", one of which is the invention of procedures that "enable both condensing and opening up" (219). Like the problem of simplifying while presenting complexity, this was a recurrent concern of Eric's. Here he starts by citing Robert Creeley's comment on the "incredible condensing of speech" in the *Cantos* and his description of the ideogrammatic method as how to "*present* rather than comment upon".[22] Then he suggests that "Pound needed a Confucian poetics, for the poet as citizen in history and as an aid to the ruler" (218). To this end, Eric argues, Pound engaged in cultural retrieval, as "necessary for social intelligence and epic composition", and in cultural translation as a means of forwarding "the great intelligence" (221). The *Cantos*, accordingly, treat the past "as a bank for the retrieval of examples of good and evil behaviour": through "fragmentation, ellipse, synecdoche and paratactical juxtaposition, it then produces "a displacing, disruptional palimpsest and counterpoint" (220).

The context for this "de-nationalised epic", Eric argues, is a specifically American anxiety: "that American promise would not be fulfilled, that the continental expansions would not be justified... that the European inheritance would not be the transplantation for a new and finer civilisation" (221). *Greenfield Hill* had set "American happiness in contrast to European oppressions" and had prophesied "the future glories of America" (222). Even Whitman, while opposing "tyranny and slavery of every kind" (229), with his vision of post-bellum healing "through westward expansion" gives permission for "manic conquest" (230). For his part, Pound makes "certain cultures interpenetrate" to "produce the new" (235). However, Eric's essay bears the traces of its own anxiety: it refers early on to how certain "key terms" in *Drafts and Fragments* are "inherited by the whole work" and act as "mnemonics for the reader" (221). But this confident statement is ghosted by an anxiety just audible in a later allusion to the modern American epic's reliance upon "the cooperative reader, in training for the athletics of poetry... with a memory capable of holding the factors, the evidences, of coherence" (224). Here Eric is, perhaps, thinking not only of Pound, Williams, Olson, Zukofsky, Enslin and Ginsberg, but also of the demands made by his own poetry.

UNFOLDING ANATOMIES:[23]

The decade after my own return to London also saw Eric's emergence as a poet: *Inside the Whale* appeared from Writers Forum in 1971, followed by *Shelter Island* from Turret Books (1971) and *the he expression* from Aloes Books in 1973. *Two Elegies*, which appeared in 1974 from Mike Dobbie's Poet & Peasant Press, was followed in quick succession by *Local Movement* (Writer's Forum, 1974), *Against Tyranny* (Poet & Peasant, 1975), *1922 Earth Raids* (New London Pride, 1976), *Homage to Braque* (Blacksuede Boot Press, 1976) and *A Faithful Private* (Genera Editions, 1977).

Picking up on the poems dedicated to poets, artists, composers and film-makers in *the he expression*, Eric produced, through this decade, a series of poems – eventually published as *Elegies* (1981). Eric prefaces his elegies with a note on the form: "Greek elegies were directed to war and love, and were not poems of lamentation". His own elegies were a series of celebrations: Paul Blackburn, Muriel Rukeyser, Lorca, Melville, Vallejo… They also address "war and love". The series begins with an elegy dedicated to Pound and Kerouac, and the technique clearly derives from Pound. Like the elegies that follow, it is highly allusive, collaging a range of informations with personal memories in densely paratactic constructions. As the dedications suggest, the elegies deal with art, politics, nature and what Eric called, in his 1989 "Notes on 'Poetics'", "my love of being in the non-human Other: jungle, the sea, mountains" (40-41). "Elegy 11: Ford", for example, begins by evoking Ford Madox Ford's wartime experience, as refracted through that of Tietjens in Ford's war tetralogy, *Parade's End* (*Selected Poems* 60-62). It begins with the situation Ford and Tietjens find themselves in at the Front ("one dread knocked out another") and progresses towards their post-war respite ("a garden to make fine/ marrows large as barrels"). This fractured narrative is juxtaposed to others, including a vignette from Eric's own war-time experiences in southeast Asia:

> we came to a white sand   village underswept by tides
> quiet offshore fishing prows and sterns upcurved
> beyond number   women painted dyes in waxed cloth
>   blue from sky and sea
>   orange and brown from fruit and earth

This brief glimpse of "a vanished sanctuary" is juxtaposed to an armed robbery and other fragmented wartime narratives before concluding with the Poundian (and Fordian) question, "is there any/terrestrial paradise", perhaps answered by the renewed glimpse of a place where "people whom they like/ …/ take their ease/ in shadows and coolness".

Eric's most Poundian early work, however, is the long poem *Tunis* (1977). This is an abbreviated version of the long poem as research project. Starting off with a collage of fragmentary references to various North African voyages and trade-routes, that construct a maritime navigation of Tunis, the first section proceeds through the destruction of Carthage to the later archaeological recovery of sepulchres, statues and bones of human sacrifices (and the glimpse these give into the religious culture of Carthage). The second section begins with the fragmentary evocation of Roman gladiators in the amphitheatre and then presents a modern experience of *circenses* and triumphal arches as ruined remains, which includes the location of that experience in relation to "unheard deserts" southwards, Byzantium to the east, "foul kingdoms of the chained" to the west, and an imagined projection "over Atlantis":

> to a Pole strung continent of Indians
> and North Celts and north Vikings
> draw iron and pine keel across a flat ocean

This final line, with its stylistic allusion to Anglo-Saxon poetry, also thereby echoes the start of the *Cantos*.

The subsequent reference to an overland journey by station-wagon provides the occasion for an array of information about the post-Roman history of the area, culminating in "what urges jihad private and satisfying/ waiting in a state of prophecy" and an evocation of the region's music of drum and flute. The remaining sections move through short, fragmentary, sensuous memories of modern Tunis to a contemplation of conditions in "a single party country" where dancers are "under edict" and poets and actors perform in the open air with "lookouts posted".[24] These conditions are underlined by the state visit of another dictator, President Nicolae Ceausescu:

> two presidents between black shades
> uniformed children cheer outriders
> > > raise flags on order

The poem works through arrays of information and (as here) the exemplary, resonant incident. It works through textual allusion: "I came", presented as a citation, in this context recalls Augustine's "From Carthage then I came" – and its citation by T.S. Eliot in *The Waste Land*.[25] Similarly, the glancing references to Dido and Aeneas and to "Trojans / the matter of Britain" serve to remind us of Virgil's *Aeneid* and the medieval stories of the Trojan foundation of London, which were part of "the matter of Britain", the medieval romances given that name by scholars. The end of the poem, however, is striking for its tender sensuousness:

> boukha on our lips
> > > > figs on our breath
>
> as inside honey
> here they tell of dates so fine
>
> sunlight glows within

Here we have "direct treatment of the 'thing'", "no word that does not contribute to the presentation", and "composition in the sequence of the musical phrase" ("A Retrospect", 3). As Eric had learned from Pound, the thing itself was enough without recourse to symbolism. At the same time, the poem ends with this Poundian attention to light.

Eric's other major Poundian work of this period is *A Book of Herne* (1981). This takes off from childhood memories of Harrison Ainsworth's 1844 novel, *Windsor Forest*, read in an edition with illustrations by George Cruikshank, that turned into a sequence exploring the stag man, the green man, and other forms of this figure, positioned between the human and non-human or transformed from human to non-human, drawing in a range of cultural materials including the Gundestrup cauldron, the figure of Cernunnos, *Sir Gawain and the Green Knight*, *The Merry Wives of Windsor*, and modern instances from Jackson Pollock to films such as *The Deer Hunter* and *The Wicker Man*. The opening poem crosses *Windsor Forest* with the poetry of Sir Thomas Wyatt, the Phantom Hunt, and the transformation of Actaeon into a stag (from Canto IV) in an address to the hunter and the hunted, chthonic energies and desire. Subsequent poems meditate upon green-man capitals, masks and bench-ends from European churches and cathedrals, Native American deer-masks, Ovid's *Metamorphoses*, Orpheus and Dionysus to produce what the final poem presents as a liberation "from stifling motherly fathering home corruption" and "this luxury state" (96) to the achieved condition of being outlaw and at home.[26]

In a perceptive review of *A Book of Herne*, Gavin Selerie observes that the title of the first poem, "Windsor Forest", "may come straight from Ainsworth but it suggests an ironic contrast to Pope's domestication of the English landscape" in his poem of the same name (Selerie, 1982, 43). Thus, Herne's horns "seem to serve as a shamanic helmet" (Selerie, 1982, 44), while the sound of the hunt, for example, becomes "the fertility spirits which medieval Christianity tried to suppress: 'Windsor Forest' unleashes these energies and offers no simple way out" (Selerie, 1982, 45). Selerie also addresses the wide range of sources on which the poem draws, and observes: "the synthesis is not made easily and this is clearly part of Mottram's method; just as the writing is an act of discovery… the reader has to negotiate difficult planes and cope with the pull of opposite forces" (Selerie, 1982, 45). In line with this reading, the volume ends with a citation from Robert Duncan: "A multiphasic experience sought a multiphasic form".

Where the poems discussed so far have used a version of Pound's open-field scoring of the page-space, "Elegy 15: Neruda" takes the different form of a series of verse paragraphs. These register, in a non-linear array, fragmentary details of Neruda's life, an evocation of the conditions of the Chilean nitrate and copper miners, "the Kennecott and Anaconda stranglehold" (Mottram, 1978). Above all, it presents, in effect, another vision of an "earthly paradise": a socially and politically committed poetry with an appreciative working-class audience:

> in silent atmosphere the Chilean workers and peasants listen to poems
> they requested by title   what more can a poet want

Here "Elegy 15" speaks to one of Eric's recurrent concerns. Eric begins his "Notes on 'Poetics'" by suggesting that, since the 1960s, "poetry readings have become a seriously effective event in a poet's life in Britain". He mentions the Mordern Tower readings organised by Tom and Connie Pickard, and then he recalls a particular reading he gave:

> In the interval of a reading in Ric Caddel's invitation series in Durham, an elderly working-class man asked me what this line and that word meant. We sat over our beers to discuss matters. (Mottram, 1989, 37)

This is in line with Eric's support for working-class poets and his consistent support for trade unionists such as the miners.[27] This is a modernism that does not align itself with aristocratism. However, in his essay "Man Under Fortune", Eric noted the problem that Pound faced: "that the range of information in the *Cantos* may not overlap that of the reader at every point", and there was, accordingly, a need for handbooks and exegesis (82). Since his death, Eric's work has suffered a critical neglect. Part of the problem is the sheer quantity of poetry he produced, but part, too, is the range and density of allusion and reference in his work. Another factor has been the shift from processual, "content-specific" poetry to language poetry (Barry, 1993, 198).

COMPANIONS IN VOYAGE[28]

In the space available, I can deal with only a handful of people linked to Eric to explore the transmission of a Poundian influence. I have, therefore, chosen five people whose relations to Eric reflect different linkages, different degrees of influence and different aspects of that influence. There are many more individuals who could have been addressed here.[29]

Allen Fisher came to Pound ten years before he knew of Eric or Eric's work. His surviving copy of the *Cantos* is the 1970 New Directions edition of *Cantos I-CXVII*, which replaced his earlier incomplete Faber volume.

His first connection with Pound was through Pound's Chinese translations, which he read alongside books by Ginsberg, Kerouac and Snyder (Pound, 1953). He also had various recordings of Pound on long-playing records, including Pound reading from his translation of *The Confucian Odes*. Fisher describes the *Cantos* as "one of the seminal books" of his reading life and identifies Pound as one of his "main teachers" – "albeit indirectly".[30] It was through Pound that he read Homer, *The Seafarer*, Golding's translation of Ovid and Gavin Douglas. The impact of Pound on Fisher can be seen in his book *long shout to kernewek* (1965) – in the ambition of the long poem, in the placing of the self amid contemporary and historical materials, in the use of citation, in the use of particulars rather than metaphor.

As this description suggests, this influence also feeds into the *Place* project.[31] This is made explicit early in the poem. In Place IV, a meditation on sources and outcomes, figured in terms of the Thames and one of its tributaries, the Falcon Brook, Pound is used to articulate the argument in terms of textual resources: "the source in the springs/ is not the actual source/ but the first visible source/ so that if Pound said it/ it is original" is answered by "so that if Pound said it/ it is part of what has been said/ leading us on to what will be said"(41). The "Lakes" section begins with "for Ezra Pound / written before his death": here a sense of the sedimented past is played against a focus on movement forwards, expressed through the Taoist idea of the Way, complicated by the modern scientific idea of the multiverse (60-62). A later poem in Book One, "to Pierre, dec. 72", which begins "now it's Pound dead", returns to this material (86-88). This time, movement through time is also figured in terms of generations, "children and forefathers", and inheritance – from Pound to Olson, and then to Fisher and Pierre Joris: "it isn't Pound dead/ that must cause this/ it ishe is not done/ we are left not to close the shop" (87).

Fisher first met Eric Mottram in 1971 after he had published *Before Ideas, Ideas*.[32] The existing influence of Pound on Fisher was reinforced by conversations with Eric in the period after 1971. What Fisher particularly remembers is Eric's annoyance with any idea that Pound's fascism should affect our reading of his work. As in his essays, where he is always careful to describe him as a right-wing monarchist, Eric would cite Eliot as an example of a similar political problem. However, the subtler workings of Fisher's relationship with Eric can be seen in connection with Eric's essay in *Chapman* discussed above. Fisher still has his copy of the magazine, but he had been reading Lao Tzu around 1961 and Alan Watts' *The Way of Zen* in 1962, around the time when he first encountered Pound through his Chinese translations. He subsequently purchased at least two editions of the *Tao Te Ching* (Lau's in 1963 and the edition by Gia-Fu Feng and English in

1972). As with Pound, conversations with Eric (and Eric's essay) seem to have re-opened this earlier interest and fed into the two poems relating to Pound and the Way in *Place*.

Clive Bush, a former research student and later colleague of Eric's at King's recalls that Eric "adored" Pound: "the importance of intelligence... the invention of different rhythms... the precision of the imagist and post-imagist poetics".[33] Above all, for Eric, "Pound was part of the American tradition of the long poem" that includes Crane, Williams, Rukeyser, Stevens, Olson and Duncan "which he thought was one of the best things produced in America". The seriousness and ambition this represented was in sharp contrast to the "little Englander" narrowness of Owen, Auden, Larkin which dominated official verse culture. For Bush's own work, "Pound's programme was fundamental": "the range, learning and intelligence... the breaking of traditional forms... and the fearless embrace of other cultures" all appealed to him, but it was above all as a technician, as "someone who can pack energy into a line", that Pound provides him with an exemplary model. The continuing presence of Pound can be seen in Bush's most recent work, *Pictures after Poussin* (2003).[34] A sequence of poems based, as the title suggests, on the paintings of the seventeenth-century French painter, Nicholas Poussin, but, like the *Cantos*, ranging over different times and cultures – the biblical, the classical, eighteenth- and twentieth-century French, and contemporary US – and contemplating that most Poundian of topics "The Earthly Paradise" (62-5). As he says of Poussin, Bush "mixes the chronologies of our looking" (10). The poems have an impersonal, objective style that, nevertheless, as is particularly marked in the final poems in the sequence, places the personal within a wide cultural field. This is combined with a continual formal inventiveness from poem to poem and a confident use of the page-space as a semantic marker and tonal register that is directly in the tradition of the *Cantos*.

Peter Barry, who was a student of Eric's at both King's College and in the MA programme at the Institute for United States Studies kept detailed notes on the "American Imagination of Synthesis" graduate course that Eric taught. Barry observes that, early in the course, when talking about Henry Adams, Eric drew attention to the role of Adams in the *Cantos*. He also emphasised Adams' interest in energy and the generation of energy, and he foregrounded Adams' response to the electric dynamo at the Chicago Exhibition of 1900, which he compared to the role of the image of the Virgin in medieval cathedrals as a unifying source of energy. Eric's particular take on this material was Adams' personal failure "to be educated to the field of multiplicity" and the more general US failure through the sacrifice of human lives to "technological over-elaboration".[35] The Adams material – and

Eric's method of synthesising an array of materials and ideas – had a great impact on Barry.[36]

Later in the course, when Eric was discussing John Cage and indeterminacy, the *Cantos* were used as a paradigm marker. Barry mentions a quotation, whose source is not identified in his notes, "Nothing in life requires a symbol", which he relates to Eric's insistence that "nothing can stand for anything else".[37] In his notes, this quotation is juxtaposed to a reference to the *Cantos* and the use of "examples rather than symbols". As Barry observes, "Pound seems to figure as the basic paradigmatic example of the fundamental Mottramesque principles".[38] In the third term of the course, Eric turned to the trope of the city as paradise, and the *Cantos* featured heavily. After discussing the city as earthly paradise in Canto XVII, cities as temples of light, and the temple at Rimini built by Sigismundo and his wife, Eric turned to *Patterson* and the *Maximus* poems and the possibility of renewing the city. As Barry observes, the list of modern American epics is very familiar, but what is interesting is the presentation of the *Cantos* as the first "city poem" and the emphasis on the *Cantos* as initiating the open-ended exploratory epic set up in such a way as to incorporate accident as well as design. As a result of the MA course, Barry worked for some time intensively on the *Cantos*, an influence that can be seen in his early work *Breton Days*, a consciously Mottramesque "locatory action", which fuses the contemporary with historical researches.[39]

One of this younger group of poets who has worked most consistently within a Poundian poetic tradition is Gavin Selerie. Selerie was not taught by Mottram, but was introduced to him in 1978 and became part of the group associated with Sub-Voicive. Selerie had read Pound's lyrics as a teenager and had bought the *Selected Poems* and *The Cantos* as extra-curricular reading while an undergraduate. He had followed this up with Pound's essays, letters, guides; Pound criticism such as *The Pound Era*; and the work of Charles Olson. Thus, although he did not come to Pound through Mottram, his prior knowledge of the Pound tradition no doubt facilitated his engagement with the Sub-Voicive group. In addition, although Pound was an important part of his formation, Pound is never simply a poetic model – and Pound's influence has been overlaid by others, particularly that of Olson. Where Pound's influence persists is in the conception of the poem as a lengthy research project; in the engagement with history; in the use of other voices and texts within a long poem; and in the use of concrete particulars and non-metaphorical language. *Azimuth* (1984) is divided into seven sections, each based on a particular "Root Place". In effect, the volume consists of series of locatory actions, each involving historical research of the particular place, mixed with personal experiences. Mottram's blurb for the book places it in the tradition of "Pound, Olson and Zukofsky" and presents it as a search for values "in the face of a violently consumerist addictive society". *Roxy* (1996) takes off from the name that provides the title to undertake a multi-layered engagement with popular music, cinema, theatre, the visual arts, architecture and fashion. Above all, it both embodies and critiques the idealization of the feminine found in the literature Pound draws on – the troubadour songs and the poetry of courtly love. *Le Fanu's Ghost* (2006), the most substantial of these research projects – with its exhaustive researches into the Sheridan and Le Fanu families (and their various writings) – is also the most Poundian in its handling of information and its constant formal inventiveness.[40] In contrast to Pound, however, all of these long poetic projects are involved in the interrogation of forms of absolute authority. (*Roxy*, for example, was written in response to what Selerie calls the "Thatcher-Murdoch era" and is very aware of the new political and social elites seizing power.)

Frances Presley has written "If I hadn't read Pound I don't think I would have become a poet".[41] Like Allen Fisher and Gavin Selerie, she came across Pound's work while still at school: "I heard about Ezra Pound, ordered some books from the public library, and was transfixed by the poems of *Lustra* and *Cathay*". What impressed her was the wit, the epigrammatic element, and the Imagist techniques: "it was my first experience of free verse which mattered". She read G.S. Fraser's brief study of Pound and everything of Pound's she could get hold of.[42] Pound's letters, at this time, were available only in carefully edited and selected form, and Presley probably accepted the standard view of the time that the *Cantos* didn't work as a whole and that only Cantos I-XXX and the *Pisan Cantos* were worth bothering with. This reading of Pound's work in the late 1960s provided the basis for Presley's poetics. In particular: "The 'Dos and Don'ts' of Imagism" and *The ABC of Reading* would dominate my reading and writing for years to come". Above all, what she took from Pound (as she indicated in her 2004 "Literary Statement") was "the emphasis on compression; the concept of the image; and the desire to 'make it new' – and the movement away from the lyric 'I'."

During 1975-76, Presley studied for an MA in Comparative Literature at the University of Sussex and wrote her dissertation on Pound, Apollinaire and the visual arts. A conference on Pound at the University of Keele in 1976 brought her face-to-face with the full extent of Pound's fascist politics, and she responded to this with "The Ezra Pound Papers" (*Myne*, 171-3). By this time, she had also spent a year in the United States and begun to study the new American poets, and this would lead her in turn (during the 1980s) to marginalised women poets such as H.D. Presley moved to London in 1980 and began to attend Mottram's readings and lectures, but her interest in Pound had already begun to wane before this time. This coincided with a growing interest in gender and gender politics which both informed her poetry and made her more critical of the Pound tradition and masculinist poetics. Something of this – and her ambivalent feelings, as a woman poet, towards Mottram – can be gauged from her poem "The Dream" (*Myne*, 110). On the other hand, she had met Peterjon Skelt in 1972, and he remained an important figure in her poetic life. Skelt had written an MPhil thesis on Lee Harwood under Eric's supervision, and, in 1986, set up North and South Press with his wife Yasmin, David Annwn and Presley. As the early catalogues show, Eric was very much the press' *éminence grise*, and the press became a major publisher of Eric's work. Where Selerie's early interest in Pound – and subsequent interest in the Pound tradition – aligned him with a London poetry sub-group influenced by Eric, Presley's involvement in these networks was combined with the development of a poetics in informed opposition to that tradition.

Notes

[1] Ezra Pound, Canto XCVIII, cited by Eric Mottram, "'Man Under Fortune': Bases for Ezra Pound's Poetry," in R. W. Butterfield (ed.), *Modern American Poetry* (London: Vision, 1984), 82. Pound is citing his own statement, in his essay "A Retrospect": "The mastery of any art is the work of a lifetime". See T.S. Eliot (ed.), *Literary Essays of Ezra Pound* (New York, NY: New Directions, 1968), 10.

[2] See Eric Mottram, *Live All You Can* (Twickenham: Solaris, 1992), 12-13.

[3] Personal communication, 20 January 2012.

[4] See Eric Mottram, "The British Poetry Revival, 1960-1975" in Robert Hampson & Peter Barry (eds), *New British poetries: The scope of the possible* (Manchester: Manchester University Press, 1993), 15-50.

[5] See Denise Levertov, *The Poet in the World* (New York, NY: New Directions, 1973); final quotation, Eric Mottram, "Entrance to the Americas".

[6] "Inheritance Landscape Location", 101. Mottram cites Guy Davenport, "Pound and Frobenius" in Lewis Leary (ed.), *Motive and Method in the Cantos of Ezra Pound* (New York, NY: Columbia University Press, 1954).

[7] Peter has given his own account of this period in "Eric Mottram as Critic, Teacher and Editor" in Peter Barry, *Poetry Wars* (Cambridge: Salt Publishing, 2006), 144-59. Ken supplied a brief reminiscence to Peterjon and Yasmin Skelt (eds.), *Alive in Parts of the Century: Eric Mottram at 70* (Twickenham/Wakefield: North and South, 1994), 39.

[8] See Robert Hampson and Will Montgomery, "Innovations in Poetry" in Peter Brooker, Andrzej Gasiorek, Deborah Longworth, Andrew Thacker (eds), *The Oxford Handbook of Modernisms* (Oxford: Oxford University Press, 2010), 64-84.

[9] My own most Poundian project, *Seaport*, was written in the 1970s. It fits exactly Eric's description of the method of *The Cantos* in "Man Under Fortune": "pieces of information are suspended together within an overall intention, both local and part of the epic process" (Butterfield, 89).

[10] Catherine Seelye (ed.), *Charles Olson & Ezra Pound: An Encounter at St Elizabeths* (New York, NY: Grossman Publishers, 1975) was crucial here: it carefully maps Olson's direct engagement with a man whose poetry he valued, and whose politics he detested.

[11] Canto XCI, Ezra Pound, *The Cantos* (London: Faber, 1975), 613.

[12] For the full text of this essay, see Amy Evans' contribution to the present volume, 00-00. I am grateful to Amy for drawing this essay to my attention.

[13] See *The Secret of the Golden Flower*, trans. Richard Wilhelm, 1962. Allen Fisher notes that Eric was "ambivalent about Jung": "we both were particularly critical of Jung's ideas of a collective unconscious, particularly as they had filtered through to writers like Joseph Campbell", but "we both had time for Jung's research into alchemy and synchronicity" (email, 22 February 2012).

[14] I am grateful to Gavin Selerie for pointing me towards this essay.

[15] Eric derives Pound's idea of the "complex" from Bernard Hart's *The Psychology of Insanity* (Cambridge, 1912). As he makes clear, he is drawing on Martin Kayman's PhD thesis "Ezra Pound and the Phantasy of Science" (York, 1978) for this information.

[16] See Ezra Pound, "How to Read", *Literary Essays*, 15-40, 25, and Pound's introduction to his Cavalcanti translations in *The Translations of Ezra Pound* (London: Faber, 1970), 23.

[17] See Ezra Pound, *Antheil and the Treatise on Harmony* (Paris: Three Mountains Press, 1924).

[18] Basil Bunting, Pound obituary in *Unmuzzled Ox* IV.2 (1976).

[19] See Charles Bernstein, "Stray Straws and Straw Men", *Open Letter*, 3.7 (Summer 1977), 94; republished in Charles Bernstein, *Content's Dream: Essays 1975-84* (Los Angeles, CA: Sun & Moon Press, 1986), 40-49, 40.

[20] Eric derives the term "heroic vitalism" from Eric Bentley's *A Century of Hero Worship* (Boston, Mass. 1957). Eric defines it later as "the active belief in political unity under the control of singular mystic force" (103).

[21] Hugh J. Silverman, *Telos*, 29 (Fall 1976), 127.

[22] Robert Creeley, *The Collected Essays* (Berkeley, CA: University of California Press, 1989), 97.

[23] Eric Mottram, *Inside the Whale* (London: Writers Forum, 1971), no pagination.

[24] In *our education is political* (London: Mainstream, 1997), an edited transcript of a 1993 interview by Wolfgang Görtschacher, Eric recalls in detail his time in Tunis, including his visit to the university: "I noticed the notice-boards were empty, because there was a law against people gathering together for meetings" (23).

[25] T.S. Eliot, *Collected Poems 1909-1962* (London: Faber, 1963), 74. See also Eliot's note which refers the citation to Augustine's *Confessions*: "to Carthage then I came, where a cauldron of unholy loves sang all about mine ears" (84).

[26] In a letter to Robert Duncan (10 January 1972), in the context of discussing what "productive life could mean" for the working classes, Eric referred to "The horror of stabilized entrapped family sociality as the alternative to labour which most people have". See Amy Evans and Shamoon Zamir (eds), *The Unruly Garden: Robert Duncan and Eric Mottram, Letters and Essays* (Bern: Peter Lang, 2007), 63.

[27] At the Poetry Reading Benefit in support of the striking miners, organised by Tom and Connie Pickard in February 1972, Eric read "Elegy 15: Neruda". See *The Unruly Garden*, 84.

[28] *A Book of Herne*, 25.

[29] In "The British Poetry Revival", Eric notes "everywhere the steady lessons of Ezra Pound" being picked up on (39). One subtext of the essay is the responsiveness of post-1945 working-class poets to this tradition – Tom Raworth, Roy Fisher, Allen Fisher, Barry Mac Sweeney, Tom Pickard etc.

[30] Allen Fisher, email, 24 January 2012.

[31] *Place* was a ten-year project, occupying the 1970s, which was published in separate volumes over 15 years. A complete edition was published by Reality Street Editions in 2005.

[32] Allen Fisher, *Before Ideas, Ideas* (London: Edible Magazine, 1971). This consists of three poems written in 1967 with an additional text added in 1970. The three poems are accompanied by quotations from *The Maximus Poems* at the foot of each page. The poems are placed "firmly in the world" and suggest what might be meant by "practical eros" (Mottram, 1972).

[33] Clive Bush, email, 20 January 2012.

[34] Clive Bush, *Pictures after Poussin* (Hereford: Spanner Press, 2003) with artwork by Allen Fisher.

[35] Eric Mottram cited by Peter Barry, email, 26 January 2012. I am very grateful to Peter for the very detailed account of the course in this email.

[36] As early responses, see Peter Barry, "Open Field Notes", *Alembic* 4 (Winter 1975/76), 10-11, and "Tramwayman", extracts from which appeared in the same issue.

[37] Cf Mottram, "The British Poetry Revival", 24.

[38] Peter Barry, email, 26 January 2012.

[39] Peter Barry, *Breton Days* (London: Share, 1973). Compare Ken Edwards *Lorca: An elegiac fragment* (Orpington: Alembic Editions, 1978). The influence of the MA course can, perhaps, also be seen in Barry's later critical work, *Contemporary British Poetry and the City* (Manchester: Manchester University Press, 2000).

[40] For my extended review of this volume and *Roxy*, see *Jacket*.

[41] Frances Presley, email (23 February 2012).

[42] G.S. Fraser, *Ezra Pound* (1960). Frances notes what she sees as "special pleading" in Fraser's account of Pound's politics.

Works Cited

Barry, Peter, *Breton Days* (London: Share, 1973).

——. "Open Field Notes", *Alembic* 4 (Winter 1975/76), 10-11.

——. "Allen Fisher and 'content-specific' poetry", in Robert Hampson and Peter Barry (eds), *The New British poetries*, 198-216.

——. *Contemporary British Poetry and the City* (Manchester: Manchester University Press, 2000).

——— . *Poetry Wars* (Cambridge: Salt Publishing, 2006).

Bernstein, Charles, "Stray Straws and Straw Men", *Open Letter*, 3.7 (Summer 1977), 94; republished in Charles Bernstein, *Content's Dream: Essays 1975-84* (Los Angeles, CA: Sun & Moon Press, 1986), 40-49,

Bush, Clive, *Pictures after Poussin* (Hereford: Spanner Press, 2003).

Creeley, Robert, *The Collected Essays* (Berkeley, CA: University of California Press, 1989).

Edwards, Ken, *Lorca: An elegiac fragment* (Orpington: Alembic Editions, 1978).

Eliot, T.S., *Collected Poems 1909-1962* (London: Faber, 1963).

Evans, Amy and Shamoon Zamir (eds), *The Unruly Garden: Robert Duncan and Eric Mottram, Letters and Essays* (Bern: Peter Lang, 2007),

Fisher, Allen, *Before Ideas, Ideas* (London: Edible Magazine, 1971).

——— . *long shout to kernewek* (London: New London Pride Editions, 1975).

——— . *Place* (Hastings: Reality Street, 2005).

Hampson, Robert, *Seaport* (Exeter: Shearsman Books, 2008).

Hampson, Robert & Peter Barry (eds), *New British poetries: The scope of the possible* (Manchester: Manchester University Press, 1993).

Hampson, Robert and Will Montgomery, "Innovations in Poetry" in Peter Brooker, Andrzej Gasiorek, Deborah Longworth, Andrew Thacker (eds), *The Oxford Handbook of Modernisms* (Oxford: Oxford University Press, 2010).

Kenner, Hugh, *The Pound Era: The Age of Ezra Pound, T.S. Eliot, James Joyce and Wyndham Lewis* (London: Faber, 1972).

Levertov, Denise, *The Poet in the World* (New York: New Directions, 1973).

Moody, A. David, *Ezra Pound: Poet*, vol. 1. "The Young Genius 1885-1920" (Oxford: Oxford University Press, 2007),

Mottram, Eric, "Pound, Olsen and the Secret of the Golden Flower", *Chapman* II.2 (Summer 1972), 20-31, 55-64.

——— . *Inside the Whale* (London: Writers Forum, 1971), no pagination.

——— . *Shelter Island & the Remaining World* (London: Turret Books, 1971).

———. *the he expression* (London: Aloes Books, 1973).

——— . "Entrance to the Americas: Poetry, Ecology, Translation" (London: Polytechnic of Central London, 1975).

——— . "Sixties American Poetry, Poetics and Poetic Movements" in Marcus Cunliffe (ed.), *Sphere History of Literature in the English Language*, vol. 9. "American Literature since 1900" (London: Sphere, 1975), 271-311.

——— . "Inheritance Landscape Location: Data for British Poetry 1977" in "British Poetry Conference" booklet (London: Polytechnic of Central London, 1977).

——— . *Tunis* (Sheffield: Rivelin Press, 1977)..

——— . *Elegy 15: Neruda* (London: Spanner, 1978).

——— . *A Book of Herne* (Colne: Arrowspire Press, 1981).

——— . *Elegies* (Newcastle: Galloping Dog, Press 1981).

——— . "Pound, Merleau-Ponty and the Phenomenology of Poetry" in Ian Bell (ed), *Ezra Pound: Tactics for Reading* (London: Vision Press, 1982), 121-47.

——— . "'Man Under Fortune': Bases for Ezra Pound's Poetry," in R. W. Butterfield (ed.), *Modern American Poetry* (London: Vision, 1984).

——— . "Notes on 'Poetics'", *The Journal of Comparative Poietics*, I.1 (Spring, 1989), 37-44, 40-41.

———. *Selected Poems* (Twickenham / Wakefield: North and South Press, 1989).

——— . "Ezra Pound in his Time" in Jacqueline Kaye (ed.), *Ezra Pound and America* (Basingstoke: Macmillan, 1992), 93-113.

——— . *Live All You Can* (Twickenham: Solaris, 1992).

——— . "Pound, Whitman and the American Epic Transmission" in Andrew Gibson, *Pound in Multiple Perspective* (Basingstoke: Macmillan, 1993), 216-44.

——— . "The British Poetry Revival, 1960-1975" in Robert Hampson & Peter Barry (eds), *New British poetries: The scope of the possible* (Manchester: Manchester University Press, 1993), 15-50.

———. *our education is political* (London: Mainstream, 1997)..

Ezra Pound, *Antheil and the Treatise on Harmony* (Paris: Three Mountains Press, 1924).

———. *The Translations of Ezra Pound* (London: Faber, 1953).

———. "A Retrospect" in T.S. Eliot (ed.), *Literary Essays of Ezra Pound* (New York: New Directions, 1968), 3-14.

———. "How to Read", *Literary Essays*, 15-40.

———. *The Translations of Ezra Pound* (Enlarged edition)(London: Faber, 1970).

———. *The Cantos* (London: Faber, 1975).

Frances Presley, "Literary Statement", BEPC, University of Southampton, 2004.

———. "The Ezra Pound Papers" in *Myne: new & selected poems & prose* (Exeter: Shearsman Books, 2006).

Catherine Seelye (ed.), *Charles Olson & Ezra Pound: An Encounter at St Elizabeths* (New York: Grossman Publishers, 1975).

Gavin Selerie, Review of *A Book of Herne* in *Palantir* 22 (1982), 44-48.

———. *Azimuth* (London: Binnacle Press, 1984).

———. *Roxy* (Hay-on-Wye: West House Books), 1996.

———. *Le Fanu's Ghost* (Hereford: Five Seasons Press, 2006).

Hugh J. Silverman, *Telos*, 29 (Fall 1976).

Skelt, Peterjon and Yasmin Skelt (eds.), *Alive in Parts of the Century: Eric Mottram at 70* (Twickenham/Wakefield: North and South, 1994).

Alexander Howard

COMPACTS, COMMERCE, AND A FEW REMARKS CONCERNING ANDREW CROZIER

> Behind all this, but at some remove, is the influence of Ezra
> Pound, I'm sure, although the materials his poetry arranges
> are very different, and rather more wilful.
>
> (Crozier, *PNR* 73)

British poetry changed in the 1950s. Out went the inquisitive, healthy sort of avant-garde heterogeneity that had informed much British poetry during the inter-war years and beyond. In came an altogether more insular, apprehensive version of British poetry that was virulently opposed to earlier modes of dynamic literary experimentation. Andrew Crozier and Tim Longville describe this postwar literary shift in the introduction to their jointly edited poetic anthology, *A Various Art* (1990). They suggest that "the poets who altered taste in the 1950s did so by means of a common rhetoric that foreclosed the possibilities of poetic language within its own devices: varieties of tone, of rhythm, of form, of image, were narrowly limited, as were conceptions of the scope and character of poetic discourse, its relation to the self, to knowledge, to history, and to the world" (Crozier and Longville 12). Crozier and Longville detail the negative effects of this deliberate and debilitating strategy of poetic foreclosure. They argue that postwar British poetry came to be viewed

> "as an art in relation to its own conventions – and a pusillanimous set of conventions at that. It was not to be ambitious, or to seek to articulate ambition through the complex deployment of its technical means: imagery was either suspect or merely clinched to argument; the verse line should not, by the pressure its energy or shape might exert on syntax, intervene in meaning; language was always to be grounded in the presence of a legitimating voice – and that voice took on an impersonally collective tone. To its owners' satisfaction the signs of art had been subsumed within a closed cultural programme" (Crozier and Longville 12).

Whilst Crozier and Longville do not explicitly name the aesthetically timorous individuals who wanted to foreclose the possibilities of poetic expression, it is clear they have in mind the so-called Movement writers who came to literary prominence in Britain during the early 1950s. Taking a dim view of modernist experimentation and the supposedly pernicious influence of international avant-gardism, Movement writers such as Philip Larkin and Kingsley Amis desired a comprehensive "redefinition of taste" when it came to matters concerning British poetry and poetics (Crozier and Longville 12). Crozier and Longville point out that this conservative and distinctly parochial redefinition of literary taste "had to be enacted by means of a wholesale rewriting of and reorientation towards the history of modern poetry, and this included the virtual suppression of parts of it" (12). Crozier and Longville stress that these interrelated acts of revisionist historical "rewriting" and conservative poetic "reorientation" had profound consequences for the generation of aesthetically ambitious and radical younger British poets emerging in the wake of the Movement (12). This younger literary generation, "confronted with such a depthless version of the past, found that as English poets the ground had been pretty well cut from beneath their feet. To accept the version of English poetry then sanctioned would be to become like a fly on a wall that had just been built." (Crozier and Longville 12). Reacting against this highly unsatisfactory state of affairs, the generation of radical British poets who began to publish in the 1960s attempted to maintain and reaffirm literary and aesthetic links with all that the earlier Movement writers had worked so tirelessly to suppress and deny.

The influential poet, editor, and Ferry Press publisher Andrew Crozier played an especially important role in the concerted cultural counter-offensive launched against the stifling formal and rhetorical literary constraints set in place by the Movement. Crozier's disdain for his parochial and conservative literary predecessors – those who wanted to turn British poetry into what he once memorably described as "a reserve for small verbal thrills, a daring little frill round the hem of normal discourse" – is reflected in his various critical writings (Crozier, *CEL* 229). Consider his retrospective assertion that the characteristically modernist "sense of consciousness as something complex, [and] even multiple" is conspicuously absent in the poetry of the Movement (Crozier, *PL* 114). Crozier posits that in the poetry of the Movement writers, "[t]he self is represented, instead, as a site of singularity, and the discourses of their poetry are generated accordingly" (*PL* 114). In addition, "[t]he self-consciousness of the subject establishes the frame-work of poetic utterance, whether it concerns the subject's awareness of its own self-identity, or the subject refers propositionally to things outside itself" (Crozier, *PL* 114). In either case, "meaning is conceived as objective, and the subject is the mediator of the experience of knowledge from which meaning is held to arise" (Crozier, *PL* 114). Subsequently, "[t]he singularity of the self goes hand in hand with its role as mediator, so that it becomes an abstraction, radically apart from whatever enters the field of poetic discourse" (Crozier, *PL* 114). Furthermore, "[t]his mediation takes place between meanings and their objective sources, is short-circuited, so to speak, within the subject, whose role, both in the utterance of the text, and in relation between text and reader, is directive. The reader is directed to respond to the poem in only a receptive spirit, not in the spirit of dialogue" (Crozier, *PL* 114).

This detailed treatment of the conceptual assumptions and formal processes underpinning the "directive" literary output of the Movement is useful as it provides an initial means with which to contemplate Crozier's decidedly different approach to (and understanding of) poetry. Crozier's aforementioned reference to a certain "spirit of dialogue" is pertinent. Whilst the consciously "directive" – and reductively "restrictive" – method adopted by the Movement writers set out to preclude the possibility of meaningful, inter-subjective literary discourse, Crozier sought to foster the conditions for spirited aesthetic collaboration and poetic "dialogue" in his various literary and editorial endeavours. Consider the crucial role that Crozier played in the foundation and development of *The English Intelligencer* (1966-68). Established by Crozier, the *Intelligencer* was a conceptually and formally provisional – and ostensibly democratic – literary "worksheet" that was circulated amongst a select band of like-minded younger British poets. According to Neil Pattison, the radical poets featured in the *Intelligencer* worksheet looked to "engage directly and critically with their contemporaries, to find their place in relation with the present, and sought through that engagement to push out towards new encounters" (iii). In his own estimation, Crozier

was trying to create an occasion for which I would be a contributor on no grander scale than anyone else invited to it. The scheme began simply with the accessibility of a duplicating machine and mailing system, facts to which I was a casual bystander, and it seemed valuable to preserve that condition. At the beginning then I regarded myself as just executive. You might argue that from the first the scope conferred upon the *Intelligencer* implied an editorial interest at work, but I did feel that we were held in the germ at least of something common, i.e. the choices seemed dictated, and open to further dictation from the looked-to participants (*TEI*, 203).

Although the quasi-editorial role that Crozier assumed during the worksheet's developmental stages complicates our understanding of the purportedly egalitarian dimension of the *Intelligencer*, it should not prevent us from appreciating what he wanted to achieve with this singular document of postwar British poetry and poetics. Drew Milne suggests that the Crozier-led *Intelligencer* represented "a bold and adventurous attempt to organize and develop a new collective poetics, based on the model of the San Francisco worksheet *Open Space*, involving a transformation of the mode of publishing and notion of audience, and the attempt to engage an ambitious avant-garde project." Whilst it is important to note that things did not turn out exactly as planned, one must recognize that the *Intelligencer* left an indelible mark on postwar British poetry. Crozier's seminal worksheet represented a formative attempt to combat the damaging poetic parochialism and aesthetic conservatism of the culturally dominant exponents of Movement writing. Operating in a intensely experimental textual environment, and delighting in the possibilities provided by a uniquely stimulating "spirit of dialogue" (Crozier, *PL* 114), the diverse group of young writers included in the *Intelligencer* strove to articulate a collective model of staunchly experimental postwar British poetics that was receptive to outside influences and alternative avant-garde traditions: European *and* American.

Crozier and Longville retrospectively describe how "American examples provided lessons in the organization and conduct of a poet's public life, indicating how poets might take matters of publication and the definition of a readership into their own hands by establishing their own publishing houses and journals" (12). Crozier and Longville also emphasise the fact that the aesthetic choices made by the group of young writers associated with the *Intelligencer* "cannot be separated from the wider context of English interest in the 1960s in American music, painting, and writing" (12). In particular, they suggest that one of the ways in which the younger generation of experimental British writers who emerged in the 1960s were recognisable to one another "was an interest in a particular aspect of post-war American poetry, and the tradition that lay behind it – not that of Pound and Eliot but that of Pound and Williams" (Crozier and Longville 12). These observations concerning a communal poetic interest in certain aspects of modern American literary history are particularly significant when applied to Crozier. As a Fulbright scholar enrolled at the State University of New York at Buffalo in 1964, Crozier was alert to contemporary developments in American modernist and avant-garde poetry at the very outset of his literary and editorial career. Buffalo evidently made quite an impression on the young Crozier. The postwar American poet Stephen Rodefer acknowledged as much in an introductory note to his early literary collaboration with Crozier, "English Schooldays." Rodefer argues that "[t]o have lived most of your life in southeast London, to come then for the first time to the United States, only shortly to New York, and then to Buffalo, New York, to stay for a year, then back to London – that has to be an experience of some consequence" (9).

In hindsight, it is readily apparent that the consequences of Crozier's formative American "experience" were indeed lasting and profound. In correspondence dated 15 November 1966, Crozier articulates his interest in the possibility of a formally radical and energetic type of British experimental writing comparable to that which he had encountered whilst in North America.[1] Crozier's early correspondence can be read as indicative of his long-standing commitment to the investigation of American poetry. Throughout his subsequent career as writer, editor, and publisher, Crozier maintained a subtle, but consistent poetic dialogue with touchstones of American modernism such as William Carlos Williams and Charles Olson.[2] Perhaps incongruously, this dialogue also included the perennially controversial figure of Ezra Pound. Crozier's poetic dialogue with the creator of *The Cantos* appears incongruous for a number of different reasons. Consider the sheer political distance between the two poets: Pound, the unrepentant advocate of Italian Fascism; Crozier, the politically committed son of British Communists. Notions of distance also come into play when discussing the profound poetic differences that exist between Crozier and Pound. Crozier's decidedly demotic poetry has little in common with the monumental type of verse produced by Pound. Crozier acknowledges this dissimilarity in the opening two lines of a poem printed in *Pleats* (1975):

> Rarely able to sense the pregnancy of cosmos
> these days I make a number of local compacts
> veiled desire for whole ground
> the non-reductive
> smoke from the same chimney and a garden fire
> matter rising to its final state
> turning along the wind and dispersing
> out of sight (*AWE* 178)

I think it possible to read Crozier's opening admission that he is rarely able to perceive "the pregnancy of cosmos" in relation to Pound's oft-cited remark concerning his desire to "bust thru from [the] quotidian into [the] 'divine or permanent world'" (*EPP* 625). Crozier's wry account of his personal and poetic limitations serves to distinguish his literary sensibility from that of his American predecessor. He was well aware of the inherent poetic and personal folly that lay behind Pound's grandiose – and ultimately tragic – attempt "to bust out from the kosmos" (Pound, *TC* 764) in the simultaneously "noble, pathetic, [and] deranged" *Cantos* (Crozier, *PNR* 29). Having recognized Pound's dilemma, Crozier set out to forge "a number of local compacts" that avoid the various pitfalls faced by the older modernist poet. As well as serving to differentiate his poetic sensibility from that of Pound, Crozier's decision to fashion "a number of local compacts" resonates when considered in relation to his interest in other aspects of American literary modernism.

Crozier's interest in what one could describe as a localist – or perhaps a particularist – sort of poetics is important in this respect.[3] On the one hand, Crozier's forging of "local compacts" recalls the earlier investigation into poetic localism that had been carried out by Pound's long-suffering friend and aforementioned modernist contemporary, Williams.[4] On the other hand, Crozier's "local compacts" might be said to evoke the sort of radical localism privileged by the loosely aligned exponents of Objectivism. Crozier played a crucial role in the critical recovery of the historically neglected Objectivists.[5] Crozier discusses the Objectivist poets at length in his literary criticism. He argues that the work of the Objectivists can be viewed "as an attempt, not altogether well timed, to incorporate and extend the innovations of the first generation of modernists at a moment when that generation was losing momentum and cohesion" (*CR*, 99). More specifically, Crozier situates the particular brand of second-generation modernism of Louis Zukofsky and his fellow Objectivists in relation to Pound's earlier poetics of Imagism.

Crozier notes that the loosely aligned group of young Objectivist poets – Zukofsky, Rakosi, Reznikoff, Oppen – initially appeared in the pages of Pound's modernist little magazine *The Exile* (1927-28). This group of young experimental poets emerged "at a moment when Pound was anxious to consolidate and put on record the achievement of the previous fifteen years, and was looking for American disciples into the bargain." (Crozier, *MAP* 144). Pound evidently had high hopes for the Objectivists. "Pound wished this small force of younger poets to manifest itself as the new generation, and arranged for Zukofsky to edit the February 1931 issue of [Harriet Monroe's] *Poetry* for this purpose" (Crozier, *MAP* 144). Pound's well-documented enthusiasm and initial support for this "small force" of younger American poets ensured that Objectivism came to be viewed as a poetic subsidiary of Imagism. Crozier argues that this association is reductive and unhelpful: "it might appear that Objectivism was the continuation of Imagism under another name; indeed, this has been suggested more than once, but this will not do" (Crozier, *CR* 97). In his estimation, "no matter how inevitably that might be felt at the moment of juncture between one generation and the next, there remains an ineradicable generational difference, and this seems to me to go a long way towards defining what Objectivism was historically" (Crozier, *CR* 98). Social experience and identity defined the Objectivists. Crozier highlights the fact that "[t]he principal 'Objectivists' of 1931 were Jewish, they were susceptible to left-wing politics, and if they did not all join the Communist Party the influence of its politics made itself felt in what they wrote" (*CR* 98). As is well known, "[t]heir literary careers slowed down or came to a temporary halt by the 1940s. The sense that any development represented by Objectivism was precocious, even premature, contributes to our understanding of its history, and the later careers of its protagonists" (*CR* 98). Crozier insists that we historicise Objectivism "in relation to a general literary situation and a moment at which poets of different generations could be identified in terms of shared principles, and that its history consists of the literary trajectories of a few poets, who are then the exemplary Objectivists, around that moment" (*CR* 98).

George Oppen was one such "exemplary" poet. Crozier discusses Oppen's first volume of poetry – *Discrete Series* (1934) – at length in his literary criticism. Crozier's critical account of *Discrete Series* is important as it underscores the significant conceptual distance between Pound and Oppen. Crozier notes that Pound "is the presiding influence in *Discrete Series*, even though Oppen's field of reference may remind us more of Williams than of Pound, and this influence is most discernible when we trace the basic strategies of Oppen's writing" (*MAP* 148). However, "Pound's influence does not result in any very clear resemblance, for Oppen adopts Pound's method only to throw it into reverse" (Crozier, *MAP* 148). In Pound's imagistic poetry, "we find a discourse constructed through the juxtaposition of elements, normally drawn from different conceptual orders of reality, the spiritual, and the mundane. These elements are not so much opposed or contrasted as shown in terms of their possible equivalence, the completion of this discourse lying in some further, unstated term" (Crozier, *MAP* 149). Crozier argues that "[t]he advantage of this method for Pound, which we might epitomise as the reciprocity of image and ideogram, is that elements so used, by virtue of their difference, can be scaled up or down, either by setting them parallel to other series of elements, or by subdivision into new series" (*MAP* 149). At the same time, Crozier recognises that "[t]he disadvantage of [Pound's] method is the monolithic unity of concept it entails; its inclusivity breaks down under the weight of its own inertia – as we find in the *Cantos* – when it is developed beyond certain limits. This is experienced either as incoherence or as vulnerability to counter-discourses" (*MAP* 149). Having outlined the various advantages and disadvantages pertaining to Pound's chosen method of poetic juxtaposition, Crozier turns his attention to the early work of Oppen. He reasons that the poems published in Oppen's first collection "have a binary structure similar to that of the Poundian image, but whereas in Pound the elements correlated are different but equivalent, in Oppen they are similar (ontologically identical in some cases) but opposed" (Crozier, *MAP* 149). Moreover, "[i]t is out of the collision between different versions of similar events, the discovery of mendacity or misrepresentation where discourses compete, that the meanings of *Discrete Series* arise" (Crozier, *MAP* 149). In effect, these assorted "collisions" and resultant "discoveries" serve to insulate Oppen's early poetry against the "monolithic unity of concept" that ultimately dominates Pound's *Cantos*.

Something similar can also be said of Crozier's poetry. Crozier has precious little time for the inertia inducing "monolithic unity of concept" that he identifies in the high modernist poetry of Pound. Crozier wants to keep things mobile.[6] Hence his desire to fashion a number of formally modest and fluid poetic "compacts" between coinciding "counter-discourses." Establishing these small-scale "compacts" between differing aesthetic, conceptual, and philosophical discourses affords Crozier the opportunity to explore the non-hierarchical dimensions and communicative potential of synchronous poetic language.[7] Crozier's recourse to non-hierarchical aspects of poetic language sits in contradistinction to the organisational systems that underwrite many of Pound's later *Cantos*. Increasingly judgemental and resistant to counter-discourses, Pound manipulates poetic language in order to establish a decidedly hierarchical system of aesthetic, moral, economic, and political values in the later sections of his *Cantos*.[8] These various hierarchical value systems impact negatively on the direction of Pound's poetry, and as a result, the later *Cantos* become rigidly instructive, dogmatic, and programmatic. The authoritarian creator of the later *Cantos* has no real interest in forging communicative poetic compacts and dialogues with his long-suffering readership. In fact, we might even go as far to suggest that Pound seeks actively to foreclose potential routes of communicative poetic commerce in the increasingly attritional and rebarbative *Cantos*. Pound does this in an attempt to pre-empt and negate any questioning of his aesthetic, moral, economic, and political rectitude. Bearing this fact in mind, we might also reason that Pound's decision to close down potential routes of constructive poetic dialogue in the later sections of his modernist epic signals the end of any potential "compacts" with naturally inquisitive, radical younger avant-garde writers such as Crozier.

But it soon becomes clear that Crozier was more than willing to engage with Pound in spite of the elder poet's unpalatable despotic tendencies. Crozier's previously cited observation concerning the construction of "local compacts" is significant in this regard. This remark hints at the underlying dialogue that exists between Crozier and Pound. Crozier's "compacts" bring to mind Pound's famous poetic "Pact" with Walt Whitman:

I make a pact with you, Walt Whitman –
I have detested you long enough.
I come to you as a grown child
Who has had a pig-headed father;
I am old enough now to make friends.
It was you that broke the new wood,
Now is a time for carving.
We have on sap and one root –
Let there be commerce between us. (*P* 90)

Much as Pound did with Whitman before him, Crozier makes an ambivalent poetic (com)pact with the patriarchal and "pig-headed" Pound. Crozier's willingness to engage in poetic "commerce" with Pound is apparent at the outset of *The Park* (August 1968).[9] Crozier's periodical opens with the following epigraph:

The real life in regular verse is an irregular movement underlying. Jefferson thought the formal features of the American system would work, and they did work till the time of General Grant but the condition of their working was that inside them there should be a <u>de facto</u> government composed of sincere men willing the national good. When the men of understanding are too lazy to impart the results of their understanding, and when the nucleus of the national mind hasn't the force to translate knowledge into action I don't believe it matters a damn what legal forms or what administrative forms there are in a government. The nation will get the staggers (Pound, *JM* 94-95).

This passage is taken from Pound's notorious *Jefferson and/or Mussolini* (1936). Paul Morrison reminds us that this treatise strove "to undo – or, as we now say, deconstruct – the opposition between the most seemingly opposed of historical figures" (165). In this highly controversial text, Pound celebrates Jefferson and Mussolini "for their freedom from ideological fixity, their commitment to the life of practical action (which involves the subordination of means to ends), and their sense of the organic totality of things" (Morrison 165). Pound's emphasis on the need for "sincere" political men of "practical action" is clearly evident in the passage reproduced in *The Park*. Pound elaborates on the character of these ostensibly "sincere" and "practical" political men elsewhere in *Jefferson and/or Mussolini*. Recognizing that "any means are the right means which will remagnetize the will and the knowledge," these are decisive and autocratic public figures of a distinctly authoritarian persuasion. In the specific case of Mussolini, "[this] authority comes, as Eirugina proclaimed authority comes, 'from right reason' and from the general fascist conviction that he is more likely to be right than anyone else is" (Pound, *JM* 95, 110). Given Crozier's leftist political affiliations, how are we to construe his provocative decision to lead with this explicit reminder of Pound's problematic political ideology? The answer lies not in the political specificity of Pound's contentious statement, rather it lies in what it represents: the important yet frequently overlooked legacy of political thinking in poetry.[10] That is, Crozier absents himself from the gestural politics of Pound's statement, whilst fully recognizing the integral role politics plays in his wider modernist project. As we know, this all-encompassing approach – together with the political – sets the marker against which many subsequent twentieth-century avant-garde poetries – including Crozier's – would be measured.

Notes

[1] These comments appear in the aforesaid *Intelligencer*. Crozier mentions the fact that "when I began to be interested in the possibility of a writing in this country of the same order that I could see achieved in North America, which is a concern you appear to share, an immediate referent at least was the activity associated with the magazine *Migrant*. So I am disappointed to see no carry over from that in your pages, say in new work by Roy Fisher, or Michael Shayer, or Gael Turnbull. What is the reason for this omission? Are you pursuing a policy of deliberate exclusion? I hope not, for I doubt that we are yet strong enough to sustain such divisiveness" (TEI 165).

[2] Crozier was greatly interested in the poetry of Charles Olson. As an undergraduate student reading English at Christ's College, Cambridge, Crozier edited an "American Supplement" to *Granta* (March 1964). Indebted to Olson's increasingly influential model of post-war poetics, "Supplement" featured the work of Louis Zukofsky, Denise Levertov, Robert Duncan, Ed Dorn, Fielding Dawson, Larry Eigner, Douglas Woolf, Robert Kelly, John Wieners, Robert Creeley, and Ron Loewinsohn.

[3] According to the postwar Scottish poet Douglas Oliver, "Crozier has always shown us an artist's restorative attention to the visible. Over and over, his poems find profusion within the smallest details of our worlds: precise perception of particulars

yet awareness that our minds are tugged each instant by the universal geometries because, like Penrose, a poet doesn't know out of what quantum mystery an act of mind comes to birth" (110).

[4] Complex and contested conceptions of localism also come into play in the work of Charles Olson. For more details see Robert von Hallberg's 1978 account of Olson's work (especially 57-59).

[5] Crozier's rediscovery of the almost entirely forgotten Objectivist poet Carl Rakosi is a case in point. Crozier edited Rakosi's *Poems 1923-1941* (Sun & Moon Press: Los Angeles, 1995). Crozier first encountered Rakosi's poetry in Kenneth Rexroth's *Assays* (1961). Having made a mental note of this initial encounter, Crozier began to collect Rakosi's poetry whilst enrolled as a Fulbright scholar at Buffalo. Crozier also tried to find out as much as possible about Rakosi. This process was complicated by the fact that Rakosi had changed his name (to Callman Rawley). Despite these difficulties, Crozier eventually succeeded in finding Rakosi. Crozier interviewed Rakosi in 1968. Rakosi later cited Crozier's interest as a key factor in his decision to return to poetry.

[6] Something of this desire for motion is dramatized in Crozier's prose poem "Driftwood and Seacoal" (1984). According to Douglas Oliver, "Crozier's first perception is of apparent rigidity of forms, of sameness, stiffening his personages into identical figures rather like miners by the sea shore. He is working again from a photograph, this time of miners in Sunderland and, as he told me recently, he had a mental picture of falsely recognizing his father for a moment walking in such a setting. Consequently, his attention is called back to the individual figures. This sets rigidity adrift, slow motions begin to drift too according to the utter change in what seems so constant" (112).

[7] Robin Purves' comments regarding Crozier's *The Veil Poem* resonate in the context of the present discussion. Purves argues that the opening passage of Crozier's poetic sequence is "immediately reminiscent, in its limited content and improvising rhythms, of Imagist poetry and more reminiscent still of the way its technical procedures would be extended by the work of the American poet, George Oppen." Purves also addresses the related topics of "counter-discourses" and use of poetic language in his discussion of Crozier's poem. Purves argues that the implied subject of this poetic sequence "is composed inside sets of coinciding discourses given a carefully modulated timbral consistency, and is tied together at points by the knot of personal reference without the poem falling into the traps Crozier identifies in his own criticism." In Purves' estimation, Crozier also recognizes that "[t]he advantage and opportunity of poetic language, as opposed to epistemological investigation, is that it can formulate ideas by the linguistic imbrication of moods, times, places, thoughts that philosophical discourse would want to separate and arrange in a hierarchy and a chronology." On a related note, in a interview with Andrew Duncan (published in *Don't Start Me Talking*), Crozier suggests that "[i]t seems to me one of the most interesting thing about poetic language is its conjunction of bringing together of larger or smaller poetic units. Or bringing together of elements into smaller and larger units. Thus drawing attention away from the largest unit as the ultimate verification of what meaning may be, which I think is one of the things which a notion of full and complete utterance or a bit of a sentence or a bit of sententiousness or an intended communication falls short of, or overlooks" (ACR 139-40).

[8] Pound's interest in aesthetic and literary systems of hierarchical value should be read in relation to his well-documented engagement with economic and political

matters. Peter Nicholls reminds us of the fact "Pound's direct engagement with the pressing political and economic questions of his day could not long postpone the emergence of a polemical axis to the poem. Once the diagnostic tendency had been fully established it was only a matter of time before "history" would mutate into a more programmatic narrative of right or wrong choices. Increasingly the poem would concern itself with definitions of just authority, even as the writing began to close down questions about its own judgmental legitimacy. Where the early Cantos had invited the reader's skepticism, now the poem began to demand a certain faith; and as Pound began to discover in Mussolini a stronger, more authoritative self-image, so the poem acquired an intransigent, often hectoring tone" (145).

[9] Crozier edited *The Park* whilst lecturing at Keele University. *The Park* was itself a continuation of *The Wivenhoe Park Review* (1965-67). Crozier edited *The Wivenhoe Park Review* with Tom Clark whilst based in the Department of Literature at the University of Essex. Both versions of Crozier's periodical featured an impressive selection of work by both British and American poets including Carl Rakosi, Charles Reznikoff, Steve Jonas, Charles Olson, J.H. Prynne, Tom Raworth, Jack Spicer, and John Wieners.

[10] Crozier's interest in the legacy of political thinking further contextualizes his engagement with Objectivism.

Works Cited

Crozier, Andrew. *All Where Each Is.* London: Agneau 2: Allardyce, Barnett, 1985. Print.

———. *An Andrew Crozier Reader.* Manchester: Carcanet, 2012. Print.

———. "Carl Rakosi in the 'Objectivists' Epoch." Heller, Michael, ed. *Carl Rakosi: Man and Poet.* The National Poetry Foundation: University of Maine, Orono, ME, 1993: 95-113. Print.

———. "Correspondence" *The English Intelligencer.* 15 October 1966: 165. Print.

———. "Inaugural and Valedictory: The Early Poetry of George Oppen." Butterfield, R. W., ed. *Modern American Poetry.* London: Vision Press Limited, 1984: 142-157. Print.

———. Letter to Peter Riley. *The English Intelligencer.* 24 January 1967: 203. Print.

———. "Styles of the Self: the New Apocalypse and 1940s Poetry," Mellor, David, ed. *A Paradise Lost: the Neo-Romantic Imagination in Britain, 1935-1955.* London: Lund Humphries & the Barbican Art Gallery, 1987: 113-116. Print.

———. "Resolving Paradox: J.F. Hendry, *A World Alien.*" *PN Review* 9: 2, 1982. Print.

———. "Thrills and frills: poetry as figures of empirical lyricism." Sinfield, Alan, ed. *The Context of English Literature: Society and Literature 1945-1970.* London: Methuen & Co Ltd, 1983: 199-233. Print.

———. "The Young Pound." *PN Review* 5: 2, 1979: 27-29. Print.

Crozier, Andrew, and Tim Longville. "Introduction." Crozier, Andrew, and Tim Longville, eds. *A Various Art.* Paladin: London, 1990. Print.

Hallberg, Robert von. *Charles Olson: the Scholar's Art.* Cambridge, MA: Harvard UP, 1978. Print.

Oliver, Douglas. "Andrew Crozier's Perceptions." *fragmente* 18, Summer 1998. 110-117. Print.

Milne, Drew. "Agoraphobia, and the embarrassment of manifestos: notes towards a community of risk." *Jacket* 20 Dec 2002: n. pag. Web. 16 February 2012.

Morrison, Paul. "*Jefferson and/or Mussolini*," Tryphonopoulos, Demetres P. and Stephen J. Adams, eds., *The Ezra Pound Encyclopedia.* Westport, CT: Greenwood Press, 2005: 165-167. Print.

Nicholls, Peter. "'To Unscrew the Inscrutable': Myth as Fiction and Belief in Ezra Pound's *Cantos.*" Bell, Michael and Peter Poellner, eds. *Myth and the Making of Modernity: the Problem of Grounding in Early Twentieth-Century Literature.* Amsterdam – Atlanta, GA: Rodopi, 1998: 139-152. Print.

Pattison, Neil. "Introduction: 'All Flags Left Outside'" Pattison, Neil, Reitha Pattison, and Luke Roberts, eds. *Certain Prose of the English Intelligencer.* Cambridge: Mountain Press, 2012: i-xxiv. Print.

Pound, Ezra. *The Cantos.* London: Faber and Faber, 1986. Print.

——. *Ezra Pound to His Parents: Letters 1895-1929.* Oxford: Oxford University Press, 2011. Print.

——. *Jefferson and/or Mussolini.* New York: Liveright, 1970. Print.

——. *Personae: Collected Shorter Poems.* London: Faber and Faber Limited, 1990. Print.

Purves, Robin. "What Veils in Andrew Crozier's *The Veil Poem.*" *Blackbox Manifold* 2 Jan. 2009: n. pag. Web. 17 March 2012.

Rodefer, Stephen. "A Note." Crozier, Andrew. *Loved Litter of Time Spent.* Sum Books: Buffalo, NY, 1967, 9. Print.

Mark Scroggins

The "half-fabulous field-ditcher": Ruskin, Pound, Geoffrey Hill

The public careers of the two close contemporaries J.H. Prynne (born 1936) and Geoffrey Hill (1932) might furnish an illuminating study in the sociology of late modernist poetry. As we enter the second decade of the new millennium, each of the two men is widely held up by American poets and academics as one of the most important English poets writing – but rarely by the same poets and academics. Prynne's career has been a study in public reticence and the dogged pursuit of ever more recondite experimental modes; his reputation has spread by word of mouth, as it were, and has been nourished by the very almost mystical regard in which his writing is held by a coterie of very devoted readers, some of them his former students. Hill, on the other hand, has followed well-trodden career paths to his now almost assured canonical status: a first at Cambridge, followed by a quarter-century teaching at the University of Leeds and briefer stints at Emmanuel College, Cambridge (as Fellow) and at Boston University (as University Professor); a long series of books from major trade and university presses (Penguin, Houghton Mifflin, Oxford University Press, Yale University); and finally, the Oxford Professorship of Poetry in 2010.

Prynne's poetry has been disseminated – aside from his first (now disavowed) collection – by "little" presses, usually in the form of small-print-run pamphlets (later collected in the imposing mass of his *Poems*, issued in successive editions in 1982, 1999, and 2005). His works are eagerly awaited by a small but vocal readership, praised and debated on the internet and the blogosphere: but they have nothing like the exposure of Hill's collections, which receive front-page, full-length reviews in the major literary weeklies and notices in most of the major newspapers. What is striking, however, is that these two poets – the one (Prynne) enveloped in an air of hieratic Mallarméan mystery, the other (Hill) touted as the "finest British poet of our time" and "England's best hope for the Nobel Prize"[1] – are both discussed more often than not precisely in terms of their *difficulty*.

That readerly "difficulty," I would argue, while it takes very different forms in Prynne's and in Hill's works, locates both men squarely within a modernist tradition. As I said at the outset, they are both late-modernist poets, and while their works draw upon different aspects of the various revolutions in literary language and form pioneered in the early decades of the twentieth-century, the very obduracy of their writings testify to the fact that literary modernism has yet to be assimilated to literary culture as a whole: that the revolutions begun by Pound, Stein, Williams, Eliot, Loy, and so forth remain a stumbling-block to reviewers and readers for whom the psychological and formal transparency of the Victorian and post-Victorian novel stands as a measuring-stick for literary achievement.[2] From a hundred years' distance, however, it is sometimes easy to forget the degree to which the modernists drew upon the Victorian culture that they so often vociferously rejected. While we can readily see the techniques of Dickens, Thackeray, and George Eliot repeated in today's bestselling "literary" novelists, it is a more complicated undertaking to trace the influence of the great Victorian cultural critics in the "high" modernist poets and those who have followed them.

§

Geoffrey Hill made his early reputation with a poetics of traditional form, of dense syntactic compression, and of formidable cross-grained cultural reference. If Hill's poetry has become less metrically strict, more earthily demotic, and less formally and syntactically costive through much the second half of his career – roughly, that is, from his move to the United States in 1988 to his present retirement in Cambridge – his work remains as densely referential, as forbiddingly intertextual as ever. He may sing the very personal praises of antidepressants in *Speech! Speech!* (2000) or indulge in an abrasive *"eat shit"* in *The Triumph of Love* (1998), but he remains a late modernist "quoting" poet in the direct line of Eliot and Pound, a poet whose work involves the continuous evocation of a wide range of historical and literary allusion.[3]

By my reckoning, the body of Hill's poetry contains a half-dozen or fewer overt citations of the Victorian social critic John Ruskin (1819-1900). This count, however, belies the importance of Ruskin's social and aesthetic thought, and of Ruskin's general stance as a cultural critic, to Hill's own memorializing project. In many ways, Hill is a late Ruskinian, but a Ruskinian whose Ruskin stands in a crucial relationship to the thought of a poet whose own Ruskinism was largely unconscious: Ezra Pound. It would be going too far to say that Hill's Ruskin is in some way *mediated* through Pound; Pound, however, stands as a crucial Ruskinian precursor in Hill's meditations on the responsibility of the poet, and of the civic weight assumed by the artist in making art – meditations which find some of their most profound sources in Ruskin's own thought.

Ruskin, once an almost oppressively dominant figure on the Victorian cultural landscape, is these days less read than invoked.[4] He made his name in the middle decades of the nineteenth-century and won an enormous readership with the five volumes of *Modern Painters* (1843-1860), the three volumes of *The Stones of Venice* (1851-1853), and the aesthetic manifesto *The Seven Lamps of Architecture* (1849). Ruskin looked at visual art and architectural ornament with an incomparably keen eye, and communicated his insights – in particular his sense, derived from his evangelical background, of the revelation of the divine in natural phenomena – in extraordinarily musical and evocative prose – "purple" passages that would be excerpted, anthologized, and admired throughout the last decades of the century.

From approximately 1860 onward, however – with the publication of the essays on political economy that would be collected as *Unto this Last* – Ruskin's focus shifted from artistic and cultural criticism to a broader critique of existing social relations, an at times savage attack on Victorian progressivism, materialism, and *laissez-faire* economics. While Ruskin continued to write art criticism and served as Oxford's Slade Professor of Art, the examination of individual works of cultural production became less important for him than a high-minded and quixotic attempt to set right the exploitative and soul-draining conditions of contemporary British society. His most notable efforts in this direction were the founding of the Guild of St. George in the 1870s, a number of books of political economy and social criticism, and *Fors Clavigera*, the series of monthly letters "to the Workmen and Labourers of Great Britain" he published regularly from 1871 to 1878 (and thereafter intermittently), which Guy Davenport has called a "kind of Victorian prose *Cantos*" (and which might be profitably considered as a proto-blog).[5]

By the time of his death in 1900, after a series of mental breakdowns and a decade of uncommunicative dementia, Ruskin had become a cultural institution, an inescapable presence in Anglophone thought and letters. Hundreds of thousands of copies of his books were in print, and a "Library Edition" of his writings, which would run to thirty-nine massive volumes, was in preparation. If contemporary artists found him less than relevant, in part due to his lack of sympathy for Impressionism (exemplified by his infamous 1878 attack on Whistler), some still remembered his championing of Turner and his early support of the Pre-Raphaelites. Ruskin's ethical teachings were a primary influence on *fin-de-siècle* British socialism; members of the first British Labour Party to gain seats in Parliament in 1906 cited *Unto This Last* more often than *Das Kapital* as an influence upon their political views (Goldman 58). And if the aestheticism of Pater, Whistler, and Wilde took elements of Ruskin's aesthetic teachings in a direction he would have found repugnant, his socio-aesthetic principles had been vigorously promulgated, in a popular and distinctly socialist form, by William Morris and his Arts and Crafts movement (see Hough).

The young Ezra Pound, invested as he is in Whistlerian notions of artistic autonomy, has rather little directly to say about Ruskin, and what he has to say ranges from ambiguous to dismissive. In *"Yeux Glauques,"* the sixth section of *Hugh Selwyn Mauberley* (1920), Pound sets the stage for a consideration of the early reception of the Pre-Raphaelites by noting that

> Gladstone was still respected,
> When John Ruskin produced
> "Kings Treasuries"; Swinburne
> And Rossetti still abused. (*Poems and Translations* 552)

"Of Kings' Treasuries" is the first lecture of Ruskin's *Sesame and Lilies,* published in 1865 and his single best-selling book. While the syntax of this quatrain might initially imply that Pound is placing Ruskin in the same camp as the despised Liberal Prime Minister William Gladstone, a closer examination of "Of Kings' Treasuries" – a full-throated exhortation to cherish the cultural heritage preserved in books, along with a virtuoso demonstration of what seventy-five years later would come to be called "close reading" – and a consideration of Ruskin's role in promoting Pre-Raphaelite art suggest that he occupies a rather more positive space in the stanza's balancing of "blasts" and "blesses" (see Wilmer). Eight years later, in a brief essay on urban planning, Pound is rather more dismissive of Ruskin's social and technological conservatism: "Ruskin was well-meaning but a goose. The remedy for machines is not pastoral retrogression. The remedy for the locomotive belching soft-coal smoke is not the stage coach, but the electric locomotive..." (*Selected Prose* 224-5).

Ruskin is largely absent from Pound's social and critical vocabulary: he has no place among such luminaries as Confucius, A. R. Orage, or Major Clifford Douglas. But this is because, paradoxically, Ruskinian principles are so pervasive that they have become the very premises of Pound's thought, accepted but unrecognised. There is an absolute congruence between Ruskin's statement, in his Inaugural Lecture as Slade Professor at Oxford (1870), that "The art of any country *is the exponent of its social and political virtues...* The art, or general productive and formative energy, of any country, is an exact exponent of its ethical life" (*Works* 20.39) and Pound's suggestion in *Guide to Kulchur* (1938) that "that finer and future critics of art will be able to tell from the quality of a painting the degree of tolerance or intolerance of usury extant in the age and milieu that produced it" (27). What the two men share, that is, is a sense of "culture" as an "organic" totality in which aesthetic productions reflect social relations, in which the general health of a society can be gauged by a close analysis of its artworks, and in which the health of the arts depends upon the health of the society as a whole (Coyle 49).

This sense of the organic dependence of artistic style upon social conditions, as Kenneth Clark points out, is absent before the nineteenth century (see Williams 140). It first emerges in the architectural criticism of A.W. Pugin (1812-1852), but it finds its most eloquent, and incomparably most influential, exponent in Ruskin. If the Aestheticists made a great splash in the last decades of the century by insisting upon the absolute autonomy of the arts, they did so not merely because they were reacting against a vulgar Victorian moralising, but because they were swimming against the current – or reversing the polarities – of a more sophisticated organicist conception of culture that had become widely diffused and deeply embedded in contemporary critical and social thought. As Graham Hough points out, Pater and the later aesthetes in essence accepted Ruskin's conception of the interdependence of art and morality (in the broadest sense); they merely "insisted on treating morals from the point of view of art," thereby inverting Ruskin's own emphasis (*The Last Romantics* 18).

It is this organicist conception of culture that Pound, after his early flirtation with aestheticism, returns to and embraces – without recognizing it as Ruskin's. Ruskin becomes the unacknowledged model for Pound's conception of the man of letters as culture-hero, as cultural warrior striving to clear a space for the production of healthy arts by reforming the ills of society. Artists, as Pound famously claims, are the "antennae of the race" (*ABC* 73), and poets in particular are responsible for a kind of linguistic hygiene, a policing of the instruments of social interaction. They cannot fall into mere aestheticism or simple self-expression, but must constantly strive to cut through the cant of public discourse, holding up examples of more rational and humane ethical relations than those exemplified in society as it now stands.

The precise doctrines shared by Ruskin and Pound – while both men execrate usury and hanker for authoritarian, paternalist systems of government, the specific details of their social programs are radically different – are rather less important than their shared sense of the writer's task as an agent of cultural hygiene, as an active force for the renovation of society, its regrounding upon more sturdy economic and, ultimately, ethical foundations. When Ruskin uses his platform as Slade Professor of Art to exhort his undergraduates that "The England who is to be mistress of half the earth, cannot remain herself a heap of cinders, trampled by contending and miserable crowds" (*Works* 20.43), his stance is essentially identical to

Pound's in the Preface to *Guide to Kulchur*, where he announces that "It is my intention in this booklet to COMMIT myself on as many points as possible.... Given my freedom, I may be a fool to use it, but I wd. be a cad not to" (7).

Hill is one of the few English poets emerging in mid-century who has taken Pound's work seriously. His work, unlike that of the poets of the "Movement," has never shied away from the readerly challenges and cultural referentiality associated with "high" modernism. Indeed, in addition to its Poundian textures of dense referentiality, in recent years Hill's work has assumed an insistent rhetoric of *laus et vituperatio* (praise and execration; see, among others, *Triumph of Love* 12) which places it in close company with Pound's. Hill encourages us to place his *laus et vituperatio* in the tradition of Lucian, of Dryden and Swift; but one of its most proximate sources, one might venture, are the "Blasts" and "Blesses" issued by Pound and Wyndham Lewis in the first issue of *Blast* (1914).

It is precisely through the invocation of Ruskin that Hill is able, in his poetry, to make his most incisive engagement with the paradoxes of Pound's career. The references to Ruskin in Hill's critical prose have until recent years been rather few, but they have become far more frequent over the past two decades. Ruskin's appearances in Hill's poetry have been rare but crucial. In section XXV of *Mercian Hymns* (1971), Hill "broods" on the eightieth letter of *Fors Clavigera*, in which Ruskin recounts his 1877 visit to a Worcestershire cottage in which two women are engaged in nail-making. It is a resonant moment in Ruskin's text (the very title of *Fors* can mean "Nail-bearing Fate"), and it perhaps unconsciously echoes the opening passage of Adam Smith's *Wealth of Nations*, which illustrates the division of labour through the similar example of pin-making (14-5). Ruskin celebrates the women's delicate efficiency at their task: "no dance of Muses on Parnassian mead in truer measure; – no sea fairies upon yellow sands more featly footed"; but he regrets not so much their straitened wages as the fact that "their forge-dress did not well set off their English beauty; nay, that the beauty itself was marred by the labour..." (*Works* 29.174-5) Hill, brooding on this episode in *Mercian Hymns*, "speak[s] in memory of my grandmother, whose childhood and prime womanhood were spent in the nailer's darg." "It is one thing to celebrate the 'quick forge,'" he writes, "another to cradle a face hare-lipped by the searing wire" (*Collected Poems* 129). Ruskin, this passage seems to reflect rather acidly, has missed the point of the "nailer's darg": he has reduced or displaced the *human* costs of labour and production onto a purely *aesthetic* plane. But is of course a mark of how seriously Hill takes Ruskin that he is "brooding" over *Fors Clavigera* in the first place.

In later works, Hill will brood more deeply on the Ruskinian inheritance, particularly as it manifests itself in Pound's example. In his sequence "Pindarics (*after Cesare Pavese*)" Hill "reads through" and comments upon the anti-fascist Italian poet's diaries. Section 18 addresses a brief quoted passage from Pavese: "*Fundamentally the fine arts and letters did not suffer under fascism; cynically accepting the game as it was*" (*Without Title* 52). "The nature it seems of that intelligence / is to be compromised," Hill writes: "P. (Ces) blamed Ruskin for the fascist state." (He alludes without quoting to another passage in Pavese's diaries: "The banality of totalitarian ideologies reflects the banality of the humanitarian theories that produced them. Tolstoi, Ruskin, Gandhi…" [*Business* 196, entry dated 10 May 1941].) Hill clearly has little patience for such spongy thought: "take your hook | and prune away among the vine-steads, clever man," he addresses Pavese, with no little sarcasm. But the conjunction of Ruskin's social thought and the "fascist state" brings in a middle term – the American poet most famously associated with Italian fascism, Ezra Pound. "Pound / was a Ruskinian," Hill writes,

> so it works out, so it
>
> fits and sits fair to being plausible;
> which is our métier.

Anyone with even a nodding acquaintance with Hill's fierce, almost disabling sense of rectitude, will recognize the savage irony in invoking "plausibility" as the poet's "métier." The work of the poet and poet-critic, as Hill interprets this inheritance from Pound, is not *plausibility* but *truth-telling*. To blame the fascist state on thinkers elements of whose thought might have been appropriated by fascism – as in the case of the French poet Charles Péguy, to whom Hill dedicates *The Mystery of the Charity of Charles Péguy* (1983) – is a failure of distinction, a failure of the poetic faculty itself.[6]

But if Hill works to exonerate Ruskin from the charge of being a proto-fascist, he will waste no time on the fruitless task of exonerating Pound. The ultimate misdirection of Pound's ethical energies, how his desperate quest for a solution to the West's social crisis led him to outright, full-throated – and never really retracted – support of Mussolini's regime, is one of the most-repeated stories of twentieth-century literary history. Perhaps the most telling conjunction of Ruskin and Pound in Hill's poetry, section CXLVI of *The Triumph of Love*, addresses just this issue. The section ends with a moving paean to Ruskin:

> Ruskin's wedded
> incapacity, for which he has been scourged
> many times with derision, does not
> render his vision blind or his suffering
> impotent. Fellow-labouring master-
> servant of *Fors Clavigera*, to us he appears
> some half-fabulous field-ditcher who prised
> up, from a stone-wedged hedge-root, the lost
> amazing crown. (*Triumph* 80)

Some straightforward glosses are in order: "wedded incapacity" refers to Ruskin's unconsummated marriage with Effie Gray; as "Master" of the Society of St. George, Ruskin regularly referred to himself in *Fors* as a "fellow-labourer" to the "Workmen and Labourers of Great Britain" to whom the letters were addressed.

Earlier in the section, Hill contrasts Ruskin to Pound on the basis of a verse from Deuteronomy:

> *Cursed be he that removeth his neighbour's mark*:
> Mosaic statute, to which Ruskin was steadfast.
> (If Pound had stood so, he might not have foundered.)

This passage (Deuteronomy 27.17) is a text – in the sense of a "text" around which a sermon revolves – which Hill takes as "implicit in [Ruskin's] major writings": "Cursed *be* he that remooueth his neighbours land-marke: and all the people shall say, Amen" (*Collected Critical Writings* 387). Hill is certainly right in reading the defence of private property as a central Ruskinian theme. The basis of his distinction between Ruskin and Pound in this passage, however, lies not in any particular shared principle, but rather in the *steadfastness* that Ruskin displays, and which Pound fails to maintain. Both Pound's and Ruskin's ethical projects, in worldly eyes, must be seen as failures: But Ruskin fails, not because he falters from his focus on remaking British society into something more humane and ethical, but because of the very unreachability of his goals and the fallibility of his instruments – the "fellow-labourers" who time and again prove unable to live up to his expectations, his own too-highly-wrought mental constitution, which eventually comes unstrung with the strain of his labours. Pound, in contrast, fails by letting his focus waver from a concern with the moral and technical weight of his own poetic technique, by allowing his attention to be consumed by the poisonous labyrinths of anti-monetarist and anti-Semitic conspiracy theories, allowing his imagination to be dazzled by "boss" figures such as Sigismundo Malatesta and Benito Mussolini.

Hill's own rehabilitation of Ruskin is by no means a matter of complete assent; most crucially, he finds he can no longer accept without qualification Ruskin's notion of "intrinsic value," once one of his own critical touchstones – a notion which I would tentatively identify as the "lost amazing crown" of the earlier passage. Hill's argument about intrinsic value, which surfaces in *The Enemy's Country* (1991, from lectures delivered in 1986) and occupies a central space in *Inventions of Value* (2008, mostly from lectures delivered between 1998 and 2001), is a subtle one, and his position changes over time. "Until recently," Hill writes in 2001, "I was an essentially an adherent of 'intrinsic value' as delineated by Ruskin. I am now much less sure of my position…" (*Collected Critical Writings* 484-6). Ruskin himself, Hill notes, seems as convinced of the "intrinsic value" of some things as Hobbes is of the "inhaerent virtue" of the dead Sidney Godolphin to whom *Leviathan* is dedicated; but that very dedication on Ruskin's part to the "intrinsicality" of value wavers in *Fors Clavigera* 37, when his never-precise definition of value seems almost to merge with the proto-labour-theory of Locke's *Second Treatise of Government* (see *Collected Critical Writings* 388-90).[7]

Hill's discussion of Ruskin in the lectures of *Inventions of Value* and his invocations of Ruskin in *The Triumph of Love* and "Pindarics (*for Cesare Pavese*)," then, play upon the *elegiac* force of Ruskin's invocations of "intrinsic value," an "unwobbling pivot" for socio-economic comm-entary that has proved to be a broken reed. In the face of Ruskin's failure, and even more so in the face of Pound's folly, Hill finds himself reflecting again upon the improbability of the poet's actually *influencing* society. "Still, I'm convinced," Hill writes in *The Triumph of Love*, "that shaping, | voicing, are types of civic action" (*Triumph* 36): the tenor of that poem as a whole, however, makes this assertion seem little more than whistling against the wind. And any such "civic action," in the midst of a culture gripped by an accelerating historical amnesia, is by necessity a rear-guard action of memory and reminding, of what David Jones called "anamnesis." By the end of that long poem, Hill has come to concede that the poet's task, *qua* poet, can be no more or less than to preserve a rigid fidelity to his own language so that his works might serve as acts of witness and memorialization. And this, of course, has been the tendency of Hill's poetry all along, from the formal elegies and Holocaust poems of *For the Unfallen* (1959) and *King Log* (1968) right through the impassioned homages of *Without Title* (2006). It is surely a diminished conception of poetry's mission, especially in the light of the society-changing power that Ruskin and Pound attributed to letters; but it is a little better than the bleak view of poetry that closes *The Triumph of Love*: "a sad and angry consolation" (*Triumph* 82).[8]

Notes

[1] Back-cover blurbs (by respectively John Hollander and *The Spectator*) from Hill's *Selected Poems*.

[2] While it's not my concern here to attempt a full consideration of the varied receptions of Hill's and Prynne's work, I suspect that the "cult" of the poet's personality has much to do with the matter. Prynne has been for much of his career a "faceless" poet; none of his books, even the collected *Poems*, have presented an image of the poet, and until a few years ago it was impossible even to find a photograph of him on the World Wide Web. Hill's dour visage, in contrast, has been almost ubiquitous: the cover of the 2006 Yale UP *Selected Poems* presents an almost life-sized photograph of him, with neither title nor author's name: the poet's words have vanished into his physiognomy.

[3] On modernist poetry and quotation, see Diepeveen, *Changing Voices*; on modernism and citation more generally, see Sartiliot, *Citation and Modernity*.

[4] The secondary literature on Ruskin is enormous. The best brief introductions remain Landow's *Past Masters* volume and Bell's luminous *Ruskin*.

[5] "The House that Jack Built," *Geography* 45. Davenport's argument for the centrality of *Fors Clavigera*, and of labyrinthine structures in general, to modernism is almost certainly overstated – but remains endlessly suggestive.

[6] As Hill puts it in a note to *The Mystery of the Charity of Charles Péguy*, "It has been said that 'Péguy's socialism re-emerged as the national-socialism of Barrès and Sorel'; but fascism, in whatever form, is a travesty of Péguy's true faith and position. He did not, in the end, have a great deal in common with Sorel; quarrelled with him; was certainly not anti-semitic" (*Collected Poems* 206).

[7] The most thorough examination of Hill's reading of Ruskin on this issue is Waithe, "Hill, Ruskin and Intrinsic Value."

[8] Hill quotes James Thomson ("B. V.")'s translation of an 1823 letter by Giocomo Leopardi commenting on the modesty of Torquato Tasso's tomb.

Works Cited

Bell, Quentin. *Ruskin*. 1963; New York, NY: George Braziller, 1978.

Coyle, Michael. *Ezra Pound, Popular Genres, and the Discourse of Culture*. University Park, PA: Pennsylvania State UP, 1995.

Davenport, Guy. *The Geography of the Imagination: Forty Essays*. San Francisco, CA: North Point P, 1981.

Diepeveen, Leonard. *Changing Voices: The Modern Quoting Poem*. Ann Arbor, MI: University of Michigan Press, 1993.

Goldman, Lawrence. "Ruskin, Oxford, and the British Labour Movement 1880-1914." *Ruskin and the Dawn of the Modern*. Ed. Dinah Birch. Oxford: Clarendon P, 1999. 57-86.

Hill, Geoffrey. *Collected Critical Writings*. Ed. Kenneth Haynes. Oxford: Oxford University Press, 2008.

——. *Collected Poems*. New York, NY: Oxford UP, 129.

———. *Selected Poems*. New Haven, CT: Yale UP, 2006.

———. *The Triumph of Love*. Boston, MA: Houghton Mifflin, 1998.

———. *Without Title*. 2006; New Haven, CT: Yale UP, 2007.

Hough, Graham. *The Last Romantics*. 1947; London: Methuen, 1967.

Landow, George P. *Ruskin (Past Masters)*. Oxford: Oxford UP, 1985.

Pavese, Cesare. *This Business of Living: Diaries 1935-1950*. Piscataway, NJ: Transaction, 2009.

Pound, Ezra. *ABC of Reading*. 1934; New York, NY: New Directions, 2010.

———. *Guide to Kulchur*. 1938; New York, NY: New Directions, 1970.

———. *Poems and Translations*. Ed. Richard Sieburth. New York, NY: Library of America, 2003.

———. *Selected Prose 1909-1965*. Ed. William Cookson. New York, NY: New Directions, 1973.

Prynne, J. H. *Poems*. Edinburgh and London: Agneau 2, 1982.

———. *Poems*. South Fremantle, WA: Fremantle Arts Centre Press / Folio (Salt); Newcastle-upon-Tyne: Boodaxe Books, 1999.

———. *Poems*. South Fremantle, WA: Fremantle Arts Centre Press; Tarset: Bloodaxe Books, 2005.

Ruskin, John. *The Works of John Ruskin*. 39 volumes. Ed. E. T. Cook and Alexander Wedderburn. London: George Allen, 1903-1912.

Sartiliot, Claudette. *Citation and Modernity: Derrida, Joyce, and Brecht*. Norman, OK: University of Oklahoma Press, 1993.

Smith, Adam. *An Inquiry into the Nature and Causes of the Wealth of Nations*. Ed. R. H. Campbell and A. S. Skinner. 1976; Indianapolis, IN: Liberty Fund, 1981.

Waithe, Marcus. "Hill, Ruskin and Intrinsic Value." *Geoffrey Hill and His Contexts*. Ed. Piers Pennington and Matthew Sperling. Oxford: Peter Lang, 2011. 133-150.

Williams, Raymond. *Culture and Society, 1780-1950*. New York: Anchor, 1950.

Wilmer, Clive. 'Sculpture and Economics in Pound and Ruskin.' *Ruskin and the Twentieth Century: The Modernity of Ruskinism*. Ed. Toni Cerutti. Vercelli, Italy: Edizioni Mercurio, 2000. 169-187.

Joshua Kotin

Blood-Stained Battle-Flags: Ezra Pound, J.H. Prynne and Classical Chinese Poetry

1

In a two-part essay for *To-day* in 1918, Ezra Pound describes the special "completeness" of classical Chinese poetry (*EW* 303). Discussing "The Jewel-Stairs' Grievance," he claims that "upon careful examination we find that everything is there, not merely by 'suggestion' but by a sort of mathematical process of reduction. [...] You can play Conan Doyle if you like" (*EW* 299). (To prove his point, he includes a "reduction" of the poem in *Cathay* (1915).) Discussing, "South-Folk in Cold Country," he notes that the only information the "writer expects his hearers to know [is] that Dai and Etsu are in the south, that En is a bleak north country" (*EW* 299). "Given these simple geographical facts, the poem is very forthright in its manner" (*EW* 299). Pound's point, here, is that we do not need any special training to evaluate these poems. Their value is universally available – and universal. The canon is irrelevant. Homer and Sappho have no bearing on Li Bai, of course; but if we accept Pound's claims, neither do the writers of the Sui or Tang dynasties.

Cynics might argue that expertise matters for Pound only insofar as he happens to possess it. He is his own ideal reader, and his pedagogy promotes his skills and worldview. This may be true in general. But in this specific case, the attribution of completeness derives from Ernest Fenollosa's account of classical Chinese poetry. Chinese poetry makes expertise unnecessary because it appeals to innate and universal properties of mind. The most well-known aspect of Fenollosa's account concerns the iconicity of the Chinese ideogram. In the lectures that would become "The Chinese Written Character as a Medium for Poetry," he argues:

> Chinese notation is something very much more than [...] arbitrary symbols. It is based upon a vivid short-hand picture of the operations of nature. In the algebraic figure, and in the spoken word, there is no natural connection between thing and sign; all depends upon sheer convention. But the Chinese method proceeds upon natural suggestion. (*CWC* 80)

As Pound declares in *ABC of Reading*, "The Chinese 'word' or ideogram [...] is based on something everyone KNOWS" (*ABC* 22). The character for "man," for example, is a picture of a "man upon his two legs." Understanding requires openness and sensitivity to the natural world, not knowledge of literary history – or even knowledge as such.

But iconicity is only a small part of Fenollosa's account. He devotes most of his essay to outlining the qualities of classical Chinese poetry relevant to English verse. Metaphor is central. The ideogram juxtaposes concrete images to communicate abstract ideas. "The known interprets the obscure": metaphors give "colour and vitality, forcing [words] closer to the concreteness of natural processes." "Ripple" combines signs for "boat" and "water," "Male," signs for "rice-field" and "struggle." This procedure conveys the interrelatedness of all things: "A true noun, an isolated thing, does not exist in nature," he writes, "[t]he eye sees noun and verb as one: things in motion, motion in things..." Verbs are concrete: "'is' not only means 'to have,' but [...] 'to snatch from the moon with the hand.'" Negative particles are absent; verbs serve in their place. (The "sign meaning 'to be lost in the forest'" expresses "a state of non-existence.") Chinese syntax follows "the transferences of force from agent to object, which constitute natural phenomena." "The sentence form," he asserts "was forced upon primitive man by nature itself. It was not we who made it; it was a reflection of the temporal order of causation. [...] The type of sentence in nature is a flash of lightning" (*CWC* 54, 55, 46, 46, 46, 46, 50, 49, 47).

Fenollosa's priority in the essay is not Sinology, but a poetics of natural law. "I trust that this digression concerning parts of speech may have justified itself," he writes, "It proves, first, the enormous interest of the Chinese language in throwing light upon our forgotten mental processes [...] Secondly, it is indispensable for understanding the poetical raw material which the Chinese language affords" (*CWC* 53). This is the essay's aim: to illuminate mental processes and provide raw materials. At its core, it is a manifesto for renewing English poetry. (In 1936, Pound appended the subtitle "An Ars Poetica" to the first stand-alone edition of the essay.) To give the manifesto urgency, Fenollosa deploys a subtle chauvinism. "The Chinese problem alone is so vast that no nation can afford to ignore it. We in America, especially, must face it across the Pacific, and master it or it will master us" (*CWC* 42). The warning reinforces Pound's own sense of art's political significance. If the health of a society is proportional to the accuracy of its language, China is both guide and threat: it provides the key to saving western culture, while forecasting the culture's obsolescence.

Fenollosa's account of classical Chinese poetry offered a way to universalise Pound's poetics and, as a result, confirm his understanding of its political efficacy. Rather than learn to identify the essential in a work of art, one could access it directly. Rather than train one's critical capacities, one could transcend them.

In the "Wisdom of Poetry" (1912), Pound writes, "The function of an art is to free the intellect from the tyranny of [...] set moods, set ideas, conventions; from [...] experience induced by the stupidity of the experiencer and not the inevitable laws of nature" (*EW* 191). Chinese, in short, promised a solution to the problem of stupidity.

The poems in *Cathay* aim to make good on this promise. Consider "The Beautiful Toilet," which juxtaposes stanzas as an ideogram juxtaposes constitutive parts. The first stanza pictures a woman passing through the door of her home, wary of entering the garden. The second describes her youth, marriage, and isolation. The contrast captures her imprisonment, but also her agency and self-awareness, the careful pressure she exerts against circumstance. A sense of intimacy pervades the poem:

> Blue, blue is the grass about the river
> And the willows have overfilled the close garden.
> And within, the mistress, in the midmost of her youth,
> White, white of face, hesitates, passing the door.
> Slender, she puts forth a slender hand,
>
> And she was a courtezan in the old days,
> And she has married a sot,
> Who now goes drunkenly out
> And leaves her too much alone.
>
> *By Mei Sheng.*
> *B.C. 140.* (*C* 7)

Juxtaposition also governs the content of individual stanzas. The overfilled garden contrasts with the flowing river; the woman's hesitancy with the motion of her hand; her past life with her present marriage. Even the repeated colours and conjunctions increase the tension between rest and motion, the woman's passive and active engagement with the world. The poem collects these concrete images to fashion a dynamic environment, providing a subtle music to make it cohere. The application of Fenollosa's techniques is flexible, fitted to the resources of English.

Or consider the opening of "Sennin Poem by Kakuhaku," a poem first published in *The New Age* in 1916 and revised for the expanded edition of *Cathay* published in *Lustra* (1917):

> The red and green kingfishers
>   flash between the orchids and clover,
> One bird casts its gleam on another. (*L* 90)

The first line places the kingfishers before us; the second captures their flight between the orchids and clover. In the third, the birds light each other's way. The diction is concrete. The images are distinct, yet interrelated. Four discrete surfaces reflect light to illuminate the scene. The orchids and clover provide a reference point to track the birds' flight. Force flows from agent to object. "Between" marks both movement and relation. The images are not culturally specific: kingfishers, orchids, and clover populate every continent (save Antarctica) and are thus available to every mind's eye. Context is unnecessary: readers need no special knowledge to understand the poem. This is universality as timelessness: an ancient poem perpetually present.

2

"A late stage of decay is arrested, and embalmed in the dictionary," Fenollosa writes. "Only our scholars and poets feel painfully back along the thread of our etymologies and piece together our diction, as best they may, from forgotten fragments" (*CWC* 54). This is a call to revitalize words by rediscovering their relation to nature. One advantage of the ideogram is that it does this work for us: "Its etymology is constantly visible" (*CWC* 54). Its roots are on display in its juxtaposition of material appearances to convey moral and intellectual facts.

But embedded in this account of the ideogram's relation to nature is an account of its relation to history. Fenollosa continues:

> After thousands of years the lines of metaphoric advance are still shown and in many cases retained in the meaning. Thus a word, instead of growing gradually poorer and poorer as with us, becomes richer and still more rich from age to age, almost consciously luminous. Its uses in national philosophy and history, in biography and in poetry, throw about it a nimbus of meanings. (*CWC* 54)

"[I]deographs," he concludes, "are like blood-stained battle-flags to an old campaigner" (*CWC* 54). In other words, ideograms display a history of use. This is not history made perpetually present, but history as a genealogy of overlapping texts and contexts. By using an ideogram, we contribute to its meaning. By studying Chinese history, we illuminate its range of reference. Completeness is a fallacy. A "nimbus of meanings" recalls the symbolism Pound sought to destroy.

This sense of conventionality is central to the poetics of contemporary English poet J.H. Prynne. From his early *Kitchen Poems* (1968) to his recent *Kazoo Dreamboats* (2011), his poetry examines how use affects the meaning of words, and how the meaning of words structures our experience of the world.

Readers are expected to learn specialized vocabularies, locate obscure references, research etymologies. Scholarship is a way to imbricate reader and text, text and world – to coordinate a collective inquiry into the pliancy and power of language.

Prynne's poetics finds its own analogue in contemporary scholarship on classical Chinese poetry. Discussing the Tang and Song lyric, Stephen Owen writes, "in the Chinese poem, fullness lies outside the text, as the end of the reading process. At its least complacent, a T'ang or Sung poem moves toward a fullness that is never attained" (70). Readers negotiate a text's relation to a world beyond its purview or control. Such negotiation is always ongoing, requiring expertise in a text's "cosmology and [...] literary tradition" and sensitivity to the dynamics of its reception (70). Readers confront a world of evolving norms, not precise word-object relations.

According to Prynne, texts that embrace their incompleteness are "metonymic." "Metaphoric" texts, in contrast, aspire to total self-sufficiency. In a review of Anne Birrell's edition of *New Songs from a Jade Terrace* (1983, 1986), an anthology of Chinese love poems compiled by Hsü Ling around 545 CE, Prynne describes Pound's promotion of metaphor:

> The Poundian theory of image had insisted on direct treatment of the thing without an ascribed or intended meaning but metaphoric with an immediacy excluding even the act of comparison itself. Absolute metaphor was thus energetic and succinct, autonomous within the context of its presentation, and connected to it not by links of reference or idiom but by feeling and inner rhythm. [...] Chinese poetic practice, and the Chinese language itself, became for Pound at a critically formative stage in his career a demonstration against metonymy. (367)

This is Pound's fantasy: texts that transcend the contexts of their production and reception. Denotation occludes connotation; autonomy is a function of completeness. *New Songs from a Jade Terrace* exposes this fantasy as such, revealing the metonymic character of *Cathay*'s sources. Prynne continues:

> Literary figuration in Palace Style Poetry, and in the earlier kinds of writing assembled in the *Jade Terrace* anthology, emphasizes what [Bernhard] Karlgren has in a more general context aptly called 'metaphor with a history'. The stylistic history, or occasionally the cosmology or other typological ordering, comprises the precursory system which makes the use of coded metaphor a metonymic rather than metaphoric procedure; and it is the subtlety of intelligible allusion,

varied and superimposed, which here shews the power of metonymy
both to support metaphor and exceed it. (368)

The anthology provides this stylistic history, illuminating the extensive network
of associations and allusions that compose the poems.[1] As a result, Pound's
source texts (many of which are translated by Birrell) come to resemble the
"blood-stained battle-flags" described in Fenollosa's essay.

As an object lesson on metonymy, Prynne reads "The Beautiful Toilet"
against the contexts supplied by anthology. Pound's version, quoted in full
above, opens:

> Blue, blue is the grass about the river
> And the willows have overfilled the close garden.
> And within, the mistress, in the midmost of her youth...

When read in isolation, Prynne writes, "the presence of the willows is suggestive
of delicate but over-luxuriant enclosure, the qualities of nature metaphorically
transferred to the isolation of the mistress by a brilliant internal chiasmus of
sound-values (*wil̄ōws, ōverfilled*)..." (369–370).[2] The enclosure, in other words,
represents the mistress' captivity. When read in the anthology, however, the
scene has a different valence. Entitled "Green, green riverside grass," the poem
appears in a collection of nine anonymous first- and second-century lyrics, and
then again in seven imitations dating from the third to the sixth centuries, CE.
By consulting the anthology's notes, we learn that "willow" is a pun for "to
detain, to keep someone from going away on a journey" (Birrell 333). From the
poem's position in the anthology, we learn that it represents an early stage in a
"transfer of poetic values from the unsophisticated feeling for nature to a hyper-
sophisticated and self-conscious acknowledgement of artifice." The mistress'
desire contrasts with nature's self-sufficiency. As Prynne observes, she "has not
been able to keep her playboy husband from roving off and leaving her alone"
(371). Her desire reflects the very stylistic changes the anthology documents.

Context, here, does more than modify a poem's meaning: it constitutes it.
Prynne observes:

> Birrell translates [...] not simply the traditionally quasi-simple poems
> from which the Chinese lyric traces some of its origins, but rather these
> same poems as seen in retrospect by the Liang court poets and as put
> into the anthology by Hsü Ling. It is what they read plus their reading
> of it which she reconstructs and transmits." (374)

Images and themes in later poems reconfigure their source texts. For example, the use of "willow" in Hsiao Kang's six-century "Peach Pink" has retroactive significance. The poem makes the subtle irony of "The Beautiful Toilet" explicit:

> Peach pink, plum white like dawn cosmetics.
> I disgrace my wrecked self next to the fresh willow.
> I wouldn't mind living a while, then dying before you –
> But I'd be in despair without my west Reincarnation scent! (256)

The line "I disgrace my wrecked self next to the fresh willow" provides a heavy-handed gloss on the delicate "willows have overfilled the close garden / And within, the mistress…" The willow, here, marks the speaker's "wrecked" sophistication. Death is mere inconvenience compared to a life without cosmetics. In the light of this poem, the woman in "The Beautiful Toilet" becomes responsible for her abandonment and the artificiality of the art that documents it.

What kind of reading is this? Authorial intention does not govern significance; neither does the literal meaning of the words on the page. Poems respond to ever-changing norms. Consider yet another example from "The Beautiful Toilet." For readers in the West, the dead metaphor "weeping willow" is an inevitable, if unintended, part of the poem's meaning. "Willow" recalls "weeping," and by means of pathetic fallacy characterizes the mistress' lament. The process is metonymic and anachronistic. The effect is unavailable in the original Chinese and likely anathema to Pound. Yet it impacts our reading – as a node of significance or an object of suppression or both. Birrell's anthology modifies Pound's translation in a similar way. After reading *Jade Terrace*, "The Beautiful Toilet" becomes yet another stage in the on-going history of a living text. The anthology supplements the poem (it does not supplant it) by embedding it in the metonymic relations that properly concern its object. This is what Prynne means by "the power of metonymy both to support metaphor and exceed it."

As a practical poetics this embrace of convention has significant implications. It requires us to give up a conception of poetic immortality as a kind of timelessness. It also forces us to accept partial responsibility for a poem's meaning. Indeed, one may ask whether we can talk about *a* poem at all. (Does a poem retain its identity as it changes over time?) This kind of responsibility can be pleasurable and empowering, but also exhausting and banal. As we read we must moderate between intention and effect, denotation and connotation. Every poem is endlessly occasional, and we are part of its most recent occasion. We must illuminate its contexts and reception history as we moderate the impact of our own position in culture. This is difficult work. (Preference for "The Beautiful

Toilet" over "Green, green riverside grass" may not only be a matter of aesthetics, but of convenience as well.) Scholarship can mitigate this difficulty: Birrell, for example, does much of this work for us – she even translates the poems. But often we are on our own, in a library with a strange text, struggling to justify our work – or simply understand it.

Prynne's poetry acknowledges this state of affairs. It invites us to participate in a collective project as it asks us to examine the factors that determine whether we accept it – ideology, class, temperament, chance, etc. To put this point another way: to read Prynne's poetry is to confront the problem of social action. An inquiry into the nature and potential of linguistic convention solicits a theory of agency. This, in part, is the beauty of Prynne's work: how it exemplifies the intricacies of personhood in a specific historical moment. For Pound, in contrast, agency is not a concern – his poetry is not open to justification. This is one aspect of its beauty: how it constructs a fantasy of intrinsic value – value that is not contingent on the beliefs or actions of individual readers.

Notes

This essay is excerpted from a longer essay titled, "Reading Ezra Pound and J.H. Prynne in Chinese."

[1] Prynne describes the anthology's editorial apparatus: "Dr Birrell [...] combine[s] a plain-text presentation of each poem with a detailed and extensive apparatus, not of commentary on each poem or representative samples of them [...], but of notes on idioms, images, names of persons and places and tunes, distinctive locutions, fables and particular associations, all arranged alphabetically at the end of the book. This she has combined with summary biographical profiles of the poets and their interconnections, and with an index of her adapted titles alongside their literally translated originals, which allows the identification of those later poems which imitate or 'harmonise with' previous originals (most of them included in the earlier chapters of this anthology)" (364–365).

[2] In his reading of the poem, Prynne cites Hugh Kenner's *The Pound Era* (194).

Works Cited

Birrell, Anne, ed. *New Songs from a Jade Terrace: An Anthology of Early Chinese Love Poetry.* Harmondsworth: Penguin, 1986. Print.

Fenollosa, Ernest, and Ezra Pound. *The Chinese Written Character as a Medium for Poetry: A Critical Edition.* Ed. Haun Saussy, Jonathan Stalling, and Lucas Klein. New York, NY: Fordham University Press, 2008. Print. (*CWC*)

Kenner, Hugh. *The Pound Era*. Berkeley, CA: University of California Press, 1971. Print.

Owen, Stephen. *Traditional Chinese Poetry and Poetics: Omen of the World*. Madison, WI: University of Wisconsin Press, 1985. Print.

Pound, Ezra. *ABC of Reading*. New York, NY: New Directions, 2010. Print. (*ABC*)

——. *Cathay*. London, Elkin Mathews, 1915. Print. (*C*)

——. *Early Writings: Poems and Prose*. Ed. Ira B. Nadel. New York, NY: Penguin, 2005. Print. (*EW*)

——. *Lustra*. New York: privately printed, 1917. Print. (*L*)

Prynne, J.H. "China Figures." *New Songs from a Jade Terrace: An Anthology of Early Chinese Love Poetry*. Ed. Anne Birrell. Harmondsworth: Penguin, 1986. Print.

Ryan Dobran

Myth, Culture and Text:
Ezra Pound's Homer and J.H. Prynne's Aristeas

The relation between the work of Ezra Pound and J.H. Prynne has been mediated primarily by the poetics of the American poet, Charles Olson. This mediation is not purely a matter of critical historiography, for it is Olson who, incidentally, became close with Pound in 1946 during the latter's stay at St. Elizabeth's Hospital, and who began corresponding with Prynne in 1961. Olson's poetics have largely guided the discussion of Prynne's early poetry, and the three poets are often seen as comprising a tradition of modernist and neo-modernist (or late modernist) writing.[1] One of the most visible reasons for this is because all three authors shared, at one time or another, a desire for the poetic text to embody knowledge; indeed, for the poem to be a kind of knowledge-making process.

As Fellow and, later, librarian at Gonville and Caius College in Cambridge, Prynne acted as scholar to Charles Olson's *Maximus* project throughout the 1960s, sending dozens of photocopied articles and books to Olson: prospectuses and slides of water-damaged eighteenth-century Port Books, nineteenth-century cosmography, G.S. Kirk's *Heraclitus*, and fascicles of the Cambridge Ancient History series, to name only a few.[2] Prynne was directly responsible for the production of a workable typescript for what later became *Maximus IV, V, VI* (1968). Much of this material makes up the ambient background through which Prynne's *The White Stones* drifts. Although poetic research and the use and abuse of external texts are notable markers of a Poundian tradition shared by Olson and Prynne himself, my purpose in this brief essay is to set the predominant figure of Olson aside in order to discuss what I find to be one of the major points of intersection between Pound and Prynne on the concrete level of the poetic text: their respective uses of ancient Greek literature in translation. When I say "use" I mean something like the explicit and purposive activity of establishing a connection to an aspect of ancient Greek culture, religion and science in a non-trivial way; that is to say, a substantial investment of time and effort. In Pound's case, I would suggest that his work creates a hegemonic effect of *paideuma* when he calls on the *Odyssey* to be one of the mythological frames of *The Cantos*. Although Pound thought of his ideogrammic method as analogous to scientific study, and was familiar with the anthropology of James Frazer and Leo Frobenius, he does not adopt an anthropological perspective but rather uses the *Odyssey* to support the beauty and power of mythological thinking. By way of contrast, I would suggest that Prynne uses the various texts that comprise the record of the seventh-century BC poet-traveller, Aristeas, in order to understand the limits of mythological thinking. Whereas Pound preserves the status of the mythological *as* mythological, Prynne seeks to contextualize the mythological with a third person narrative intercalated with texts drawn from ancient, anthropological, archaeological and philological sources. Pound collapses historical distance by his combinatory writing style whereas Prynne preserves historical distance. As the latter wrote to Peter Riley on 14 February 1967 in *The English Intelligencer* shortly before publishing "Aristeas": "What went on before that ['economies of exchange'] I prize beyond measure, but I could not want it back or any version of cultural nostalgia" (Pattison et al 77). "Aristeas" may rewrite the travels of Aristeas through the tradition of Herodotus' and Pliny's legendary reports, but this mythical language is countered by the presence of anthropological detail, which views these descriptions as part of an ideologically irrecoverable material culture. However, this contrast is not as clear-cut as one would like, and so I propose it here as a starting point, rather than a final thesis.

While there has been much intimation and perhaps some tacit consensus about the importance of Pound's work to Prynne, this connection has received little serious attention. Although it is occasionally remarked that there is something Poundian about Prynne's work, it is imperative that this relation be diagnosed not merely by pointing out a resemblance, but by understanding the distinctions and divisions within that resemblance.

In one of the few reviews of Prynne's first retained collection, *Kitchen Poems* (1968), Pound's *Cantos* were a point of comparison:

> Mr. Prynne's "kitchen" is basically economics: the backroom where not only wars but all our individual jobs and hopes and fears are calculated, graphed and statistically defined. He shares the distrust of this generalizing process – affecting both our language and our thinking – which comes from the tradition of Pound, from the great Cantos against usury. (Holmes 25)

Despite the reviewer's misunderstanding of the significant differences between Pound and Prynne in terms of their political and economic commitments, critics have largely followed this grouping. Prynne's work has been continuously placed in the neo-modernist or late modernist wing whose antecedents are Pound, Williams and Olson, rather than Eliot and Stevens (Corcoran 164, 174-178). Others have relegated him within a distinctly British Poundian tradition whose forerunners are Basil Bunting and Charles Tomlinson (Giles 11). More recently, in *Late Modernist Poetics: Pound to* Prynne, Anthony Mellors has argued that Prynne's poetry of the late 1960s continues a Poundian tradition whose "eclecticism and difficulty form a hermeneutic basis for cultural renewal"

(Mellors 2-3). Despite such suggestive reports, the relation between Pound and Prynne has tended to repair and polish the massive discrepancies in poetic texture, political attitudes and thinking which separate them. What *is* similar seems to be the way in which they refer, whether explicitly or covertly, to mythological, historical and scientific contexts, producing a kind of palimpsestic texture. Both writers augment our sense of what kinds of syntax, rhythms, visual patterns, and diction constitute the architecture of the poem, and both do so at a fundamental level, the kind of level which actively shapes the thinking of their readers. Indeed, one of the shared features of these two writers is that their work disrupts the revisionist urgency for a new theory of "modernism". I want to try and steer clear of what appears to be an increasingly desperate "modernist" election agenda, near the end of its tenure, and look specifically, if in only a short and general way, at these two poets' poetic work.[3] My hunch is that the trench between them is richer than the bridge, so to speak, and one major difference stems from their divergent thinking about myth and culture.

As is well known, Canto 1 rewrites a brief passage of book 11 of Homer's *Odyssey*, when Odysseus, driven by Circe, arrives on the shores of the "Kimmerian lands" (Pound 4).[4] In order to communicate with Tiresias, Odysseus and his men perform the *nekuia*, which involves pouring "libations" of "mead and then sweet wine, water mixed with white flour", prayer, and the "dark blood" of sheep sacrifice.[5] The aim of this blood-tribute is to bring out Tiresias. The darkness and obscurity which surrounds the arrival of Pound and his cohort on "Kimmerian lands" in Oceanus, the edge of the known and living world, provides a kind of structural analogy to the way in which *The Cantos* will be organized. Leon Surette comments that the *nekuia* that begins Pound's epic "serves as a paradigm of ritual enlightenment". Furthermore, he writes that the entirety of *The Cantos* may be seen as a kind of catalogued "struggle of enlightened individuals to bring their wisdom into the world in the face of the hostility of an indifferent populace and corrupt authorities" (68). I would continue Surette's line of criticism and say that the darkness of Kimmerian lands provides a further analogy of such ritual enhancement, that of the light of knowledge-making which the representation of the textual surface seeks to produce, and the dark, grotesque ignorance, which is its background.

In Canto 1 we read:

> Sun to his slumber, shadows o'er all the ocean,
> Came we then to the bounds of deepest water,
> To the Kimmerian lands, and peopled cities
> Covered with close-webbed mist, unpierced ever
> With glitter of sun-rays
> Nor with stars stretched, nor looking back from heaven
> Swartest night stretched over wretched men there. (3)

Pound follows the Homeric depiction of Oceanus, down to the mythical depiction of the "Kimmerian lands" at the entrance to Hades. It has been suggested that for Pound the rite of the *nekuia* which follows the arrival on "Kimmerian lands" is an iconic procedure: the ghosts who drink the blood of animal sacrifice and speak to Odysseus are analogous to the cast of personae, historical and mythological, who Pound will interview, castigate, and nominate as characters in the mental theatre of *The Cantos*. The visual gravity and rough music of Pound's Anglo-Saxon verse eventually contrasts with the deflationary mention of "Lie quiet Divus" during Tiresias' speech to Odysseus:

> And he strong with the blood, said then: "Odysseus
> "Shalt return through spiteful Neptune, over dark seas,
> "Lose all companions." And then Anticlea came.
> Lie quiet Divus. I mean, that is Andreas Divus,
> In officinal Wecheli, 1538, out of Homer.
> And he sailed, by Sirens and thence outward and away
> And unto Circe. (4-5)

Once more Anticlea's ghost form is silenced to allow an awareness of Andreas Divus' Renaissance Latin translation of Homer to surface. Pound sifts through pages of the same volume, from Divus' *Odyssey* to Georgius Dartona's Latin translation of the second Homeric Hymn to Aphrodite, which begins "Venerandam". Shortly thereafter the rewriting is abandoned as the colon breaks into the white space of the page. Despite Pound's self-conscious promotion of these source-texts, he nevertheless adopts the bibliographical code of a fragment for his song. The self-directed irony in Canto I creates a pathos of history by imitating the torn or burnt edge of a manuscript and by observing the dilemma of the synecdochal, of how the part comes to impossibly represent the whole. This pathos is related to a distinctly mythical method which, despite its clever humour, nonetheless secures the authority of its utterance by recourse to Homeric mythology. While Pound here includes a conceptual awareness of translation and materiality, he does not allow this material to obstruct the ritual of enlightenment. In some sense, his silencing of the materiality of Divus' translation, on which he bases his own rewriting, reveals Pound the artist as the interlocutor of a panoramic and cascading continuum of temporalities, which are not parts of a chronology, but rather synchronized under the aegis of the artist's craft. That is to say, for Pound form functions as an artificer of material, as though the latter contents were all, basically, stone, and therefore capable of being shaped in any number of ways. But what precisely this "stone" is has been a matter of dispute. Is there a *paideuma* or periplum that offers a logic to Pound's intertextual montage? It is rather as though the absence of a logic derives from the tacit and at times explicit belief in the beauty of a spirit which animates different historical personae at the artist's will. This mythological spatialisation of temporal relations also "takes place" within Dante's *Inferno*, Malatesta's Tempio, in Kung's mountain, or in a vortex of light and colour. That Pound does not allow one mythological tradition to predominate, that his use of myth is pluralist, does not diminish its relation to the production of an authoritative culture. Its incessant confusion of distinct material cultures and contexts of power may have comedic, if not also satirical, effects.

Mythological thinking occurs not only in Pound's tacit nomination of Homer's authority as a kind of stable ground of reference and assurance, but also in Pound's reliance upon what he seems to believe is a secure and clarifying textuality. *The Cantos* do not merely contain or rewrite history so much as obscure temporal relations, seemingly grounded on the assumption that these excerpts of the past brought to the foreground of poetic texture will be instantly recognized as wisdom. That is to say, "Knowledge of the past is therefore the same as wisdom" (Meletinsky 160). The intensity of this vision obstructs causality, so that individual contexts operate as shells into which Pound inserts his commentary and combinations. The story of what happens must be given a mythological shape; for example, the anecdotal folktales created in Canto 16: of Hulme reading Kant in German in the hospital, or mourning the loss of great sculptural objects owing to Gaudier's demise (71).

The opening of Pound's Canto 47 reopens Circe's edict to Odysseus – to go the "Kimmerian lands" and seek the testimony of Tiresias, "Who even dead, yet hath his mind entire!" Tiresias is "So full of knowing that the beefy ['living'] men know less than he" (236). Pound remarked upon this line in his *Guide to Kulchur*: "I hope that elsewhere I have underscored and driven in the greek honour of human intelligence 'Who even dead yet hath his mind entire'" (Terrell 184; *Guide to Kulchur* 146). Pound's notion of intelligence can be rather confusing, but I only want to highlight the way in which Tiresias is summoned as a metonymic token for a cultural detail relating to knowledge. In Canto 47, this epitaphic phrase is a "sound" that "came in the dark". This knowledge is "the shade of a shade", and yet "must thou sail after knowledge / knowing less than drugged beasts" (236). Pound's concept of knowledge is a kind of experiential pursuit through darkness in order to illuminate one's surroundings: "Properly, we shd. read for power. [...] The book shd. be a ball of light in one's hand" (*Guide to Kulchur* 55). It shows how the myth of Odysseus through Circe is modelled on the cultivation of obscurity in order to present an illumined relation. Pound's repetition and parallel clause-structures often have the effect of creating a cycle of perception through which this experiential knowledge of myth gets practiced. That is to say, the cognitive practice of Pound's reader is ritualistic, with the *nekuia* establishing a transhistorical montage of ghosts. Just as the ritual allows the ghosts to personify the transcendence of spatio-temporal limits (recall Odysseus' surprise at Elpenor's ghost-form) in order to create concurrent structures of perception which are historical in subject, but which are not rendered historically, so is the measure of Odysseus' pursuit of knowledge the measure of civilization: "By this gate art thou measured" (236-237). Pound writes in *Guide to Kulchur*:

> To act on one's definition? What concretely do I myself mean to do? I mean to say that one measure of a civilization, either of an age or of a single individual, is what that age or person really wishes to *do*. A man's hope measures his civilization. The attain-ability of the hope measures, or may measure, the civilization of his nation and time. (144)

I would speculate that the kind of intuitive and experiential knowledge embodied by the figure of Tiresias and Odysseus is the agent of this drive towards civilisation. Civilisation culminates in the egocentric, wilful action of the individual. But the knowledge of one's own civilisation is necessarily relative to others: "*A man does not know his own ADDRESS (in time) until he knows where his time and milieu stand in relation to other times and conditions*" (83). Pound's views on "time" have been described in detail, and here I only want to take notice of this structure of historical relativism which creates patterns of concurrence that are necessarily obscure. Indeed, Pound's spatialisation of temporal values places contrary, syntactical pressure against the linear necessity of English word order (see Harmon). This creates a contradiction at the centre of Pound's ideogrammic method, which is supposed to excoriate the dead cells on the surface of the mind, in order to prepare it for the proper subject of knowledge (*Guide to Kulchur* 51).

Canto 8 reflects back upon this spatialisation by alluding to one of the final lines of *The Waste Land*: "These fragments you have shelved (shored)" (28; see Eliot 70).[6] Pound's jape mocks the metaphor of the shipwreck that imbues Eliot's psychology of the intertextual retreat into "Shanti", while emphasizing the material connection between shelves and the books from which he gathers his textual fragments. Ensconced within the conceptual environment of the library, the pseudo-scholarly labour of producing a revisionist history of Malatesta both derides and proudly cues the philology that disgusts him.[7] Despite Pound's cues to the textual materials and the jagged edges of their montage on the page, he wants to re-stage Greek myth as an exemplary way of being and of understanding the beauty of the natural. His disdain for philology is due to the vacuous literalness of its textual scholarship, its lack of spiritual embodiment of the text. It is not active. It has no power. The poems are thus organized around the egocentric irony of the maverick-scholar-poet. For Pound, the poet's mind should be intratextual, written into history. And Pound's coherence depends, in no trivial way, upon his self-authorising relation to cultural supremacy, embodied in his rewriting of various historical exemplars of supremacy, whether Malatesta, Mussolini or Kung.

The lands outside the purview of the central Greek homeland are the limits of the recognisable world.[8] Prynne takes up an interest in precisely this geographical and conceptual threshold. Before "Aristeas, in Seven Years", Prynne composed several shorter poems in response to this body of research. For example, the poem "In Cimmerian Darkness" responds to the mythical trope of the Cimmerians, which, as we saw in Pound's Canto I, views this land and their people as a limit of civilisation, both literally in the sense that at various times in the second and first millennia BC they existed nomadically on the outskirts of the Greek colonies north of the Black Sea, and figuratively in Homer's depiction of them at the entrance to Hades. Prynne's allusion is perhaps more local to the English tradition than Pound's, but, more importantly, finds Cimmerian darkness by no means hellish, but joyous. He responds to the opening of Milton's "L'Allegro", but unlike Milton who invites us *out* of the "dark Cimmerian desert" to rejoice in "Jest and youthful jollity", for Prynne, "Cimmerian darkness" offers a specious, but nevertheless exhilarating "dip" into another "age":

When the faint star does take
    us into the deeper parts
    of the night there *is*
      that sudden dip
and we swing across into
      some other version of this
    present age, where any curving
    trust is set into
the nature of man, the green raw and fabulous
love of it, where every star that shines,
    as he said, exists
in love,[9] [...] (74)

The darkness which hovers over Pound's "Kimmerian lands" as the land of the dead and the entrance to Hell is rather a source of jubilation for Prynne. Prynne's interest in the emergence of Indo-European peoples on the Euro-Asiatic steppe coincides with his interest in Aristeas from Proconnesus, whose epic *Arimaspea* (presumably) recounts his seven years with various Scythian or quasi-Scythian tribes as well as the Issedonians. Aristeas is the first recorded instance of a European traveller having contact with central Asiatic peoples, who apparently drew from their folklore and shamanistic practices.[10] It seems likely that the Hyperboreans, worshippers of Apollo, who may have been the aim of Aristeas' travels, were the Chinese (Bolton 100-101 and Vassileva 69-78). Prynne defined the area of his concern earlier in *Kitchen Poems*, where he contrasted "true expansion" to imperial acquisition:

> the true expansion
> is probably drift, as the Scythians
> being nomadic anyway for the most part
> slipped sideways right across the Russian
> steppes, from China by molecular friction
> through to the Polish border. (14)

Scythia denotes the area between the Danube and Don rivers. As a people, the Scythians may be distinguished between the western peasants and the eastern nomads, divided roughly along the river Dnieper, which from the Black Sea splits modern Ukraine moving north through Belarus and south Russia (Jettmar 23; Rice 20-24). Prynne's "Scythians" designates the broadest possible sense of that term. Prynne views the nomadic "drift" and its "molecular friction" as both "true" and natural.

The Cimmerians as a historical people are at the very root of our knowledge about the emergence of Indo-European culture on the Euro-Asiatic steppe. Here, "In Cimmerian Darkness", however, they long for the stars, and their incessant skyward gazing is reminiscent of Longinus' *On the Sublime* 10 in which Longinus pits Aristeas' *Arimaspea* unfavourably against Homer's *Iliad*. It is one of the few extant fragments of the poem. I merely want to take note of the way that lines three and four connect to Prynne's staging of "darkness":

> Here is another thing also that fills us with feelings of wonder,
> Men that dwell on the water, away from the earth, on the ocean.
> Sorrowful wretches they are, and theirs is a grievous employment:
> Fixing their eyes on the stars, their lives they entrust to the waters.
> Often, I think, to the gods they lift up their hands and they pray;
> Ever their innermost parts are terribly tossed to and fro. (201)

The body of research brought together for "Aristeas" informs the writing of other poems in *The White Stones*. Prynne's poem "In Cimmerian Darkness" is antithetical to the use of the phrase in Homer, Milton and Pound. The perception of the faint star compels the physiological "dip" of the "innermost parts", which heave in the gut, brought on by rough seas. Later in the poem, the "divine" is mediated by "the cups / of our radio telescopes" that "stand openly / braced to catch the recoil". However playful, Prynne is conscious of the notion of "vacancy" (75) as a necessary condition for the reception of the starry divine.

His speculative effort to understand what the "divine" might be to the semi-nomadic peoples outside the recognisable limits of the Greek world, north of the Black Sea, is one of several concerns in "Aristeas". Such concerns are nodes of research and speculation that structure the poem. While, in one sense, the poem is built on this research and the speculative commentary it elicits, there is a steady narrative voice which guides its reader through the referenced material and only occasionally breaks its pattern. There is an inviting set of tours and detours through the discourses and iconography of Buriat, Siberian and Eskimo shamanism; the ecology of nomadic settlement; the anthropology of the lost peoples known as "Cimmerians"; and the imaginative reconstruction of Aristeas as both poet and shamanic figure. "Aristeas, in Seven Years" seems to have imitated the Poundian style of contextual juxtaposition, albeit in a much less abrasive and paratactic manner. The poem features a list of "References" to which the curious glossator may seek further context and information. The poem declares itself a knowledge-making process analogous to a scholarly text, and yet it is unclear as to what the status of these external texts is: do they support the writer's commentary that they intercalate? do they display an ironization of the construction of scholarly knowledge, as Pound's often do? If Prynne's sense of poetic coherence relies, in general, less on eliciting a cognitive reaction by a combinatory method, and more on a kind of linguistic *competence*, with its implied attention to English grammar as a system by which the social practice of individual thinking occurs, his poem "Aristeas" is unique. While it may be said that in *The White Stones* Prynne tries to imbue the English language itself with a kind of mythical aura and therefore rarely uses proper names as beacons for cultural direction, "Aristeas" remains exceptional in his *oeuvre*.[11] Although it is by no means an easy poem, it does exhibit an unusually centrifugal focus on Aristeas.[12]

Like Pound, Prynne is drawn to the use of texts in his work, whether explicitly marked or covert, and in the late 1960s, Prynne shares with Pound a need for an explicit didacticism. "Aristeas" is one of only three poems in Prynne's ongoing body of poems to append a list of "References".[13] This is not only apparent in the properly constructed bibliography, itself more reminiscent of Eliot's appended "Notes" to *The Waste Land* than Pound's source intralineation,[14] but also in various direct implorations found throughout *The White Stones* (1969) and *Kitchen Poems* (1968): We should "Know the names" (16) or "mean the / entire force of what we shall come to say" (108). The purposefully intimidating reference list indicates, in a manner not unlike Pound's, the poet's recourse to scholarly authority. But how is it performed? And how might it differ from Pound's work? I would propose that Prynne's use of scholarship has an effect analogous to that found in scholarship itself. There is an institution of expectation at work, a selective fidelity to experts in the field, among which the poet does not include himself. There is a dispassionate and provisional trust in these sources that seems to place Prynne's poem on the solid ground of the social and natural sciences. Because the subject and environment of Aristeas is fundamentally obscure, there is significant clearance for versified speculation.

But perhaps the most notable distinction between Pound and Prynne is the latter's interest in the material culture of the outer limit of the Greek world, against the former's zealous urgency for recovering myth as the well-lit path out of ignorance and corruption. The seven years of Prynne's title represent Aristeas' disembodiment and voyage into the Euro-Asiatic Steppe:

> Leaving the flesh vacant then, in a fuller's shop,
> Aristeas removed himself for seven years
> into the steppes, preparing his skeleton and the
> song of his departure, his flesh anyway touched
> > by the in-
> > vading Cimmerian
> > twilight: "ruinous"
> > as the old woman's
> > prophecy. (92)

Note the way in which "Cimmerian twilight" refers to the nomadic ecology across a terrain. The "Cimmerian / twilight" touches Aristeas, in the sense of divine inspiration. And the key to understanding the divine in this poem is to follow the reference in the bibliography to a lengthy philological dissertation on Proto-Indo-European (PIE) *deiwos, whose purpose is to investigate this term's semantic history before it came to mean "god".[15] This diachronic strain, which includes both "Zeus" and "Jupiter", develops into the set of English words we associate with "god": "deity", "divine", and also the Greek prefix *theo-*. Hopkins begins her study by establishing that *deiwos was once an adjective. By creating various schematic diagrams of cognatic uses in Sanskrit, Greek, Italic, and others, Hopkins creates an array of signification. She concludes from her data that *deiwos signified "sky", "bright one" and, in several cognates, "day".[16] M.L. West has recently stated the concept more clearly than Hopkins: "The name *dyeus originated as one of a number of words built on the root *di/dei "give off light" and located in the semantic sphere "brightness of heaven, heaven, daylight, day" (167). Hence the nomadic figures each embody a "singular" vantage "as the clan is without centre" (Prynne 92), because they are defined by "the extent of day", "where the / sky holds" (93).

"Aristeas" is the subject of an excellent essay by Simon Jarvis, who makes several points worth considering: that Prynne's use of references is less like assemblage and more like writing because Prynne creates a dialogue between the primary text ("Aristeas") and those of his referents; that Prynne's method of juxtaposition is ambiguous because of its need to avoid a non-dialectical confusion of pro and contra positions, e.g. pro-nomadic and contra-Mediterranean imperialism. I would like to take issue with two points, however.

Firstly, Jarvis maintains that Prynne does not mean to say that Aristeas *is* a shaman, but that the relation between Aristeas of Proconnesus and the shaman, whether Evenk, Buriat, or Siberian, is a "structural analogy". Jarvis is here careful not "to endorse the view that Aristeas was a shaman, but to suggest at the poem's outset a structural analogy between the risks taken by Aristeas in abandoning his settled community and his settled personality and those taken by the shamans in the religion of those with whom Aristeas wishes to catch up" (Jarvis). Yet it is precisely this notion of the "Greek shaman" that Prynne takes seriously. His comparison may be unfamiliar, but it is by no means novel.

In a chapter entitled, "The Greek Shamans and Puritanism" from *The Greeks and the Irrational*, E.R. Dodds speculates upon several anthropological sources to make his link between the emergence of the Greek notion of *psyche* and the interaction of the Greeks with shamanistic culture on the outer perimeter of the Greek colonies in Scythia, just north of the Black Sea. Dodds conjectures that these shamanistic practices, which the Greeks encountered in Scythia "might" (and he doubly emphasizes the "might") have influenced, if not articulated, the concept of the psyche, the notion of a divine self within the self which can "travel" without the body. What Dodds calls "psychic excursion" is that practice, common to all forms of shamanism, Siberian or not, by which the soul travels to the underworld or some other world, to consult the animal and ancestral spirits, typically to divine some knowledge, to purge the clan of sickness, or some other purifying ritual. For Dodds, the influence of shamanistic practice is prevalent not only in the figure of Aristeas, but also in Pythagoras, and perhaps Empedocles and Orpheus. At the end of the Archaic Age, Dodds argues that a psychology of puritanism arose out of the "opening of the Black Sea to Greek trade and colonisation in the seventh century" (142).[17] In some sense, this type of transport is also present in Odysseus' visit to the "Kimmerian lands". Although Dodds' link is speculative, it remains the kind of text which Prynne may have read but could not have included in "Aristeas" because it makes the kind of speculative conjecture which "Aristeas" itself makes.[18]

It seems quite clear, if not obvious, that Aristeas *is* a shaman in "Aristeas". Terms like "analogy" give the reader little purchase on this poem, and rather sequester its subject into a kind of allegory of experience rather than the experience itself. And I would suggest that Prynne's use of external scholarship stems from a desire to remove allegory. Hence, the management of these source materials represents not only the experience of negotiating one's perception of a fundamentally obscure and irrecoverable pre-literate culture, but it suggests Prynne understands that the methodological terms of pre-literate cultural reconstruction are themselves infused with a theory of knowledge devastatingly foreign to their subject. Nevertheless, Prynne's use of common-place designations – tree, river – are also translations from a particular practice of shamanistic performance, so that they blend the imagined environment of the English reader with the cosmological microcosm of the shaman's spirit-theatre.

The tree and river are names for objects of a specific experience. The common English words attain a kind of heightened metaphysical status, as landscape features imbued with magical transport: they fit into an elaborate ceremony whose architecture is built from the materials of the immediate landscape, but whose substance is infused with spiritual cognate-forms. Besides the present context of "Aristeas", Prynne's poetic language may be said to mirror quite closely this semantic stratigraphy. The words are not merely signs that require the translation of marks and sounds into imagined spaces, but referential names which create a context of practice, just as the shaman's drum is both instrument and the river-boat on which he paddles (Anisimov 86).

In "Aristeas", Prynne is thinking of Pound. He modifies *Hugh Selwyn Mauberley*'s "The age demanded an image / Of its accelerated grimace" (*Personae* 186) to "The spirit demanded the orphic metaphor / *as fact*" (Prynne 92). As Pound rewrites Homer's *Odyssey*, Prynne seeks to develop a lyrical narrative of "Aristeas" based upon his readings of Herodotus and contemporary studies of ancient geography and anthropology. The way in which Prynne describes Aristeas disembodiment, what Mircea Eliade calls the very definition of shamanism ("the technique of ecstasy"[19]) is significant:

> Gathering the heat to himself, in one thermic
> hazard, he took himself out: to catch up with
> the tree, the river, the forms of alien vantage
>
> 1   *and hence the first way*
> > by theft into the upper world – "a
> > natural development from the mixed
> > economy in the drier or bleaker
> > regions, where more movement was
> > necessary"[20] [...] (90)

Beyond the pseudo-scientific "thermic hazard", which might signify the risk of catching fire, or the risk of being without the necessary conditions for homothermic survival in regions of extreme cold or self-deprivation, I want to make reference to "the tree, the river, the forms of alien vantage" beyond their common significations. This line refers to several items in the shaman's tent, which is the place especially constructed for the shaman and his clan's communication with the spirit-world. The "tree" refers specifically to a young larch, a coniferous tree erected in the middle of the shaman's tent – this is called the *turu*, or world-tree. The "river" refers to the shamanistic clan-river by which the shaman paddles into the lower world, the *khergu*. The whole tent represents a kind of total universe. I think that at this time the archaic myth-practice is important to Prynne because it remains a unity of the spirit and matter; it has no requirement of a symbolic relation. Furthermore, the "forms of alien vantage" refer, I think, to the story of Aristeas travelling in the form of a raven, so that this "alien vantage" indicates a topographical relation to the earth; both Aristeas and the geographer share a bird's eye view. Prynne writes that "with the merest black / wings he could survey the / stones and rills in their / complete mountain courses," (91). I get the sense that in Pound's work various mythological names and visions are registered as dreams of a vision of a rejuvenated past: as in Canto 74, "'to carve Achai' / a dream passing over the face in the half-light"; this dream registered in the same breath as "Time is not, Time is the evil" (464). Prynne is no stranger to dream imagery, but he tries to imbue an empiricism within the image, so that its quality of enigmatic speech stems from a stratigraphic relation: a layer of common description, and then probing deeper, a layer of intertextual reference to shamanism, whether Aristeas or the Netsilisk Eskimos.

The action of "catching up" may refer to the Siberian Evenk word *khamat-mi* "to catch up with", "to overtake", which "in relation to the shaman, [is] the special dance for attracting game and securing success in the hunt, executed by the shaman in pantomime form" (Anisimov 109). But catching up, not in the sense of moving forward from an anterior position, but of becoming modern, of advancing by creating larger structures of permanent settlement and possession, is related to the "lost" peoples, the Cimmerians, who remained a fiercely nomadic culture north of the Black Sea. Hence, Prynne draws on a double signification here, which is darkly parodic: how the Shamanic catch-up means not only spiritual dance, but the way in which the eradication of the nomadic cultures is brutally handled.

Prynne draws on an article by Tadeusz Sulimirski to summarise their hypothetical chronology. Sulimirski identifies three periods in Cimmerian history, which spans 1000 years. They are "consequent on great disturbances caused by the drive of eastern peoples in the thirteenth century and then again in the eighth century B.C., which each time affected the whole steppe belt of Eastern Europe" (62). The problematic archaeological record of the Cimmerians attests to a nomadic culture; not one driven by the expansion of a centrally governed location, but shifts of culture provoked by Scythian aggression. I would like to make mention that a comparison of Prynne's notes in the poem (93) to their original source in Sulimirski's article reveals a mistake. Prynne's poetic notes deflate the uncertainty and careful condensation of Sulimirski's summary. Moreover, by placing "invaded / by the Scythians" after the second time period, Prynne mistakes Sulimirski's description of the transition between the first and second periods for the general condition of the second. Here, Prynne's diagrammatic use of historical information evokes an authority very similar to Pound's own. Prynne's poetic extension of this information does not really depend on this periodisation – he is more interested in how the shamanic ritual imbues the substance of bone with the notion of spiritual travel. But his condensation of Sulimirski's Cimmerian history appears confident that its presentation should dictate something definite. It should, in some way, be recognized as important to our understanding of "Cimmerian wandering" (93). That this type of nomadism is deemed "ruinous", which is for Prynne in scare quotes, reveals only the way in which

> any settled and complaisant fixture
> on the shoreline would regard the movement of
> pressure irreducible by trade or bribery. (93)

The politics of nomadism in England were not a realistic option to Prynne in 1967, but the central Asiatic cultures living at the edges of the ancient Greek world represented fierce independence from what Prynne called "Apollo's price". Prynne's "Aristeas" is a kind of elegy, not for Aristeas, but for the visionary capacity of shamanistic ritual and the politics of the nomad, whose has no use for controlling the gold as money; to them it "was no more / than the royal figment" (94). Their "need to catch up as a response to cheap money" suggests that the desire to mine and utilize the land's resources placed a violent pressure on the principles of nomadic life.

In addition to the synaesthetic force of the image, Pound seeks figures of authority, whether to idolise or excoriate. He is concerned with administering the kind of knowledge that *must* be that of the members of a literary civilisation. For his project Pound requires a kind of immediate saturation of clarity, which induces conviction, a beauty that will coerce purpose, so to speak, so that we are drawn into a myth of finding the lighted path through the darkness of history, to seek out the overwhelming authority of the *tao*, Mussolini, Malatesta, or Homer. The contradiction between the ideology of authority and the cultivation of a poetic textuality which often contains very little rhetorical authority because of its distractive parataxis, is one of the most persistent features of Pound's work. If Pound models his aesthetics on exemplary figures, be they mythological or historical, Prynne is less insistent on the power of the individual. Prynne attempts to rewrite a poem largely non-extant to reveal the coordination of myth and historical materialism.

The connection between Pound and Prynne may be staged upon their attempt in different ways of deriving a sense of an archaic mind-set, whether from Homer's Odysseus or Tiresias, or the Evenk or Buriat Shaman. Pound creates a lateral, dynamic plane of macaronic texture and spatialised time, whereas Prynne tries emphatically to return myth to its material culture, not in order to evacuate the spiritual, but in order to organize its powers towards the recognition of matter as the root of spirit.

Notes

[1] For discussion, see Owens; Rodríguez; Sheppard 58-65; and Mellors 1991 and 2005.

[2] A list of which may be found in Maud 153-156, 175, 178, 180, 193-194, 306n14, 319n28.

[3] It is perhaps worth mentioning that one of the first major English critical responses to Pound was the book by Prynne's teacher and colleague Donald Davie whose *Poet as Sculptor* (1964) acknowledges Prynne as a kind of source for the book's sixth chapter on Cavalcanti: "Some pages of Chapter VI derive immediately from conversations with J.H. Prynne" (vi). An early critic of Pound's work at the University of Cambridge in the early 1960s, Prynne is also part of Pound's English reception-history. Prynne's study of Pound involves a critique, however, and what separates Prynne's critique from Olson's is that Prynne's is not merely political or cultural. Prynne takes issue with the very foundation of Pound's and Fenollosa's theories of the ideogram, which, in some respects, comprises Pound's chief poetical innovation, an interesting discussion of which may be found in Marriott 49-63. On 9 May 1963, Prynne wrote to Olson about his conversations with Davie: "This is just a snippet note, to enclose some things which might interest you. These have been sparked off by discussion between myself and Donald Davie about Pound and the kinetic thrust of the verse line. My aim was to convince Donald of how wrong Fenollosa was about the transitive dynamics of Chinese sentence-structure, and also even to suggest that Pound himself came (in practice) to realise this: that the monolinear sequence allows too little breadth of narrative, too little space in which to deploy the larger patterns of awareness. The locus, that is, as well as the vector (or, as I revert to it, the noun as well as the verb). The overall Poundian structure, even, as a form of parallelistic gerundial patternment". I am grateful to Melissa Watterworth Batt and the staff at the Dodd Research Center for their assistance during my viewing of these materials. It is also worth mentioning that Prynne also supervised Peter Nicholls' dissertation on Pound, "The relation of Ezra Pound's social and economic thought to the writing of *The Cantos*" (unpublished doctoral dissertation, University of Cambridge, 1983), later published as *Ezra Pound: Politics, Economics and Writing: A Study of The Cantos* (1984).

[4] See Terrell 1-4. On Pound's Canto 1 and the *Odyssey*, see especially the work of Hugh Kenner, *The Pound Era* 147-149 and 349-351 as well as "Pound and Homer"; Karachalios; and Kahane.

[5] On the background of the *nekuia* (or *nekyia*), see Tsagarakis 45-69.

[6] Compare also Eliot's comment in "The Metaphysical Poets" that the "ordinary man's experience is chaotic, irregular, fragmentary" (198).

[7] Cf. Canto 14 wherein the philologist is the petrifier of history, a member of those hellish "unamiable liars": "pets-de-loup [wolf-farts], sitting on piles of stone books, / obscuring the texts with philology" (63).

[8] In his *Geographica* (1.2.10), the Greek geographer Strabo writes: "Quite simply, the men of Homer's time regarded the Pontic Sea as a kind of second ocean, and they thought that those who sailed there took themselves beyond the limits of the inhabited world just as much as those who went any distance beyond the pillars of Heracles" (quoted by West 157).

[9] The last three lines of this excerpt allude to John Clare's "The Exile", the first stanza of which reads:

> Love is the mainspring of existence. It
> Becomes a soul whereby I live to love.
> On all I see, that dearest name is writ;
> Falsehood is here – but truth has life above,
> Where every star that shines exists in love. (387)

[10] See Needham 170-172 and Minns 110-115. For a collation of all of the fragments from Aristeas' *Arimaspea*, see Bolton 207-214.

[11] Citation of Prynne's poems will follow parenthetically from the most recent edition of *Poems* (2005). For such an argument, see Anthony Mellors, "Literal Myth in Olson and Prynne", *fragmente* 4 (1991), 36-47. On the notion of imbuing English with mythical authority, there is a playful remark in "Song in Sight of the World", when, after expressing a love for Apollo, and then alluding to the various metamorphic devices of Norse myth, Prynne writes: "We are poor in this, but I love / and will persist in it, the equity / of longing" (77).

[12] The absence of Bolton's monograph on Aristeas in Prynne's "References" is probably not an oversight, but an intentional omission. Bolton refutes that Aristeas is a kind of shaman (133) and refutes that the *Arimaspea* is a shamanistic poem (134). He is also dismissive of the relation between myth and reality, as can be seen in his statement that the reason for the Arimaspi being cyclopic "does not matter" (85).

[13] The other two being "The Glacial Question, Unsolved" from *The White Stones*, and much more recently, *Kazoo Dreamboats* (2011). The essay "A Note on Metal" (1968) has endnotes (132).

[14] Indeed, in the original publication of "Aristeas, In Seven Years", the "References" are not given at the end of the poem, but in the following issue of the circular.

[15] The English "god" is not etymologically related to *deiwos. What I conjecture here is that Prynne attempts to transfer the sense of a pre-Christian religion into common English. That he tries to do this covertly is of particular interest.

[16] G.S. Hopkins, "Indo-European *Deiwos and Related Words" *Language* 8.4 (Language Dissertation 12) (1932): 5-83.

[17] Prynne's concern for the birth of the mind-soul in Western thinking is pointed out by the poet Douglas Oliver, who became close to Prynne and Dorn in the 1970s. See Oliver, "J.H. Prynne's 'Of Movement Towards a Natural Place'".

[18] In his study, Bolton is critical of Dodds' reading of Aristeas as a shaman, or even the Arimaspea as a "shamanistic poem" (133-134).

[19] See Eliade 4. He also writes about Aristeas specifically within a shamanic context (388-389).

[20] In this excerpt, Prynne quotes from Phillips, "A Further Note on Aristeas", one of his references: "The origin of nomadism in its first stage, before the horse was ridden, is not confined by the Russian prehistorians to any particular region of the steppe, but is regarded as a natural development from the mixed economy in the drier or bleaker regions, where more movement was necessary to find grazing than any kind of agriculture allowed. Specialised nomads could then inhabit regions impossible for cultivators" (my bold, 160).

Works Cited

Anisimov, A.F. "The Shaman's Tent of the Evenks and the Origin of the Shamanistic Rite." *Studies in Siberian Shamanism*. Arctic Institute of North America; *Anthropology of the North: Translations from Russian Sources 4*. Ed. Henry N. Michael. Toronto, ON: Toronto University Press, 1963, 84-123. Print.

Bolton, J.D.P. *Aristeas of Proconnesus*. Oxford: Clarendon Press, 1962. Print.

Clare, John. *Poems*. Vol. 2. Ed. and introd. J. W. Tibble. London and New York, NY: J.M. Dent, 1935. Print.

Corcoran, Neil. *English Poetry Since 1940*. London and New York, NY: Long-man, 1993. Print.

Davie, Donald. *Ezra Pound: Poet as Sculptor*. London: Routledge & Kegan Paul, 1964. Print.

Dodds, E.R. *The Greeks and the Irrational*. Berkeley, CA: University of California Press, 1951. Print.

Eliade, Mircea. *Shamanism: Archaic Techniques of Ecstasy*. Trans. Willard R. Trask. London: Routledge & Kegan Paul, 1964. Print.

Eliot, T.S. *The Annotated Waste Land with Eliot's Contemporary Prose*. Ed. Lawrence Rainey, 2nd ed. New Haven, CT and London: Yale University Press, 2006. Print.

Giles, Paul. *Atlantic Republic: The American Tradition in English Literature*. New York: Oxford University Press, 2006. Print.

Harmon, William. *Time In Ezra Pound's Work*. Chapel Hill, NC: University of North Carolina Press, 1977. Print.

Holmes, Richard. "Poetry: inside history of small conflicts" [Review of Brian Jones, *Family Album*; Robert Bly, *The Light Around the Body*; J.H. Prynne, *Kitchen Poems*; Anselm Hollo, *Selected Poems: Paavo Haavikko*; Penguin Classic *Poems from the Sanskrit*, trans. John Brough]. *The Times* Saturday *Review*. 29 June 1968, 25. Print.

Jarvis, Simon. "Quality and the non-identical in 'Aristeas, In Seven Years'." *Jacket* 20 (December 2002). 10 May 2011. <http://jacketmagazine.com/20/pt-jarvis.html> Reprinted from *Parataxis: modernism and modern writing* 1 (1991), 69-86.

Jettmar, Karl. *Art of the Steppes: The Eurasian Animal Style*. Trans. Ann E. Keep. London: Methuen, 1967. Print.

Kahane, Ahuvia. "Blood for Ghosts? Homer, Ezra Pound, and Julius Africanus." *New Literary History* 30.4 (1999), 815-836. Print.

Karachalios, E. R. "Sacrifice and Selectivity in Ezra Pound's First Canto". *Paideuma* 24.1 (1995), 96-106. Print.

Kenner, Hugh. *The Pound Era*. Berkeley: University of California Press, 1971. Print.

——. "Pound and Homer." *Ezra Pound Among the Poets: Homer, Ovid, Li Po, Dante, Whitman, Browning, Yeats, Williams, Eliot*. Ed. George Bornstein. Chicago: University of Chicago Press, 1985, 1-12. Print.

Longinus, *On the Sublime*. Trans. W. Hamilton Fyfe and rev. Donald A. Russell in *Aristotle: Poetics. Longinus: On the Sublime. Demetrius: On Style*. Loeb Classical 199. Cambridge, MA: Harvard University Press, 1995. Print.

Marriott, D.S. "An Introduction to the poetry of J.H. Prynne (1962-1977)." Diss. U. of Sussex, 1993. Print.

Maud, Ralph. *Charles Olson's Reading: A Biography*. Carbondale and Edwards-ville, IL: Southern Illinois University Press, 1996. Print.

Meletinsky, Eleazar M. *The Poetics of Myth* [1976]. Trans. Guy Lanoue and Alexandre Sadetsky. New York, NY and London: Garland, 1998. Print.

Mellors, Anthony. *Late Modernist Poetics: from Pound to Prynne*. Manchester and New York, NY: Manchester University Press, 2005. Print.

——. "Literal Myth in Olson and Prynne." *fragmente* 4 (1991), 36-47. Print.

Minns, Ellis H. *Scythians and Greeks*. Cambridge: Cambridge University Press, 1913. Print.

Needham, Joseph. *Science and Civilization*. Vol. 1. Cambridge: Cambridge University Press, 1954. Print.

Nicholls, Peter. *Ezra Pound: Politics, Economics and Writing: A Study of* The Cantos. London and Basingstoke: Macmillan Press, 1984. Print.

——. "The relation of Ezra Pound's social and economic thought to the writing of *The Cantos*." Dissertation. University of Cambridge, 1983. Print.

Oliver, Douglas. "J.H. Prynne's 'Of Movement Towards a Natural Place'." *Grosseteste Review* 12 (1979), 93-102. Print.

Owens, Richard. "'The Practical Limits of Daylight': Charles Olson and J.H. Prynne." *Worcester Review* 31 (2010), 135-148. Print.

Pattison, Neil, Reitha Pattison and Luke Roberts, eds. *Certain Prose of the English Intelligencer*. Cambridge: Mountain Press, 2012. Print.

Phillips, E.D. "A Further Note on Aristeas." *Artibus Asiae* 20.2-3 (1957), 159-162. Print.

Pound, Ezra. *Guide to Kulchur*. New York, NY: New Directions, 1970. Print.

——. *Personae: The Shorter Poems of Ezra Pound* [1926]. Rev. edn. Ed. Lea Baechler and A. Walton Litz. New York, NY: New Directions, 1990. Print.

——. *The Cantos*. New York, NY: New Directions, 1993. Print.

Prynne, J.H. to Charles Olson. 9 May 1963. Series 2, Box 206, Folder 1963. Charles Olson Research Collection, Archives and Special Collections at the Thomas J. Dodd Research Center, University of Connecticut Libraries. Print.

——. "A Bibliography for ARISTEAS, IN SEVEN YEARS." *The English Intelligencer* 2 (1967), 377. Print.

——. "Aristeas, in Seven Years." *The English Intelligencer* 2 (1967), 276-279. Print.

——. *Kazoo Dreamboats*. Cambridge: Critical Documents, 2011. Print.

——. *Poems*. North Fremantle, WA: Fremantle Arts Centre Press; Tarset: Bloodaxe Books, 2005. Print.

Rice, Tamara Talbot. *The Scythians*. London: Thames and Hudson, 1957. Print.

Rodríguez, Andrés. "Enlarging History: the Poetry of J.H. Prynne." *Sagetrieb* 10:3 (Winter 1991), 83-107. Print.

Sheppard, Robert. *The Poetry of Saying: British Poetry and its Discontents 1950-2000*. Liverpool: Liverpool University Press, 2005. Print.

Sulimirski, Tadeusz. "The Cimmerian Problem." *Bulletin of the Institute of Archaeology* 2 (1959), 45-64. Print.

Surette, Leon. *The Birth of Modernism: Ezra Pound, T.S. Eliot, W.B. Yeats and the Occult*. Toronto, ON: McGill-Queen's University Press, 1993. Print.

Terrell, Carroll F. *A Companion to the Cantos of Ezra Pound.* Vol. 1. Berkeley and Los Angeles, CA: University of California Press, 1980. Print.

Tsagarakis, Odysseus. *Studies in Odyssey 11.* Hermes-Einzelschriften 82. Stuttgart: Franz Steiner Verlag, 2000. Print.

Vassileva, Maya. "Greek Ideas of the North and the East: Mastering the Black Sea Area." *The Greek Colonisation of the Black Sea Area.* Ed. Gocha R. Tsetskhladze. Stuttgart: Franz Steiner Verlag, 1998. Print.

West, M.L. *Indo-European Poetry and Myth.* Oxford: Oxford University Press, 2007. Print.

West, Stephanie. "'The Most Marvellous of All Seas': The Greek Encounter with the Euxine", *Greece and Rome* 50.2 (2003), 151-167. Print.

Gareth Farmer

"Obstinate Isles" and Rhetorical Sincerity: Veronica Forrest-Thomson and Ezra Pound

> He is not here he has outsoared the shadow
> of our right. 'tis life is dead not he. And
> ghastly through the drivelling ghosts on the bald
> street breaks the blank day of critical interpretation
> staining the white radiance of eternity.
> (Forrest-Thomson, "In Memoriam Ezra Pound"
> *Collected Poems* 132)[1]

Don't allow "influence" to mean merely that you mop up the particular decorative vocabulary of some one or two poets whom you happen to admire. (Pound, "A Retrospect" 5)

If as Pound [...] said, "technique is the only gauge of man's lasting sincerity" clearly this sincerity cannot be a matter of "telling the truth" but a matter of organising "the truth" and, as far as poetry is concerned, the truth has as much to do with "beauty of the means" as with "beauty of the thing". It is, of course, "beauty of the means" that has so much been neglected in recent ordinary language poetry. (Forrest-Thomson, "His true Penelope was Flaubert" 5)[2]

"Can you find," Veronica Forrest-Thomson writes in her late poem, "In Memoriam Ezra Pound," "four ice-cream cornets hidden / in this elegiac picture?" Alert readers will pick up the literary sleights of reference in her question – to Wallace Steven's "The Emperor of Ice-Cream," (Stevens 64) and to Max Jacob's *Le cornet à dés*. One of Forrest-Thomson's challenges to the reader of this poem is whether we can find other echoes in this self-consciously literary poem. P. B. Shelley is there, of course, in elegiac mood, lamenting Adonais-Keats, awakening from the dream of life and whose soul now "stains the white radiance of eternity" (Wu 1972). And the "drivelling ghost" of Tennyson is caught standing outside Arthur Hallam's "[d]ark house" on that "unlovely street," where "drizzling rain / On that bald street break the blank day"; so many "fatal young men" with which to stock an elegy (Tennyson 135). But the elegy is also, of course, to Pound; the subtitle reads *"obit first November / nineteen seventy two."* Forrest-Thomson was paying tribute in her inimitable way to the great poet and one of her most prominent poetic models who died on the first of November 1972 at the age of eighty-seven.

Pound's influence pervades Forrest-Thomson's critical and creative writing, from her earliest poetry and theoretical statements, to her last poems and the essays on which she was working at the time of her death at just twenty-seven in 1975. This piece examines Pound's influence on Forrest-Thomson's work from several angles. I start by sketching Pound's presence in Forrest-Thomson's early critical work, drawing some context for her later, mostly unpublished writing. I then examine the lessons Forrest-Thomson learned from Pound in some of her early, unpublished poems, as well as two later works. In the second part of this piece, I introduce some excerpts from Forrest-Thomson's as yet mostly unpublished writings on Pound, one of which was left unfinished by the time of her death. In this closing section, I have tried to provide interesting and challenging excerpts from these unpublished pieces. The aim of providing these excerpts is both to introduce this important work to a wider audience, but also to argue that some of Forrest-Thomson's insights into Pound's relationship with nineteenth-century poetic form and rhetoric contribute to contemporary debates about poetic form.

Towards the end of her life, Forrest-Thomson became increasingly preoccupied with what could be called formal and rhetorical sincerity and affect. Forrest-Thomson's own elegy to Pound poses a question with which she was troubled right up until her death: how far can elegy, and even the use of inherited language and poetic rhetoric, be considered "sincere"? How far, in other words, can quoted and distorted extracts of sedimented sentiment carry a weight of emotional and intellectual sincerity in the gestural dilutions of literary echo? Clearly elegy is always full of rhetorical flourish, not least in the filtering and purifications of mythical identification and metrical distancing. But what exactly happens in poetic form to create the elegiac affect and how can this be, well, affected? In introducing moments in Forrest-Thomson's work influenced by Pound, I intend to get a tentative grip on her conviction that one of Pound's major innovations was to re-examine the "beauty of the means" of nineteenth-century poetry and find a way of using these means for contemporary poetic practice. For Forrest-Thomson, Pound taught twentieth-century poets to engage seriously and sincerely with nineteenth-century poetic forms and practice in order to tap into concomitant forms of powerful and "sincere" literary affect.

I

The literary allusions in Forrest-Thomson's late elegy, "In Memoriam Ezra Pound" and her professed literary fealty to Pound are unsurprising given his central role in the development of her poetics. In his essay, "A Retrospect" Pound entreats the aspiring poet to "be influenced by as many great artists as you can, but have the decency either to acknowledge the debt outright, or to try to conceal it" (5). Forrest-Thomson's earliest recorded statements about poetry use Pound's edicts, and she is, at least, decent enough to try and conceal them as her own. Thanks to the foresight of Anthony Barnett, the editor of both of Forrest-Thomson's *Collected Poems*, a document entitled "Attitudes and Beliefs" which she wrote between the ages of sixteen and nineteen has been preserved. Veronica's mother, Jean Forrest Thomson, sent the document to Barnett during his research for the 1990 *Collected Poems and Translations*.[3] "My Attitudes and Beliefs" is comprised of five sections: "My Attitudes and Beliefs – About Life in General"; "Desirable Attitudes and Attributes"; "My Ideas About Poetry in Particular"; "Personal Poetry Projects and Purposes", and "Work Guides". The document develops from an early outline of her general philosophical positions, to theories of poetry and a series of guidance notes for practice. For ease of reference, I shall refer to the document as her "manifesto". Whilst the term may seem incongruous when compared with the mature documents of poetic movements over the centuries, the papers do amount to Forrest-Thomson's early expression of a personal manifesto for poetic practice. The manifesto was obviously a working document as annotations reveal that Forrest-Thomson returned to it in subsequent years, adding thoughts and changing or excising words and sentences.

The manifesto offers Forrest-Thomson's own statements on poetics, many of which are based on or inspired by Pound's edicts. Her definition of the "critical faculty" in the middle of document, for example, concludes with the emphatic statement: "As for the criticism of others, it can be helpful but one should never pay attention to anyone who hasn't him/herself produced a notable work" (11). In "A Retrospect" Pound instructs: "Pay no attention to the criticism of men who have never themselves written a notable work" (4). Elsewhere, Forrest-Thomson writes that poetry should not be involved in "description which can be done better by photography, nor indication of visual reaction which can be done better by painting; but recreation in terms of language rhythms and relationships to make a new word-object" (13). Her position recalls Pound's own when, in "A Retrospect," he writes: "Don't be descriptive; remember that the painter can describe a landscape much better than you can, and that he has to know a deal more about it"

(6). Further, in annotations in the section she called "Work Guides" towards the end of the document, Forrest-Thomson lists her influences including: "Pound – Ideogrammic method," adding, assertively, "but keep out proper names" (15). If what she calls Pound's ideogrammic method – a catch-all if slightly misleading description of one branch of his poetics – was to be an acknowledged influence on her poetry, Forrest-Thomson wasn't happy to simply copy the lessons of her master; keeping out proper names – those with which *The Cantos* are stocked – was her assertion of her own tentative move within the space cast by Pound's shadow.

Forrest-Thomson's assertive positioning in relation to other writers" poetics is a characteristic response of her entire poetic project. Forrest-Thomson was a voracious reader and much of this reading was subsumed into her critical writing. She was also a vigorous experimenter with poetic modes. Hence, Pound's influence is clear in a number of her earliest poems, some of which are still unpublished. For example, another document sent to Barnett by Forrest-Thomson's mother is a loosely assembled collection of typed and hand-written poems called, "Veronica – Some Teenage Poems" (hereafter, "VTP") and which contains poems written between the ages of fourteen and twenty-two (c. 1961-1970).[4] Some of the earliest poems appeared posthumously in the *Adam International Review*, while many of the later poems are published in her pamphlets and the two *Collected Poems* ("Poems of Youth" 46-49).

Early poems in this document such as "Image of Art," "Chinese Characters in Autumn," and "Trees" are clearly the young poet's attempts at imagist poetry. The poems are written in dialogue with, or as a challenge to, Pound's injunction to stay away from description and to leave painterly habits to the painters. While Forrest-Thomson clearly wants to experiment with imagist modes, the allure of elegant description with overtly painterly techniques is strong. In "Image of Art," for example, she ponders in strained and poetical syntax of portrait of Christ's face: "Why should this last" and "For whom so perfect rounded / Is this image ?" (3 – the gap between the final word and the question mark is in the original). Forrest-Thomson contemplates the shape and longevity or significance of the portrait, but is also very conscious of a poet's inability to render the image of Christ's face. "The face of Christ," she writes, "Languid under over-worldly lids / Stirs from the spurning earth." These are ambitious lines for any poet, let alone a sixteen-year-old. The evocative repeated /u:/ sounds and image of the "Languid [...] lids" contribute to the brooding presence of this portrait. The line "under over-worldly" is canny. The sense of the whole line is of the other-worldly nature of the portrait and the jarring sensation a reader experiences when confronted with this perceptual mind-twisting phrase is tactical. The phrase contributes to a complex image of Christ who is burdened under the weight of mankind's sins. Forrest-Thomson appreciated the perceptual complexity of the image and in such poems she challenged her own powers of description and her own poetic capacity. Forrest-Thomson was striving for an "intellectual and emotional complex" in concise, or not "prolix" language, as Pound prescribes in "A Retrospect" (4 and 3 respectively). Pound set the challenge; a young Forrest-Thomson tested her abilities.

Some of Forrest-Thomson's other early poems are recognisably imagist in both theme and language. The opening stanza of the "Trees", for example, written at the age of seventeen, reads:

> Trees stand like sticks
> against the darkling purple
> of the late day;
> Whorls of whirling smoke hover
> like guardian angels
> over the greying roof;
> Yawns are cracking the
> stuffy air inside. ("VTP" 7)

The influence of H.D. is clear here, specifically in the fourth line which is surely an allusion to the poet's famous erotic poem "Oread": "Whirl up, sea – / whirl your pointed pines" (17). H.D.'s nymphs become Forrest-Thomson's "guardian angels" of smoke clouds billowing over a grey roof. The small poem resembles an imagist vignette: an image rigid against a natural backdrop; here "trees" against a purple sky. The fact of using a simile as a way of drawing disparate data together is made explicit with the comparative "like," arresting what could have been an imagist poem proper: "whorls of whirling smoke hover; / guardian angels over greying roofs." Forrest-Thomson combines three distinct images, eliding any direct parallel and connecting them with the imagist punctuation mark *par excellence*, the semi-colon.

"Chinese Characters in Autumn" is another early poem overtly alluding to Pound and imagism. The poem describes a forest landscape in winter as resembling a "hieroglyphic / skeleton" (5). The opening stanzas are synesthetic and allude to Pound's poetic injunctions as well as his work on Ernest Fenollosa's *The Chinese Written Character as a Medium for Poetry*. The poem begins:

> A clove-scented, balding pomander
> in October,

Burnt-sienna taste of cinnamon
on iced melon,
A Druids' alphabet of trees
spells Chinese
caricatures of each reality;
And I
signing a sketchy individuality,
provisioned, uneasy,
cornered in a page of windy sky. (5)

The gardening terms, the clear and precise use of language, as well as the use of the analogies of the "Druid's alphabet" and the "Chinese / caricatures," all signal the influence of Pound and H.D. Forrest-Thomson was surely testing the imagist technique of "direct treatment of the "thing" ("A Retrospect" 3) as well as Pound's "phanopoeia" or "casting of images upon the visual imagination" ("How to Read" 25). The compounded "clove-scented" and "Burnt-sienna taste" are, respectively, visual and sensual images; both types of "image," in Pound's formulation, to cast on a reader's imagination. Forrest-Thomson's deliberate confusion of perception toward the end – where "reality" becomes somehow enfolded as a page in a book – seems to represent a challenge to herself to get the scene down on paper. The final lines – "signing a sketchy individuality," and the description of the landscape as "cornered in a page" – are versions of, as Ming Xie neatly summarises Pound's ideogrammic technique, the "verbal action [which] involves the perception of dynamic relations in process" (212). Here the dynamic relations are made between perception and the act of creating the poem. Further, Pound and Fenollosa are clearly evoked in Forrest-Thomson's choice of title, the reference to the ideogram, the paratactic syntax and the self-consciously visual or painterly language. Forrest-Thomson uses such poems to test Pound's stylistic lessons.

Pound's influence continued to dominate Forrest-Thomson's work throughout her life. In her later poems, however, a youthful earnestness to emulate or experiment gives way to a parody of the form of *The Cantos*. She also relinquished her early reticence to use proper names. "Letters of Ezra Pound", for example, which features a number of quotations from Pound's letters, is a case in point.[5] On the surface, "Letters of Ezra Pound" appears to copy the collage-like style of *The Cantos*. However, such poems are stylistically distinguished from Pound's by Forrest-Thomson's incorporation of an additional level of self-commentary *on* style that registers, I would suggest, a form of discomfort towards insincerely inhabiting inherited modes. Forrest-Thomson's self-commentary, unlike Pound's own, resembles the activity of what Margaret Rose has described in a book on literary parody as "metafiction": a process whereby, as Simon Dentith neatly summarises it, a text "holds up a mirror to its fictional practices, so that it is at once a fiction and a fiction *about* fictions" (14-15).[6] "Letters of Ezra Pound" begins:

> In order to be clear about aesthetic words
> you have to describe ways of living.
> said Wittgenstein
>   who was "indifferent to his surroundings".
> remembering the date (1969) on the calendar
> an attempt to condense the James novel
> (a young American T.S. Eliot,
> write him at Merton, Oxford.
> I think him worth watching
>   and
> his *Portrait of a Lady* is very nicely drawn.)
> in the literary scene of Allen Ginsberg
> (Apocalyptic tradition of Whitman, of course)
> could only be tried here
> (If you people at Cam can do
>   anything
> in the way of a milieu.)
> The need of old forms, old situations,
> as Yeats wrote (1929)
>   also,
> Ezra when he recreates Propertius
> escapes his scepticism. (CP 64)

If Pound attempts to escape his scepticism by an unfettered and committed approach to and through "old forms, old situations," Forrest-Thomson's statement of such registers her own. An allusion to Wittgenstein is spliced together with quotations from D. D. Paige's *The Letters of Ezra Pound* as well as literary anecdotes.[7] The lines describing Eliot are quoted verbatim from Paige's *The Letters*, while those about the "date" and "Cam" are also Pound's statements, but with key nouns changed (Paige 81). The condensing of the James novel is Pound's description of the style of *Mauberley*. In a letter to Felix E. Schelling in 1922 he writes: "Mauberley is a mere surface. Again a study of form, an attempt to condense the James novel" (Paige 248).[8]

The suggestion that a style can be condensed into both describable and, therefore, usable, patterns is a theme of Pound's logopoeia. As Jane Hoogestraat remarks, Pound's refinement of his poetic theory to coin the term "logopoeia" was in response to his reading of Jules Laforgue (259). Pound somewhat awkwardly defines the term in his 1929 essay, "How to Read":

> LOGOPŒIA, "the dance of the intellect among words", that is to say, it employs words not only for their direct meaning, but it takes count in a special way of habits of usage, of the context we expect to find with the word, its usual concomitants, of its known acceptances, and of ironical play. It holds the aesthetic content which is peculiarly the domain of verbal manifestation [....] It is the latest come, and perhaps most tricky and undependable mode. (25)

Pound's emphases on the context, "habits of usage" and the separable "direct meaning" are perhaps unnatural distinctions, but his comments reveal the persistence in certain ideals of authorial control over a poem's effects and over its forceful context. However, his jerky, prolix and neologistic way of getting to and defining the term are syntactic and phenomenal registers of the tricky and undependable identity of poetic "context." Theoretically at least, the poem employing logopoeia will attend to language's aesthetic (material) content and set habits of usage such as clichés, inherited phrases and scraps of language into controlled, "ironical play." But, if logopoeia is "the dance of the intellect among words," maintaining the dance step is, as Forrest-Thomson's poetry reveals, hard won and fraught with pitfalls and potential failure.

"Letters of Ezra Pound" can be described as a "study of form" and an attempt to copy aspects of others' form and style. But while Pound's technique was to try and transform style into his own, Forrest-Thomson incorporates comments on style into the poem. Pound attempts to emulate; Forrest-Thomson consciously reflects on emulation. Unlike Pound's occasional, self-conscious interjections on style in *The Cantos*, the primary subject of Forrest-Thomson's poem – and the subject of the quotations she chooses – are the cultivation of literary style and diction. The typography and arrangement of "Letters of Ezra Pound" are also forced into free verse, as if in parody of the visual arrangements of materials found in *The Cantos*. The poem operates as what could be called a schematic diagram of Pound's varying styles rather than an emulation of it. Compare, for example, the opening of Pound's *The Pisan Cantos*:

> The enormous tragedy of the dream in the peasant's bent shoulders
> Manes! Manes was tanned and stuffed,
> Thus Ben and la Clara *a Milano*

> by the heels at Milano
> That maggots shd/ eat the dead bullock
> DIGONOS, Δίγονος but the twice crucified
> > where in history will you find it?
> yet say this to the Possum: a bang, not a whimper.
> > with a bang not a whimper.
> To build the city of Dioce whose terraces are the colour of stars. (445)

Pound's literary splices and details coalesce through a mixture of registers and tenses, all connected by an attendance to a controlled rhythm and repetition, culminating in the final, sentence and the delicately chosen last word. The details – from the founder of the Manicheans (Manes), Mussolini, to twice-born Dionysus and Eliot (Cookson 132) – complement each other as Pound builds cumulative images and resonances. The shifts in form, so Pound wrote in a 1939 letter to Hubert Creekmore, were to "facilitate a reader's intonation" as the words and phrases were poised and arranged to shift the pace of the work (Paige 418). Forrest-Thomson's arrangement is less balanced and more erratic, although her foregrounded "and," "anything" and "also" do emphasise a basic, conjunctive connection between fragments.

The major differences between the passages are those of tone and register. Pound primarily pursues his subjects by uniting historical details and bringing them together into inter-illumination. So, in the lines above, Pound pursues the fusion of the humble local and the fetid particular with a divine or sublime symbolism, developed through the imperial Mussolini turned on his heels and Eliot's famous deflation, and framed by the polarised images of the crippled "peasant" and the "Dioce" city in the "stars." Pound's indented lines enhance the contrast by high-lighting the shift of emphasis – from the elegant sounding "Ben and la Clara *a Milano*," to the demotic, "the heels at Milano," for example. By contrast, the opening lines of Forrest-Thomson's poem are awkward and lack Pound's finesse. As well as beginning with a banal, prosy excerpt from Wittgenstein, the resort to the standardised and homogenous past participle of reported speech – "said" – and the full stop and lowercase word – "living. / said Wittgenstein" – are both abrupt and jarring. The dead-pan tone is enhanced by the seeming banality of the quoted excerpt – "indifferent to his surroundings" – the "indifference" of the subject as well as the continuing neutral tense of the report, "who was." Similarly, the word "remembering" creates a past perfect tense space which inharmoniously contrasts with the contemporary "date (1969)" (Forrest-Thomson's present tense) and which parodically undermines Pound's original expression of the memory of seeing Eliot in 1914. The gerund – "remembering" – also creates the anticipation of the complementary word, "attempt*ing*" which would have been a more elegant expression, instead of "an attempt." The roughly arranged collage form is presided over by a faux authoritative tone ("Whitman, of course") and scepticism attaches to the lines, registering a discomfort of disunity. Forrest-Thomson imitates both Pound's authoritative and emphatic statements on style and his style itself, all the while commenting on the nature and necessity of literary style itself.

Forrest-Thomson draws attention to composition by selecting quotations *about* composition, such as: "describe ways of living," and "the need of old forms, old situations." Rather than organise the poem around the use of particular forms and setting up tensions between these forms as in her early poetry, Forrest-Thomson's emphasis here is on the subject of form as well as the activity of conscious arrangement. The poem exemplifies modernist practice but also anxiously stands back and reflects on itself *as* such. The dangling word "and" illustrates this process most vividly:

> I think him worth watching
> > and
> his *Portrait of a Lady* is very nicely drawn. (64)

The word is part of one original sentence, but Forrest-Thomson splits this sentence and uses it to exemplify the bringing together of clauses. In doing so, she creates tensions between the first and second clauses and, by extension, between all the details of the poem. At the same time, Forrest-Thomson comments on the operation of such a word in the poem as indicating the activity of writing a poem composed of fragments. The relative insignificance of "and" is reversed and becomes ironically vital: it describes and illustrates a commentary on composition itself; a conjunction as a symbol for a conjunctive mode. The poem is doubly about style: it takes Pound's descriptions of style and tries to render these in a mode comparable to his own as well as commenting on the process. The poem's parenthetical date and anecdote appropriation couched in a chatty idiom aims to transform "old forms, old situations" into what Forrest-Thomson called in her "Note" to her 1971 collection, *Language-Games* the "historical present" and the "present act of articulation" of the poem (CP 165). But this chatty style isn't entirely comfortable – as if the turn to the demotic of the present day is a step too far across what Andreas Huyssen has termed the "great divide" between high and low cultures indicative of postmodern practice (Huyssen *passim*).

After a few poems featuring Wittgenstein's work in the collection *Language-Games*, Forrest-Thomson's poem "Idols of the (Super)Market" (CP 81-

82) returns to the themes of "Letters of Ezra Pound," bringing together a variety of fragments and quotations to reflect on a selection of, she puts it, misquoting part of a novella by Henry James, *Lessons of the Masters* (81).[9] The poem is a wry commentary on the inheritance of manners and decorum of particular literary figures and "Idols"; as she puts it, those masters who look to the "Sacred Fount" to provide inspiration (81). Nevertheless, the poem also features reflections on poetic decorum and style, those themes that, as I have argued elsewhere, Forrest-Thomson took very seriously indeed.[10] Her seriousness about a poet's imperative to learn from past masters and preserve traditional devices is evident in her continual return to such subjects throughout her poems. Pound was himself notoriously derisory about the state of what Forrest-Thomson describes wryly in "Idols of the (Super)Market" as "Eng. Lit." (81) wherein, as he (Pound) puts it, writers' "unrewarded gropings, hopes, passions, laundry bills, or erotic experiences" were frequently "thrust on the student or considered germane to the subject" ("How to Read" 15). Forrest-Thomson was troubled by the impact of quotations in her poetry, particularly those derived from Wittgenstein which made an attachment to metaphysical order and literary tradition more difficult to maintain. Forrest-Thomson, like Pound, was interested in the preservation of lessons as to the refinement and definition of what constitutes poetry and much of her critical work attempts to get to grips with the characteristics of what has been called "poetic decorum". Unlike Pound, however, Forrest-Thomson repeatedly registers her scepticism about how far such poetic decorum was possible in a contemporary context. While her critical work refined and developed much of Pound's critical project, her poetry went one stage further and explored and ironized the relevance or applicability of such poetic decorum to contemporary practice.

II

Forrest-Thomson forged her poetics from a variety of critical positions, at the centre of which, overtly and covertly, stood Pound. Her early manifesto also situates Pound's ideas amongst various nineteenth-century poets and poetic theories that give a clue as to her later essays on his work. For example, Forrest-Thomson claims in her manifesto that "[t]he first requirement of art is that it be articulate" (11). Her statement echoes A. C. Swinburne's own in his review, "Matthew Arnold's new Poems" in the *Fortnightly Review*, October 1867: "[t]he essence of an artist is that he should be articulate" (Connolly 32). Further, throughout her manifesto Forrest-Thomson repeatedly calls for poetry to render the "equation of a situation" (16), writes of the "equation of a poem" (16), of it achieving a "perfect balance" (16), and for it to "assent emotionally and feel formally" (13), all familiar tenets of modernist theory in general and Pound in particular. Further, her call for poems to "cleanse the perceptions" (13) also reveals a distinctly Mallarméan strain to her aesthetics. Similarly, mimicking Pound's much-pondered statement that "technique is the only gauge of man's lasting sincerity," Forrest-Thomson also remarks in the manifesto: "without [...] sincerity the work of art will be a lie and distortion" (12). Forrest-Thomson was involved from an early age with examining and extending Pound's commitment to formal or rhetorical "sincerity" and its possible connections with nineteenth-century poetic practice.

In 1978, Manchester University Press published Forrest-Thomson's *Poetic Artifice: A Theory of Twentieth-Century Poetry,* three years after its author's death. This book draws connections between the poetic practices of Pound and Eliot and, later, John Ashbery and J.H. Prynne, and their nineteenth-century forbears. Forrest-Thomson would go on to develop these connections further in her later, unpublished work. In *Poetic Artifice,* Forrest-Thomson aims to:

> talk about the most distinctive yet elusive features of poetry: all the rhythmic, phonetic, verbal, and logical devices which make poetry different from prose and which we may group together under the heading of poetic artifice. If prose often resembles the "natural" language of ordinary speech, poetry is resolutely artificial, even when it tries to imitate the diction and cadences of ordinary speech.
> (*Poetic Artifice* ix)

These "elusive" and "artificial" features, as well as the poetic "logical devices," Forrest-Thomson calls "poetic artifice." From her early, intense study of poetry Forrest-Thomson had built up the conviction that, as she puts it in *Poetic Artifice,* "[t]he question always is: *how* do poems work" (x). Her conviction dovetails with, or derives from, Pound's conviction of the heightened importance of the "beauty of the means" before "beauty of the thing." However, this "resolute artificiality" is very deliberately developed in opposition to the "prose tradition in verse" that Pound was to later extol ("The Prose Tradition in Verse" 371). While Forrest-Thomson derived some of her terminology in *Poetic Artifice* from Pound's mid-career essays (for example, her ideas of the "image-complex" and "disconnected image-complex," both explored throughout *Poetic Artifice*) his main influence was in his early experiments with a variety of metrical and formal modes. As Pound exhorts in "A Retrospect," a poet should work towards achieving a mastery of metres in order to develop their art (9). Forrest-Thomson's *Poetic Artifice* represents what could be described as a "retro-aesthetic", rejuvenating, as she puts it, the "distinctive yet elusive features of poetry" of the nineteenth century in order to revitalise contemporary practice.

As with her manifesto, *Poetic Artifice* situates Pound's relevance within an historico-poetic arc ranging from Shelly, through Tennyson and Swinburne and up to Ashbery and Prynne. All of these poets, according to Forrest-Thomson, were rhetorical and formal innovators, concentrating on formal means to achieve poetic beauty. If the manifesto and *Poetic Artifice* fleetingly equate Pound's aesthetic project with nineteenth-century poetry, her unpublished manuscripts make the connection much more explicitly. Forrest-Thomson's literary executor, Jonathan Culler, has recently donated a number of Forrest-Thomson's unpublished typescripts to the Girton College, Cambridge Library Archive. These include the first two and half chapters of a book on Pound tentatively entitled "Obstinate Isles: Ezra Pound and the Late Nineteenth Century" and a long essay called "His True Penelope was Flaubert: Ezra Pound and Nineteenth-Century Poetry." This essay, parts of which have recently been edited and published in the *Chicago Review* (Hansen and Farmer), distils a number of the arguments fleshed out in the first two chapters of the book. Before quoting a few indicative excerpts from "Obstinate Isles," I would like to give a brief overview of Forrest-Thomson's project on Pound.

In short, Forrest-Thomson concentrates on Pound's early poetic practice, primarily those poems collected in *A Lume Spento* and, as Eliot described them in the 1928 *Selected Poems*: "early poems rejected by the author and omitted from his collected edition" (189). She views Pound's early poetry as distilling and extending the poetic techniques of Tennyson and Swinburne, but also those of Robert Browning, D. G. Rossetti and other poets of the late nineteenth century, particularly Arthur Dowson. If this idea isn't particularly novel, what *is* novel is Forrest-Thomson's detailed demonstration of this influence and her argument for the precise ways in which Pound both imitated, inherited but also extended these techniques. The precision and vigour of her "fanatical" ("HTP" 29) close analyses are designed in large part to circumvent lazy critical practices such as concentration on content over analysis of poetic form and overly casual and unsubstantiated claims about poetic influence.[11] Channelling Pound's own witty dismissals of contemporary critics, for example, Forrest-Thomson writes of N. Christoph De Nagy's influential book on Pound's early poetry that:

> when [he] goes on to claim that "Browning's poetry is primarily
> a poetry of ideas" it is quite clear that he wouldn't know a poetry
> of ideas if he saw it – Dante, Lucretius, Donne, Raleigh, Sir John

> Davies, Eliot. He thinks you can make poetry of ideas simply by expounding second-rate commonplaces and ignoring the poetry altogether. (HTP 42)[12]

Strong words indeed! Forrest-Thomson wanted to challenge the critical practice of concentrating on poetry's statements about the "commonplace" and the apparent ignorance in such practice about the intricacies of poetic form. To counter such practices, Forrest-Thomson wanted to concentrate on the *means* rather than the *thing*. For Forrest-Thomson, the ideas in poetry are intimately entwined with poetic form. As such, the opening three chapters of "Obstinate Isles" examine the forms of poems by Swinburne, Tennyson, Browning, Rossetti and William Morris in some detail. Forrest-Thomson concentrates particularly on the ways in which the poets "fictionalise", that is to say, how they create aesthetically distanced poetic forms which command their own intricate and complex patterns. Her concentration on Swinburne's and other nineteenth-century poets" "fictionalising" contributed to her broader argument, outlined in a number of published essays, for poetry to provide resistance to, and to distance itself from, forms of realism.[13]

In her unpublished writing, Forrest-Thomson concentrates on the means and rhetorical uniqueness of what could be called "high" nineteenth-century poetry. Her essay, "His True Penelope" is, I believe, an early draft of what would have become the latter chapters of "Obstinate Isles." Evidence of this assertion is suggested by a helpful chapter outline Forrest-Thomson wrote for this book. The summary of chapter five, for example, reads:

> IL MIGLIOR FABBRO[.] The recapitulation of points about fictionalising etc. (1) The edge uncertain but a means of blending – P[ound]'s ideas of S[winburne] and B[rowning] how they must have pulled in opposite directions – influence of Rossetti (2) The cultivation of Pierian roses – his notion of the Nineties – discussion of his ability to take their fictionalising literally – Canzoni – *A Lume Spento* – (3) To forge Achaia – his development of new conventions – "La Fraisne" etc. Yeats and Pound. ("OI" up)

The summary can be broken down into three topics: influence; Forrest-Thomson's notion of "fictionalising" – and Pound's apparent literal interpretation of this – and, as she puts it, "his development of new conventions" out of those he inherited. To summarise these points in turn (and this is a necessarily crude reduction of her argument developed over many pages): the influence of Swinburne and Browning on Pound's work was a process of his blending or combining Swinburne's ability to create "fictional" poetic realms through the force of his emphatically artificial poetic technique and Browning's innovations in the development of personae. In Forrest-Thomson's opinion, Pound was able to "forge Achaia" and develop new poetic conventions because of his literal belief in the power and potency of these poetic techniques in the present. The phrase "forge Achaia" is important here. It refers to the opening stanzas of Pound's *Mauberley* (1920) in which he describes Mauberley's futile quest to develop an already moribund aestheticism. The passages also gave Forrest-Thomson the title of her essay. Starting from the second stanza of the opening of Pound's poem, it reads:

"His true Penelope
Was Flaubert,"
And his tool
the engraver's.

Firmness,
Not the full smile,
His art, but an art
In profile;

Colourless
Pier Francesca,
Pisanello lacking the skill
To forge Achaia. (*Selected Poems 1908–1969* 106-107)

Mauberley's craft was like the engraver's, forging glimpses – but only glimpses – from the firmness of metal forms of perfection or idealism (here associated with Achaia). When Pound twice returns to the phrase in the first of his Pisan cantos, he associates it with glimpsed perfection – "the line of the cameo / profile "to carve Achaia" / a dream passing over the face in the half-light," (*The Cantos* 464) and idealised deification – "for the deification of emperors / and the medallions / to forge Achaia" (467). The phrase – to forge – and the Greek region represent both memorialisation and perfection. The important thing here is the way in which Pound describes *glimpses* of perfection, or in Mauberley's sense, perfection and beauty "In profile."

In her unpublished essays, Forrest-Thomson examines the ways in which influence is transmitted: "His art, but an art / In profile" is a good description of imitation. What troubled Forrest-Thomson was the way in which influence and craft could be transmitted and then used *sincerely*. To paraphrase one of Pound's most quoted dicta: he was able to make poetry new by believing that poetic conventions were not something historical, where past modes are no longer possible, but were vividly present. To Forrest-Thomson, Pound treated inherited poetic techniques as vibrantly usable and alive in contemporary poetic practice. Part of Forrest-Thomson's summary of her proposed sixth chapter of "Obstinate Isles" makes her ideas of the inheritance of transmittable rhetorical sincerity clearer.

> CHAPTER SIX: EVEN IF MY NOTES DO NOT COHERE – later Cantos and how they revert (1) But these had thrones and in my mind were still uncontending – how our previous analyses and theories have made it possible to explain the resemblances – (2) H.D. once said "serinitas" (Atthis) etc. Pound's greatest myth was his myth of technique and he got that from the great fictionalising of the late nineteenth century – Eliot – Davie – Kenner thus his ends match his beginnings "Winnowed in fate's gray" "But to affirm the gold thread in the pattern" – (3) I have brought a great ball of crystal who will help me to lift it – summing up as far as possible. ("OI" up)

Forrest-Thomson's summary is interlaced with the threads of others' words. She believes that Pound's later *Cantos* – *The Pisan Cantos* and *Thrones* particularly – revert to his early practice and techniques. Sections of *The Cantos*, like *Thrones*, create forms of clarity amidst materials which, she believes, approach the "serenitas" enabled by a lifetime's toil at his craft. The sentence "H.D. once said 'serenitas' (Atthis) etc." refers to Pound's "Canto CXII" in his *Drafts and Fragments*:

> But for the sun and serenitas
> > (19ᵗʰ May '59)
> H.D. once said "serenitas"
> > (Atthis, etc.)
> at Dieudonné's
> > in pre-history. (*The Cantos* 807)

According to Jeffrey Twitchell-Waas, Pound refers here to being given a draft of H.D.'s long poem, *Helen of Egypt* (472). Twitchell-Waas remarks that Pound explains this passage from *The Cantos* in a letter he sent to H.D. in September 1959 in which he refers to "an imagist dinner in 1914 at the Dieudonné restaurant in London where H.D. made this remark about a Sappho fragment addressed to Atthis" (472).[14] Twitchell-Waas argues that, although Pound is at this stage in *The Cantos* remembering the occasion of being given H.D.'s poem, she also operates to him at the same time as "a figure [...] for a serenity lost" (472). For Forrest-Thomson, this type of nostalgia is inexorably entwined with style and technique. "Pound's greatest myth was his myth of technique," she states in the summary of chapter six. What she means by this is clarified by her argument that Pound takes the techniques and lessons of the nineteenth-century poets literally. For Pound, according to Forrest-Thomson, the myth of technique was so all-encompassing that it was the central focus of his poetic project. Arguing that Pound took his nineteenth-century forbears literally is also to state that he took them very seriously and that he believed that *sincerity* of formal clarity would lead to a form of *serenitas*.

Forrest-Thomson associated literalism with sincerity and it follows that to use form sincerely is to believe in its status as a proxy for other types of sincerity. In her introduction to "Obstinate Isles," Forrest-Thomson confronts Pound's dismissal of rhetoric, which, she implies, he not only embraced but also used in all sincerity. Forrest-Thomson argues that Pound's early poetry and later cantos were themselves using and relying on positive forms of poetic rhetoric; they "revert" as she puts it in the summary to chapter six. "I hope," she writes, "by a detailed consideration of Pound's early poetry in relation to the latter half of the nineteenth century, to help English criticism to touch bottom independently again" ("OI" 1). This will be achieved, she argues, by "an examination of the qualities of those conventions that lift poetry away from the commonplace and which both the theme of the form of the late nineteenth-century poems do stress" (1). In the next paragraph she adds: "Such poetry is called 'rhetorical' in a pejorative sense and Pound himself helped to institute this" (1). Towards the end of the introduction she writes:

> With the fairly circumscribed area defined [...] we may hope to isolate what could be meant by the "art of verse structure"; not by Pound in 1912 but as it appears in the work of those nineteenth-century poets who influenced Pound and in his own works written under their influence. ("OI" 2)

Forrest-Thomson argues for both the pre-eminence of the "art of verse structure" in Pound's early and late poetry and for the fact that he was positively investing in rhetoric. Such an argument anticipates a recent article – "Poetry and Rhetoric: Modernism and Beyond" – by Peter Nicholls. In this article, Nicholls argues for a comparable ambivalence in Pound's poetic theory towards rhetoric. He notes that rhetoric, far from being something rejected outright, was, as he puts it, "both a threat and a temptation" in modernist poetics (186). It is perhaps time, as Nicholls suggests, for a reassessment of Pound's investment in forms of poetic rhetoric and the lessons he learned from nineteenth-century poetic practice. As Nicholls implies, and Forrest-Thomson anticipates, rhetoric can no longer be treated as the default opposite to modernist innovation. It is, and perhaps always was, an integral part of the development of a variety of modernist poetics.

Early in "His True Penelope," Forrest-Thomson further clarifies her sense of Pound's complicated notion of rhetoric and its relation to the sincerity of technique. Quoting from the passage cited at the head of this essay from Pound's "I gather the limbs of Osiris," Forrest-Thomson argues:

> If, as Pound has just said, "technique is the only gauge of man's lasting sincerity"[,] clearly this sincerity cannot be a matter of "telling the truth" but a matter of organising "the truth" and, as far as poetry is concerned, the truth has as much to do with the "beauty of the means" as with "beauty of the thing". It is, of course, "beauty of the means" that has so much been neglected in recent ordinary language poetry. ("HTP" 4-5)

Concentrating on the "beauty of the means" necessarily brings a poet closer to rhetorical sincerity. Throughout her later critical writing, Forrest-Thomson returns to the notion of formal complexity and sincerity. She takes great delight in revealing apparently simple stanza or verse forms as comprised of intricate and masterful arrangements achieving rhetorical sincerity. Complexity of rhetoric is inexorably associated with sincerity. Hence, she writes, of Rossetti's poem "The One Hope":

> Thus what seemed at first a very commonplace use of stanza, line, phrase, arrangement is now revealed as extremely sophisticated. I think we have to concede that Rossetti has passed the test of *lasting sincerity of technique* which sets him in a strong position with respect to other sincerities whatever, in the this artificial realm, these may be. ("HTP" 7 – my emphasis)

Forrest-Thomson refers to emotion or sentiment, of course, and Rossetti is forgiven any subsequent emotional identification as he has proved himself in the arena of rhetoric. She writes: "If there is a single characteristic that distinguishes these masters [Swinburne, Tennyson and Rossetti] from all others it is their continued, even tenacious, dwelling in the palace of art" (9). Similarly, of Dowson's lyric "Amor Umbratilis" she writes:

> I said that in this poetry "sincerity" equalled "rhetoric" and Dowson's poem clearly demonstrates this; by observing the artificialities of fiction the poet remains true with his technique of manner to the technique of content or, by putting it another way to attain the beauty of the thing by concentrating on the beauty of the means. ("HTP" 21)

Sincerity equals rhetoric because truth is attached to a commitment to technique and manner. Achieving beauty is a matter of concentrating, sincerely, on the means and manners of poetic technique. In this way, beauty of content – whatever that may be – is glimpsed "In profile," as Pound put it. Forrest-Thomson describes a form of indirect directness, a sincerity of content – an affective form, perhaps – which is produced by concentration on technique. Writing of a small poem by Dowson a little earlier in "His True Penelope," Forrest-Thomson sums up what she means by this form of indirectness: "What is relevant here is Dowson's mask of direct lyricism in simple stanza which forces us to recognise an attitude that is far from simple lyricism and a stanza that is far from simple" (HTP 20). Through studied use of apparently simple techniques and manners, a poet may be able to create a highly complex attitude; it is simply a matter of controlling complexity. Forrest-Thomson's insights into forms of complex sincerity tied up with poetic form anticipate the work of poets such as Denise Riley who, in both her poetry and critical writing, confronts this notion of adopting masks of lyrical directness and who theorises these complex attitudes towards both inherited language and linguistic affect.[15] Forrest-Thomson's energetic and detailed critical work on nineteenth-century poetry and its influence on Pound, much of which is unpublished, offers us some provocative and prescient ways into thinking about the intimate relations between poetic form and lyric expressivity.

I shall end this piece with the final stanza and ultimate dangling line of Forrest-Thomson's "In Memoriam Ezra Pound." The poem is a moving homage to Pound as well as an emulation, an imitation and a parody of his styles and it mobilises a number of Forrest-Thomson's critical insights into Pound's work developed in her published and unpublished writings. Given more space, I would attempt to show how the poem both extends and contradicts Forrest-Thomson's own theoretical edicts. We might wonder, for example, after reading her criticism, what happens to the referenced "he" entwined in this manic elegy. We might also consider how aspects of verse technique, particularly sound and sight repetitions, gather the lines up into what might be called a "complex rhetorical sincerity affect" evading irony and the playful surface of literary contortions. We might consider how the space between "dead" and "instead" in the penultimate line evokes the abrupt but inevitable death the elegy so emphatically evades. And we might wonder whether Forrest-Thomson knew this and decided to undermine such rhetorical sincerity by a whimsical apostrophe to Carol Reed's 1949 film, *The Third Man* in the final line. But these issues are for other exegeses. The sub-heading of the poem reads, "*obit first November / nineteen seventy two.*" Forrest-Thomson was twenty-four – three years from her death – and with still a lyfe so shorte and so much crafte yet to lerne:[16]

He is not here he has outsoared the shadow
of our right. 'tis life is dead not he. And
ghastly through the drivelling ghosts on the bald
street breaks the blank day of critical interpretation
staining the white radiance of eternity, every
little pimple had a tear in it, a fear of many
coloured glass, the noise of life strains the white
radiance of an elegy. How does the stress fall
on an autumn day. Remember remember the first
of November where history is here and nowhere:
the room in Poictiers where no shadow falls
on the pattern of timeless moments. Forget
the gate of white is the gate wherein our past
is laid. These books are radiant as time
against the shadow of our night where no
shadow falls. He is not dead.   Instead.

Give me back my swing. O Ferris wheel. (CP 132-133)

Notes

[1] Poems quoted from *Collected Poems* will hereafter be represented as CP followed by page references. Thanks to Allardyce, Barnett, Publishers for permission to quote from the poems.

[2] Hereafter to be represented parenthetically as as "HTP". I shall also be referring throughout this article to Forrest-Thomson's unpublished and unfinished book on Pound, provisionally entitled *"Obstinate Isles": Ezra Pound and the late nineteenth century* (hereafter represented parenthetically as "OI"). Many thanks to Girton College, Cambridge Library Archive and to Jonathan Culler and the Estate of Veronica Forrest-Thomson for allowing me access to these documents and for permitting my full quotation from them. Forrest-Thomson is referring to Ezra Pound, "I Gather the Limbs of Osiris IX: On Technique". *The New Age* 10, no. 13 (January 25 1912): 298: "technique is the only gauge and test of man's lasting sincerity." For published excerpts from these essays, see Hansen and Farmer: 10-35.

[3] The document was made available to me courtesy of Anthony Barnett and permission to quote from it has kindly been granted by both Barnett and Jonathan Culler. During my conversations with Barnett, Culler and Forrest-Thomson's brother, Miles Thomson, I have established that no other copies of this document exist, the originals having been lost or destroyed. Unless otherwise stated, I have kept the lineation and punctuation of the originals, but have silently corrected some orthographic errors. The document is unpaginated and Forrest-Thomson switches between using single and double sides of the A4 paper. I have numbered the pages containing typescript or handwriting, but this numbering is by no means authoritative.

[4] This document was also given to me courtesy of Anthony Barnett. A copy of this document has also subsequently come to light in Jonathan Culler's Forrest-Thomson papers which are now housed in the Girton College, Cambridge Library Archive. Many of the poems in VTP have dates and ages next to them written in what appears to be Forrest-Thomson's handwriting; she may, therefore, have collated the document herself. Another possibility is that Forrest-Thomson's mother assembled and annotated the document after her daughter's death. "VTP" has page numbers, but these numbers only refer to the recto side of A4, despite the fact that there are numerous hand-written poems on the verso. As with the manifesto, I have decided to number the pages containing text sequentially.

[5] "Letters of Ezra Pound" was uncollected during Forrest-Thomson's lifetime. According to Barnett, it was published in the magazine *Solstice*, no. 9 (Cambridge, 1969) (CP 175). It is not entirely clear why Forrest-Thomson chose to leave this poem out of her 1971 collection *Language-Games*. It would have fitted well with comparable poems such as "Idols of the (Super)Market" and "Notes to Chapter 1, 002," both of which she did include.

[6] Dentith refers to Margaret Rose. *Parody/Metafiction: An Analysis of Parody as a Critical Mirror to the Writing and Reception of Fiction*. London: Croom Helm, 1979.

[7] Wittgenstein writes: "In order to get clear about aesthetic words you have to describe ways of living" ("Lectures on Aesthetics" 11). The distinction between Forrest-Thomson's "to be" and Wittgenstein's "to get" signals a difference between their perspectives on language. While Forrest-Thomson's "to be clear" implies a working towards a definitive clarity, Wittgenstein's "to get clear" gives the impression that the process of clarification itself reveals a form of clarity.

[8] There are numerous other references to Pound's letters in the poem. For example, in a letter to Harriet Monroe dated 30th September, 1914 Pound praises Eliot remarking that "It is such a comfort to meet a man and not have to tell him to wash his face, wipe his feet, and remember the date (1914) on the calendar" (Paige 80). On 4th May, 1933, Pound wrote to John Drummond to advise on a possible new publishing venture and remarks: "P.S. If you people at Cam. can do anything in the way of a nucleus, I'll do what I can to bring in the scattered and incongruous units of my acquaintance" (329).

[9] Forrest-Thomson alludes to Henry James. *The Lesson of the Master and Five Other Stories*. London: Heinemann and Balestier, 1892.

[10] Farmer, Gareth. "Veronica Forrest-Thomson, Poetic Artifice and the Struggle with Forms." Unpublished PhD thesis, University of Sussex, 2012.

[11] It is worth reminding ourselves of Pound's own scepticism about influence here (which I quote at the start of this piece): "Don't allow 'influence' to mean merely that you

mop up the particular decorative vocabulary of some one or two poets whom you happen to admire" (Pound, "A Retrospect" 5).

[12] The actual quotation is: "Browning's poetry, primarily a poetry of ideas [...]" (De Nagy 106).

[13] See, for example, Veronica Forrest-Thomson. "Dada, Unrealism and Contemporary Poetry." *20th Century Studies* 12, (December, 1974): 77-93.

[14] The letter to which Twitchell-Waas refers is printed in Timothy Materer. "H.D., Serenitas, and Canto CXIII." *Paideuma* 12.2, 12.3 (1983): 275-80.

[15] See, in particular, Denise Riley. *The Words of Selves: Identification, Solidarity, Irony.* Palo Alto, CA: Stanford University Press, 2000 and *Impersonal Passion: Language as Affect.* Durham, NC & London: Duke University Press, 2005.

[16] The allusion is to the line: "The lyfe so short, the craft so long to lerne" from the opening of Geoffrey Chaucer's "The Parliament of Fowls" (Chaucer 385). The line is quoted by Pound in his "A Retrospect" (10) and also appears in Forrest-Thomson's handwriting at the back of the 1990 *Collected Poems and Translations.* While the quotation reveals an obvious affinity between Pound and Forrest-Thomson, it is, of course, much more poignant in the latter's case.

Works Cited

Chaucer, Geoffrey. "The Parliament of Fowls." *The Riverside Chaucer.* Ed. Larry D. Benson. Oxford: Oxford University Press, 1987. 385-394. Print.

Cookson, William. *A Guide to The Cantos of Ezra Pound.* London: Anvil Press, 2001. Print.

Connolly, Thomas Edmund. *Swinburne's Theory of Poetry.* Albany, NY: State University of New York Press, 1964. Print.

Dentith, Simon. *Parody.* London: Routledge, 2000. Print.

H.D. *Selected Poems.* Ed. Martz, Louis L. Manchester: Carcanet Press, 1988. Print.

De Nagy, N. Christoph. *The Poetry of Ezra Pound: The Pre-Imagist Stage.* Bern: Francke, 1960. Print.

Farmer, Gareth. "Veronica Forrest-Thomson, Poetic Artifice and the Struggle with Forms." Unpublished PhD thesis, University of Sussex, 2012.

Forrest-Thomson, Veronica. "My Attitudes and Beliefs." Allardyce, Barnett, Publishers Archive. Print.

——. "Veronica – Some Teenage Poems." Allardyce, Barnett, Publishers Archive; Girton College, Cambridge Archive. Print.

——. "His True Penelope was Flaubert: Ezra Pound and Nineteenth-Century Poetry." Unpublished typescript. Girton College, Cambridge Archive. Print.

——. "Obstinate Isles: Ezra Pound and the Late Nineteenth Century." Chapter summary, introduction and chapters 1-3 of a proposed book. Unpublished typescript. Girton College, Cambridge Archive. Print.

——. *Language-Games.* Leeds: School of English Press, University of Leeds, 1971. Print.

——. "Dada, Unrealism and Contemporary Poetry." *20th Century Studies* 12, (December, 1974): 77-93.

——. "Poems of Youth." *Adam International Review,* Vol. xxxix, Nos. 391-3, (1975): 46-9. Print.

——. *Poetic Artifice: A Theory of Twentieth-Century Poetry.* Manchester: Manchester University Press, 1978. Print.

——. *Collected Poems and Translations.* Ed. Anthony Barnett. Lewes: Allardyce, Barnett, Publishers, 1990. Print.

——. *Collected Poems.* Ed. Anthony Barnett. Exeter: Shearsman Books; Lewes: Allardyce Book, 2008. Print.

Hansen, Michael, and Gareth Farmer, eds. "Veronica Forrest-Thomson: Three Essays." *Chicago Review,* no. 56:2/3 (Autumn, 2011): 10-35. Print.

Jane Hoogestraat, "'Akin to Nothing but Language': Pound, Laforgue, and Logopoeia." *ELH,* Vol. 55, No. 1 (Spring, 1988): 259-85. Print.

Jacob, Max. *Le Cornet à dés.* 22nd ed. Paris: Gallimard, 1945. Print.

Materer, Timothy. "H.D., Serenitas, and Canto CXIII." *Paideuma* 12.2, 12.3 (1983): 275-80. Print.

Nicholls, Peter. *Modernisms: A Literary Guide.* 2nd ed. Basingstoke: Palgrave Macmillan, 2009. Print.

——. "Poetry and Rhetoric: Modernism and Beyond." *The Oxford Handbook of Modern and Contemporary American Poetry.* Ed. Cary Nelson. Oxford: Oxford University Press, 2011. 173-94. Print.

Paige, D. D., ed. *The Letters of Ezra Pound 1907–1941.* London: Faber and Faber, 1951. Print.

Pound, Ezra. *Selected Poems.* Ed. T. S. Eliot. London: Faber and Faber, 1948. Print.

——. "A Retrospect." *Literary Essays of Ezra Pound.* Ed. T. S. Eliot. London: Faber and Faber, 1954. 3-14. Print.

——. "How to Read." *Literary Essays of Ezra Pound.* Ed. T. S. Eliot. London: Faber and Faber, 1954. 15-40. Print.

——. "The Prose Tradition in Verse." *Literary Essays of Ezra Pound.* Ed. T. S. Eliot. London: Faber and Faber, 1954. 371-377. Print.

——. *Selected Poems 1908-1969.* 2nd ed. London: Faber and Faber. 1977. Print.

——. *The Cantos.* 14th ed. New York, NY: New Directions, 1998. Print.

Rose, Margaret. *Parody/Metafiction: An Analysis of Parody as a Critical Mirror to the Writing and Reception of Fiction.* London: Croom Helm, 1979. Print.

Stevens, Wallace. *Collected Poems.* London: Faber and Faber, 1984. Print.

Tennyson, Alfred Lord. *Selected Poems.* Ed. Aidan Day. London: Penguin, 1991. Print.

Twitchell-Waas, Jeffrey. "H. D.'s *Helen in Egypt* as a Response to Pound's *Cantos.*" *Twentieth Century Literature,* Vol. 44, no. 4 (Winter, 1998): 464-483. Print.

Wittgenstein, Ludwig. "Lectures on Aesthetics." *Lectures and Conversations on Aesthetics, Psychology and Religious Belief.* Ed. Cyril Barrett. Oxford: Blackwell, 1966. Print.

Wu, Duncan, ed. *Romanticism: An Anthology.* Oxford: Blackwell, 1999. Print.

Xie, Min. "Pound as Translator." *The Cambridge Companion to Ezra Pound.* Ed. Ira B. Nadel. Cambridge: Cambridge University Press, 1999. 204-223 Print.

Laura Kilbride

"REAL GAMES WITH BOOKS":
ON ANNA MENDELSSOHN AND EZRA POUND

Η γλώσσα τιμάει το πρόσωπο
["the way of speaking honours the face/person"]
– traditional

? It's complicated. More so now than when a Greek (or a Celt or a Chinese) wrote. Then the forward slash stood for options not division: an "undefended heart,/ flows right down into my hand..."[1] "The age demanded an image..." and "Hugh Selwyn Mauberley" is a mask which continually slips".[2] It is not my intention to be archaeological – "Bless thee, *Bottom*!... thou art *translated...*!"/ "This [article] was written after the fall of the wall"[3] – yet the question remains: were we to discover this slippage again, in another time another place, would we consider the set-up "political"? If so could we?

– "...but Anna Mendelssohn says that Pound and Eliot are fascists [!]"
– "Where did you get that from?"
– "she SAYS so, in *Implacable Art*."[4]

"To anyone who wants poems to give them answers/ not that they ask interesting questions" (34) she does not. Yet a position "im-" "not, opposite of" + "placabilis" "easily appeased", working out of old wars "without understanding, covenant-breakers, without natural affection, *implacable*, unmerciful"... towards the last "dinky century" ("France is and will remain the *implacable* enemy of Germany...") is for sure struck.[5] Where she stops and glares at Pound is where we might start. Yet the desires which range from exhibit A, to "the historical personage Anna Mendelssohn", to "our Anna" remain unsupported by critical protocol. Sean Bonney greets her, but opinions diverge.[6] Connie Scozzaro is upfront about the problem of autobiography, but "this is not the principal focus of my interest in transmutation". Eleanor Careless, reading Mendelssohn's last pamphlet *Py*, is encouraged by "an association between poet and persona..." but stops here fearing "simplification".[7] Esther Leslie prefers the truth of masks, introducing "Grace Lake – as we should call her in reference to her poetic persona..."[8] That a problem so completely central – the root, essentially, of all our gasping over "lyric" –should have been so quickly recuperated as to appear awkward is a crying shame. Fortunately, Mendelssohn's work evades simplification and the problem is never allowed to become a cliché.

Instead ancient questions are put again with a gathering urgency: "Everything works counter to memory/ so that there are no answers to questions of a personal nature"; "how can there be love when there is no memory"? (59); "western art, is vastly/ construed to be in opposition to personal papers…" (37). The first page notes these poems are "from Implacable Art", the large tab pointing towards a larger body of work, perhaps a life lived (1). The index does not remove the problem of how to navigate these scrapbooked text blocks which run from tableau text as image – a civil servant in a bowler hat [?] (33) – to poems translated into French (89). Poems gather under then outstrip their titles – often escaped first lines – shot-through with emboldenings and underlinings, interrupted by facsimiles of poems in the poet's handwriting, prose, columnar arrangements and drawings – Delaunay-esque, cubist, cartoon-ish, unstill life ("greyhounds in the field, paws printed, tails sized") – ranging from plans for paintings towards things we can never assume were intended to be "finished".

In this "selection" some things feel more provisional than others, particularly the joke rhymes ("the mat is not the cat./ and neither does it sit on that) (97) and the slack line-breaks (34-8). It is significant that they feel "funny" rather than bad. I've no call to "correct" the clunky rhythm's grate in what could be a failed sea-shanty: "There is nothing wrong with a high heart/ As long as it hangs not alone/ Whilst heavy men mock and moan…" (44) or re-lineate according to any worked out distinction between poetry and prose ["tone it down would you please leave the full stop/ The line has been drawn by the temperature…"(22)]. Instead, these poems feel as if they are meant to be contingent.

What results is not *écriture* ["Oh not cixous!" (19)], nor the agonised search for the authentic moment of writing as in Tom Raworth's "Stag Skull Mounted": "this is my handwriting", but linguistic spread. Here is a poet thinking in language, through and around the current political and economic situation… the durations of which we are led to understand autobiographically.[9] The book is "for my parents, Morris & Clementina," (dedication). And there are moments at which the voice tips to acknowledge certain events… Yet at this point we draw back, almost but not quite so far back as "exhibit A". Not enough is known or there is no reason to associate this provisionality, this contingency, this effect of preserved-presentness with sincerity. And "Here… I float" – does it matter?

Yes, [and again] YES! Reading *Implacable Art* "one had reason to believe" that the strength of this poetry lay in the force of its protest. And since protest depends on a connection – however fraught – between the way of speaking and the person ["People who talk about revolution and class struggle without referring explicitly to everyday life, without understanding what is subversive about love and what is positive in the refusal of constraints, such people have a corpse in their mouth..."][10]: "everything is difficult, and all right". Out of this comes a question: what has to be assumed, either of poetry or of the self, for a poem like "I object" (22) to carry its title? And what might this protest have to do with the poetry of Ezra Pound?

§

"hahamklag farbre birtwhistling práal eileen cantos/ battre" (35). This isn"t finger-pointing, but as close as the reader gets to Anna's "says so". Removed for further study, these lines are crazy, but that doesn't mean that we can't read whatever we desire. So we sit up at "cantos", which terminate on a line by themselves and take a jump, reflecting that – stylistically at least – these poems look a lot like the *Cantos*... – and would we make the link between contingency and sincerity without Pound's odyssey? Now "Of Lorca" begins to resemble that sprawl with its indentations, line-breaks, initializations – a glance reinforced by its quasi-parodic already-undone allusions, where "sf" can stand for "science fiction", "sarah farell", "Sigmund Freud"... (21)

There's spattering enough of other languages ["I'm a happy continental"] and though *Implacable Art* isn't a re-run of the masque which is *Personæ* ["in Medéa mé"], there are points of reference enough ["Tancred and Garibaldi always slept together..."] and a dearth of dropped speechmarks to ensure we make the connection between, for example, the Russian situation as an alternative crib to speak from in "My Chekhov's twilight world" (98) and the mask ["Ezra is a crowd; a little crowd"...][11]

Of course, we resist this as we play into Olympian hands. This produces a polarisation: Mendelssohn both is and is not directly engaged in an argument with Ezra Pound, because the poem both is and is not Mendelssohn speaking. This is alright until the poem "Europa" (29), where the Imagist mode ("Use no superfluous word, no adjective, which does not reveal something... the natural object is always the *adequate* symbol... Use either no ornament or good ornament..."[12]) rumoured in the first half is tipped out of its blasted-heath-sweet pairs by "human compassion" towards a protest which will take as many lines as it needs:

> a little insight
> no great light

somewhere
circulating

sorrow helps
& trust in

human compassion.

what does not help
is the piling up
of pretence
& incapacity
for self-effacement.

although
even when
one's face
has been effaced
the light
being false
of face
to the true one

For seven lines I am happy to talk about "the speaker" etc…, but after this point I am moved towards the critical equivalent of taking her word for it. "Human compassion" is the spanner in the works, and self-effacement is the pivotal instability or pun. If pretence "does not help" then we must assume that self-effacement – the erasure of self – can only be a hindrance. Yet talking about our "incapacity/ for self-effacement" changes everything: it is just as unhelpful not to be able to self-efface. Hence it is here that "self-effacement" becomes – by virtue of its relation to "pretence" – unstable, for self-effacement is both the erasure of self and putting one's face on: "Have you noticed that the mirrors in department stores are depressing?" (133). We shouldn't dwell on this, however, because "even when" "one's" theoretical third person face has been effaced the light is anyway false to the true "one"… I'm inclined to smirk at the way "light" – our happy natural symbol – carries over ["our shadows in the electric light"] but really am none the wiser. What I mean to say is that the poem splits into two halves: if I were to offer terms I might call the first impersonal – in W.B. Yeats' formulation: the "I" identified within the poem need not be identified with "the bundle of accident and incoherence that sits down to breakfast..." – the latter personal. Yet the former necessarily sabotages and makes impossible the latter. Sharon Cameron notices this bi-polarity as a given in her series of essays which aim to investigate impersonality. For the writers she discusses (among them Simone Weil and T.S. Eliot) personality is not necessarily opposed to personality. Instead this "falling outside the boundary of the human particular" provides "a means of emerging from a point of view."[13] It is here that anyone's sense of confusion begins, and danger sets in.

§

"The innocence of the aesthetic domain perishes in Eliot and Pound."[14] – this last sentence of Maud Ellmann's *The Poetics of Impersonality* might be our first. Here she sketches the groundwork for "impersonality" in ways that are ripe for further thinking about how "the idea of impersonality leads a double or 'diphasic' life in their aesthetics..." It is impossible to reproduce her theses here which are meticulously worked out in local readings, and anyway: "It would be an exaggeration to say that Pound had a 'theory' of impersonality, for he prefers to send ideas straight into action: and slogans like 'imagisme' and 'vorticism' belong in manifestos rather than dissertations in philosophy..." However, on writing after strange gods, she proves extractable:

> Though other critics argue the proportions, even the most sympathetic separate the artist [Pound] from the man, to counteract the scandal of his politics. Indeed Donald Davie points out that American society asserted "an absolute discontinuity" between the poet and the man when Pound received the Bollingen Prize for the *Pisan Cantos* in 1949. Pound himself has argued that "one of the great maladies of modern criticism is that first rush to look for the person, and the corresponding failure EVER to look *at* the thing (ABCR, (147))" However, he has made his person so objectionable, that his readers gladly turn their gazes to the thing... Ironically, these critics reassert the contradictions of the work in the very trouble they take to disavow them...[15]

Ellmann's critique of how "impersonality" works itself out in writing after Pound and Eliot is immensely useful when attempting to explain the impulse and shape of Anna's "protest". At the same time, her solution to the question of how not to repeat the personality/impersonality distinction in criticism provides suggestions as to how to read Anna's poems (129):

Eliot and Pound both show that it is impossible to overcome the self, but this does not mean that their work is merely a disguise for their biographies. Their poetry should be regarded neither as their mirror nor their hiding place, but as the laboratory for the fabrication of themselves... (198)

Ellmann's attempt to come to terms with "impersonal" writings was in some sense begun by Donald Davie. In his lecture "Poetry and Sincerity" (1965) Davie re-presents "impersonality – the idea that the 'I' in a poem is *never* immediately and directly the poet" – as the overriding "rule" governing the reading and writing poetry.[16] "To this rule there was a necessary and invaluable corollary: that the question "Is the poet sincere?" was always an impertinent and illegitimate (2). Speaking with one eye on poets such as Lowell and Ginsberg, Davie asks "Must we abandon this rule?" and concludes: "I think we must".

The lecture struggles to relinquish the (for him principally) Poundian poetic/politic. Davie considers the various corollaries (impersonality only applies to poetry written up to 1780 and not after... personality, as opposed to impersonality, encourages a gossip column approach to poetry... it "opens the door to the exhibitionists"... and gives precedence to the Baudelairean poet at the expense of the Wordsworthian...) but remains completely open about the difficulty of doing so: "For my own part, much of the time I bitterly regret having to give it up as regards the poetry of our own time..." Eventually, however, the personal wins out: "we must welcome the change from poetry seen as the extent body of achieved poems, to poetry seen as a way of behaving, a habit of feeling deeply and truly and responsibly..."[17]

It would be no disservice to Davie to suggest that this tremendous statement derives as much from his realisation that we are, in a sense, already past all that, as from his politics: "The question", he writes, "has already been settled off-campus". Davie's insights are offered with the pinch of hindsight, which suggests what a monstrous anachronism it is to be writing about Mendelssohn in terms of Ezra Pound (and this quite apart from the dim sense that the more modest modern "irony" was surpassed by the arcade, and is now just surviving in the mirrored hall of the society of the spectacle). Yet the legacy of that irony remains to be seen. As Davie suggests, impersonality continues to turn up in unexpected places:

The confessional poet is his own biographer, and his poems are his autobiography like any other autobiographer he selects what he will reveal and suppresses much more. And insofar as the confessional poet thus presents only a trimmed and slanted image of himself, he may still be thought to be revealing to us not a personality but a *persona*. This is to use the term "persona" in an extended but thoroughly legitimate sense.

Davie's re-definition suggests the inescapability of impersonality, yet this does not cancel the fact of an attempt at escape. In doing so he describes the Janus-like character of much post-Poundian poetry: "We can spread the nets of rhetoric wide enough to catch them in the act, but this is to belie the impetus behind their writing…"

§

"Concentration camp styles. along mill road. 1998" (80): I take this line as a limit-case for this confusion ranging on danger. It proves impossible to separate the personal from the impersonal – three clauses, presumed jottings, are supplied with a place and a year all in the mode of a journal. If Simone Weil's notebooks engage in what Cameron calls "desituating strategies" which aim to departicularise the writing self, Mendelssohn's jottings work in the opposite direction.[18] I take this line personally [who, me? – I was ten. Although our space is co-habitual…] and yet – there is no "I", no speech-marks, nothing idiosyncratic, nothing joined up – no jubilant death-mask to cry: "(seriously though)/ I, Veronica did it". One is caught then on an old impasse. And perhaps the problem here is also a matter of personal taste: for who would desire to lay claim to a fashion originating in the concentration camps? (Fashion?) At Davie's suggestion, the old syllogism breaks down, and we glimpse the full implications of a term like "the confessional mode" – how easily the personal becomes personae.

The personal is recuperated by the impersonal, yet the impetus behind it remains. It is this will to make the impersonal personal that drives and survives in Anna's work: "She plays real games with books and I don't do those stupid mimicry acts…" (133). In these, she continually outpounds Pound, or so I take the lines: "cantos/ battre": where *battre*, in Ital. dial. means (Romanesco?) "to knock", but more likely and appropriately French: "to beat/defeat/ break", or – most suggestively, as in a *jeux des cartes* – "to shuffle". This implacability is focused in the poem "pladd. (you who say either")" (17-19) where to read really is to enter the language laboratory.

Pladd. Plural+ add? Or past participle of "to plead"? In which case – who is pleading/ pled, and who is listening/ listened? For compassion, like protest, necessarily depends upon a connection between speaking and personhood. Or is this a phonetic transcription of "plaid": a cloth made from overlaying strips and figurative for layers? The title identifies and perhaps accuses "you" for the shoulder-shrug and your impartiality.

"nothing can be clear when knowing the associations/ are read by unread people…" starts on a meta-poetical comment about that old-boy's network allusion ["accumulating pats on the back from big brothers" (3)], but tacks, paratactically, the real world of scandal/ accusation back on: "exposées, exposures." The line which describes "new poems for old" is less revolutionary than a straight swap, while "groovy" feels like a personal interjection, as with her later "groan". "scratch luck/ nothing matches the theoretical tuck" rhymes fortune productively with surgical manipulations, lays waste to the former, puts us in mind of "exposures": which is neither here nor there the media's method of assassination, or of establishing face, but both.

The mix of registers is interspliced with one-word clauses, flinging objects from the real (we presume) (biographical?) world: "nutmeg. primus stove. raised eyebrows…" – and we are only halfway. Pun, phonetic transcription, onomatopoeia, allusion, uncertainty, incidence and metapoetical comment undo and relate. The voice isn't, and then it shifts, it actually scat-sings: "planna vanne. Plin plor plon pladverbially/ plodding along with a net in sturdy boots…" then stops: "adolph who?" Of course this is typical of Anna, whose "plaesthetics" (129) necessarily involve "spreading my mask/ around my middle" (129). Out of the shuffle emerge full bars, written in "I": "I wait, I walk with life too great to beat,/ out into the cold, out into the street, out…", and outside it:

> a Self that one is pullulating in on this
> Subject of editorally infiltrated Capitals,
> my years of care are not matched by much
> other than steel and martyr'd hatred.
> Ploy…

Out of this shuffling pack, two impulses cross and diverge, first towards the division between voice and person, and once more against it.

Mendelssohn's brilliance lies in her attempt to beat/defeat/break/ shuffle the political unaccountability of impersonality, perhaps in her attempt to write a self attempting to do all these things. Writing of *Four Quartets* Cameron supposes Eliot's representation of "experience that is particularized without being particularized as someone's" as the poem's "most radical discovery": "Thus the passages develop affect with respect to a loss that is not a particular person's loss."[19] None of this could or would wash with Anna. Her attempt to "battre" ("better"?) the *Cantos* demonstrates "How T.S. Eliot's words are borne out" (53).This protest will be continually undone by a juncture between γλῶσσα and πρόσωπο, yet this poetry believes in their unity on the strength of what must be: Am I far away from those/ I love? Is this someone else's?" (19). Her poems open on the contradiction or truth that there is, at the same time that there cannot be, any distinction between books and world. As she writes in "Poetry does not deserve evil keepers":

> whoever gave you charge
> of this country's poetry
> has given full reign to atrocity
> of both literary and human fame… (45)

– "Did I mention that she hated Ezra Pound with an almighty fury?"[20]

Notes

[1] Anna Mendelssohn, *Implacable Art* (Applecross, WA & Cambridge: Folio / Equipage, 2000), 115. References are to this edition and will be given in the text.

[2] Ezra Pound, *Selected Poems and Translations* (London: Faber, 2010) 111; Donald Davie, quoted in Maud Ellmann *The Poetics of Impersonality* (Cambridge, MA: Harvard University Press, 1987) 149-50.

[3] T.J. Clark, *Farewell to An Idea: Episodes From A History of Modernism* (New Haven, CT: Yale University Press, 1999) 8.

[4] Victor Hugo, *Les Misérables* Book I, Chapter XII (passim).

[5] *Romans* 1:31; Adolf Hitler, *Mein Kampf* (Munich: Franz Eher Verlag, 1925-26).

[6] Sean Bonney, "'Minds do exist to agitate and provoke / this is the reason I do not conform' – Anna Mendelssohn" in the *Poetry Project Newsletter*, February/ March 2011, 17-19, available here:< http://poetryproject.org/publications/newsletter>[last accessed v. i. MMXII.].

[7] Connie Scozzaro, "On 'In The Minority of One'" *The Paper Nautilus* 2, October 2011 37; Eleanor Careless "'I shall not prove and neither shall I be proven': *PY*" *The Paper Nautilus* 2, October 2011 45.

[8] "Bouleversed Baudelairizing: On Poetics and Terror" (London: Veer 2011) 28.

[9] *Collected Poems* (Manchester: Carcanet Press, 2003) 78.

[10] Raoul Vaneigem, *The Revolution of Everyday Life*, trans. Donald Nicholson-Smith (London: Rebel Press, 1983) 26.

[11] Wyndham Lewis, *Time and Western Man* (Santa Rosa, CA: Black Sparrow Press, 1993) 68.

[12] Website of the Poetry Foundation< http://www.poetryfoundation.org/ poetrymagazine/article/335[last accessed v i MMXII].

[13] Sharon Cameron, *Impersonality: Seven Essays* (Chicago, IL: University of Chicago Press, 2007) viii; 14.

[14] Maud Ellmann, *The Poetics of Impersonality* (Cambridge, MA: Harvard University Press, 1987) 199.

[15] ibid, 137-8 .

[16] Available here:< http://www.google.co.uk/#sclient=psy-ab&hl=en&s ite=&source=hp&q=donald+davie+poetry+sincerity&pbx=1&oq= donald+davie+poetry+sincerity&aq=f&aqi=&aql=&gs_sm=e&gs_ upl=101l4478l0l4728l29l1 8l0l2l2l0l278l3248l0.12.6l2ol0&bav=on.2,or.r_gc.r_ pw.r_cp.,cf.osb&fp=3c19b6e5f907be2d&biw=1008&bih=424>[last accessed v i MMXII]. My thanks go to Michael Kindellan for putting me on to this essay.

[17] ibid.

[18] ibid., 111

[19] ibid., 149.

[20] Peter Riley, to myself; private email correspondence, xii. xii. MMXI.

Allen Fisher

ATKINS STOMP

1.
"I don't know how humanity stands it
I think I'm in danger of losing altitude
In a **catacomb**, hope for future bliss
My hand writes on a tangent to cup spills.
At bottom a low trellis, beyond it a narrow lawn
Climbs a stool to feed meter for gas
"The enormous tragedy of the dream
No capacity to express demands for tomorrow.
Next door she say she wants to scrub my potatoes
Escape over the gate with a peach
On poster a dove sips neon
Disease promoted as health. London.

A cat walks garden wall to the railing
the path still goes from the gate
Sent in the 'district support unit'
Trees and shrubs with dead foliage in summer.
"Take that smile off your face
Two pound of maggots wouldn't reach tench,
        that kind of rigid
Laced on the **koran** a flowering meadow
Repast glows in the heads.
Ate all I famished
"three young men at the door
, digged a ditch round me
A tree in the centre, then a low wall.
Bounce a ball against a brick hammering pavement
Decides between gas and hot air
We exhume the past, dissolve parliament
"I don't know how humanity stands it
Walked down the table to where the chairman sat
Organising rain with a sponge push
Bone heads in rows
Shits on daffodils showers them with sod.

2.

How they purchase will depend on their choice of food
Huge profits from 'Landspeed'
Started with anecdote lead on conservative angst
Destruction of flora in a circle unexplained.
Splintered beauty
A kid hops the walkway,
says two elves can beat a wolf, and repeats it
Behind the front, a row of trees and flowers.

"having run into the future on a bicycle
Beat of two forks pulsed out of phase
They decided **therapy** should involve poetics
Helicopter over paradise.

Explanation jotted on a menu
the moon in her tender green meadows
Wooden heads   heads of watermelon
Turtled by ribald-rid offenders.
Lifted menu popped it into her bag
Dicing down Mayall Road
Research into **primeval** echoed polyphony
"I been told the process ain't nacheral.

An opaque greenery shifts vision
Different colours arrayed in a bar
Thought that hinges on definition
Pollute fumes from rose ash glow.
Sad to feel the ribs of his cow
Dead honeysuckle twined round the railing
Housing seen to **diminish** rapidly
Encircled by a ribbon of officers.
The air was made open
Helicopters over paradise
Are you kidding?
Essential repeat mauves in the head.

3.

The alleged ubiquity of confusion
Rain no longer of the process
An oil-soaked **naiad** rages through blood
A runner play stream grouse project.
Pulse of two beams beaten out of phase
Distinguishes smoke from fire
Those are voices singing is an illusion
A dense hedge made only for looking.

Tackled the chairman on the lending leap
Says two elves can beat a wolf and repeats
Listen to the baste of the reggae
The stars differing colours
come into the park they say is dead
Amid hopes drown our hearsay with one keg
From my feet you can name me as a traveller
Cross town to be with you, Let's fuck
I have a understanding of selling and buying food
Escape over the gate from a tiger
Opens the air to its **vacation** thuds of apples
Stimulation animates through absorption box.

Reorganises into war and pride
Remains cube a sponge from a carpet
Spent in the disturbance resort bullet
The wall has not been opened.
From an inability to communicate
A siren
Increasing speed into a **cul-de-sac**
A cascade instabled from a sponge.
More geese than swans
From an inability to communicate to
another locked within
Population inversion amplifies in beat.

4.
The allay of ubiquity
Two pounds of anchor wouldn't reach bottom,
      that kind of tide
Massaged my **igloo** says breathe into pain
Unable to say the simplest.
Spits on window sills flowers them from pods
Pushed back a few feet, replaced by a vegetable wall
The actual colours and shapes of unspoiled
Without resort to says words can be born.
In the space of the picture the boots
Explored by means of *touch*
From bed to the **levee**, tarragon scent over omelettes
A runaway greenhouse effect.
Touch, a complex including eyes and ears
Distil bananas in a dustbin
Sent in the disco retort spoon it
Stimulates emission across spontaneous drive.
What's more she say she plants blood for tomatoes
Boiled boots for dinner with ballet shoes
high seas move over curvature towards carpet
Asymptotic touch a massage with a sponge.
Coherences limit of spatial depth
Rimes with foot to feed the metre for gas
The strange wilfulness that describes essentiality
Doppler waste in person ample pies in heat.
up to the gate, and from the fence we can see outside
I sink in anger a refuses attitude
, something about being singular i think
Studies shoes to understand where he has been.
The alleged ubiquity of pi
Dissing bricks now insanity's standardised
"It's a DITCH all right.

from Allen Fisher (1985) *Brixton Fractals*, London: Aloes Books
[collected in Allen Fisher (2004) *Gravity*, Cambridge: Salt Publishing].

Juha Virtanen

ALLEN FISHER READING:
FACTURE, "ATKINS STOMP", AND EZRA POUND

In the first book of his early tour de force, *Place*,[1] Allen Fisher writers:

> I read Pound who calls me to read Dante
> who gives me better sight to read Duncan
> who suggests that I read Pound (Fisher, 2005: 46).

The three lines candidly convey multiple interpretations. A *prima facie* reading could construe them as a synoptic view of the types of learning and erudition involved with some of the poets from the British Poetry Revival.[2] The short poetic unit combines contributors from Donald Allen's *The New American Poetry 1945-1960* (1960) with the poetries of high modernism and beyond, which provides a brief glimpse to the nexus of materials that contributed to the poetics of *Place*.[3] During an interview in 2009, Fisher described how, in addition to Olson's open field composition,[4] the "expansiveness", "range" and "feel" of *Place* was also influenced by "Pound's *Cantos*, Williams' *Paterson*, Zukofsky's *A*" as well as "Gary Snyder, James Koller and Lew Welch" (Fisher, 2009). In this respect, the lines represent one aspect of Fisher's "process showing", whereby the research carried out for a particular project is incorporated into the work itself. Yet, alongside this possible construal, these lines also evince a significant feature of Fisher's aesthetics as a whole. As Peter Barry observes, the poet's oeuvre demands a "sustained participatory engagement" (Barry, 1993: 200) from the reader, which Fisher himself identifies as the necessary business of poetry. Any significant work of art requires the viewer's "engagement to create it, to produce it" (Fisher, 1985b: 165) and consequently, the actual production of the art process is open to continuous transformation. In "The Mathematics of Rimbaud" (1982) Fisher describes this condition in terms that appear analogous to his readings of Pound, Dante and Duncan:

> as soon as a formal model is intelligible, [and it] admits semantic realisation where meaning is apparent, that meaning changes in relation to the meaning another may give it, or in relation to living after the first realisation of the meaning. And the meaning may take on a multiplicity that is summated or left impossible and so forth (Fisher, 1982: 2)

In this essay, my intention is to outline how this active and transformative readerly engagement is performed within Fisher's own poetry, particularly in relation to the resources he deploys. In light of the themes of this anthology, I will focus specifically on the materials involving Ezra Pound. To begin, I will outline a contextual framework through analysing sections within *Place: Book I* where Pound is explicitly mentioned; I will then contrast these examples with "Atkins Stomp" from *Gravity as a consequence of shape*, where Fisher adopts a slightly different technique in its stance towards the modernist poet; ultimately, this will enable me to speculate upon the ethical ideals behind Fisher's poetic "facture".

Place exists through myriad discourses; its complex nexus of resources and reportage conducts – in Robert Sheppard's words – a "multiple archaeology" (Sheppard, 2005: 61) of the "dynamegapolis" (Fisher, 2005: 320) that is contemporary London. The violent realities of this space are investigated through local history, topography, geology, mathematics and countless other systems of knowledge. Alongside these researches, the poems draw upon the works of Blake, Wordsworth, Pope as well as more contemporary authors. In fact, although several critics[5] have noted Fisher's references to Olson and Mac Low, writers such as Snyder, Jack Spicer, Kirby Malone, Robert Kelly, Eric Mottram and Ulli McCarthy (now known as Ulli Freer) are all included among the dedicatees featured throughout the book. Likewise, while the first book asserts that the speaker is not "Maximus, but a citizen of Lambeth" (Fisher, 2005: 11), the early sections of *Place* address Pound more often than they do Olson. "Making an Essay out of Place" includes a poem dedicated to Pound, and earlier, the poet is mentioned during a section concerning the lost rivers of London:

> if I take a river to its source
> > and in the case of the Falcon Brook
> > this is 2 springs
>
> & follow its course
> > from head to tail
> > to the Thames
>
> I may arrive from at least three projections
>
> > > the source in the springs
> > > is not the actual source
> > > but the first visible source
> > > so that if Pound said it
> > > it is original

this originality has come because of previous accumulation

the tail   into the Thames
           is not the final result
           but the last visible result
           before we consider the Brook   Hidaburna
           as the source   or A source

and the Thames as the course
           toward an ocean or cloud
           so that if Pound said it
           it is part of what has been said
leading us on to what will be said
                    (Fisher, 2005: 41).

Barry's study of *Place*, which reads this poem as a "guardedly optimistic" (Barry, 1993: 211) treatise on the possibilities of salvaging the future, associates these lines with Pound's use of Frobenius' *paideuma*. In *Guide to Kulchur* (1968), Pound defines the term as a "the gristly roots of the ideas that are in action" (Pound, 1968: 58), which Barry aligns with the movements of Falcon Brook and the Thames; like the river, Pound's ideas do not emerge *ex nihilo*, but as a result of "previous accumulation". In this context, perhaps the "source in the springs" is comparable to the tradition that Pound heralded as the "beauty which we preserve" (Pound, 1974b: 91). Consequently, the investigations of the underground rivers might be paralleled with Pound's research into the lyric traditions of the Melic poets, the *canzoni* from Provence, Chinese ideograms[6] and several other moments of verbal exactness that have been obscured by history.

Although these parallels are convincing, the passage also appears suspicious about Pound. Each time the section refers directly to the poet, it does so through a language of conditionality. Fisher's citizen of Lambeth is not Maximus, but nor is he willing share Pound's "mystical belief" (Tytell, 1987: 39) in a tradition of letters. Whereas Pound argues that a "return to origins" (Pound, 1974: 92) will lead to an invigorating arrival to nature and reason, *Place* does not traverse through history with a sense of nostalgia or preservation.[7] Instead, Fisher's poem asserts that London's political superstructures[8] have not significantly changed since the times of antiquity:

In republican Rome
centre of political gravity in an executive
           limited only by law the nomosic addition

citizen auctoritas elected by the rich
      a class with inherited training arenas
with disproportionate voting power   (Fisher, 2005: 348).

Additionally, as demonstrated by the change from the definite to the indefinite article in describing the river's "source", Fisher seemingly rejects systems of knowledge that seek to assert a conclusive, singular discovery. When the poem's investigations of Falcon Brook disclose such findings (e.g. "it is original"), this is done under the hypothetical guise of Pound. By contrast, when a later section, which is dedicated to Pound – but not related through him – concludes with a scene from contemporary London, the tones are less definite:

                    through   the new road near
Palace where fresh shingle bites underfoot
         into clean sand   the Water Board digs
            i count 5 layers
       the bottom layer may not be oldest
                (Fisher, 2005: 60)

The speaker is reluctant to declare that the strata have reached a final destination. Initially, his uncertainty might appear relevant only for this particular encounter and observation. However, if one engages with *Place* according to the poetics outlined in "The Mathematics of Rimbaud", this passage invites a re-consideration of the preceding surveys regarding Falcon Brook and the Thames. Effectively, the poem twists back on itself, and generates new "meanings" through the parallels that emerge as these two sections cut across one another. As a consequence, the uncertainty about the stratum found in Crystal Palace begins to permeate the declarations Pound *might* have made about the lost sources of the river. This process highlights two crucial differences between Pound and the poetics of *Place*. At a micro level, reading these two sections in conjunction suggests that the *paideuma* of Fisher's poem is not made of gristle; its roots more appropriately exist in a perpetual state of proposal and breakage from that proposal. At a macro level, these non-linear convergences are indicative of Fisher's resistance toward closed totalities. Because the reader is invited to "join the text at any point" (Sheppard, 2005: 61), its meanings may "take on a multiplicity" that refuses to settle. Ultimately, as the author of *Place* wishes to "grasp the world/ without gripping it" (Fisher, 2005: 343), he is unburdened by unviable expectations to "make it cohere" (Pound, 1987: 810).

To summarize, although Fisher's expansive poetry shares Pound's "breadth of cultural ambition" (Bush, 1997: 106) in terms of its scope and methodology, it also rejects the "monumental and totalising tendencies" (Lopez, 2006: 126) exhibited in *The Cantos*. More specifically, Fisher seems troubled by Pound's desire to attain this totality. In fact, he asserts that *The Cantos'* greatest achievement is its lack of design, and that the best qualities of Pound's work are its moments of enthusiasm and spontaneity.[9] These proposals provide a curious context for the references to Pound in "Atkins Stomp", one of the 14 poems in *Brixton Fractals*,[10] which was published in 1985 as the first section of Fisher's *Gravity as a consequence of shape* project. On the one hand, the poem confronts some of the most troubling aspects in Pound's oeuvre. On the other, I suggest, it opens them to a series of transformations enacted through Fisher's readerly engagement.

Because Fisher plans his poetry as extensive projects, each "with a different criteria [sic]" (Fisher & Milne, 1994: 30), the techniques of "Atkins Stomp" understandably differ from the poems in *Place*. Aside from the clear distinctions in the form and register of the poem, its approach towards Pound also assumes a different methodology. Although the examples above situate Fisher's speakers in an array of dialogues with Pound, the resources for *Place* do not contain a single reference to texts by the poet. *Brixton Fractals*, by contrast, features *The Pisan Cantos* (1994)[11] and extracts from Pound's wartime speeches for Radio Rome.[12] Both of these are quoted in "Atkins Stomp", although as Ken Edwards points out,[13] the exactness of these citations is not always clear. Some, however, are easier to identify. For instance,

> At bottom a low trellis, beyond it a narrow lawn
> Climbs a stool to feed meter for gas
> "The enormous tragedy of the dream
> No capacity to express demands for tomorrow   (Fisher, 1985a: 29)

contains an instantly recognizable echo from the first line to Canto LXXIV. The same poem is referred to again in "I don't know how humanity stands it/I think I'm in danger of losing altitude" (Fisher, 1985a: 29). Likewise, it is incorporated within

> Ate all I famished
> "three young men at the door
> ,digged a ditch round me
> A tree in the centre, then a low wall   (Fisher, 1985a: 29)

as well as in

> "having run into the future on a bicycle
> Beat of two forks pulsed out of phase
> They decided therapy should involve poetics
> Helicopter over paradise.   (Fisher, 1985a: 30).

Alongside these references to Canto LXXIV, the concluding lines of the poem, "Dissing bricks now insanity's standardized/'It's a DITCH all right'" (Fisher, 1985a: 32) refer to "Last Ditch of Democracy" – the first of the broadcasts Pound recorded for Radio Rome in 1941. A fragment from an undated script, "Homesteads", is also incorporated to the lines "Research into **primeval** echoed polyphony/'I been told the process ain't nacheral'" (Fisher, 1985a: 30).

In other words, the resources to "Atkins Stomp" simultaneously present Pound at his best and his worst. *The Pisan Cantos* develop the "enthusiastic mode" (Herd, 2007:100) of Pound's poetry to a highly skilful degree. When these poems were written in captivity at the US Army's Disciplinary Training Centre (DTC) in 1945, Pound was cut off from libraries, and only had access to a select few source materials. Thus, he was forced to extemporize his compositions largely from memory,[14] which resulted in stark, concise juxtapositions that featured a peculiar breadth of allusions.[15] Yet, these poems can also seem engulfed by Pound's dubious politics, which – when combined with the anti-Semitic undertones of "Last Ditch of Democracy" and other radio broadcasts – may complicate any aesthetic reception of the work as a whole. Indeed, although scholars have tried to examine Pound's views in light of his mental state during the 1930s and 40s,[16] and even if *The Pisan Cantos* ultimately force "the angry propagandist to surrender all but a few cragged redoubts" (Kenner, 1971: 474), Pound's fascist affiliations frequently lurk behind the quotations in "Atkins Stomp". In Canto LXXIV Pound's "enormous tragedy of the dream" quickly leads to a lament for Mussolini's death, where the poet scornfully labels Il Duce's Partisan executioners as "maggots" (Pound, 1987: 439). Furthermore, the "dream" itself includes a possible referent to Pound's admiration of the Fascist leader. Terrell argues that the line recalls Mussolini's speech from 1935, in which he promised each Italian peasant access to home ownership.[17] Thus, the immediate context for the opening of Canto LXXIV calls to mind Pound's impassioned support for Mussolini[18] in works such as Jefferson and/or Mussolini (1936). The approximate background for "three young men at the door/, digged a ditch around me" is equally troubling. At first, the lines in Canto LXXIV recount an act of kindness by the guards at the DTC; the aforementioned ditch is in fact dug to keep damp away from the frail poet.[19] This scene, however, is immediately followed by attacks against Zion, Isaiah and King David, where the latter is associated with Pound's distrust of economic "interest" (Pound, 1987: 443). The broader context of the extract may therefore be read in parallel with the "Jew millionaires" (Pound, 1978: 9) that Pound attacks during "Last Ditch of Democracy". Consequently, Fisher's selections face a predicament that is shared by many of those who read *The Pisan Cantos*: is it possible to regard these poems as an act of self-criticism, or is Pound still unwilling to fully renounce his "dream"?[20] A wider survey of the resources in *Brixton Fractals* suggests that Fisher is not interested in an apologist reading of the modernist poet. For instance, "Boogie Stomp" (Fisher, 1985a: 57-58) refers to Olson's meetings with Pound at St. Elizabeths, which led Olson to describe the "full shock" of realising "what a fascist s.o.b Pound is" (Olson, 1975: 43). In light of Fisher's source materials, perhaps a similar encounter takes place within "Atkins Stomp".

Of course, while the references in "Atkins Stomp" are difficult to extricate from Pound's fascist utterances, it seems unlikely that Fisher would wish to incorporate the full context of these quotes by way of synecdoche.[21] At the same time, Pound's works are a prominent presence within the poem, as it both opens and closes with quotations from them. How exactly does Fisher wish to use these materials? The introduction to *Brixton Fractals* states that its bibliography is not used authoritatively,[22] but only as a way of indicating the "indirect" (Fisher, 1985a: 4) perceptions of the poems. Thus, by designating his resources as participants to the "perception and memory" (Fisher, 1985a: 4) of the text, Fisher once again alludes to the active readership he outlines in "Necessary Business" and "The Mathematics of Rimbaud". In this respect, the quotations from Pound could be construed as an attempt to negotiate between the poet's accomplished aesthetics and reprehensible politics. Perhaps the lines concerning "two pound of maggots" (Fisher, 1985a: 29) and "two pounds of anchor" (Fisher, 1985a: 32) feature a tacit acknowledgment of the dualities Olson faced during his visits to St. Elizabeths:

> In language and form [Pound] is as forward, as much of a revolutionist as Lenin. But in social, economic and political action he is as retrogressive as the Czar.   (Olson, 1975: 53).

However, Fisher's use of quotations is more specific and complex than this. He does not simply include them as juxtapositions to the other voices of the poem; nor do they exactly correlate with the linguistic slippage implied by bricolage.[23] Rather, I propose that Fisher's methodology is somewhat similar to a Situationist détournement, in so far as the "ideas and realizations" of the quoted resources can be "multiplied at will", and made to clash with several "social and legal conventions" (Debord & Wolman, 1981: 11).

To clarify this proposal, I would like to return to the aforementioned reference to "having run into the future on a bicycle". Fisher derives the line from a section in Canto LXXIV[24] where Pound draws upon his personal recollections. The section recounts the poet's visit to Oxford in 1913, during which he heard William Lawrence tell John Kettlewell about running into Prince Edward on his bicycle. In response, Kettlewell suggested that it was a pity the accident had not killed the future sovereign.[25] Pound incorporates the anecdote in brief, but when he comes to describe the crash, Canto LXXIV reads: "having run into the future non-sovereign Edvardus/on a bicycle" (Pound, 1987: 458). Fisher, as we have seen, removes this historical referent entirely. Consequently, although the line in "Atkins Stomp" is openly identified as Pound's, it bears little connection to its original meaning. Rather, the bicycle ride calls to mind the beginning of "Banda", the first poem in *Brixton Fractals*:

> Took chances in London traffic
> where the culture breaks
> tone colours turn from exhaustion
> emphasised by wind,
> looking ahead for sudden tail lights
> a vehicle changes
> lanes into your path and birds,
> over the rail bridge, seems purple.
> A mathematician at the turn of the century
> works out invariant notions in a garden
> every so often climbs a bike,
> makes a figure of eight around
> rose bed to help concentration
> then returns to the blackboard.   (Fisher, 1985a: 1)

As the figure of the mathematician is partially based on David Hilbert, the "figure of eight" could be a reference to the unresolved Reimann Hypothesis.[26] Therefore, the parallels between "Banda" and the bicycle in "Atkins Stomp" are possible to read as a representation of an ungraspable system of knowledge. More broadly, however, this convergence demonstrates how *Brixton Fractals* cuts through space and time, and simultaneously takes place across a multiplicity.[27] The effects of this plurality proliferate across the lines in "Atkins Stomp". For instance, the "helicopter over paradise" suddenly assumes numerous forms: it recalls the paradoxical ambiguity about paradise that Pound addresses in Canto LXXIV,[28] yet it also acts as an echo of the Brixton riots in the early 1980s.[29] Moreover, the helicopter's presence in both "African Boog" and "Birdland" extends the signification of the line to include the violent realities of "surveillance" and "social intransigence" (Montgomery, 2011: 17). In sum, like the earlier sections of *Place*, the relations between the lines in *Brixton Fractals* are striated. Of course, several space-times cut across *The Pisan Cantos* as well, as the "life of the DTC passing OUTSIDE" (Pound, 1962: 17) the poems impinges and breaks into their flow. In this respect, Canto LXXIV also becomes a cage[30] in which Pound tries to measure his individual autonomy. Similarly, the "experiential multidimensionality" (Sheppard, 2005: 200) in *Brixton Fractals* also sets itself against the violent forces that permeate life in inner cities. However, whereas Pound searches for "control and order" (Nicholls, 1984: 166) as a mode of self-preservation, Fisher's poem seeks to divert the meta-narratives and superstructures of contemporary London in an effort to undermine them.

Although the term does not appear in his early theoretical work, Fisher commonly identifies his aesthetic practice as "facture", a term he derives from art history. Traditionally, the expression is used to discuss an artist's handling of the brushstroke and how their "materials are worked descriptively and expressively" (Zurier, 2009: 29). Although Fisher's theory is more closely aligned with the constructivist tendency of incorporating the technical means of production in the work itself,[31] the ethics behind his "facture" are quite distinctive. He contrasts the term with concepts such as "create" or "make" and argues that while these acts imply "completions and finished products", facture remains open and includes "the viewer in the production process of the art" (Fisher, 2012: 1). This is comparable to David Summer's recent work, where the "language of facture is" described as "notional metaphors" (Summer, 2003: 74) that stress the reflective capacities of the mind in formulating concepts and relations. Summer expands his proposition by referring to the development of tools during hominid evolution. He argues that the facture of these implements "not only allowed adaptation" but also "created the expectation of further" (Summer, 2003: 109) adaptations, thus multiplying agency by enabling the activities that make these alterations possible. The readerly engagement Fisher outlines in "The Mathematics of Rimbaud" and *Necessary Business* promotes this continual adaptation as well. The poems of *Place* and *Brixton Fractals* insist that their ideas and realisations can multiply through each moment of reception. However, as I have attempted to demonstrate, these reading practices are also enacted within the poems themselves. Through his interrogations and transformations of details from Canto LXXIV, Fisher diverts Pound's utterances by dismantling their rebarbative ideologies in order to reappropriate them to a new socio-political milieu.

In doing so, "Atkins Stomp" reveals a complex relationship between its resources. *Brixton Fractals* was published six years into the Thatcher administration's project of deregulation and privatisation, which exponentially deepened Britain's social inequalities by adhering to a narrative of "two nations", one consisting of "a privileged" set of "good citizens" and "hard workers", the other of ethnic minorities, inner city residents as well as "the non-skilled working class outside of the South-East" (Jessop et al, 1988:87). As Gilmour argues, even when unemployment rose to a peak of 3,133,200 in 1986,[32] Nigel Lawson's chancellorship neglected the poor. Indeed, Lawson regarded the less fortunate as "necessary sacrifices to the achievement of an enterprise society based on self-sufficiency, thrift [and] entrepreneurial instincts" (Gilmour, 1992: 133). The violence of Thatcherism also emerges in Fisher's poem:

> Explanation jotted on a menu
> the moon in her tender green meadows
> Wooden heads heads of watermelon
> Turtled by ribald-rid offenders.
> Lifted menu popped it into her bag
> Dicing down Mayall Road
> Research into primeval echoed polyphony
> "I been told the process ain't nacheral. (Fisher, 1985a: 30)

As I indicated above, the concluding remark is sourced from Pound, but this section of "Atkins Stomp" also draws upon an article published in *Investor's Chronicle* on July 1st, 1983. Specifically, Fisher refers to an encounter between Thatcher and Robert Leigh-Pemberton before the latter was appointed as the new Governor of the Bank of England. After the disagreements she had experienced with the previous Governor, Gordon Richardson, the Prime Minister sought to nominate Leigh-Pemberton as he appeared more "in tune" (Quaglia, 2008: 28) with her policies. Although the article refrains from stating it explicitly, it would appear as if Thatcher's decision was informed by a business lunch in 1980, during which Leigh-Pemberton jotted his views about bank lending on a menu that Thatcher subsequently deposited in her bag.[33] Fisher includes images of this exchange in close proximity to "Dicing down Mayall Road", which formed a part of the front-line for the Brixton riots in 1981. In doing so, the poem forms a causal link between the economic policies of Thatcherism and the social deprivation that contributed to the causes of the riots. *Brixton Fractals* clearly harbours a deep mistrust for the world of finance. In fact, this position is not entirely dissimilar from some of Pound's suspicions regarding the power of economic forces;[34] the final section of Canto XLVI outlines the "one hundred thousand violent crimes" (Pound, 1987: 235) that the Great Depression inflicted upon the vulnerable. However, whereas Pound witlessly associated these brutal techniques with his deplorable theories of usury, Allen Fisher's reading performs a more careful analysis. His critique identifies Thatcher and the market economy as a process that – Fisher suggests – simply ain't nacheral.

Notes

[1] Book I of *Place* was first published by Aloes Books in 1974, and continued in various serial pamphlets, before finally culminating in the belated publication of *Unpolished Mirrors* by Reality Studios in 1985. In 2005, Reality Street published a collected edition of the project. My references are from this edition.

[2] See, for example, Eric Mottram's "The British Poetry Revival, 1960-75" (1993)

[3] Of course, Place draws upon a far more expansive list of resources (see Fisher, 2005: 409-416)

[4] Also see Mottram's article, "Open Field Poetry" (1977). Although Olson is included as one of the examples, Mottram makes relatively few references to "Projective Verse". Instead, he illustrates his arguments by drawing upon a wide range of sources, including Williams, Pound, Einstein, Rexroth, Duncan, Fenollosa, Mac Low, Ashbery, Heisenberg, Whitehead, Ginsberg and several others.

[5] See, for example, Clive Bush's *Out of Dissent* (1997). Robert Hampson's "Producing the Unknown" (1993), Redell Olsen's "Postmodern Poetry in Britain" (2008) and Sheppard's *The Poetry of Saying* (2005).

[6] See Fenollosa's *The Chinese Character as a Medium for Poetry* (1968)

[7] Barry (1993:211) also rejects the notion that *Place* believes in a sentimental escape to a "natural" past.

[8] I am drawing upon the Marxist sense of the term. See, for example, Marx & Engels (1970: 47)

[9] I am paraphrasing the suggestions Fisher made in conversation with staff and students from Royal Holloway and University of Kent during a seminar on his work. The event was held at the Centre for Creative Collaboration in London, on June 14th, 2012.

[10] This chapbook was later included in *Gravity* (2004a), the first of the collected volumes for *Gravity as a consequence of shape*. This was followed by *Entanglement* (2004b) and *Leans* (2007). My references are to the original chapbook published in 1985. For more on the serial production of *Gravity as a consequence of shape*, See Sheppard (2011: 181-184)

[11] *The Pisan Cantos* were later included in a collected edition of *The Cantos*, published by Faber & Faber. My references are to the Faber & Faber edition

[12] Transcripts of these were later published in a collection edited by L.W. Doob. See Pound (1975).

[13] See Edwards (2000:11)

[14] See Makin (1985: 241)

[15] See Ayers (2004: 10-11)

[16] See, for example, Flory's *The American Ezra Pound* (1989)

[17] See Terrell (1984: 362)

[18] Also see Selby (2005: 206)

[19] See Pound (1987: 443)

[20] Nicholls (1984: 162-170) also notes upon these predicaments.

[21] See Ayers (2004: 28), where these methods are discussed in relation to "The Waste Land".

[22] Middleton (2005:42) also discusses the bibliographical methodology of *Brixton Fractals.*

[23] See Derrida (2004: 360)

[24] See Pound (1987: 458)

[25] See Terrell (1984: 383)

[26] The Reimann Hypothesis (which pertains to the location of "nontrivial zeros" in a particular function used in quantum field theory and elsewhere) is the 8th entry on Hilbert's list of 23 unsolved problems, and it remains unresolved. See, for example, Gray's *The Hilbert Challenge: A Perspective on Twentieth Century Mathematics* (2000). For a further discussion of "Banda", see the relevant sections in Bush (1997: 102-210).

[27] In part, I am drawing upon Sheppard's discussion of "facture" and "fracture" in *Gravity as a consequence of shape.* See Sheppard (2011: 181-198)

[28] See Pound (1987: 450)

[29] See Edwards (2000:11)

[30] See Ellman (1987: 190) for a slightly different formulation.

[31] See Buchloch (1984: 87)

[32] See Gilmour (1992: 84)

[33] See Anon (1983: 26)

[34] Also see Davis (1968: 71-72)

Works Cited

Anon. (1983) "New Governor of Bank will be nobody's pawn", *Investor's Chronicle* (July 1st), p. 26

Allen, D. (1960) *The New American Poetry 1945-1960*. New York, NY: Grove Press

Ayers, D. (2004) *Modernism: a Short Introduction*. Oxford: Blackwell Publishing

Barry, P. (1993) "Allen Fisher and Content Specific Work", *New British Poetries: The Scope of the Possible*. eds. P. Barry & R. Hampson. Manchester: Manchester University Press. pp. 198-215

Bush, C. (1997) *Out of Dissent: A Study of Five Contemporary British Poets*. London: Talus Editions.

Buchloch, B.H.D. (1984) "From Faktura to Factography". *October* Vol. 30 pp. 82-119

Davis, E. (1968) *Vision Fugitive: Ezra Pound and Economics*. Lawrence, KS: The University Press of Kansas.

Debord, G. & Wolman G.J (1981) "Methods of Détournement" *Situationist International Anthology* (ed. & trans. Ken Knabb). Berkeley, CA: Bureau of Public Secrets. pp. 8-14

Derrida, J. (2004) *Writing and Difference*. (trans. Alan Bass). London: Routledge

Edwards, K. (2000) "Introduction: The Two Poetries" [Online] Available from: http://www.modernpoetry.org.uk/introduction.pdf [Last accessed 17/06/12]

Ellman, M. (1987) *The Poetics of Impersonality: T.S. Eliot and Ezra Pound*. Brighton: Harvester Press

Fenollosa, E. (1968) *The Chinese Written Character as a Medium for Poetry* (ed. E. Pound). San Francisco, CA: City Lights

Fisher, A. (1982) "The Mathematics of Rimbaud", *Reality Studios* (3.1) pp. 1-5

—— (1985a) *Brixton Fractals*. London: Aloes Books

—— (1985b) *Necessary Business*. London: Spanner

—— (2004a). *Gravity*. Cambridge: Salt Publishing

—— (2004b). *Entanglement*. Toronto: The Gig

—— (2005). *Place*. Hastings: Reality Street

—— (2007). *Leans*. Cambridge: Salt Publishing

—— (2009) *Interview with A. Fisher on 27.02.2009*. London. [Digital recording in possession of author]

—— (2012) *Re: facture*. [E-mail]. Message to author. 31.05.2012

Fisher, A & Milne, D. (1994) "Exchange in Process". *Parataxis* 6 pp. 28-33

Flory W.S. (1989) *The American Ezra Pound*. New Haven: Yale University Press

Gilmour, I. (1992) *Dancing with Dogma: Britain Under Thatcherism*. New York: Simon & Schuster

Gray, J. (2000) *The Hilbert Challenge: A Perspective on Twentieth Century Mathematics*. Oxford: Oxford University Press

Hampson, R. (1993) "Producing the Unknown: language and ideology in contemporary poetry" *New British Poetries: The Scope of the Possible* (eds. P. Barry & R. Hampson) Manchester: Manchester University Press. pp. 134-155

Herd, D. (2007) *Enthusiast! Essays on Modern American Literature*. Manchester: Manchester University Press

Jessop, B. et al (1988) *Thatcherism: a Tale of Two Nations*. Cambridge: Polity

Kenner, H. (1971) *The Pound Era*. Berkeley, CA: University of California Press.

Lopez, T. (2006) *Meaning Performance*. Cambridge: Salt Publishing

Makin, P. (1985) *Pound's Cantos*. London: George Allen & Unwin

Marx, K. & Engels, F. (1970) *The German Ideology Part One, with Selections from Parts Two and Three, together with Marx's "Introduction to a Critique of Political Economy"* (ed. C.J. Arthur). London: Lawrence & Wishart

Middleton, P. (2005) *Distant Reading: Performance, Readership. And Consumption in Contemporary Poetry.* Tuscaloosa, AL: The University of Alabama Press

Montgomery, W. (2011) "Fractalizing the Front Line: Brixton in the poetry of Allen Fisher and Linton Kwesi Johnson". *Journal of British and Irish Innovative Poetry* 3.1. pp. 9-22

Mottram, E. (1977) "Open Field Poetry". *Poetry Information 17.* pp. 3-24

—— (1993) "The British Poetry Revival 1960-1975", *New British Poetries: The Scope of the Possible* (eds. P.Barry & R. Hampson) Manchester: Manchester University Press. pp.15-50

Nicholls, P. (1984) *Ezra Pound: Politics, Economics and Writing. A Study of the Cantos.* London: Macmillan

Olsen, R. (2008) "Postmodern Poetry in Britain". *Cambridge Companion to Twentieth-Century English Poetry.* Cambridge: Cambridge University Press. pp. 42-55

Olson, C. (1975) *Charles Olson & Ezra Pound: An Encounter at St. Elizabeths* (ed. C. Seelye). New York, NY: Grossman Publishers

Pound, E. (1936) *Jefferson and/or Mussolini. Fascism as I have seen it.* New York: Liveright

Pound, E. (1962) "A Prison-Letter" *The Paris Review 28,* p.17

—— (1968) *Guide to Kulchur.* New York, NY: New Directions

—— (1974b) "Tradition". *Literary Essays of Ezra Pound* (ed. T.S. Eliot). London: Faber & Faber. pp. 91-93

—— (1975) *Ezra Pound Speaking: Radio Speeches of World War II* (ed. L.W. Doob). Westport, CT: Greenwood Press

—— (1987) *The Cantos.* London: Faber & Faber

—— (1994) *The Pisan Cantos LXXIV-LXXXIV 1498.* New York, NY: New Directions

Quaglia, L. (2008) *Central Banking Governance in the European Union: A Comparative Analysis.* London: Routledge

Selby, N. (2005) *Poetics of Loss in The Cantos of Ezra Pound: From Modernism to Fascism.* Lampeter: Edwin Mellen Press

Sheppard, R. (2005). *Poetry of Saying: British Poetry and its Discontents 1950-2000.* Liverpool: University of Liverpool Press

—— (2011) *When Bad Times Made for Good Poetry: episodes in the history of the poetics of innovation.* Exeter: Shearsman Books

Summer, D. (2003) *Real Spaces: World History Art and the Rise of Western Modernism.* London: Phaidon

Terrell, C.F. (1984) *A Companion to the Cantos of Ezra Pound: Volume 3.* Berkeley, CA: University of California Press.

Tytell, J. (1987) *Ezra Pound: The Solitary Volcano.* London: Bloomsbury

Zurier, R. (2009) "Facture". *American Art* (23.1) pp. 29-32

Gavin Selerie

POUND AND CONTEMPORARY BRITISH POETRY: THE LOOSENING OF FORM

Alan Halsey begins his review of David Moody's *Ezra Pound: Poet,* volume 1, with the question "What is Pound to us, precisely a century after the publication of his first book?"[1] He then distinguishes between the significance Pound has for those "past fifty" and his relevance to a younger generation of writers. For the former his work seemed "a master key to the reading and practice of modern poetry," despite "an obsession with the archaeology of poetic form" which rendered his project less radical than the disjunctures of Stein and the Dadaists or the "blazing artillery" of Lewis. However, Halsey wonders whether those who have developed their practice out of different strands of modernism or at several removes from Pound can regard him as anything other than a "strictly 'historical' figure".

It is likely, given the dominance of other models and, in particular, the reaction against layers of allusion and a perceived intellectual elitism, that Pound is not considered as seminal a force by younger poets and readers. On the other hand a lot of his strategies may have been absorbed into experimental practice, so that the line of influence has become obscured. In an age of information overload (but not in the Canto sense), it is harder to chart such continuities, as it is to develop concentrated habits of reading.

Many of Pound's remarks about the form and texture of poetry remain relevant, but they are less likely to be taken as absolute precepts. Few would quarrel with the axiom "Use no superfluous word, no adjective which does not reveal something"; nor with the injunction: "If you are using a symmetrical form, don't put in what you want to say and then fill up the remaining vacuums with slush."[2] On the other hand, when Pound prescribes "no book words, no periphrases, no inversions",[3] one is inclined to say, depending on context. As I have argued in "Statement on Poetry" and implied in "Proxy Features" (a poem on poets and poetics),[4] there may be a need to reclaim elements which were thrown out in the modernist programme. When a liberating aesthetic hardens into dogma, it is ripe for a challenge or invites reassessment.

§ § §

I first read some of Pound's shorter lyrics as a teenager and was struck by their crafted, fluent music: the fresh and accurate charting of voice. Bob Dylan's image of "Ezra Pound and T.S. Eliot/Fighting in the captain's tower", from the album *Highway 61 Revisited* (1965), brought the issue of cultural bearings sharply into view. Towards the end of the decade my Anglo-Saxon tutor urged me to read Pound's "The Seafarer" and this took me to Michael Alexander's revision of such a mode in *The Earliest English Poems*. Pound's archaisms were not an obstruction, but I was conscious that a more purged language might function better, as he himself discovered. By 1969 I had acquired *Selected Poems*, ed. Eliot, and *The Cantos* (in the distinctive black jacket edition). Neither was on the syllabus, for we were examined on literature up to 1900, but Pound was discussed in English faculty lectures and the work was part of a core pre-contemporary culture which I came to almost in reverse, my mid-sixties obsession being the Beat poets. It seemed that one could sidestep Pound's political views, although later I learned to tackle these head-on.

The *Selected* intensified my fascination with poetry that deployed wit in an easy, immediate way. I was impressed particularly by the Chinese translations or "versions" and the imagist poems (if one can separate them from a more general deployment of that effect). *The Cantos* were a strange assemblage, at times impenetrable but mostly stimulating, a long stretch of rolling, twisting matter. I homed in immediately on Cantos 16 and 80, which remain my favourites, partly for their London focus but also for their historical sweep and etching of personality in voice. The whole Pisan section offered striking examples of intertwined motifs and references. Elsewhere, I was entranced by the beauty and precision of Canto 49. Once I had obtained the separate volume *Drafts and Fragments*, I could sense further possibilities for the lyric "moment" within a longer span. "From Canto 115", for instance, draws various strands together, yet exists as an independent unit: a meditation on the state of the world, with a concentrated clarity of image.

Having studied Latin poetry and read Greek epic in translation, I was strongly aware of the classical influence, announced in the first line of Canto 1 (with its daring start *in media res*). My reading of Renaissance epic at this point and later in the 1970s helped to place Pound's epic, for all its novelties, in the tradition of the long poem. A structure of linked episodes and of continuity within change is there already in Ovid's *Metamorphoses* and its Renaissance counterparts. Pound's more radically shifting work, with layers of allusion and history in pieces, is a twentieth century equivalent: a story that involves wrestling with experience and searching for truth, against a background of world war and rapid technological "advance".

Content to be carried by the texture of language, I did not worry much about allusions I could not grasp. Nevertheless, I remained curious and alert to the emergence of relevant background information. From the mid-1970s I started acquiring critical matter, including Hugh Kenner's *The Pound Era* and Guy Davenport's *Cities on Hills*. I had some stimulating discussions with David Moody, c. 1973-77, and met Eric Mottram, who proved a font of useful comment (see below). I also encountered William Cookson from whom, over the years, I bought issues of *Agenda*. Long conversations with Alan Halsey helped to shape a sense of what Pound does and how this might be of use to contemporary poets. For instance, we talked about the crucial development that marks *Ripostes*, or (more fully) *Lustra*, off from an earlier, more stilted, style. As indicated in his Obit. for Ford Madox Ford, the latter's negative reaction to *Canzoni* sent Pound back to "the living tongue".[5]

For many poets of my generation, Pound's prose, amplified by some of Bunting's remarks, served as a poetic primer. Although Olson and Dorn's practice was closer in time, the groundwork laid by earlier modernists seemed fully relevant, at least in terms of sound and rhythm. Useful material included Pound's letters as well as his essays, guides and critical books. The *Paris Review* interview, which I first read in 1973, was an additional resource. I should also mention the Pound/Spann anthology *Confucius to Cummings*, acquired in America in 1968. This is how I first encountered the Troubadour poets, Villon and Ford Madox Ford, but the end-matter and occasional commentary were also illuminating. For a guitarist and songwriter, the emphasis on the close association of verse and music was attractive.[6] If Pound's dicta tend to be too absolute, there was much in these works to prompt further engagement with language. Given the prevailing conservatism of British poetry, Pound's articulation of what is valuable in the tradition and his model of a re-formed poetics still resonated in a later era. As Robert Duncan argued with regard to *The Cantos*:

> We couldn't have a more extreme instance of democratic comp-
> osition than we had out of that man who kept hoping he'd rescue
> himself by having totalitarian order.[7]

Olson and Ginsberg negotiated a way through the negative features of Pound's ideology, and these manoeuvres fed into the experimental British scene from the late 1950s on.[8]

I began to glimpse an alternative poetry situation in the mid-1960s, via the Penguin Modern Poets series and then, in 1969, through Michael Horovitz's anthology *Children of Albion*. This dovetailed with experience of poetry and music, including concerts given by groups such as Pete Brown and his Battered Ornaments. I attended a few London poetry readings but was more actively engaged with the theatre and music aspects of the counter-culture. While visiting London frequently in the years 1968-78, I lived elsewhere, in Oxford, the Sussex Downs and Vale of York. Hence I was absent from the Poetry Society radical realignment and subsequent "wars". I met Jeff Nuttall, Horovitz and others, but my poetics, at least in a Poundian context, was formed more privately. I heard Geoffrey Hill read parts of *King Log* and *Mercian Hymns* at a small gathering in York around 1976. This helped to validate a referentiality and multiple voicing which I was already using. The work of W.S. Graham also offered a channel through Pound, recovering a regular pulse and internalizing the weight of allusion.

Before describing my engagement with a London poetry scene that intersected with Pound, I should explain a parallel interest. In March 1968, while living in the USA, I had discovered the work of Olson, via Donald Allen's *The New American Poetry*. Back in England I acquired the first two *Maximus* volumes and subsequently borrowed tapes of Olson's Berkeley and Vancouver readings, with additional material by Duncan and H.D.[9] These opened up a different prospect on the long poem and aspects of Pound's poetics. When I moved back to London in 1978 I had just visited Gloucester, Massachusetts, where I saw many of the features explored in *Maximus*. Somewhat bruised by postgraduate study at the University of York but wishing to maintain an involvement with poetry, I was introduced to Eric Mottram, an authority on both Pound and Olson.[10]

Mottram not only kept alive elements of modernism, in retrospect, but encouraged an equivalent contemporary advance. I meshed quickly with a group of poets associated with the King's College and Sub-Voicive readings. Among those influenced by Pound were Mottram, Allen Fisher and Robert Hampson, who all produced extended sequences. Others, such as Frances Presley, responded more to the lyric, in its non-Romantic aspect, and briefer imagist flashes.[11] Carlyle Reedy, speaking of her "own attempt to get as near as possible to a condensed ... observation", counts "even some Pound" as a worthwhile model.[12] One could argue that Pound's most significant legacy is his deployment of the line unit, and in this sense the list would embrace most of the poets operating in an alternative or experimental sphere during the period under discussion. Habits of syntax and punctuation are particularly relevant here. However, the tracing of lines of influence needs to be specific. By the 1970s the use of a field of materials to create a dense intertextual web was a well-tried strategy which was ripe for renewal. Allen Fisher's *Place*, Robert Hampson's *Seaport*, and my own *Azimuth* and *Roxy* are examples of this span of operation. Iain Sinclair's *Suicide Bridge* and Maggie O'Sullivan's

A Natural History in 3 Incomplete Parts show other possibilities of linguistic and historical exploration.

During the same period I was in touch with poets associated with the Cambridge scene, some of whom adapted Poundian practice or shaped their art in reaction to it. If Olson was more of an influence, one should remember Prynne's input to Donald Davie's *Ezra Pound: Poet as Sculptor*[13] and Veronica Forrest-Thomson's engagement with Pound in *Poetic artifice* and elsewhere.[14] There is not space here to deal with the complexities of that mediation. However, I shall deal with some poets outside the London orbit later in this essay.

The reaction against an overriding narrative ego and attendant referential apparatus, which manifested itself in the 1980s and 1990s, seemed to displace both Pound and Olson as prime models for experiment. Eric Mottram, for instance, felt that poets needed to work "in response to the developments initiated by Derrida and the French intellectuals."[15] Others challenged what they saw as "informational overload" in the modern verse epic and the given necessity for natural or direct speech.[16] A different mood was in the air, and this can be gauged by a comparison between, say, Allen Fisher's *Place* (completed 1980) and *Brixton Fractals* (completed 1985).[17] From a long perspective, however, that shake-up did not erase the lingering effect of high modernism. Rather, its processes were transformed so as to destabilize authorial absolutes and embed information more fully in the linguistic moment. Raworth's pulp procedures, for instance, still retain layering and appositional placing of fragments. A dialogue with Language poetry initiated by Ken Edwards and others did not suppress features which could be usefully redirected, such as the persona and dramatic monologue. The London scene, strongly weighted towards performance, continued to nourish or tolerate work which had an evident link with the Fenollosa/Pound "Noh" plays or *The Cantos*. Only in the new millennium, with the fallout from a result-oriented rather than curiosity-driven education process, did a break from earlier experimental practice become such that information-relevance and related habits of inquiry could not be assumed. This shift will be examined below.

Since the modernist long poem has been much preoccupied with place, I should – in Olson's words – "come back to the geography of it".[18] Without literally conjuring spirits, an involvement with the topography of north-west London has been crucial to my poetic progress. A near-decade in Ladbroke Grove (1979-1987) sparked research into the Kensington location of many modernist writers and artists, actually an extension of the Victorian geographical base.[19] I paced the streets by habit and ended up teaching a local history course that involved considerable reference to Pound, Ford, Lewis and H.D. This led to investigation of Violet Hunt and her circle. Figures as diverse as Gilbert Cannan, May Sinclair, Radclyffe Hall and Edward Wadsworth lived within walking distance of each other. Some, like Brigit Patmore, lived north of Notting Hill Gate. Peter Brooker's term "bourgeois enclave"[20] rather obscures the varied existence across a borough that stretched from the Chelsea border to Kensal Green Cemetery. Thus, Pound's "rotting hill", coined in response to a Wyndham Lewis letter of 1948, registers decline but also an older paradox.[21]

Despite shifts in sensibility, there are continuities from, say, 1850 through to at least the 1980s.[22] I trace some key links up to 1940 in an essay on Canto 80.[23] But the later period includes other interesting parallels. Eric Mottram, for instance, lived in Vicarage Gate after returning to London in 1966, and made contact with Bernard Stone, whose bookshop was in Kensington Church Walk.[24] Carlyle Reedy ran a poetry workshop in Notting Hill from 1967-72. David Miller, based in Colville Terrace, promoted Reedy's work and probably introduced her to Ken Edwards, who lived around Westbourne Grove in the 1970s, publishing under the imprint Share Publications.[25] Michael Horovitz was another inhabitant of Colville Terrace. Christopher Logue lived in Denbigh Close, off Portobello Road, from the 1950s through several decades. There are layers of experiment here and, aside from the historical and social dimension, of interest in itself, I have looked for techniques that are applicable in an altered context. Part of the modernist legacy involves a radical take on "aboutness", so that place operates as a sliding frame or as an element rather than the defining subject. This has proved useful for poets who engage more fully with mass culture. If Pound "trash talked London" (David Ayers' phrase),[26] and if a milieu that once spawned artistic revolt has become (re)gentrified, there are features of his "manor" – cf. urban slang sense – which remain poetically relevant.

§ § §

It is helpful to get a historical sense of the ways in which Poundian practice has been adapted or modified in Britain. Clearly, Bunting was the major figure who preserved and developed Pound's ideas of form. The older poet particularly admired his "eye for detail".[27] Bunting proved a crucial link with writers such as Tom Pickard and Barry MacSweeney who emerged in the 1960s. Despite a ritualistic formality in performance, he was approachable, ready to share technical knowledge and left-wing by inclination. His influence extended into the '70s and '80s, with poets such as Richard Caddel and David Annwn seeking sound textures that are both intricate and clear. A notable gathering of those affected was the "Bunting at Eighty" celebration at University of Warwick in 1980.

Although each has an individual mode, Pound and Bunting share assumptions about poetic language: such that I cannot remember which of the two taught me the power of the active (over passive) voice and, for all the need to avoid an absolute pattern, the relative weakness of unstressed line endings. Pound's suppression of overt linkage carries through to the late modernist *Briggflatts*, which, at one level, was written as a demonstration for younger poets to read.[28] Years before, Bunting found in a dictionary the phrase Pound used as a slogan: "DICHTEN=CONDENSARE".[29] The injunction to be terse and the model of abbreviation left their mark on poets such as Pickard, and in another way upon some who have embarked (as the modernists) on long projects. But there is difference and development. One of Bunting's disagreements with Pound, that the latter tended toward reflection rather than presentation,[30] forms part of a possible revised agenda. By the same token, there has been opposition to Bunting's elaborate knitting or knotting of sounds, which is considered too far from the conversational or too purely sonic.[31]

As already implied, W.S. Graham provides an example of a poet who read Pound closely and absorbed procedures without resorting to imitation. Around 1950 he says he has "been shaken up in the last three years by study of Pound and Eliot, analysing the structure of their verse and form." Graham is impressed by their use of "different textures of thought and idiom in the same poem (like montage)".[32] Elsewhere he insists that the re-inhabiting of archaic forms must be marked by an awareness of relative context.[33] Earlier, he writes of his irritation with commentators who concentrate on the argument of Pound's *Cantos* rather than its "language apparatus".[34] In 1969, he admires the "'stepping' texture" of Pound and his "contemporary disciples", although he has reservations about "too many legs of varying numbers".[35] Graham met Pound twice at St Elizabeths in late 1951/early 52 when they "talked fairly technically, which he seemed to love."[36]

Graham had come through a neo-romantic 1940s context to a firmer, exploratory mode, as achieved in "The Nightfishing" (written 1948-49; revised 1950). Here diction and rhythm reflect Pound's reworking of older forms, for instance in "The Seafarer", while there may be a debt to *The Cantos* — as well as *Four Quartets* — in the layering pattern of overall structure. The character of the writing is, nevertheless, original. Graham continued to develop his concerns and technique through later sequences which involve interlocking parts. In grappling with language and perception, he increasingly pares down a larger scale of reference so that immediate space is the operative field. As Tony Lopez has observed, there are parallels with Beckett's late-modernist stance.[37]

Graham's last work seems to have been written in 1980; he died in 1986. As that decade progressed, he became increasingly relevant to British poets seeking an appropriate mode of expression for a changed climate: post-high modernist, post-mid-century and post-looser cultural experiment. Fittingly, as a writer preoccupied with order and flux, he is featured in Iain Sinclair's anthology, *Conductors of Chaos* (1996). Lopez, in a brief introduction, mentions Graham's impact upon Denise Riley, John Wilkinson and Kelvin Corcoran.[38] I also found Graham's fluency of tone within set structural limits a useful index of possibility.

Tom Leonard (born 1944) is a poet who might more usually be linked with William Carlos Williams. Yet, writing about W.S. Graham, particularly in relation to Beckett, he has a diversion upon Pound that suggests another line of influence on his own work:

the deliberate cultivation of the oblique: not so as to be obtuse, but because the functional basis of his art is not didactic, but musical...

the eye rests on the ideogram, and the brain is informed, not of what the ideogram "means", but that it is simply something-that-means-something-relevant, that is ancient, that is "graceful". Its function is rhythmic.

Pound's art – all this in *The Cantos* – musical in that its vitality lies in a constant play of differing registers including phoneticised American and the Latin, Greek, French etc., set within the overall patrician.[39]

Reading this, it is possible to see how the modernist "doing of voice", with parallel interest in music and dance, feeds through into contemporary performance. The epigraph to Maggie O'Sullivan's "Of Mutability" divides a line from Canto 57: "seeking a word to make/change".[40] The magical in O'Sullivan's or Geraldine Monk's work is less hermetic than it is in Pound and Yeats, and its processes are more radically inventive, yet this play of forces is related to earlier experiment.

§ § §

Geographical location is one way of grouping poets who have been inspired by Pound to develop a rhythm "which corresponds exactly to the ... shade of emotion to be expressed"[41] or in broader terms achieve "*freshness of language*".[42] Another angle would be publication contexts. An obvious example here is the cluster of poets published in *Agenda*; intermittently, *PN Review* might also be classed as sympathetic to Pound-influenced poets. A more dynamic context is the axis represented by Five Seasons Press (Hereford) and West House Books (Hay-on-Wye, then Sheffield). A common thread here is the typesetter and poet Glenn Storhaug, whose knowledge of printing relates to a sense of how poetry operates. In addition to running Five Seasons Press, he has designed and typeset much of the work published by West House Books. His method of enabling a poetry text to reach the reader is partly informed by familiarity with key modernist books. When I said that my experience of *The Cantos* could not be divorced from the setting in which I first encountered them (new Collected edition, second impression, 1968), Storhaug recalled George Barker's remark that "All poetry should be set in Bodoni."[43]

Despite this line of influence, it must be stressed that different eras demand their own forms of "making it new". The poets in this loose association have gone through phases of development, moving beyond or apart from a Poundian model. What unites them is a care with the placing of words and an engagement with historical or mythic material, shaped through current contexts. In discussing their work I shall include reference to books published by other presses such as North and South.

An interest in Chinese and Old English poetry led Glenn Storhaug to develop his own style of imagist poetics, discernible in *Sailing from Stavanger* (1975).[44] The more recent *for silver see blue* (2003) also has a central nautical theme, whereby northern and Mediterranean scenes are traversed in a difficult yet finally redemptive current. Allusions to *Pearl* and *Pericles* are intertwined with satellite-telephone instructions and other contemporary jargon. Family and personal experience is refracted through myth or historical matter, and the play of sound is defined with sculptural precision. Close description of physical objects is accompanied by zanier scanner effects. A zen-like concern with process makes for complexity and clarity. Functioning in the present, this work draws recognisably on the ideogrammic method.

Alan Halsey is a poet who has read Pound deeply over the years, attuned to the satiric and ironic within lyric folds and deep-piled historical matter. Drawing on a language well that yields a range of specialist vocabularies, he teases out the implications of discourse. Many of his texts from the 1980s, for instance, probe the working of monetarist economics, as a force that has got within nearly every system of thinking and behaviour. Halsey has written a number of book-length sequences which display affinities with the modernist long poem, primarily, perhaps, *The Cantos*. These include *Sections Drawn Across the Vortex* and *The Text of Shelley's Death*.[45] However, his lightness of touch and quick-moving strategies align him as much with the authors of *The Dunciad* and *Don Juan*. As *Lives of the Poets* shows, he is equally fascinated by neglected writers working at the margin.[46] The deployment of pieces, including collaborative work, is reminiscent of eighteenth-century miscellanies. Halsey has sought to avoid "over-preparing the event" and is reluctant to supply more than brief pointers to sources or implications. Even the longer, more ambitious projects are, as it were, de-programmed. That said, the Poundian fragment and intersection with older literature remain a reference point, as in some of Halsey's recent versions from or takes upon Classical poetry.[47] There is a continuing concern with history, particularly in modes of juxtaposition, and an inclination to focus on the jumble of things: objects in their places, often seen fleetingly or obliquely. Thus a "Dante's Barber Shop" in Sheffield becomes the context for an exploration of *De Vulgari Eloquentia*.[48]

Halsey ran the Poetry Bookshop in Hay-on-Wye for seventeen years before moving to Sheffield, where he continues to reside. He shares a geographical base with David Annwn, who, despite strong Welsh associations, has lived in Wakefield for many years. Both in linguistic texture and scope of material, Annwn's work owes a debt to Poundian procedure, although this may emerge also via David Jones and Basil Bunting. The habit of quoting and alternating Middle English and Troubadour poetry in contemporary contexts seems to have influenced poems such as "To the Makere of Plays" from *King Saturn's Book* (1987).[49] Like most poets of his generation, Annwn finds Pound's fascism and racism repugnant; yet even this can be used. Closing his *Selected* with "In Drax", he enrols Pound against E.P.'s own political and gender philosophy ("'We should be men'... Give me a new sign of beginning").[50] But it is in the longer sequences that overlays, underlays, versions, rejections, infractions of and collisions with Pound are more fully realised. This starts with "Clefs from the Deadlock Boutique" in *Danse Macabre* (1997),[51] but goes much further in the trilogy: *Turbulent / boundaries* (1999), *Blake's Kayak* (2000) and *euro6oros* (2002). Pound himself is eclectic but, by the time of that latter sequence, Annwn is pushing the manic centrally-justified line through territories unthought of in a pre-I.T. age.[52] As in *Bela Fawr's Cabaret* (2008), the esoteric jostles with street-talk and rougher business.[53]

I have collaborated with Alan Halsey and David Annwn on several books and, while our approaches are individual, there is a residual core of shared experience. We have, in different ways, absorbed and moved on from

221

a modernist dynamic that challenged a dull world but remained in thrall to other oppressive features. It would be arrogant to claim exemption from the same charge; perhaps, rather than advance, we should speak of possibilities of negotiation in a different climate. During the years since 1972, I have produced three books which could be regarded as long poems.[54] These feature repeated motifs, variations on a theme and montage technique. Effects are cumulative. Whether walked or imagined, place provides a base focus (cf. the musical term "divisions on a ground", used as a title for the penultimate poem in *Music's Duel*). The poetry is, to borrow Peter Barry's useful term, "content-specific",[55] although I have argued for a dual level of operation, whereby function and meaning are not merely dependent upon particular data.[56] Pound continues to be an important influence, both at the level of the line and the larger structural unit.

I have referred to my involvement with north-west London, not a sentimental attachment but a fact of daily existence. It runs through *Azimuth*, *Roxy*, various texts collected in *Music's Duel*, and the current project *Hariot Double*. Historical and linguistic collage recall modernist practice, with some specific parallels. T.S. Eliot told George Barker that "when he wrote *The Waste Land* he always had the seedy Praed Street area of Paddington in mind."[57] This is not far from the area I cover – with an overlay of voices – in the sequence *Southam Street*.[58] However, as Eric Mottram noted, the tonal level here has an almost documentary-like neutrality which inheres in the material;[59] no intellectual system is imposed. That may apply equally to my longer works, and it could be seen as part of a post-modernist shift.

§ § §

A key feature of Pound's practice is extensive allusion. Bunting admitted that the degree of literary reference in work by Pound, Eliot, and himself would "weigh against us as the century goes on." By contrast, Yeats' references "are those you can find in the life around you," resulting in an easier reception for the poetry as cultures shift.[60] Equally, however, Bunting insists that sheer sound will carry work such as *The Waste Land*: "the thing's a thing in itself, it doesn't need to be something else".[61]

Peter Nicholls has written acutely about the difficulty posed by Pound's use of allusion in *Hugh Selwyn Mauberley* and *The Cantos*. As he observes:

> our culture has become increasingly remote from what Pound simply assumed were the principal reference points for any thinking person – Homer, Sappho, Horace…

[But] the real problem for… new readers of *Mauberley* goes beyond one of mere reference [since]… knowledge [of figures in context] won't in itself explain the allusive habit of mind that finds it attractive to couple [names] together in this way.[62]

Citing Robert Alter's view that allusion "is not merely a device… but an essential modality of the language of literature", Nicholls argues further that the layered procedures of Eliot and Pound provide "a necessary complexity of response to modernity".[63] The essay concludes with a consideration of Susan Howe's "poetics of erasure and disfigurement" where, on the one hand, "sources live their real life only in the text" and, on the other, an "exegetical itch" is induced.[64]

There are, undoubtedly, other ways of using the "zigzag" or "labyrinthine" structures which Pound developed.[65] Robert Sheppard makes some interesting remarks about such strategies in "Poetic Sequencing and the New: *Twentieth Century Blues*".[66] Wendy Mulford writes briefly about "multi- and non-linear" texts in the "After. Word" to *Out of Everywhere*, with reference to work by, among others, Geraldine Monk and Maggie O'sullivan.[67] Younger poets in the present volume may offer further possibilities. Given the relative unfashionability of the big project, I have chosen to highlight work that, for all its ideological reorientation, is indebted to *The Cantos*. An example already cited is Robert Hampson's *Seaport*, which has a weight of public concern lacking in much poetry written today, at least in the linguistically innovative sphere. Although the focus is mainly upon one city, Liverpool, the socio-economic and political currents evoked in the poem apply broadly through space and time. Thus, in a mid-nineteenth-century context, Hampson quotes the following comment: "Both Whig and Tory governments did as little as possible,/thinking it wrong to interfere unnecessarily with trade."[68] Cue: coalition policy, 2012. Again, in an early 1980s context, a voice or graffiti scrawl asks: "*who owns the banks?*"[69] In pressure this economic narrative is reminiscent of Pound, but there is a Marxist drift to the presentation of forces and events, as in the treatment of slavery, the emigration trade and the Toxteth "riots".[70] Radicalism of perspective is embodied in the structure of the poem which, while basically chronological, twists and turns to perform a critique of exploitative control. The fact that the sequence is unfinished – of section III, only two fragments have been published – adds to its open nature.

In Hampson's provisional text – this term describing its nature as well as its current state – the reader is sharply aware of the medium of language. This results partly from variation in form (long stepped and dispersed lines as against one or two-word columns),[71] but also from a spinning scale of reference. The issue of expression and how to hold material in focus is foregrounded in "The Chart",[72] which responds to *Moby-Dick* via Olson's *Call Me Ishmael*. A consideration of Melville's prose structures, and the encyclopaedic aspect of the chapter on Whales, has implicit relevance to Hampson's analytical and descriptive procedures. This process balances weight of "matter" with fluency of perception, allowing accident to cohere and enabling discovery.

Eric Mottram sums up Pound's limitations by remarking that "He cannot reach beyond totalization into its necessary critique".[73] The challenge that contemporary poets face is to match Pound's acuteness of ear and depth of cultural vision, while not imposing an extraneous order. Mottram cites Derrida's argument that "the nature of the field... excludes totalization... [because] there is always more."[74] One could argue that, after Ashbery et al, the sense of that field as play has gone so far that a tangible relevance should be recovered, not as separable "subject-matter" but as active process. This need not involve a reversion to received, uniform or absolute "meaning"; nor does it necessarily pull the linguistic/contextual back to the representational. Many of the texts mentioned above show that there are de-centred ways of treating a range of materials and, *through* poetic language, possibilities for complex engagement.

Notes

[1] "The Resuscitator as a Young Volcano", www.stridemagazine.co.uk, Jan, 2008.

[2] "A Retrospect", in T.S. Eliot ed., *Literary Essays of Ezra Pound* (London: Faber, 1954), 4, 7.

[3] Letter to Harriet Monroe, January 1915; D.D. Paige ed., *Selected Letters of Ezra Pound* (London: Faber, 1950), 48-49.

[4] www.archiveofthenow.org; Gavin Selerie, *Music's Duel: New and Selected Poems 1972-2008* (Exeter: Shearsman Books, 2009), 301.

[5] William Cookson ed., *Ezra Pound: Selected Prose 1909-1965* (London: Faber, 1973), 432.

[6] Having heard a singer perform "The Song of Wandering Aengus" in the mid-1960s, I acquired Yeats' *Collected Poems* and discovered the "Crazy Jane" sequence; I then became interested in Pound's use of the song form, along with his remarks in "The Tradition" (*Literary Essays*, 91-92) and elsewhere.

[7] "Robert Duncan's Interview" in *Unmuzzled Ox*, 4:2 (1976), 82.

[8] See, for example, Gavin Selerie ed., *The Riverside Interviews 6: Tom McGrath* (London: Binnacle Press, 1983), 83-84, 136.

[9] My contact here (c.1975) was Tony Ward, who had obtained the tapes from the University of Essex. I acquired my first Pound recording, *The World's Great Poets* vol 2

[Spoleto, 1967], around 1980. With its inclusion of Cantos 16, 49 and 115, this was equally illuminating.

[10] The link-person may have been Martin Kayman, a fellow postgraduate student at York, or Barry Miles. Mottram strongly believed in the necessity for "training" in order to gain "literary or poetic bearings". See Peterjon Skelt ed., *Prospect into Breath: Interviews with North and South Writers* (Twickenham & Wakefield: North and South, 1991), 29 and elsewhere. Mottram told me, in conversation, that "the reader has a responsibility to inform himself" of the process and reference-field which a poem uses, directly or implicitly.

[11] Presley discusses the impact of Pound upon her work in Peterjon Skelt ed., *Prospect into Breath: Interviews with North and South Writers*, 124-27. Her text "The Ezra Pound Papers" (1976) is in *The Sex of Art: Selected Poems and Prose 1973-1986* (Twickenham & Wakefield: North and South, 1987), 23-25.

[12] "Working Processes of a Woman Poet" in Denise Riley ed., *Poets on Writing: Britain, 1970-1991* (London: Macmillan, 1992), 262.

[13] See chapter 6 of Davie, *Ezra Pound: Poet as Sculptor* (London: Routledge & Kegan Paul, 1964), some pages of which "derive immediately from conversations with J.H. Prynne" (vi); this is probably the section on the breaking down of the line, accentuated by typographical layout (112-19).

[14] *Poetic Artifice* (Manchester: Manchester University Press, 1978), chapter 3. See also Forrest-Thomson's "In Memoriam Ezra Pound", from *Collected Poems and Translations* (Lewes: Allardyce, Barnett, 1990), 82-83.

[15] Quoted by Gavin Selerie, "A Letter from London" [May, 1985], in *North Dakota Quarterly*, 54:4 (Fall 1986), 130.

[16] See Charles Bernstein, "Undone Business" [pub. 1984] in *Content's Dream* (Los Angeles, CA: Sun & Moon Press, 1986), 333; and Bob Perelman, *The Marginalization of Poetry* (Princeton, NJ: Princeton University Press, 1996), 43 – a section which draws upon Robert Grenier's "On Speech" (1971) and ideas from Ron Silliman's "The New Sentence" (1979). Silliman's anthology *In the American Tree* (Orono, ME: National Poetry Foundation, 1986) exercised a considerable influence upon certain UK poets.

[17] *Place* (Hastings: Reality Street Editions, 2005); *Brixton Fractals* republished in *Gravity* (Cambridge: Salt Publishing, 2004). See also the note on Fisher in Adrian Clarke & Robert Sheppard eds., *Floating Capital: new poets from London* (Elmwood, CT: Potes & Poets Press. 1991), 122. The editors' concern over the fetishisation of place is perhaps anticipated, if obliquely, in a letter from J.H. Prynne to Olson (28 September, 1962). Prynne explains that he has passed through Gloucester but did not stop, on account of "a cordial dislike of [its] visible surface" (Box 173, Charles Olson Research Collection, University of Connecticut).

[18] "Maximus to Gloucester, Letter 27 [withheld]", in George Butterick ed., *The Maximus Poems* (Berkeley & Los Angeles, CA: University of California Press, 1983), 184.

[19] Pound remembered the district, wittily abbreviated to "KENS", as "SWARming" with writers and intellectuals (letters to Patricia Hutchins, 1956-58, quoted in her *Ezra Pound's Kensington: an Exploration 1885-1913* [London: Faber, 1965], 22, 71). Hutchins herself lived here in the 1940s and 1950s.

[20] *Bohemia in London: The Social Scene of Early Modernism* (London: Palgrave Macmillan, 2007), 63. The "bourgeois" tag is valid for Pound's immediate vicinity.

[21] See Lewis' footnote in Paul Edwards ed., *Rotting Hill* (Santa Barbara, CA: Black Sparrow Press, 1986), 95, and the editor's comment, 290. Pound's phrase, "amid the dry knot of rotting hill" occurs in a letter of 3 February, 1948 (Timothy Materer ed., *Pound/Lewis: The Letters of Ezra Pound and Wyndham Lewis* [New York, NY: New Directions, 1985], 239).

[22] On the latter period, see Rupert Loydell's remarks in "Even the Bad Times are Good: Rupert Loydell & Robert Sheppard", www.stridemagazine.co.uk, Jan, 2012.

[23] "'And now, why?': London Ghosts and their Haunts", forthcoming in Walter Baumann & William Pratt eds., *New Essays on Ezra Pound and His World* (New York, NY: AMS).

[24] See Peterjon Skelt ed., *Prospect into Breath: Interviews with North and South Writers*, 16.

[25] Robert Hampson, based in North London, was in regular touch with both Miller and Edwards, visiting them in Notting Hill; partly out of this association came the magazine *Alembic* (1973-79), edited by Edwards, Hampson and Peter Barry.

[26] Made in a response at the closing plenary session, "Ezra Pound and London" conference, University of London, 9 July, 2011.

[27] Pound's comment is relayed in a letter from Bunting to Tom Pickard, 4 October, 1970; quoted in Peter Makin, *Bunting: The Shaping of His Verse* (Oxford: Clarendon Press, 1992), 325.

[28] Specifically Tom Pickard and Gael Turnbull. See Bunting, letter to Dorothy Pound, 11 June, 1965; quoted in Peter Makin, op. cit., 124. The notebook manuscript of *Briggflatts*, which Bunting gave to Pickard, is in the Poetry Collection, SUNY Buffalo. This draft contains much that was removed in the published text.

[29] *ABC of Reading* (London: Routledge, 1934), 77.

[30] Letter from Bunting to Pound, 4 January, 1936; quoted in Peter Makin, *Bunting: The Shaping of his Verse*, 76-77. I absorbed the gist of this argument around 1980, via Bunting himself or Tom Pickard.

[31] See, for instance, Frances Presley's comments in David Annwn, "Her Pulse Their Pace: Women Poets and Basil Bunting" in James McGonigal & Richard Price eds., *The Star You Steer By: Basil Bunting & British Modernism* (Amsterdam: Editions Rodopi B.V., 2000), 141. Presley felt that these remarks were taken slightly out of context and clarified her critique, with emphasis on gender, in a review of *Briggflatts*; *Poetry Wales* 45: 3 (Winter 2009/10), 59-60.

[32] Letter to Edwin Morgan (undated), in Michael & Margaret Snow eds., *The Nightfisherman: Selected Letters of W.S. Graham* (Manchester: Carcanet Press, 1999), 118

[33] Letter to Robin Skelton (31 January, 1957), in *The Nightfisherman: Selected Letters of W.S. Graham*, 157; cf. 95.

[34] "From a 1949 Notebook given to Elizabeth Smart", in *Edinburgh Review* 75 (1987), 25.

[35] Letter to William Montgomerie (24 September, 1969), in *The Nightfisherman: Selected Letters of W.S. Graham*, 230.

[36] Letters to Elizabeth Smart (26 November, 1951 and 17 January, 1952) in *The Nightfisherman: Selected Letters of W.S. Graham*, 133-34.

[37] The Poetry of W.S. Graham (Edinburgh: Edinburgh University Press, 1989), 127.

[38] *Conductors of Chaos: a Poetry Anthology* (London: Picador, 1996), 211.

[39] "Journeys" in *Edinburgh Review* 75 (1987), 85.

[40] *In the House of the Shaman* (London & Cambridge: Reality Street, 1993), 35.

[41] Ezra Pound, "A Retrospect", in *Literary Essays*, 9; section originally published as "Prolegomena" (1912).

[42] *Writers at Work: The* Paris Review *Interviews* (Harmondsworth: Penguin Books, 1972), 97.

[43] I have not been able to trace the source of this comment, but the setting of Barker's own books confirms the preference.

[44] *Sailing from Stavanger* (Oxford: Evenlode Press, 1975).

[45] *Sections Drawn Across the Vortex* (Hay-on-Wye: Binnacle, 1996); *The Text of Shelley's Death* (Hereford: Five Seasons Press, 1995). Halsey discusses the impact of Pound on some of his earlier work in an interview, "Words Caught on the Run", *Colorado Review* 24: 1 (Spring 1997), 161-72.

[46] *Lives of the Poets* (Hereford: Five Seasons Press, 2009); additional "Lives" appear in *Even if only out of* (London: Veer Books, 2011), 59-63.

[47] See *Term as in Aftermath* (Toronto/Tokyo: Ahadada Books, 2009) and *Even if only out of* (2011). It is also worth noting the influence of the Stone Text rubbings from Pound's *Confucius* on Halsey's graphics – an area that has been little covered in discussion of his work.

[48] *Marginalien* (Hereford: Five Seasons Press, 2005), 283-321.

[49] *King Saturn's Book* (London & Wakefield: North and South, 1987), section XVIII.

[50] *The Spirit/That Kiss: New and Selected Poems* (Twickenham & Wakefield: North and South, 1993), 67.

[51] David Annwn, Kelvin Corcoran, Alan Halsey and Gavin Selerie, *Danse Macabre* (Wakefield & Sheffield: Ispress and West House Books, 1997), 31-37.

[52] *Turbulent/boundaries* (Sheffield: West House Books, 1999); *Blake's Kayak* (Wakefield: Ispress, 2000); *euro6oros* (Wakefield: Ispress, 2002).

[53] *Bela Fawr's Cabaret* (Sheffield & Toronto: West House and Ahadada Books, 2008).

[54] *Azimuth* (London: Binnacle Press, 1984); *Roxy* (Hay-on-Wye: West House Books, 1996); and *Le Fanu's Ghost* (Hereford: Five Seasons Press, 2006). The last work, perhaps, explodes the genre; yet key aspects remain operative.

[55] Robert Hampson & Peter Barry eds., *New British poetries: the scope of the possible* (Manchester University Press, 1993), 211-12.

[56] *Backstory: the Making of Roxy* (1997; rev. 2000), 12; *Music's Duel*, 324. Robert Hampson engages with this issue, comparing the terms "float perception" (Allen Fisher) and "ambient significance" (Eric Mottram), in "cris cheek in Manhattan", www.pores.bbk.ac.uk/1.

[57] Bookride.com, 29.10.2007. Paddington is classified as part of north-west London in Pevsner's *The Buildings of England* series.

[58] *Southam Street* (London: New River Project, 1991); written 1985-86 and reprinted in *Music's Duel*.

[59] Letter to the author, 16 October, 1991; another letter of 1st February, 1992, referring to *Tilting Square*, speaks of "performance" which is "tactful rather than insistent".

[60] "A Conversation with Basil Bunting", in *Poetry Information* 19 (Autumn 1978), 40.

[61] "Basil Bunting: The Last Interview", in *Bête Noir* 2/3 (Spring 1987), 41.

[62] "The Elusive Allusion: Poetry and Exegesis", in Peter Middleton & Nicky Marsh eds.,

Teaching Modernist Poetry (Basingstoke: Palgrave Macmillan, 2010), 10-11.

[63] ibid., 12, 15.

[64] ibid., 21-22.

[65] These terms are taken from Guy Davenport, *The Geography of the Imagination* (London: Picador, 1984), 56.

[66] *The Why Project* (Portland, OR: Anabasis, 1992).

[67] Maggie O'Sullivan ed., *Out of Everywhere* (London: Reality Street Editions, 1996), 239-42.

[68] *Seaport* (Exeter: Shearsman Books, 2008), 29. The work was written in the late 1970s/early 1980s.

[69] ibid., 64; cf. Allen Ginsberg on Pound's view of the money system in Gordon Ball ed., *Allen Verbatim: Lectures on Poetry, Politics, Consciousness* (New York, NY: McGraw-Hill, 1974), 173-77.

[70] In considering this reversal of political bias, it is helpful to remember that Christine Brooke-Rose found affinities between Pound's and Marx's economic pronouncements. See *A ZBC of Ezra Pound* (Berkeley & Los Angeles, CA: University of California Press, 1971), 232-36.

[71] See, for instance, the opening pages of Part IV (*Seaport*, 47-50).

[72] *Seaport*, 33-34. This piece leads into Melville/Liverpool matter, based on Redburn and background biographical detail.

[73] "Man Under Fortune: Bases for Ezra Pound's Poetry", in R.W. Butterfield ed., *Modern American Poetry* (London: Vision Press, 1984), 90.

[74] ibid., 90-91. The quotation is from Derrida, *Writing and Difference*, 289.

Gavin Selerie

FROM *HARIOT DOUBLE*

Remember, Remember

A rider with a red beard
from the North (a lie)

> dust in the courtyard

> conference aside
> (*sawsed mee with a Gudgeon*)

> then to dinner
> with company enough

Lower, Hariot, Torperley
spoke of the stars & channels

Captain Whitlocke, the young Lord
fooled with spoons

Cosin Thomas, casually here
asked *what newes of the parlemente?*
(a bayte to discover
what matter has seeped)

> he not collecting rents
> but under this noble name
> leasing a cellar
> for fuel

we may not know what we know
(*best witchcraft is Geometrie*)

lines cut crosswise
make their match angles equal

and the go-on says
reasons fit, *of which of whether*

    a pumpkin slit
    is a forked flash

Syon, the fourth of November last,
smudged dots between two half-circles:
to have been there is enough,
a body stuffed in a bottle
with the cork rammed home

Seal up *Master Herriotts studie door & chests*

To fling a figure of a king's life
makes he (the doer) *a funeral beaste*

Lord in limbo

Questions, have we enough
from a trail of gunpowder: as quho
caste the King's nativity—combust
in the ascendant, a human signe
joyn'd to the taile of the Dragon—
and if ever milorde did affirme
he would take the Catholicques part.

Ther was a discourse
but he remembreth not particulars.

Some jealous quipster breathes a name.
The court glowes like rotten wood
which beetles bore unseen.

How whispers make halberds.
Any spiall of purpose gives entercourse
with actors lined in a cupboard.
To dispell this scent you'd need go
to the Chilterne Hilles.

Rawleigh, 'father of wiles', is caged already.
Two roomes in the Bloody Towre
with a door open to the garden.

A barge brings Percy, shoots beneath
the arch to slipp'ry steps, *don't stride*
too short into the water. By iron tread
he's gated as a friend, behind portcullis teeth
and a rampart—that *gallery*
noisome with savour of ditches.

Next, by persuasion, Martin Towre,
over against the Mount. No river view
through window bars in thick walls.
'Boullen' carved in stone
beneath a rose. What you may learn
out of the grate.

Why Martin? At th'east ende,
a name transferred from another tower.
Bird or man who dwells aloft,
migrant to strait quarters.

The first comminge is full of passion
from wharfe to vault,
a duskish cylindre through infinite space:
the plotte which holds
a file of ancestors, a father's bones.

Your Majestie, that is soe greate a Scholler
cannot but know how impossible it is
to prove a negative.

It were fair walking on the leads. Turne
from Ordnance roofs, cannonball pyramids,
a pen of ample state, to hamlets & fields
over the moat—the Minories, East Smithfield,
greene out to Epping and Essex.

A pegg in a hole for everie span
of this pavement.

You can eyelet the breast, fitte the will
to its lodging, scan what's brittle
in baffled glory. So castell'd
a league from tottering favor,
you may this lot inlarge, chyl-cold
to extirpe anie care.

The Three Magi

It's a fine tale, *Heriot, Hues & Warner*
round a table in the Tower
at the earle's chardge, so they might *converse*
singly or together, as Sir *Walter* did. These
and *Nath. Torperley*, forming *an academy*
in prison.

From charts obscure
the *Atlantes* of the Mathematic world
talk seeds, spots
at the heart of a land
where you cannot freely philosophize.

Brasen spheres and a skull cleaved
to get the working clear

       tentare, tendere—
       feel, try, tempt

       a stretch
       into
       mist

School of spirits summoned
for deepe searching
in cob-castle.

Wallis has it from Wood
who fixes it (enlarged) from Aubrey
who spins it (gossipy) from Pell and writer anon.
who gets the germ (perhaps) from Dr R[h]ead,
Hariot's last physician:
Chirurgicall Lectures of Tumors & Ulcers (1635).

If there was a *handsome table*, these men
came severally at intervals.
But truth tips (like theirs) a *gyddie platt*:

this world, its parts runne
as an old shippe that has had
all or most of her peeces changed.

For a *wardour's* trick in the yard
(nightwatch)
magick at the smallest jarre
drifts down

flames crackle, wheels whir,
lips murmur or hum

Some calculator sees his shadow—
one's carried a boatload of fusty books,
found a skeleton grasping an howre-glass
on his Lo.'s Turkey carpet,
marked the face of a tapestry
breathing on stone.

Sixteen years to probe, the life restrained
is a walker of peaks and streams
whose *black velvet gowne* is *laced with gold*.
None who *might* steps beyond,
as a *sonne dyall* on the south wall
declares.

Just say these fellows
are points on a board, touching
when the moment allows.
Out of a slashed nought, *north* driven
the brain yaws
to measure and explain.

David Vichnar

P. S.: Pound and Sinclair's Intertextual Ley Lines

1. As Pound noted in his portrait of the artist as an ironic man, the demand of the twelve years that had come to constitute his London "age" was first and foremost that of the "image." *Hugh Selwyn Mauberley* surveys his 1908-1920 London period, employing his Imagist/Vorticist techniques, yet is marked by a sense that, like the era, so the techniques are exhausted, over, ready to be metamorphosed. Parallels with Joyce's 1904-1915 Triestine exile abound: both were periods of aesthetic programmatics, of initially modest writerly successes met with immodest critical hostility, of frustrating journeys back home which only underscored the growing sense of alienation. Both Pound and Joyce had arrived in their cities of exile at the age of twenty-two, both with the aspiration of becoming poets (which Joyce, of course, was wise enough to abandon soon and Pound wise enough to stick to), and neither left until they'd made their breakthrough – Joyce having published, at long last, *Dubliners* and embarked upon the serialisation of *A Portrait of the Artist as a Young Man* (on Pound's insistence, in Harriet Shaw Weaver's *The Egoist*), Pound having passed through his Imagist and Vorticist periods and already commenced his lifelong *Cantos* project. Both of their first exilic sojourns drew quickly to their closes (Joyce was left jobless and deserted after all of his pupils were conscripted during the First World War, while Pound found himself bemoaning the "botched civilisation" of London during the Post-World War I period and soon left), and finished with a tone of disgust in their writing: Joyce through Stephen Dedalus and Pound through Mauberley, both exorcising their Aesthetic propensies and ironising their fictional past selves. Although they were both to explicitly draw lines under their pasts, and both would exchange their first exiles for Paris (Pound directly from London, Joyce via Zurich), it is undeniable that both Trieste and London were to leave indelible traces on their lives and writing. During his penultimate brief sojourn back to his dear dirty Dublin in 1909, Joyce writes to his partner Nora: "Why is it I am destined to look so many times in my life with eyes of longing on Trieste?"[1] and as late as a 1932 he includes a passage in "Work in Progress" that has his "altered ego" Shem recall his Triestine descent into alcoholism with peculiar nostalgia: "And trieste, ah trieste ate I my liver!"[2] Pound is even less ambiguous; again in 1909 he writes to his college friend William Carlos Williams: "London, deah old Lundon, is the place for poesy."[3] And as late as *The Pisan Cantos*, written almost three

decades, in 1945, after the fact, Pound recalls, as well as many other London experiences, his first lodgings near the British Museum, across an alley from the Yorkshire Grey pub and the "old Kait' [...] stewing with rage / concerning the landlady's doings / with a lodger unnamed / az waz near Gt Titchfield St. next door to the pub / 'married wumman, you couldn't fool her'" (Canto LXXX).[4]

The point of these parallels is, of course, to underscore their haphazardness. One might rewrite the paragraph above replacing every Pound/Joyce analogy with an equally valid instance of difference between the two. The point is also that these parallels are willed links imposing a pattern of order upon the chaos, vicissitude and randomness that is human life. Finally, the point is that however subjective and arbitrary, such links produce poetic energy, and bestow a meaning, if not sense; meaning as such arises only out of such links and patterns, and outside the wilful impositions and biases of human sense-making lies the unthinkable, un(re)presentable. Such is, at least, the strong belief of the master parallelist and the subject proper of this brief comparative piece, Iain Sinclair. Such is, also, the underlying belief of this essay – that there is a line of energy streaming from Pound to Sinclair, a fundamental affinity between their poetical projects. Between the "pedagogical" genealogy of Pound's *Cantos*, composed of a multilingual, broadly intertextual corpus of (non)literary texts aiming to encompass the history of socio-cultural development in both the East and the West, and Sinclair's "psycho-geography" as recorded in both his poetry and prose, which consists of the reading of urban space and architecture as palimpsests of their various pasts and presents, thereby archiving their past development – both historical and fictional – and recording, re-presenting, their present effects upon the recipient psyche of the observer. The affinity, it will be shown, lies in Sinclair's insistence on radical metaphor and on direct juxtaposition of disparate ideas and images. A closer reading of a passage from his *Suicide Bridge* will reveal a debt readily acknowledged to Pound, the source of these techniques.

2. Again, biographical parallels between Sinclair and Pound abound, but touches upon just two will serve here. Sinclair, too, chose London for a self-willed exile, as the ultimate and permanent stage of his development from his early childhood in Cardiff via college years at the Dublin Trinity. His choice of London comes from within a consciously assumed literary paradigm; here is Sinclair reminiscing, in 2003, about his college years in Dublin:

Dylan Thomas was the model, in a sense – not knowing exactly how the story went, but knowing that he'd got away to London, and that was what you had to do. [...] My twin passions, really, were poetry and cinema. Dylan Thomas was the initial model, but I soon moved on to Eliot, Pound, Hitchcock, Buñuel, Orson Welles.[5]

Secondly, before becoming a literary persona, establishing himself, according to one critic, as "one of the most important contemporary writers on London,"[6] or, according to another, as "our major poetic celebrant of the city's hidden experience, its myths and subcultures,"[7] Sinclair – like Pound over sixty years before him with *A Lume Spento* (1908) – engaged in the modernist practice of self-publication, founding his Albion Village Press to publish his *Lud Heat* (1975) and *Suicide Bridge* (1979), collage texts of essay, fiction, and poetry; the texts, for obvious reason, under focus here.

Already in his 1975 poem *Lud Heat*, subtitled *A Book of the Dead Hamlets*, Sinclair launches his life-long "psycho-geographic" project of a cognitive mapping of the psychological effects produced on the perceptive human consciousness by physical environments. The two axes delineating this mapping are the Sinclair's experiences as an assistant gardener with the Parks Department of an East London borough, and the "sacred landscape" delineated by the churches of Nicholas Hawksmoor. "The most notable thing that struck me as I walked across this landscape for the first time," he recalls in conversation with Kevin Jackson, "were these run-down churches, and I suddenly realised, there's this one here and that one there, and maybe there is some connection. And then I did have this very vivid dream of St Anne's, Limehouse…" (*The Verbals*, 98). One is struck, in turn: "a vivid dream"? "Maybe some connection"? More often than not, Sinclair's progression in his cognitive mapping is one of "that was my hunch: confirmation followed" (*Lud Heat*, 28). In this, as in much else, Sinclair consciously positions himself as heir to the ancient Celtic tradition of the poet as soothsayer, of the bard whose word, governed by prophetic intuition, has the power to alter reality. As he confided to Jackson:

> By nature and temperament I'm absolutely one of those mad Welsh preachers who believes that… deliver a speech and you'll change someone's life. Or kill them. I really believe all that, but I can't go around spouting that and survive, so I'll adapt equally to the Scottish side of me, which is cynical, rational and cynical, and I believe in that as well. [...] It's Stevenson, the classic Scottish Jekyll and Hyde thing. One is really deranged and manic, the other is looking at it being deranged and manic, and commenting on it. That's the tension. (*Verbals*, 59)

Sinclair's walk around Hawksmoor's London churches in *Lud Heat* reveals a "web printed on the city and disguised with multiple superimpositions," a web "too complex to unravel here, the information too dense: we can only touch on a fraction of the possible relations. [...] It is enough to sketch the possibilities."[8] Drawing upon Alfred Watkins' theory of the ley line, according to which the ancient sites in England and Wales are aligned with one another in a network of straight routes of communication, Sinclair creates willed ley lines across a chosen area (in *Lud Heat*, this produces a "hieratic map" of London), which generate a wealth of occult materials in his texts for Sinclair to carefully counterpoint with local, matter-of-fact accounts.

That the ley line is one of Sinclair's signature tropes has been amply demonstrated in the many prose works that followed *Lud Heat* and *Suicide Bridge*. Here, three examples will suffice. His 1997 *Lights Out for the Territory*, a collection of nine loosely collected perambulatory pieces, describing lighting out for various London nooks both familiar and unfamiliar, forgotten and re-remembered. As Sinclair himself reveals halfway through, the seemingly random extravagations actually serve a specific purpose – his writerly project of map inscription:

> Each essay so far written for this book can be assigned one letter of the alphabet. Obviously, the first two pieces go together, the journey from Abney Park to Chingford Mount: V. The circling of the City: O. The history of Vale Royal, its poet and publisher: an X on the map: VOX. The unheard voice is always present in the darkness.[9]

Revisiting his ley-line approach as late as the opening of his 2001 novel, *Landor's Tower* – in which the story of a historical figure, Walter Savage Landor, is interwoven with Sinclair's frustrated attempts to write a book about Landor, along with a subplot about booksellers hunting for rare editions – Sinclair encapsulates Watkins' lesson in the following formula: "everything connects and, in making those connections, streams of energy are activated."[10] Later, Sinclair makes it explicit that his use of Watkins' psycho-geographical concept is a means to an aesthetic end steeped in modernist poetics of juxtaposition and collage:

> All of it to be digested, absorbed, fed into the great work. Wasn't that the essence of the modernist contract? Multi-voiced lyric seizures countered by drifts of unadorned fact, naked source material spliced into domesticated trivia, anecdotes, borrowings, found footage. Redundant. As much use as a whale carved from margarine,

unless there is intervention by that other; unless some unpredicted element takes control, overrides the pre-planned structure, tells you what you don't know. Willed possession. (*Landor's Tower*, 31)

A recent and compelling example of semi-non-fictional accounts of Sinclair's voyages outside of London is his 2005 *Edge of the Orison*, which, encompassing the genres of memoir, biography, art theory and literary criticism, follows the journey of the poet John Clare, who, in 1841, having escaped from a lunatic asylum in Epping Forest, walked for three days to his home in Helpston, (then) Northamptonshire, some eighty miles away. In obeisance to his aesthetics of free association and imagist juxtaposition, Sinclair uses the fact that Clare spent his last years at the Northampton asylum, and the coincidence that his journey to Helpston took place in pursuit of his first love, a certain Mary Joyce, to draw a ley line between his central quest and the chronicling of Lucia Joyce's institutionalisation at the same venue, 110 years later. Enough material for Sinclair's mind to begin its connect-work:

> What happened to Lucia Joyce in Northampton? Can her silence be set against Clare's painful and garrulous exile? Visitors came to the hospital to pay their respects, to report on the poet's health. Biographers of Lucia cut out, abruptly, after she steps into the car at Ruislip and drives north, never to return.[11]

According to this logic, Joyce surfaces in Sinclair's musings at the most unexpected instances. For example, upon pondering the river Lea, Sinclair's mind makes the sudden Imagist switch to:

> Djuna Barnes, profiling James Joyce, zoomed in on his "spoilt and appropriate" teeth. And that is this stretch of the Lea, precisely: spoilt and appropriate. Hissing trains. Occasional apologetic herons (all spindle and no heft) tipping out of dead trees like faultily assembled kites. Nothing spectacular, nothing to stop your advance on Broxbourne. "Writers," Joyce told Barnes, "should never write about the extraordinary, that is for the journalist." But already, she was nodding off. "He drifts from one subject to the other, making no definite division." (*Edge of the Orison*, 141-2)

Finally, towards the end of the journey, Sinclair pays his respects to Lucia when passing Kingsthorpe Cemetery. Ever on the lookout for the aleatory epiphany, before making the turn, "up the slope to where Lucia is buried, I find a nice marker, the grave of a certain Finnegan" (*Edge of the Orison*, 347).

3. It now remains for me to bring to light some of the ley-lines between Sinclair's psycho-geographic aesthetics and Pound's Imagist project developed into the "profounder didacticism" of *The Cantos* working through "revelation."[12] Whether one takes the young 1913 Pound by his word that image is "that which presents an intellectual and emotional complex in an instant of time,"[13] or gives more credence to the post-Imagist Pound of a 1916 letter to Iris Barry, wherein he associates Imagism with "the actual necessity for creating or constructing something; of presenting an image, or enough images of concrete things arranged to stir the reader,"[14] Sinclair's divinatory project of decoding, transcribing, and re-presenting (i.e. making present again) the occult cultural memory of a landscape fits both bills. As Robert Sheppard acutely observed, *Landor's Tower*'s self-description as a record of "multi-voiced, lyric seizures countered by drifts of unadorned fact, naked source material spliced into domesticated trivia, anecdotes, borrowings, found footage" (31), actually seems to describe Sinclair's *Lud Heat* as well as "a work like Pound's *Cantos*":

> Pound's technique of modernist juxtaposition and the ideogrammic method of *The Cantos* can be read as a literary equivalent of the ley line. Pound states that the juxtaposition of elements without syntactic linkage, by simple contiguous arrangement [...] creates new combinations.[15]

Interestingly, when speaking of the genesis of *Lud Heat*, Sinclair himself, although not invoking Pound directly, likens its composition to "cutting" down and through a "huge *Waste Land* collage" – a metaphorical parallel to Pound's real-life creative activity:

> because I started on mock-epic forms, like the huge *Waste Land* collage poem at film school, and I'd written some things in Dublin which were on a large scale, and I weeded all that out. Cut, cut, cut, till I was happiest with these small, fragmentary forms. That seemed to suit the pace of the life. Film-making was exactly the same: single frame, just click click click click... Getting everything down in a very sharp way. Writing and film were part of the same thing. [...] I wanted to move [...] to a more narrative base, a sense of a man in the world, and what happens in this room, it's all right in front of your nose. And then I moved back from that, later, into the London mythology.[16]

However, one need not settle for such metaphoric and indirect confirmations of one's hunch – nor for one of the section subtitles, "Vortex of the Dead! The Generous!" (*Lud Heat*, 96), which cannot be regarded as a solid, unequivocal intertextual line between the two. The confirmation, as always with Sinclair, comes later, in the twin-piece of *Lud Heat*. *Suicide Bridge*, which is subtitled *A Book of the Furies/A Mythology of South & East* and which, even though published only in 1979, was created simultaneously with its precursor. Its cognate character is evident both formally (a collage text of essayist prose, maps and free verse) as well as thematically: *Suicide Bridge* covers much of the same ground as *Lud Heat*, but here the mythological strata are clearly foregrounded and multiplied. The London landscape becomes peopled with Egyptian deities, kabbalistic symbols, characters from the Blakean "Albion" mythology, pop-cult figures Aleister Crowley, Howard Hughes, or JFK, but also host of 1960s counter-cultural icons: Wilhelm Reich, William Burroughs, Norman O. Brown, the Situationist International. The approach to this welter of information, again, is one of evaluative decoding based on the energy emitted (or, "admitted") by the system:

> An impenetrable maze of statistics, lost in space & time; dead ends, false corridors, pits, traps. All that matters is the energy the structure admits. Can it heat us? Is it active? Or simply a disguise for the lead sheet imprisoning the consciousness of the planet; the gas of oppression, the burnt-out brain cells, milk-centred eyes. (*Suicide Bridge*, 241)

One of the more energetically rewarding burnings-out of brain cells has taken place earlier on in the text. In the "Kotope: Down the Clerkenwell Corridor" segment, the link sought is one between Pound and the Cathars. To that end, the ancient practice of bibliomancy – of divination in which advice or predictions of the future are sought by random selection of a passage (usually from a sacred text) – is invoked, and the revelation is the following:

> no reference Davie (*Ezra Pound: Poet As Sculptor*)
> no reference Dekker (*Sailing After Knowledge*)
> must be Kenner, no alternative,
> flip open the great black book itself
> & immediately confront:
>
> "O Anubis, guard this portal
> as the cellula, Mont Ségur.

Sanctus
that no blood sully this altar"

Kotope is not amazed, that smile,
the head turning,
minions have to react: awe
a magician,
this is it, & Anubis too
the jackal-headed one,
guardian of the mysteries
so lightly approached
(*Suicide Bridge* 178)

The passage quoted is, of course, 'Canto XCII' of the *Rock-Drill* section of *The Cantos*, devoted to charting the genealogy of the "true" religious tradition, i.e. the Neoplatonic alternative to mainstream Christianity, bridging the millennium of the Dark Ages and connecting together Antiquity with Early Modern period. The question, as always, for Sinclair, is that of interpretation of the discovery:

for Wilson a simple matter:
mind discovering its power potential,
what you need you get;
for Kotope, the Way

"The four altars at the four coigns of that place,
But in the great love, bewildered
farfalla in tempest
under rain in the dark"

for the servants a Master
                    rediscovered
we must begin again: ROCK-DRILL
(*Suicide Bridge* 179)

4. "A Master rediscovered" – the final confirmation of the validity of the hunches that motivated the writing of this comparative piece. There is, however, the ultimately more relevant aesthetic affinity between Pound and Sinclair that lies deeper than intertextual linkage or acknowledged succession. Sinclair's oeuvre as a whole grows out of an awareness of the interrelatedness

between the forms and rhythms of poetry and prose. And if Sinclair (after the decade-long hiatus that followed *Lud Heat* and *Suicide Bridge*) turns to the prose medium and novel genre proper, revisiting poetry only sporadically (most recently, in his 2006 collection, *Buried at Sea*), his prose – according to the consensus among the many of his critics – is endowed with the richness, polyvalence and complexity usually described as "poetic." Thereby, he follows in the footsteps of Pound's early remarks from a 1915 letter to Harriet Monroe that "poetry must be as well written as prose. Its language must be a fine language [...] There must be no interjections. No words flying off to nothing [...] Rhythm must have a meaning. It can't be merely a careless dash off [...] There must be no clichés, set phrases, stereotyped journalese."[17] Sinclair only reverses this process: writing prose as well as poetry, turning to book-length "novels" by extending the prose sections of his poetry, yet carefully eschewing any automatism, cliché, set phrase or stereotype: "making it new" with every image.

Notes

[1] James Joyce, *Selected Letters*, ed. Richard Ellmann (New York, NY: Viking Press, 1975) 191.

[2] James Joyce, *Finnegans Wake* (New York, NY and London: Faber & Faber, 1939) 301.

[3] *The Selected Letters of Ezra Pound, 1907-1941*, ed. D. D. Paige (San Diego, CA: Harcourt Brace Jovanovitch, 1950) 7.

[4] Ezra Pound, *The Cantos* (New York, NY: New Directions Books, 1996) 522.

[5] *The Verbals – Iain Sinclair in Conversation with Kevin Jackson* (Tonbridge: Worple Press, 2003) 26.

[6] Nick Bentley, "Introduction: mapping the millennium: themes and trends in contemporary British fiction," in *British Fiction of the 1990s*, ed. Nick Bentley (Oxford: Routledge. 2005)

[7] Robert Bond & Jenny Bavidge, "Introduction," *City Visions: The Work of Iain Sinclair* (Cambridge Scholars Publishing, 2007) 1.

[8] Iain Sinclair, *Lud Heat and Suicide Bridge* (London: Random House; New York: Vintage, 1995) 16-7.

[9] Iain Sinclair, *Lights Out for the Territory* (London: Granta Books, 1997) 156.

[10] Iain Sinclair, *Landor's Tower: or The Imaginary Conversations* (London: Granta Books, 2002) 2.

[11] Iain Sinclair, *Edge of the Orison: In the Traces of John Clare's Journey Out Of Essex* (London: Penguin Group, 2005) 233.

[12] *Selected Letters of Ezra Pound*, 180.

13 Ezra Pound, "A Few Don'ts by an Imagiste," *Poetry* (March, 1913). Reprinted in "A Retrospect," *Literary Essays of Ezra Pound.* ed. T.S. Eliot (New York, NY: New Directions, 1935) 3.

14 *Selected Letters of Ezra Pound*, 90.

15 Robert Sheppard, "Everything Connects: The Cultural Poetics," *City Visions*, 34.

16 *Verbals*, 87.

17 *The Selected Letters of Ezra Pound*, 48-9.

Harry Gilonis

SECOND HEAVE – FRACTURE SYNTAX

My contribution to this book is a group of poems, and it would be hardly genre-specific to burden them with a hefty scholarly apparatus. They come from a bigger project of mine entitled *North Hills*, comprising 'faithless' versions of Chinese originals. Their willed lack of fidelity is not whimsical, but rather an attempt to get closer, paradoxically, to the spirit of their originals than traditional translations usually do. Pleasingly, Pound himself provides a clear precedent, in the end-note to the first edition of *Cathay* in which he refers to Ernest Fenollosa's papers, his source-material for that book: "I find [here] a perfect speech in a literality which will be to many most unacceptable. The couplet is as follows: 'Drawing sword, cut into water, water again flows: / Raise cup, quench sorrow, sorrow again sorry.'"[1]

There is not space to go into the matter properly here, but suffice it to say that in some regards both Fenollosa and Pound were importantly on the right track. Classical poetic Chinese very often suppresses many of the parts of speech which modify by adding specificities (number, gender, tense, mood); the original texts are in effect 'lattices' which an informed and competent reader would flesh out; possibly – and entirely licitly – differently on each re-reading. Wai-Lim Yip, in his book on *Cathay*, writes of "the special mode of representation of reality constituted or made possible by the peculiarity of the Chinese language itself".[2] What I have tried to do with the *North Hills* poems is to enact some of these (traditionally untranslatable) features of the Chinese originals; hence, traditional Western translational fidelity isn't appropriate in this context.[3] I should perhaps say that there is a direct parallel with Pound, in that these poems come out of a close and long-standing engagement with Chinese poetry, but *not* out of Sinological expertise.[4]

My poems herein have widely-differing differing ways and degrees to which they modulate both their responses to the Chinese originals *and* to versions of those made by Ezra Pound (in *Cathay* and *Lustra*). But that is a matter for readers, or even for critics, not for their author. I will here note only information germane to reading some of them:

'Liu Ch'e' – author of the Chinese original. Pound wrote his version (and that of the following piece) knowing no Chinese; both were adapted from H.A. Giles' translations (reprinted in Yip's *Cathay* book, pp. 60 & 64).

fan peace – by 'The Lady Pan', unattributed by Pound in *Des Imagistes* and *Lustra*.

'mei sheng' – a false attribution by Pound (and presumably Fenollosa). This is one of the anonymous *Seventeen Old Poems* collected in, amongst other places, the *New Songs from a Jade Terrace* anthology.

river song – here just the first of two Li Po poems Pound elided.

wife's letter – this version works from the original, but also from translations by Witter Bynner, A.C. Cooper, W.J.B. Fletcher, David Hinton, John Holcombe, Amy Lowell & Florence Ayscough, Shigeyoshi Obata, Arthur Waley and William Carlos Williams & David Rafael Wang – as well as Pound's version and Ernest Fenollosa's notes.

untitled epigraph – Pound (and presumably Fenollosa) wrongly attributed this poem to 'Rihaku' [Li Po].

friend leaving – This poem appears, under a different title, in my book of *North Hills* poems, *eye-blink* (London: Veer Books, 2010); reprinted here with grateful thanks to Veer.

stop talking – Pound conflated the last two poems of the four into one poem; I have restored the divisions. This sequence is more demotic than the other poems, reflecting its early original, which, almost uniquely in the poems translated here, employs a first-person singular pronoun.

Thanks to Richard Parker for asking for these; and for his patience and help.

Notes

[1] Ezra Pound, *Cathay...* (London: Elkin Mathews, 1915), p. 32 – cited here from Barry Ahearn, "Cathay: What sort of Translation?", pp. 31-48 in Zhaoming Qian, *Ezra Pound and China* (Ann Arbor, MI, 2003), p. 34.

[2] Wai-Lim Yip, *Ezra Pound's Cathay* (Princeton, NJ, 1969), p. 12. See further (e.g.) Yip, *Chinese Poetry* (Durham, NC, 1997), p. xiii, and David Hinton, *Classical Chinese Poetry: An Anthology* (New York, 2008), pp. xx-xxi.

[3] Pound wasn't invariably detained by it either; hence his use of "Brer Rabbit" in translating one of the *Confucian Odes* (Mao 70). [Other translators tend to say "hare", but Pound is at least lexicographically correct – see *Mathews Chinese-English Dictionary*, M6534.]

[4] By the time Pound came to translate the "Confucian Odes", he had considerable competence, conducting correspondence on lexicographical technicalities with Chinese friends – as any reader of Zhaoming Qian's *Ezra Pound's Chinese Friends* (Oxford, 2008) will know.

('Liu Ch'e')

quite a way after Liu Ch'e (156-87 BC)

(rustle) part of a silk sleeve (stilled)

(dust)   jade courtyard   (filled)

yet not foot falls ... lone, alone

leaves leave, lie there still   looking for one who is lost

left   here   no peace   (*hopeless anguish tossed*)

('Lady Pan')

quite a way after 'Pan Chieh-yü' (fl. c. 30-48 BC)

silk cut

snow white

fan shaped

garden moon

measured entry

tiny breeze

autumn falls

cold wind

'laid aside'

passion spent

(mei sheng)

anon.; attrib. by EP to 'Mei Shêng' (? between 25-220 BC)
quite a way after anon., attrib. to EP...

blue-green, blue-green   river grass

hemmed-in, hemmed-in   willows weep

ample, ample   house and girl

bright, bright   window's prospect

fine, fine   her made-up face

slim, slim   she gives her hand

she: once a working-girl

now a playboy's wife

he: a professional drunk

bed rarely occupied

river song

quite a way after Li Po (701-762 AD)

shipped oars   spices & magnolia

musicians (flutes & pipes) pooped or stern

bottles of American wine

men   drifting loose women

boat passes under yellow cranes

mindless   heartless moving

   [gulls hang suspended]

empty air holds sun   then moon

the hills an ink- blotch

looming over these characters

wealth distinction

nope, rivers don't back up to their source

wife's letter

quite a way after Li Po (701-762 AD)

young-haired and
breaking gowans
your hobby-horse
by blue greengages
together we dwelt
small fond people
lo! became spoused
never been experienced
lowering dark
heart's gate when
the scowling stopped
excused dust
pillar of faith
look   out
far   away
unstable locality
impossible water
gibbous moon
foot marks
deep green moss
tear or tear   [*pron.* 'tare or teer']
leaves falls
yellow returning
evening grass
moved heart
facing gradually
beyond gorgeous
"how is it far?"
let's meet up
out at Long Beach

stair grief

quite a way after Li Po (701-762 AD)

therefore palace grows whitened

late night soaked court lady

let down behind blind

clearly watches autumn moon

Departure Poems

untitled epigraph
quite a way after Wang Wei (*c.*700-760 AD)

light wet dust wet

brighter paler green   leaves

annihilation by wine-cup

gone west   no friends

1: river separation

quite a way after Li Po (701-762 AD)

leaves yellow crane towering

mist blooms   no willow

blue hills sail lone

long river horizon

2: friend leaving

quite a way after Li Po (701-762 AD)

blue hill horizons north

white water rounds to east

parting taken to be necessary

leaf-litter blown ten thousand miles...

cloud floating (thoughts)

sun-dropping (feelings)

we wave you leave

hhuun hhuun [neigh-saying] [crying]

3: taking leaves

quite a way after Li Po (701-762 AD)

hear say hard road west

no easy stroll / walkover

cliff facing face

horses mainly cloud

trees gnaw the path

river winds wind round city

arrival raises a glass

no checking on Oracle

4: ruined city

quite a way after Li Po (701-762 AD)

Phoenix Terrace... once, here, phoenixes...

now: air emptied, river emptied

paths to the palace under sedge

old crowned heads under dust

light divides the green hills

bright (r)egrets halve the river

floating cloud / screens / the sun

: the old city – never seen again

stop talking I

quite a way after T'ao Ch'ien (365-427 AD)

cloud clouds   (stop talking)

rain rains   (tense time)

boxed compass a murky blur

all roads lead to roadblocks

quiet room in the east end

sediment settles in the home-brew

friends remote or morose

I scratch my head to pass the time

stop talking II

quite a way after T'ao Ch'ien (365-427 AD)

clouds cloud   (*stop talking*)

a tense time as rains rain

boxed compass murky blur

most roads head for the river

at least – at least there's beer

a quiet drink up east

thinking – no, really – of friends

but no-one seems to pop by

stop talking III

quite a way after T'ao Ch'ien (365-427 AD)

trees in the park up east

new twigs on the branches again

flourishing well – much-loved,

'a harmonious spot'

as everyone says

sun, moon, pass over

palliate with a pallet

this, that, *ça m'est égal*

stop talking IV

quite a way after T'ao Ch'ien (365-427 AD)

persuasively birds fly by

interesting me in my garden

(recollecting my pen, halted, idle)

singing each to each / trading lines

we too have our friends

sufficient unto the day

might as well stop talking

nobody knows the sorrows…

Tony Lopez

Darwin in Rome: Pound and Stein

This is a work-in-progress report on a creative research project that grows out of my involvement with writing, Pound Studies and the history of modernism. My previous project (which turns out to have been a pilot for this one) was set up as a response to four twentieth-century American poets who I thought used some form of collage technique: Ezra Pound, Gertrude Stein, Ted Berrigan and Lyn Hejinian. That project was funded by the UK Arts and Humanities Research Council and was thus conceived within the framework of their definitions of research. Thinking about the challenge at that time of achieving funding for a creative project in the UK, I decided to frame an investigation that any academic assessor in "English" or "American Studies" would be sure to recognise as research. So I set up my field of study with symmetry in relation to gender and the history of modernism in the twentieth century, and located it by focusing on specific resources in a number of important literary archives. New writing from that project was published as *Covers* (Salt, 2007), and some associated critical work is published in *Meaning Performance* (Salt, 2006). Working on *Covers* I came up with an idea for an ambitious writing project of much larger scope that I held back from the *Covers* publication to give me time to develop it aside from the pressure of bringing funded work to press. I had to get the *Covers* project finished and published so that I could get on with the bigger and more interesting book.

Only More So is a large-scale non-narrative prose work composed using my own variation of the "New Sentence" method of composition described in Ron Silliman's 1987 book, a method that is derived from Gertrude Stein's *Tender Buttons* (1914) and *How to Write* (1931). Unlike the Language writers' "New Sentence" autobiographical compositions (such as Hejinian's *My Life,* 1980, and Silliman's *Tjanting,* 1981) my project is information-rich, incorporating the Poundian tradition of research-led composition developed in the Malatesta cantos and American History cantos. In blending these processes I have employed a wide range of non-literary and specialist sources relevant to issues of our time such as the legacy of twentieth-century genocide, environmental concerns, and new developments in the sciences.

So, in a very compressed introduction, I have opened up a number of topics that can't all be fully addressed here. What I want to consider first is the notion of a Poundian breakthrough, as it seems to me; a Poundian challenge to our understanding of what poetry is, demonstrated by the method and content of the cantos. This is a passage from Canto 9:

"Sence to-day I am recommanded that I have to tel you my father's opinium that he has shode to Mr Genare about the vats of the cherch... etc...
"Giovane of Master alwise P.S. I think it advisabl that I shud go to rome to talk to mister Albert so as I can no what he thinks about it rite.
(*A Draft of XXX Cantos*, 42)

Here in this quoted misspelled prose letter are, by implication, traces of a specific historical person, the rich and powerful Malatesta, a man who was in a position to employ others to get things done. What is immediately striking are the folksy "by ear" spellings: "sence", "tel", "opinium", "shode", "cherch", "shud", "no", "rite". The deliberate misspellings are an immediate fictional sign of authenticity and also of social difference, which sets up a relationship between the author Pound, the imagined writer of the original letter, the implied historical character Malatesta to whom the letter is addressed, and the reader (which term might be complicated further: consider the reader in 1933, as well as the contemporary reader). What is being communicated here? That art needs an economic structure to exist. That the economic structure in 1454 required that a man of substance needed for his own purposes to build and so he would hire workers: designers, skilled masons, labourers and so on. These skilled workers needed an employer who understood and cared about good workmanship, beauty and form, otherwise there was no scope for them to achieve it. He would need supervisory staff to deal with craftsmen and tradesmen; otherwise he would be kept from his own important duties and concerns as a *condottiere*. A good, intelligent, skilled worker uses a word like "advisable" but given the complete division of labour and lack of general education, he can't spell it, so we recognise his station. He needs to ask permission to travel because he would not be able to cover the expense himself and so he wants to make sure that he is authorised before he sets out.

"First: Ten slabs best red, seven by 15, by one third,
"Eight ditto, good red, 15 by three by one,
"Six of same, 15 by one by one.
"Eight columns 15 by three and one third
    etc... with carriage, danars 151

This is the culture of stone turned into an extensive and epic metaphor. Stonework can be seen to be true or not. Numbers are the means of power, of measuring and analysis, of precise instructions and good proportions. So the use of numbers, like the metaphorical use of stone, feeds back self-referentially into an aesthetic concern built into the poetry. The numbers are not standardised in printed language: eight, ten and three are spelled out, 15 and 151 are printed in numerals, the numerals 1 and 5 appear in each line as a chime. "Ditto" is an Italian word, from Latin, but would it be used in a list like this in 1454, or is it 1920s or 30s shorthand? It works together with "danars" to build up colour, but it also works in the contemporary voice of Pound. The relationships in the passage are obviously feudal and familial, taking in neighbours and employees, sketching in quite a complex hierarchy.

Meaning also resides in the textual form of the writing: it's not a verse narrative in which an epic hero achieves great victories but the assembled textual evidence of the activities of a great man, for whom we have surviving stone monuments. There is an implied narrative:

"MONSEIGNEUR:
"Madame Isotta has had me write today about Sr Galeazzo's daughter. The man who said young pullets make a thin soup, knew what he was talking about. We went to see the girl the other day, for all the good that did, and she denied the whole matter and kept her end up without losing her temper. I think Madame Ixotta very nearly exhausted the matter. *Mi pare che avea decto hogni chossia.* All the children are well. Where you are everyone is pleased and happy because of your taking the chateau here we are the reverse as you might say drifting without a rudder. Madame Lucretzia has probably, or should have, written to you. I suppose you have the letter by now. Everyone wants to be remembered to you. 21 Dec. D. de M."

The poem is as full of implication and irony as Browning's dramatic monologues but it is also partly a conceptual poem: it is concerned with positioning the reader – with engaging the reader in a process of equipping themselves to read. This documentary collage is offered as a poem. The poem is not written in metrical form but assembled from prose passages apparently in different hands and includes factual documentation, details, evidence – the stuff of the proto-realist novel, an epistolary – but cut into and selected – mundane, even banal language is used in this construct. The passages about the pony give us a family man who is away on important business; his building project employs a whole community. Each correspondent uses a different mode of address to Sigismundo and thus places himself in a particular relationship with the powerful man.

"All the stone cutters are waiting for spring weather to start work again".

The very seasons are a force to be compared to the will and ambition of Malatesta who has commissioned the building that affords them their identity as stonecutters.

Canto 9 is a radical departure for English language poetry, which begins to invoke a hugely ambitious conception of poetry that Pound was to work through in his developing epic. It is not a new idea that this is an intellectually demanding poetry that educates its readers into an active role in the production of meaning. There is some question about whether that active role is allowed for or made possible in the later cantos. But here the radical turn away from verse narration forces us to make a step change and read the implications of juxtaposed historical documents as epic poetry. Pound directs the collage: material is selected, cut and arranged to present meaning, and as he makes new demands on the reader he also establishes his view of moral and aesthetic superiority in the great man. Pound is creating both an historical great man and a contemporary 1930s image of the great man, which is an idea beyond the realm of aesthetics. The ambition for poetry is important, however it played out in Pound's later career.

Here is something very different but equally radical that has some equivalent demands and designs on the reader:

> What is a sentence. After a while what is a sentence. Think what is a sentence. A sentence is never displaced. By and by. Leave it alone. Come again. What is a sentence they go to have it happen that they cough. This is a sentence. They will be having this that they were annoyed. Think of a sentence nobody is more simple. Nobody is more simple. Think of a sentence nobody is any more simple than think of a sentence. Not that. What is a sentence. A sentence does make it more carefully a beginning of their kitchen.
> Without doubt.
> To please a young man there should be sentences. What are sentences. Like what are sentences. In the part of sentences it for him is happily all. They will name sentences for him. They will all call sentences sentences for him. Sentences are called sentences. Thank you very much for reading sentences. Sentences which are called sentences are laid together. This makes them sentences. For which they are intended. He will read sentences which are intended for sentences. For which they are intended.
> (Stein, "Sentences" in *How to Write*, (1931) 142-3)

Published two years before *A Draft of XXX Cantos*, this is writing that challenges our understanding of what writing is and what it is for. As I copy-type this text, the spellcheck function on *Microsoft Word* wants to autocorrect most of it. The first sentence is identified as grammatically incomplete because the word "sentence" should come with a question mark before I press the space key. "By and by" is underlined as a fragment that I should "consider revising". "Cough" should have a question mark. The word "simpler" is offered 3 times as an alternative for "more simple". "Like what are sentences" is also identified as a fragment. "Sentences sentences" needs correcting as a repeated noun, and so on.

Gertrude Stein's sentences, in her composition entitled "Sentences", are not recognisable by the most sophisticated word processing software package as permissible English sentences. They are not being used in the language game of giving information. We get the sentence: "This is a sentence", which is, I take it, in 1931 a new and pure kind of modernist poetry that refers to nothing but itself. "Sentences are called sentences". It is a kind of nonsense and at the same time a kind of breakthrough in writing. This is twenty-five years before concrete poetry. The writing is clearly composed in order to keep us involved with the surface of its construction, like certain kinds of abstract painting, it refers us back to language and is otherwise almost emptied of content, reference and progress. It is wearying to read at length.

Now one useful way of characterising the Language writers would be to identify them as poets who went back to the experimental writings of Gertrude Stein and began to adapt her discoveries in new ways, foregrounding Stein's radical achievement over those more readily assimilated modernists such as Pound, Eliot and Williams. Ron Silliman defined "The New Sentence" as a kind of disjunctive prose poetry invented in the Bay Area among a particular community of writers. It is composed in non-consecutive sentences that resist syllogistic synthesis. His account of that phenomenon relies upon a reading of Gertrude Stein's *How to Write*, using as a motto her sentence "A Sentence is not emotional a paragraph is".

Putting sentences together into units or paragraphs that have an emotional rather than logical or narrative structure is a kind of description of the New Sentence. The first version of Lyn Hejinian's book *My Life* was structured in 37 sections each made of 37 non-consecutive sentences – but this arbitrary frame based on her age at the time of writing is only one aspect of the book. The material that is collaged into it is mainly an autobiographical memoir, without many of the normal crises and self-justifications of that confessional protestant genre. A girl grows up in post-war California; you can reconstruct her story through the book. There is also a thread of homespun proverbial phrases; of philosophy and feminist theory and a good deal of self-reflexive writerly material that playfully develops the writer-reader relationship: "Are your fingers in the margin"?

In Silliman's *Tjanting* the process of writing comes even more to the fore, the reader sees the author try out and repeat various moves in the writing itself, building up phrases, adding more language and complexity as he goes. Combination and assembly is built into *Tjanting's* additive form based on the Fibonacci sequence. The work is about its own processes, as much life-experience is built of repetition and self-awareness. There is a focus on the scene of writing, on what is happening in the immediate surroundings, on what the writer is thinking of (what occurs in the process of writing). He travels around the Bay Area public transport system with his notebook, he works at home in his apartment. What has been written before is often re-processed and re-ordered. Silliman inhabits the work, and his everyday tasks, movements and errands get written in.

The book I am working on uses an arbitrary form just like Silliman's *Tjanting* and Hejinian's *My Life* – but the material is much more various. It is a slow writing project that takes Derrida's notion of intertextuality perfectly seriously and puts it into practice on a scale previously unimagined. *Only More So* was composed by collecting and editing sentences from a wide range of non-literary sources and assembling them into prose sections each of 55 sentences long. Those sections are assembled into chapters that are each 10 sections long. The work was built up as a modular sequence and is 100 sections in 10 chapters.

I have been working for some time with a variety of source materials to make collaged work in various verse forms, where the sentence is the unit of composition, and the rapid switching of registers within sentences provides for the possibility of a whole variety of emotional responses. In *Only More So* the sentences are combined in non-consecutive arrays from which the reader will always construct a kind of continuity of theme and purpose with a developing sense of resonance and self-reference within the work. The writing is genuinely and fundamentally experimental in its processes but the aim is not to display a crude, unfinished or difficult surface, on the contrary, I am aiming at a prose with the kind of finish, compression and ease of reading achieved in the verse writing in my book *False Memory* (1996, 2003). If sufficient care is taken in composition, the reader naturalises the collaged text and incorporates its particular aesthetic qualities, making connections and developing their own priorities of significance and thematic coherence.

Only More So employs a wide range of source materials such as the popular science journals *Nature*, *New Scientist* and *Scientific American*, and specialist non-fiction literature in for example history, ecology, medicine, archaeology, psychology, pharmacology, art, literary theory, architectural history, music, teacher education, sociology, environmental science, evolution and genetics, management, holocaust studies, marketing, meteorology and linguistics. No topic is sustained at a single location for more than one sentence and the sentence combinations are edited to avoid close repetitions of word, phrase or subject. There is a build up across sections of materials from the same and similar sources and the reader will recognise non-identical repetition and variations of language at some remove. The effect is a level compositional field of language in which specialised elements are presented seemingly without hierarchical organisation or imposed control.

Dispassionately objective and recognisably technical vocabulary, is brought into close proximity with other varieties of language (social and historical writings for instance, first person memories, public notices, advertising materials and instructions) whose implications point at one stage to small-scale events of personal concern but at another to issues of planetary scale. There will of course be different responses to the work based on different readerly preoccupations, but I expect that the emotional effects of combinations will be similar for readers who are engaged for some time. Scale is rapidly shifted and, because of apparently shared vocabularies, it is often initially unclear exactly which field a segment invokes. Issues such as boundaries and definitions of human consciousness and common experience are teased out of the reporting of advances in experimental psychology (exploring the mechanisms of pain and empathy, for instance) and new developments in neuroscience, together with medical and social care applications such as affective programming, prosthetic and enabling technologies and so on.

I may have invented the slowest and most laborious method imaginable of composing a prose work. The process of collecting, copying, editing and assembling individual sentences into sections precludes any possibility of getting into a fluent and continuous spate of writing. The project is about selecting and composing rather than self-expression. I am able to plan which areas of specialist reading that I'll go to for source materials and thus plan for thematic development and coherence across the larger sequence. But chance definitely plays a part in the gathering of material and in the particular combinations that can be made. The source materials reference more source materials in a process that could be exponential if everything were followed up. So there is a finding out phase of work where I am collecting as much material as I can (in libraries), reading and copying, and assembling my own source books with a great deal of copied material. This quite intensive process focuses me on the fields of work that I am drawing from and enables me get a grasp of a whole set of materials. For me writing everything out by hand is an important part of the process. Then there is a composing stage, which requires reading through all the other sections so that I am immersed in the content of the work so far, and then I can assemble the next section out of the material available, improvising the assembly from what I have collected. This is another copying process, sentence by sentence, until I get a section that works. After this is I type the section and then read it through again and edit it as a single piece. Editing is from then on a continuous process until publication.

I've described the writing process in some detail because I wanted to be clear what this work is not. I have read critical discussion of "found text" recently that seems to mean by that phrase a kind of literary allusion. I'm not really involved in that, certainly not motivated by it, which some modernist writers do seem to be. There was, a long time ago, a stage in procedural work where you would take an established literary text and deform it in some way, selecting words or parts of words, or punctuation marks or whatever to make a new text. Think of Cage or Mac Low. I'm not really involved with that; it is a method I recognise and you can always make an imaginative new use of a hackneyed method. It's the result that interests me; I'm not really interested in a work that is only about process.

It may be that this book is the first Constructivist poem composed on the pleasure principle. *Only More So* returns to and builds on the later work of Pound and Stein, but also Ian Hamilton Finlay and contemporary science; it could not have been written before 2010.

Works Cited

Lyn Hejinian, *My Life* (1980). Los Angeles, CA: Sun & Moon 1991.

Tony Lopez, *False Memory* (2003). Bristol: Shearsman Books 2012.

———. *Meaning Performance: Essays on Poetry*. Cambridge: Salt Publishing, 2006.

———. *Covers*. Cambridge: Salt Publishing 2007.

———. *Only More So*. New Orleans, LA: University of New Orleans Press, 2011; Bristol: Shearsman Books, 2012.

Ezra Pound, *A Draft of XXX Cantos*. London: Faber, 1933.

Ron Silliman, *Tjanting* (1981). Cambridge: Salt Publishing, 2002.

———. *The New Sentence*. New York: Roof Books, 1987.

Gertrude Stein, *Tender Buttons* (1914). Los Angeles, CA: Green Integer, 2002.

———. *How to Write* (1931). New York: Dover Press, 1975.

Tony Lopez

FROM *DARWIN*, A SECTION OF *ONLY MORE SO*

There is a village under Slievemore Mountain known locally as the Deserted Village. If you think about this a little, it makes perfect sense. Producers of the US drama show *24* say they will cut the number of torture scenes. Studies on the mechanism underlying this effect should provide fundamental insights into the molecular and cellular basis of memory recall. Although each simplex is geometrically flat, they can be glued together in a variety of patterns to produce curved space times. The rings in one instance retained their luminous property nearly twenty-four hours after the insect's death. These pictures seemed to deserve to be better known. Leaving the coast for a time, we again entered the forest. The frequent occurrence of murder may be partly attributed to this habit. Time moves from left to right in the representation. Dust falls in such quantities as to dirty everything on board, and to hurt people's eyes; vessels have even run onshore owing to the obscurity of the atmosphere. One reason for choosing this species of opossum as the first marsupial genome to be sequenced is its long-standing role as a laboratory animal.

Paradise is a garden. It fits us then to be as provident as fear may teach us. What we see may be accompanied by a change in the soundtrack to what Hollywood calls exit music. Exhausted by his ordeal my father burst into tears of relief. These changes were effected in such a manner that clouds, varying in tint between a hyacinth red and chestnut brown, were continually passing over the body. In the virtual world you can look at behaviour in response to the disease. Data has come to be seen and used as a singular mass noun like information or news: the data is currently being processed. This is a forensic sentence. End credits are unusual in the gallery. An intention is embedded in its situation, in human customs and institutions. Did you see Gilbert and George on Jonathan Ross? Two kinds of geese frequent the Falklands.

Humans perceive the properties of a surface by interpreting visual input. On the basis of preliminary studies, we expect to identify several thousand sites of structural variation. The ending echoes the paratextual subversion of the pre-release poster, which read: "The Birds is coming". The village was never occupied again, except as a boley village. All the little streams are bordered by soft peat, which makes it difficult for the horses to leap them without falling. Imagine Miller's naked body laid out on the white sands of a coral beach. When a histogram is positively skewed, apparent glossiness is increased. The authors argue that over time Paul Broca's conception of the area involved in speech processing has become simplified by others. Options had to be kept open at this stage so that the mind could travel hopefully towards some eventual synthesis, which lay beyond the poem's present horizon. About a third of children with autistic disorder develop temporal lobe epilepsy by adolescence. This is a legacy website of the University of Manchester; the information it carries was frozen on 30 September 2004, and may no longer be accurate. From far off we heard the flight of the BUPA swan. When the insect was decapitated the rings remained uninterruptedly bright, but not so brilliant as before: local irritation with a needle always increased the vividness of light. Laminar flow control can be used on engines, wings, fuselage and tail.

These free-floating proteins bind to specific viral or bacterial proteins, disabling the invaders or labelling them for destruction. Pleasure is their capacity to choose well-known things. A boley village was populated in summer months by young people looking after cattle that grazed on the hillsides. Bowering impersonates Vancouver. After being imprisoned for some time in a ship, there is a charm in the unconfined feeling of walking over boundless plains of turf. In addition to gloss, perceived surface roughness and translucency also depend on image statistics. Caldeira and his colleagues reason that cooling the arctic requires much less material than cooling the planet as a whole.

The end sequences of each clone are mapped to the reference sequence. To measure the activity of individual neurons, which is crucial to the study of cognitive processes such as visual attention, electrodes must be directly inserted into a monkey's brain. She said she liked it best and did she like it best or did she change her mind upon seeing the other? Air sucked in through thousands of tiny holes near the wings eliminates turbulent flow and cuts drag. There are many physical dimensions of gloss that affect the perception of surface material. An intriguing example is lithium metal. That was my foray into neurobiology. This man had been trained into degradation lower than the slavery of the most helpless animal. I observed this phenomenon on several occasions. It takes thirty turbines to reach a kill rate of one bird a year.

Robert Sheppard

THE LI SHANG-YIN SUITE
(T'ang Dynasty ?812-58)

the Lo-Yu tombs

sun   deposits   glory   then
buries   thoughts   in   night

memo to secretary Ling-Hu

far   from   Cloudy   Mountain   trees   of   Ch'in
I   send   this   message   via   two   carp
Long   absent   from   the   prince's   autumn   garden
there's   a   poet   delirious   in   the   rain !

White Beauty

now   shadows   lean   across   the   marble   frieze
&   morning   stars   crouch   beneath   the   slanting
Milky   Way   are   you   sorry   to   stare
long   long   nights   drugged   above   purple   seas ?

Jade Pool

(—)

chill   wind   blowing   through   palace   the   1
&   only   China   Doll   croons   this   morning
  O   mountain   pool   swollen   with   night   rain!
   when   shall   we   sit   at   lit   window
  his   voice   all   night   in   the   rain?

(=)

at   her   porch   by   Jade   Pool   she
hears   *Lonely   Woman*   warbled   across   the   land
where's   the   Emperor   8   horses   charging   10,000
miles   a   day   his   golden   saddles   &
jewelled   axles   aglitter   why's   he   never   returned?

no name

Phoenix   tail   motif   hangs   on   scented   drapes
Around   your   greenblue   canopy   stitched   into   night.
Sly   peep   round   slice   of   moon   fan –
Shy   voice   shushed   my   thunderous   retreat.   Now
Quiet   your   room   where   the   candle   droops.
How   far   can   your   pomegranate   blossom   scatter?
I   tether   my   horse   to   river   willow
&   await   your   word   on   the   wind.

falling petals

My   house   guest   is   gone.
                    The   master   bedroom   is   empty.
Petals   in   the   yard   spin
                    where   wind   chases   tail,   dance,
kick   up   their   soft   skirts
                    while   the   sun   sinks   low.
Oh!   I   cannot   sweep   them
                    until   hint   of   your   return.
Their   perfume   is   crushed   underfoot,
                    my   bathrobe   scented   with   tears.

cold thoughts

Gone   again.   The   river   laps
                    at   the   doorstep's   reach.   Cicadas
are   silent   on   moist   leaves
                    always   pure   &   mostly   hungry.
Thoughts   arrive.   They   lap   at
                    my   long   standing   silence,   frozen.
The   Pole   Star   draws   me
                    north;   your   southron   never   calls.
Slipping   across   the   dream's   horizon
                    you   recede   on   refluent   tide.

north among vines

When   sun's   up   on   hills

         I   seek   the   monk's   hut

Audience   of   leaves   attends   him

         I   turn   chilled   in   cloud

A   gong   intones   the   dusk

         I   lean   on   staff   listen

The   world's   a   dust   speck

         what   roomy   passions   have   I ?

October-November 2011

These versions and un-versions make use of the anonymous translations and the visual configuration of the Chinese characters, lineation and punctuation in the parallel text *Three Hundred Poems of the T'ang Dynasty*, possibly published in Hong Kong. Further background and translations by A.C. Graham were consulted in eds. Cyril Birch and Dennis Keene, *Anthology of Chinese Literature*, Harmondsworth: Penguin, 1967.

Ezra Pound invented 'Chinese poetry' for our times – and Hugh Kenner claims as much in *The Pound Era* with a chapter entitled 'The Invention of China' – and however much we applaud the pioneering of Arthur Waley (Pound's famous antagonist on the grounds of strict Sinology and accuracy), Pound's cadences ring through most attempts to 'do' ancient Chinese poetry, from Snyder to Gilonis. This has positive and negative results worthy of debate beyond this note, of course. We may feel the same about Anglo-Saxon poetry with respect to Pound, but extraordinarily that is based upon just one poem, the powerful 'Seafarer'. In the case of Chinese poetry (and philosophy) there are some stray versions (and what I call 'un-versions', synthetic approximations), as well as Chinese 'Cantos', but mostly we go to *Cathay* of 1915. (The late translations of *The Classical Anthology* seem oddly flat.) Faced with the poems in *Three Hundred Poems of the T'ang Dynasty*, a chance purchase in a charity shop, I felt drawn by the very inadequacy of (some of) the translations to version them so they might be *read*, like Pound did in fact. I re-read Kenner's account of Pound's mis-readings of the

Fenollosa manuscript at some point and felt that my own creative meddling and infidelities – both deliberate and accidental – were authorised in some way. I chose Li Shang-yin because of his supposed difficulty (though I suspect 'difficulty' became 'untranslatability' for the anonymous translators), and because it is said that he wrote genuine love poems that respect the nature of the women addressed. What most struck me about the visual appearance of the poems was the neatness afforded by the characters, a different kind of visuality from the theorising of Pound's ideogrammic method. Gaudier-Brzeska could not really have got very far with just his eyes, but he would have noticed the spatial configuration of characters per line. I have no knowledge of how this works phonetically and decided to refunction this artifice as numbers of words (including ampersands and numerals) per line (a Zukofskian borrowing, but an old trick for me), with extra spaces between words to provide some equivalence to the visual form of the texts, an artifice borrowed from some late poems of Mina Loy – although Pound's careful placing of European and Chinese language on the page of his *Cantos* lies somewhere in the background. The significance of the visual (or rather the visible) is something I have always found in Pound (as did the Niogandres concretists) rather than the imagist mirage of re-constituting the thing in itself. One anachronism ('lie quiet Divus,' a voice intercedes, 'we know where you live'), 'southron' may seem a bit subversive, stealing from Bunting, but it's the sort of trick he learnt from Pound; the '1 & only China doll' may seem egregious but I believe the translation provided the suggestive 'unique and exquisite' as adjectives for the singular and beautiful woman. All this testifies to the continuing, but dispersed, presence of Poundian poetics in the broad understanding of contemporary 'translation' and spatial (rather than temporal) prosodies.

Sean Pryor

SOME THOUGHTS ON REFRIGERATION

If Shakespeare owns *incarnadine*, Milton *pandemonium*, and Keats *sedge*, Ezra Pound ought to own *frigidaire*.[1] A poet may in certain limited senses own a word, whether by coinage or seemingly singular usage. In *Homage to Sextus Propertius* Pound refers unforgettably, and with impenitent anachronism, to "a frigidaire patent". But Pound's ownership is compromised, since *Frigidaire* is a proprietary name. It was the name given to the Guardian Refrigerator Company, the first company to develop self-contained refrigerators, when it was bought by General Motors in 1919. That same year, Pound published four sections from *Homage* in the March issue of *Poetry*. The full poem soon appeared in *Quia Pauper Amavi* (1919), but only when Pound included it in *Personæ* (1926) did he add the line about the frigidaire patent: "my cellar does not date from Numa Pompilius, / Nor bristle with wine jars, / Nor is it equipped with a frigidaire patent" (206). Propertius does use the word *frigidus*. Standing outside Cynthia's doorway, for instance, he complains that "frigidaque Eoo me dolet aura gelu" (1.16.24): "a frigid wind from the icy East pains me". But Propertius speaks of neither refrigeration nor a frigidarium, the cooling-room in a Roman bath. Beyond Pound's free and happy way with Latin, what is special about this phrase is the way it focuses the problems of innovation, property, and language. Transforming παν-, δαίμων, and *-ium* into an English word is an invention worthy of letters patent. Putting a brand-new brand name in your poem, partly as an assault on the out-dated form and content of so much contemporary verse, is a more complicated affair.

The obvious irony is that, in what must be the first use of the word by a major poet, and in what ought to have established Pound's patent in perpetuity, he, or his Propertius, disclaims the innovation and the right to profit from it. When in "Ireland's Dead" Lionel Johnson tells the holy land of Ireland that her martyred dead "thy fields incarnadine" (59), he contracts a debt to *Macbeth* which the poem probably cannot pay. (Nevertheless, the poem appears in Pound's edition of Johnson.) When Pound's Propertius adds that his humble cellar has nothing so swank as a frigidaire patent, he openly declares that someone else owns the right to produce the appliance or to license its production, and that someone else owns its name. Frigidaire registered the word as a United States trademark on 23 November 1920 (Serial Number 71117931). It is as if Pound quotes it under fair use; he contracts no debt. And yet the word becomes his. Or, better, when Pound points to *frigidaire* as if in a department-store window, he owns an angry scorn for the ownership of words. It was an unmistakably upmarket window display: in *The Times* the word first appeared, on 21 May 1925, in an advertisement for Harrods.

Pound's line is clearly involved in the general economy of *Homage to Sextus Propertius*, in the poem's audacious way with translation. It helps that *frigidaire* began, at least as long ago as the sixteenth century, as the French for *frigidarium*. General Motors then sold the word back to France as a term for a refrigerator. The question of the ownership of *frigidaire* reflects one of the poem's major concerns. Pound's Propertius defiantly opposes the official verse culture of his day, represented by martial epic in general and by Virgil in particular. Unlike the laureate of imperial money and power, Propertius refuses to sell his gift, and that is why Pound takes the poem's epigraph from Ovid's *Ars Amatoria*: "quia pauper amavi" (2.165). Such poets live and love in poverty. But Pound's line also shines light on the ownership of Propertius, on the problem of who has the right to read, print, translate, interpret, and profit – monetarily and culturally – from his poems. Rather than jealously hoarding him, Pound puts Propertius into free circulation. One might say that *Homage* takes the elegies out of cold storage; their wine is for drinking.

§

What then happens when Keston Sutherland affixes to the front cover of a slim book of poems, *The Stats on Infinity*, the abstract of a United States patent for a refrigerator door closer? Sutherland's epigraph clearly alludes to *Homage*, but the allusion works at a remove.[2] Instead of peddling the old wine of "a frigidaire patent" in a new bottle, Sutherland gives us the thing itself – except that it is a different thing, since he takes Pound's noun as a premodifier and his postmodifier as a noun. Propertius only claims not to have a refrigerator; Sutherland presents the patent for a refrigerator. (After all, what would a wine cellar want with a patent? Unless the thing to do with patents is to hoard them.) That is to say, Sutherland's allusion trades in the grammatical irreverence with which Pound reads Propertius. Is that to contract a debt, or put Pound into circulation, or both?

Spurred by the allusion, one can link Sutherland's short volume and Pound's sequence in various ways. The brief thoughts in this essay are only a small, preliminary sampling. The first poem in *The Stats on Infinity*, "The Proxy Inhumanity of Forklifts", also mixes ancient and modern, myth and history, tragedy and comedy, secular and sacred, the conventionally poetic and the conventionally prosaic:

> In 1983, over 13,000 workers' compensation claims
> to Erato I scream this bloodless anathema
> a veto on forklifts' trussed talons in its face scrub[.] (1)

Like Pound, Sutherland generates sparks by striking a classical vocabulary (*Erato, anathema*) against an Anglo-Saxon one (*scream, bloodless*). Like Pound, he sounds words' etymological overtones. "And as Ford said: get a dictionary / and learn the meaning of words" (*Cantos* 98/709). Take the poem's first line, lifted from an article on work-related injuries involving forklift trucks:

> In 1983, over 13,000 workers' compensation claims for lost-workday injuries involving forklift trucks were filed in 30 states. An estimated 24,000 forklift-related injuries were treated in U.S. emergency rooms in 1983, and an estimated 34,000 in 1985. (Stout-Wiegand 179)

Twenty years after those claims were filed, a British soldier bound an Iraqi prisoner and suspended him from the prongs of a forklift truck. By sounding the *pendere* in "compensation", Sutherland's poem shows prisoners and workers hung together, weighed on the unjust scales of violent economic and military systems. Such echoes are everywhere, and they can be deceptively soft; the barely audible verbal harmonies sound loud political dissonances.

But most of all the poems in *The Stats on Infinity*, like *Homage to Sextus Propertius*, hurl politics against sex and epic against lyric. The brutal meeting of sex and violence is also an occasion for "The Proxy Inhumanity of Forklifts": other Iraqi prisoners at Camp Breadbasket were forced to simulate oral and anal sex while a British soldier took photographs. One might look to epic for earlier representations of comparable meetings of sex and violence, and Sutherland does seem to have found the forklifts' trussed talons in Pope's *Iliad*: "His Eagle, sacred Bird of Heav'n! he sent, / A Fawn his Talons truss'd (divine Portent)" (8.297-8; cf. 12.235). But Sutherland inverts Pope's grammar, too. His talons do not do the trussing; they are trussed. (But by what, and why?) Alternatively, since Pope had clearly read it, perhaps Sutherland found the words in Dryden's *Æneis*: "*Jove*'s Bird comes sowsing down, from upper Air; / Her crooked Tallons truss the fearful Prey" (9.762-3; cf. 12.377). Who or what, if anyone or anything, was Jove in Iraq? And who will compensate the victims of gods?

On the other hand, Pound's Propertius mocks Virgil as "Phoebus' chief of police", as a hack who writes "to imperial order" (223). For the lyric poet of poverty and love, Jove is just another "old lecher" (218). And there are lyric aspects to and allusions in "The Proxy Inhumanity of Forklifts". Rather than screaming to Calliope, Sutherland's lyric *I* screams to Erato, caught between the legal machinery of the workplace and the industrial machinery of the military. A page later, love, sex, and violence come together in the echo of that scream:

> that screaming which incessant I abandon
> to straining for abandonment in you, for a motive to
> make love immune to triviality[.] (2)

This looks like flight from the death that defines the social and political world to the ecstasy of *la petite mort*, but the ambiguous grammar couples the two. Both the screaming and the abandon are incessant. There seems to be no stable figurative hierarchy to the poem: sex is like war is like sex is like war. To complicate things still further, Virgil himself invokes the lyric and amatory muse, midway through his imperial epic, precisely because she yokes love and war: "Now, Erato! thy poet's mind inspire, [...] Relate what Latium was; her ancient kings; [...] And how the rivals loved, and how they fought" (7.52-7). Like Virgil after the civil wars and Pound after the Great War, Sutherland suggests that the only way to begin to understand the past and the present, myth and history, love and violence is to set them in unreconciled relation. There is, in particular, no generic refuge from the antagonisms of the world.

§

Nor is poetry itself a refuge. Obviously to write of frigidaire patents and compensation claims is to set the shabbily prosaic tramping through the ancestral garden of poesy. This is true both formally and thematically. Sutherland has spoken about the way his recent work approximates prose, and he describes some of it as a kind of metrical prose (Kilbride). It is tempting to hear significant rhythms in putatively prosaic found objects: "In 1983", "over 13,000 work-", "-ers' compensation claims". Three trimeters, roughly iambic? Conversely, Sutherland's verse frequently spills over into prose. The abstract from the refrigerator patent is, again, a key passage. The volume's prose epigraph reappears, fives pages into the "The Proxy Inhumanity of Forklifts", as lineated verse:

> A door closer assembly for a household refrigerator
> of the type having a door

frame with a front faced surface and a door
having a confronting surface, the assembly
including a hinge plate mounted on the door
frame and having a pivot pin
mounted on the hinge plate in
a spaced relation to the front faced surface, a door
plate mounted on the door[.] (5-6)

It's the perfect practical criticism exercise. Take what seems the dullest, most mechanical prose you can find, lineate it, and – like water into ice – you have poetry. You find the rhyme of *pin* and *in*. You find the fabulous alliterations in and surreal conception of "frame with a front faced surface". And by breaking the line each time *door* appears, whether as attributive or noun, you find that the sentence's strange syntax returns to the term obsessively. Lineation transforms awkward technical description into a mesmerising mantra.

Pound could raise verse to the pitch of incantation when he wanted to, reaching for states of illumination through the cadence of consonants and vowels, stress and quantity. But he also preached Ford's gospel of the prose tradition in verse. When he pastes prose passages into the Malatesta cantos, he is interested in their rhythms, and in what those rhythms tell us about political power and machination, but the result is not like Sutherland's poem. He does not discover ecstatic chant in Renaissance correspondence. In *Homage to Sextus Propertius* – which Sutherland called "one of the greatest triumphs of versification in the English language in the twentieth century" (Kilbride) – Pound replaces Propertius' elegiac couplets with a deft mix of metrical allusion, his own strong but supple patterning, and slack prose rhythms. The odd line is so long it spills past the margin like a prose paragraph. With more or less irony, Pound then plays these modes off against conventionally poetical or prosaic diction and theme. The tripping triplets of "the moon still declined to descend out of heaven" (218) undermine that reverend symbol and object of romantic longing. They suggest wry weariness at the chaste goddess' refusal to bestow her favours, and so at sublunary Cynthia's. A line later we read: "But the black ominous owl hoot was audible" – and that bathetic predicate mocks the onomatopoeic "owl hoot". (And it mocks the ear that listens for onomatopoeia.) The hoot is not loud or low or long. In what is almost tautology, it is simply audible. And yet what does a black sound sound like? It is like Yeats' "bitter black wind", which the young Pound praised for its "transensuous" effect (*Spirit of Romance* 159). Nine years later, the Pound of *Homage* undoes the effect, exposing the too poetical device.

Sutherland's lineated patent might seem, in contrast, to discover effects and devices, to reveal the magic or the poetry of things. The very object of the patent takes on new and strange significance. Subjected to close or fanciful reading – the kind of reading lineation can seem to invite – the patent describes the volume which, as prose, it fronts and introduces. A patent (*patere*, to open) ought to facilitate opening; here, it promises to open the poems for our consumption and digestion. The door, the frame, the hinge, and the surfaces each more or less metaphorically suggest aspects of *The Stats on Infinity*, as physical object and as poetry. Indeed, the original refrigerator patent identifies its invention as an artwork. It legitimates the new device by offering a "Description of the Prior Art", of the then current design of refrigerator doors, and it explicitly extends the legal claim to cover the many "alternatives, modifications, and variations [which] will be apparent to those skilled in the art". Acknowledging Pound's prior art, *The Stats on Infinity* probes this identification. The surfaces of the volume's leaves face one another, pivoting on a hinge or binding, and the surface of the verse confronts the reader with considerable difficulties of reference and construction. In fact, the whole volume refers to and is constructed through the confrontation of surfaces: verbal, generic, conceptual, political, metallic, papery, bodily. The patent's attempt to describe an object with rigorous precision, however inelegant the resulting sentence, thus suggests new kinds of ever so elegant and rich precision. Insipid prose becomes intoxicating poetry. A language designed to limit meaning and own innovation in the service of profit becomes a language freed to circulate and metamorphose, opened to multiple meanings and collective ownership.

Pound certainly had no liking for patents; he strongly objected to the private ownership of innovation. In 1935 he wrote that the cultural heritage "is the whole aggregate of human inventions, ameliorations of seed, of agricultural and mechanical process belonging to no one man, and to no group, escaping the possibilities of any definition of patents under any possible system of patent rights" (*Selected Prose* 275). At its best, Pound's poetry offers something like that aggregate, a continual reprocessing and redistribution of thought and technique.

But Sutherland's refrigerator patent describes a device designed to effect closure. The assembly is, in the United States patent and in the epigraph, "biased by a spring in a door closing direction". Perhaps that's true of Sutherland's poetry, too. The irony would then be that the opening patent explains how the verbal invention shuts itself. You have to hold the door open. That's a tempting thing to say about the confronting surface of "The Proxy Inhumanity of Forklifts", with its reverberating echoes ("trussed talons"), its wild figurations ("trussed talons in its face scrub"), and its weird syntactic torsions (what is the antecedent of "its"?). One might have said the same thing about *Homage to Sextus Propertius* in 1919; one might still say it about *The Cantos*. And it's tempting to say that, once you've opened the door and turned the page, once you've seen the prose patent turned to verse, everything is welcoming and open and easy again. The poem that confesses its confronting surface no longer confronts.

That is too open and too easy. The inexact identification of artwork and appliance goes both ways. Modern poetry is not exempt from the logic that fetishizes innovation for profit, even the richest plenitude of thoughts and techniques. Sutherland has argued that inherited metrical forms are commodities, subject to that same capitalist logic. The six sonnets *manqués* in *The Stats on Infinity*, each consisting of twelve lines in two irregularly rhymed sestets, repackage and sell on a traditional lyric form. In "The Proxy Inhumanity of Forklifts" metre is a commodity, a "comestible blob" (Kilbride): say, for instance, in a trite, contrite pentameter: "make love immune to triviality". Not just metre, but lineation itself is a commodity. The versified patent reveals poetry to be a bloodless anathema – ἀνάθεμα in the old sense, an offering to false gods. To chant "a door" is to adore, to fetishize the language of ownership and the art of innovation. There is something inadequate about poetry's plenitude. The refrigerator is broken and the food has spoilt.

When Sutherland lineates the patent he changes a single phrase: "biased / by a spring in a door: out of order" (6). It is a disordering to change that attributive "door" to a noun, to be so imprecise about the spring's position in the mechanism. It is a disordering to swing joyfully with the rhyme in "biased / by a spring". It is a disordering when, in spring, the commanding officer of a military camp orders an "unlawful mission [...] to capture and deter looters", and when his troops plead innocence on the grounds that they had been ordered to abuse their prisoners ("Two Soldiers Guilty of Iraq Abuse"). It is a disordering when the door closer assembly of a refrigerator is broken. It is a disordering to write to imperial order. It is disordering when the best words in their best order are not good enough, when poetry cannot redeem "the corrupted and toxic stuff of ordinary or 'everyday' language" (Kilbride) – a redemption of which Pound sometimes dreamed. It is disordering to dream that it could, when ordinary life is out of order, and that is why Pound dreamt so large. There is an order in saying so.

Notes

[1] My thanks to Julian Murphet for his help with this essay.

[2] An allusion which I'm by no means first to notice. See, for instance, http://bebrowed.
wordpress.com/2011/03/19/keston-sutherlands-odes-again/

Works Cited

Dryden, John, *The Works of John Dryden*, ed. Alan Roper and Vinton A. Dearing, vol. 6, *Poems: The Works of Virgil in English, 1697*, ed. William Frost and Vinton A. Dearing (Berkeley, CA: University of California Press, 1987).

Johnson, Lionel, *Poetical Works of Lionel Johnson*, ed. Ezra Pound (London: Elkin Matthews, 1915).

Kilbride, Laura, "'Political all the way down': Keston Sutherland on Poetics, Politics and Community", *Literateur* (25 November 2011) <http://literateur.com/interview-with-keston-sutherland/> accessed on 26 February 2012.

"Keston Sutherland's Odes Again", *Bebrowed's Blog* (19 March 2011) < http://bebrowed.wordpress.com/2011/03/19/keston-sutherlands-odes-again/> accessed 28 February 2012.

Pope, Alexander, *The Poems of Alexander Pope*, ed. John Butt, vol. 7, *The Iliad of Homer, Books I-IX*, ed. Maynard Mack (London: Methuen, 1967).

Pound, Ezra, *The Spirit of Romance* (1910), rev. edn (London: Peter Owen, 1952).

——. *Selected Prose, 1909–1965*, ed. William Cookson (London: Faber and Faber, 1973).

——. *The Cantos* (New York: New Directions, 1996).

——. *Personæ: The Shorter Poems of Ezra Pound*, ed. Lea Baechler and A. Walton Litz, rev. edn (New York: New Directions, 1990).

Stout-Wiegand, Nancy, "Characteristics of Work-Related Injuries Involving Forklift Trucks", *Journal of Safety Research* 18.4 (Winter 1987): 179-190.

Sutherland, Keston, *The Stats on Infinity* (London: Crater, 2010).

"Two Soldiers Guilty of Iraq Abuse", *BBC News* (23 February 2005): <http://news.bbc.co.uk/2/hi/uk_news/4290435.stm> accessed 25 February 2012.

United States Patent 5027473, "Refrigerator Door Closer" (2 July 1991): <http://patft.uspto.gov/netacgi/nph-Parser?Sect1=PTO1&Sect2=HITOFF&d=PALL&p=1&u=%2Fnetahtml%2FPTO%2Fsrchnum.htm&r=1&f=G&l=50&s1=5027473.PN.&OS=PN/5027473&RS=PN/5027473> accessed 27 February 2012.

Danny Hayward

OR STORMING THE SHOPPING CENTRE:
POETRY, COMPETITION, POUND, *QUID*

What does it feel like to write from a margin? Where today *is* the margin, and who made it marginal? What can we say is most authentically characteristic of marginal cultural production in our own historical moment? From my own margin in London in 2012, in the middle or perhaps near the beginning of the most profound crisis for capitalist accumulation since at least the 1930s, it seems that the answer to these questions is negative and unwelcome. Cultural margins proliferate by *renouncing* the desire to storm the cultural centre whose prominence defines their marginality. As the number of margins increases, the *denial* of renunciation increases in amplitude. According to the terms of that denial, renunciation of desire for the centre is not asceticism but *realism*. And the terms with which we describe this realism belong essentially to marketing. Writing from a margin feels like catering to a niche. Thus the terms are set out. We all know that marginal activities of cultural production are no more capable of displacing industrial practices than I am of displacing Ford or Chrysler in the American automobile market, and this is not (at least it is not *only*) because the industrial practices are "too big": the question is not about size (or "productivity") but target markets. Consumers who want to buy big cars are immune to any well-meaning attempt to inveigle them into buying poems or documentation for conceptual art, and while the case of Jesus, who achieved such remarkable efficiency in his manufacture of bread, deserves a separate treatment, precedent suggests that in 2012 Jesus Lunches would soon enough be bought out by Grupo Bimbo. For what is good for Goldman Sachs is good for culture; for what begat Goldman Sachs in turn begat the Tate Modern and the Poetry Foundation. Realistically we know this.

From such basic banalities as these, recent criticism of UK poetry often infers a false conclusion, namely that competition, because it is inhibited in its application to "central" and "marginal" fields of cultural production, is no longer "relevant" for the analysis of political poetry produced at the cultural periphery. Poetry, like all the brethren of the aesthetic perimeter, is not capable of *suffering* the experience of being *outcompeted* by a cultural centre, because in the therapeutic discourse of institutional "structure" (couch architectonics for the terminally asleep), cultural "centres" no longer deign to compete with a margin whose gestures they can do no more than *recuperate*. Thus the partition walls are erected, social possibility is screened off into impossibility, what was painful becomes instead comfortingly irrelevant, and all stresses melt into the good night as surely as a weekend city break in historical Khartoum. But the existence of market *niches* does not negate competition, any more than being locked in a room negates the existence of someone outside with a key: and the more sober accountancy of cultural "impact" which goes under the heading of *efficacy* seems to me to be objectionable not only because it puts poetical afflatus in fetters and frog-marches it to the basement bash of a narcissistic coterie, or because it applies thumbscrews to infinite longing; but also (and this is a more culpable turn) because it deforms an accurate perception of real social relations, that is, the full range and potency of capitalist relations of production and exchange. Right now, the vocabulary of avant-garde "critique" declares that the will to "displace" the cultural centre is properly obsolescent. Its sobriety is shopkeeper consciousness revised to a *Gradus ad Parnassum*. The similarity is obvious. Competitive subsistence in a niche is falsely categorised as autonomy; to this end debt should be kept down, and likewise the head; humility is raised up into a metaphysics whose central purpose is to detain the idea of a true and just and *central* communist culture at the border of what we are permitted to imagine.

These are abstract terms. We admit the Winter Palace was not stormed by a "margin" just as the Bastille was not stormed by a rhomboid, but artists excluded from the culture industry go on imagining in their work what it would mean to produce an art that could compete with and destroy the centre they despise. What does that mean? For Charles Olson, the twentieth-century poet who more than any other imagined himself at the centre of things, poets must go "down through the workings of [their] own throat[s], to that place where breath comes from", but Olson was in many respects a secluded writer, and this essay will travel down the throat to find what malady arises when the breath does *not* catch (projective verse was just another failed launch) – when it does not catch but is instead squeezed out of the chest by a foreign centre, by capital as the ever expanding *true centre* of our life and as *our greatest competitor whether we like it or not*.[1]

The essay will have two parts. In the first, it will offer some brief reflections on Ezra Pound's contribution to Wyndham Lewis' journal *BLAST*, a journal that in my opinion was *not* "influenced", as has so often been argued, by the aesthetics of an anarcho-syndicalism, whose social aims its repudiated, but which desired instead to fix on everything in the aesthetics of syndicalism that it could *use*; which wished to seize those aesthetics and to put them to work in a culture which could *outcompete* and *defeat* working-class politics, of every stripe, and other enemies besides. The second part of the essay will discuss issue thirteen of Keston Sutherland's magazine *Quid*, issued in 2004 in response to the abuses of detainees at the prison camp in Abu Ghraib. Both parts will try to answer to what it means to imagine a true culture of the centre from a position on the margin. The centre is a capitalist centre, the activities of the margin are defined by the present insuperability of that truth; and at the core of the essay is an inquiry into the simplest and most corrupted image of the *relation* between these two terms, between capitalist centre and margin: the image of invasion in competition with competition itself.

§ § §

During the war period hardly anyone attracted more of Pound and Lewis' obloquy than George Bernard Shaw. Shaw in 1915 was a prominent figure: his long pamphlet, *Common Sense About the War*, was still, no doubt, what Arnold Bennett had proclaimed it to be in 1914, "the talk of the town". Shaw was, in other words, the established margin of the state of things. His socialism was domesticated enough to be discussed over tea; his plays were domesticated enough for West End success, and Pound and Lewis might well have despised him well enough on these bases alone. But *Common Sense About the War* offers also a very loquaciously extended account of Fabian attitudes towards the cultural centre, and if the second issue of *BLAST* offers something less akin to Common Sense than to psychopathic marginalia, still it will glow better with Shaw as its context.

Common Sense About the War is a history. After a brief exposé of what he deems to be the culpable because *insufficient* bellicosity of British "diplomatists", whose secretive appeasements of the Germans were "slosh and tosh", Shaw pauses to exclaim:

> I am writing history because an accurate knowledge of what has occurred is not only indispensable to any sort of reasonable behaviour on our part in the face of Europe when the inevitable day of settlement comes, but because it has a practical bearing on the most perilously urgent and immediate business before us: the business of the appeal to the nation for recruits and for enormous sums of money.[2]

Thus two purposes are decorously reconciled. The writing of the history of the build-up to the First World War is "indispensable" to "reasonable behaviour" as "reasonable behaviour" is "indispensable" for one's prospects of salvation at the divinely ordained climax of history, "the inevitable day of settlement"; but readers who surmise from this that Mr. Shaw's head has come unscrewed and has floated beyond both sandbags and clouds and into the distant skies can take solace in the assurance that not only will the pamphlet ensure good outcomes at the eschaton, but, also, will secure for "the nation" what it must urgently and "immediately" needs. What does it need? Yes: "Enormous sums of money".

Despite his progressive's agnosticism, Shaw's position here is quite conventionally protestant, which is to say that it cantilevers salvation and accumulation into a delicate equilibrium. *Things fall apart*, the *Common Sense* pamphlet reassures its polite readership, which, amid the rubble of the war, or just off to its side, and disdaining such ignoble degeneracies as the "forty tolerated homosexual brothels of Berlin" and the "half barbarous Turco and Ghoorka slaves" who fight on its behalf, is mandated with the greatest task of all: of "permeating the educated and influential classes with socialist ideas".[3] When *BLAST* 1 *blasted* Shaw's associate Sidney Webb, newly enrolled with the parliamentary Labour Party, the insult was a tribute not just to Webb's and the Fabians' irremediable drabness, to their delighted tenure in mediocrity, to their transgression of Nietzschean principles of heroic individualism in the name of the crowds of "dolts and flatheads" who flock to the "Peter the Hermits, the Luthers, the Savonarolas" of this world, in a passion to do their bidding; but it was an attack on what Webb, Shaw *et al* understood to be their pre-eminent social task.[4] Webb and Shaw's pre-eminent task, in the eyes of Wyndham Lewis especially, was to dress up history's advancing bad side so that it may nevertheless *not look too big*, and so to dissolve historical *antithesis* back into a bad anagram for *accoutrement. Now that the war is here*, the "socialists" declare, *now that we can't rid ourselves of it, now that any attempt to refuse it is diminished to the merest solipsistic moon-gazing, we "must use the war to give the coup de grace to medieval diplomacy, medieval autocracy, and anarchic export of capital*".[5] The war for Shaw is something to be *used*, an instrument which needs to be placed in the right hands (his own), a kind of wrench which when set to work with proper care and expertise might reduce the "anarchic" flood of exported capital to something more orderly and even *beautiful*, such as for example a *trickle*, whereupon the baneful stench of "medieval diplomacy" would be at last confined to its outhouse along with the ornithologist Sir Edward Grey, English Foreign Secretary, and whatever other vestigially "medieval" rotten apples can be found in the fruit bowls of the well-meaning English bourgeoisie. There is no sense when reading Shaw (it would not after all be *common-sense*) that the war, whatever it was, might not be a "thing" capable of being "used". Everything just needs its proper increment of plumbing.

Other artists had a more sophisticated account of *use* not least because they had a more refined account of hydraulics. As T.E. Hulme – another associate of Pound's and Lewis' – wrote, in his translator's preface to Sorel's *Reflections on Violence*,

> Our younger novelists, like those Roman fountains in which water pours from the mouth of a human mask, gush as though spontaneously from the depth of their own being, a muddy romanticism that has in reality come through a very long pipe.[6]

The aversion Hulme felt for the effluence of "our younger novelists", the epithet for whom he lifted from a description of Zola in Romain Rolland's *Jean Christophe in Paris*, led him in turn to a philosophy of "classical" and "pessimistic" conception, which, had he not been blown apart by a shell in 1917, might have culminated in a High Anglican resignation similar in tone to T.S. Eliot's. (His later writing promises a turn into the same chapel of echoing pomposities.) But Hulme's hydraulic dismissal of what Eliot would call the "torturing vacuity" of a certain set of "younger" Anglophone novelists, grouped by means of rhetorical plagiarism with the socialist Zola, is an attack not only on the intellectually exiguous moralism of a moribund bourgeois aesthetics, but also on the *additive* ethics of bourgeois reconciliation that says we need only graft onto the working class movement or to the war our *own* good ideas, not yet Fallen from their berth in Milton's *happie Eden*, and still nakedly unashamed of their will to political power.[7] The fact of war's "distance", and of the impossibility of "using" it to achieve whatever end or whatever "definite noble purposes" we might confect, was no more real for Hulme, who died in Oostduinkerke, than it is now for even the most remotely "privileged" poet-academic working from his office in Nevada.

BLAST I was published in 1914, five years before England acquired a significant communist party, in a period when solutions to this question, of how to overcome the distance between the real movement of the working classes and the real cocktail parties of the bourgeoisie, were still thin on the theoretical ground. *BLAST* 2, a somewhat disregarded successor, was published in July 1915, three months after Rupert Brooke's "The Soldier" was intoned from the pulpit at Saint Paul's.[8] Both of these magazines were very plainly and even ostentatiously unconcerned about their relationship to the proletariat. *BLAST*'s woodcuts, polemics and pasquinades famously mock every social type on which they can lay their *magenta oposculusi*. But what the magazine *is* interested in is the sabotage of bourgeois socialist impostures of the Shavian type. And here Pound comes in. In *BLAST* 2,

"The War Number", Pound's first poem is printed on the twentieth page. It is called "Dogmatic Statement On The Game And Play of Chess (Theme for a Series of Pictures)".

> Red knights, brown bishops, bright queens
> Striking the board, falling in strong "L's of colour,
> Reaching and striking in angles,
>   Holding lines of one colour:
> This board is alive with light
> These pieces are living in form,
>   Their moves break and reform the pattern:
> Luminous green from the rooks,
>   Clashing with "x's" of queens,
>   Looped with the knight-leaps.
> "Y" pawns, cleaving, embanking,
> Whirl, centripetal, mate, King down in the vortex:
> Clash, leaping of bands, straight strips of hard colour,
> Blocked lights working in, escapes, renewing of contes[9]

"Dogmatic Statement", like *BLAST* more generally, refused to contribute to the ritual weeping orchestrated from the pulpits of St. Paul by the clerisy of "Social Order". Pound did not decide for his readers what war "was"; nor did he decide what it had to do with him. The "invitation" to "respond" to war is a false invitation insofar as it stipulates a definition of the social phenomenon to which the artist is to respond; the autonomy of *sentiment* in the face of the enormous slaughter of proletarian soldiers and civilians, acting under the directions of competing states, each representing competing capitalist interests, is for Pound, not an autonomy much worth having.[10]

The poem "Dogmatic Statement" is also about chess. The typo with which it finishes, "renewing of contes", is, for one critic, once it has been emended to its proper "contest", "a model of... the 'tensional' aesthetic of Vorticism".[11] Patricia Rae does not say in her analysis what kind of model the poem constitutes. Perhaps it is a "model" in the way that the "twitching of three abdominal nerves", redacted in *BLAST* 1 from Pound's "Fratres Minores", is a spermatozoal "model of" the wretched yearning for transcendence evinced by "[c]ertain poets here and in France", who mistake their testicles for the ineffable.[12] At any rate the last line is in this reading certainly *not* a "response to" or (its nastier synonym) "a comment on" the war, any more than it could be a misspelling for the sake of melopoeia of *countess*, or, more to the point, any more than it could be a pun in proleptic admission of the "Social Order" which provides the title for the next poem which *Blast* presented.[13] But then in what sense is Pound's writing in *BLAST* a poetry for or against (or in any case *in*) imperialism?

The question might best be approached by a diversion. In 1916 Pound was writing enthusiastically to the would-be *Imagiste* Iris Barry a programme for aesthetic education. His recommendation of all the work that was "worth something", his "KOMPLEAT KULTURE", was in fact a very select canon indeed. More than anything, Pound was insistent that Barry commit, if she thought herself able, to learning Latin, "[t]he value being", he said,

> that the Roman poets are the only ones we know of who had approximately the same problems as we have. The metropolis, the imperial posts to all corners of the known world. The enlightenments.[14]

Pound does not then go on to elaborate in any fine detail what "imperial posts to all corners of the world" mean for the *poetry* whose reading he so ardently promotes. He does not tell us that Virgilian meter represents the binding of the racial *differend* in unity, or that the end of the line in Latin verse functions as the surrogate for fear of the imperial perimeter. The barbarian hordes are not amassing at the right margin. Experiencing the relevance of Latin verse to English composition in 1914 does not involve specifying the *exact* relationship of Latin verse technique to Roman Imperial anxieties. There is no one set of plausible synchronic resemblances. Gibbonesque memorial grutching on the topic of "the terrible irruption of the huns" is not like a trochee or an unstressed long syllable, Pound thinks; and this is not because technique is not "historical" but because the relationship between history and technique is more complex (but also more fraught) than any merely technical *vocabulary* in which we might choose to express it. The "problems" that must by implication be incarnated in the language retain only an unstated connection to the actual practice of literary craft, or to the acquisition of "the tools" for poetic construction, as Pound goes on to put it, out of sight of "Romanticism" and its numberless ruminant visionaries (Wordsworth is a "dull sheep").[15]

Because neither is "problems" a neutral term, even where the problems in question are tactfully understood to be "approximate" rather than absolute or perfectly calculable. The word has in Pound's letter a fragrance of scholasticism, and intentionally so, for poetry must have restituted to it the intellectual dignity which it lost when the poetic mind, like the holy spirit gone AWOL or like T.S. Eliot strolling "by accident" into his landlady's bedroom, sublimed itself into a hovering position above the poetic testicles.[16] By mocking poetic afflatus and reducing it to a kind of pneumatology of the groin, Pound was able to believe in the seriousness of his reading lists: mockery defended them against the satire that, in 1914, England's "enlightened" liberals were aiming at the conservatives whose favoured "science" of socio-biology had been (thus the liberals) "perverted" into a justification for military Imperialism. One of the reasons Pound had to repudiate "poetic" language, flowery and recondite, is that such writing was taken by his enemies to be a screen for bad thinking. "[T]hus, emerging from natural history, the doctrine [of Imperialism] soon takes on a large complexity of ethical and religious finery, and we are wafted into an elevated atmosphere of 'imperial Christianity', a 'mission of civilization,' in which we are to teach 'the arts of good government' and 'the dignity of labour'."[17] The liberal Fabian J.A. Hobson's criticism of socio-biology does not begin by explaining the limits of its truth, but by criticising the enthusiasts who "waft" whatever science it might contain into a theodicy designed to justify the damage of imperial expansionism. Problems which ought to be rationally managed, such as the identification of a "necessary outlet for progressive industry", cannot be rationally managed by the wafting and vapouring of rhymesters, rhapsodising over the dulcet cadences of the machine-gun fire dispensed in "the national interest" into the bodies of those decent and unassuming soldiers whose civilian appetites are required to "swell the tides of consumption". The "science of economics" is no less vitiated by such rhetoric. It is impossible to understand the insouciant ferocity with which *BLAST* 2 proposed that the Allies must win the war, because this would be the best outcome *for art*, without knowing the social registration of the reverse argument, that "art", in Nietzsche's words, is just "a faint tinkling of bells" whose fine melodies drown out the real (*aristocratic*) interests served by the social order of "things as they are".[18] The stewardship of that argument, in 1902 and in 1914, was liberal, and it was bourgeois, and Pound's decision to make the "imperial posts" crowding across the surface of the world into a "problem" for poets (and not, as it might well have been, and might be again yet still, a *joy* or a *disaster*) is then not only a defensive manoeuvre – an attempt to dissociate art from the overt euphemism of aristocratic propaganda – but a challenge, meant to force on people like Hobson the realisation that they knew *nothing about life*. But in what sense is the work in *BLAST* 1 (as much as in *BLAST* 2) a *war poetry*, more absolutely a war poetry than anything by Rupert Brooke, spinning in his necrotic sonnets the banal nationalist hysteria of a properly "English heaven"?

The poetry in *BLAST* marks the emergence of a "war" poetry whose language is *in competition* with war. It is not the re-emergence of a "Stirnian" individualism in the contortion of prosody, as it is in all the tepid recountings of Pound's and Lewis' later commitments to fascism, however significant, various (and however hateful) those commitments may have been and will forever be, and nor is it the scintillating datum serving as evidence for the anxiety of influence, the phallic posturing against the misinterpreted Father; but what it is instead is the first emergence of a poetic language which knows that if it is to survive it *must* defeat other language (and not just poetry) in an unregulated and devious and destructive competition. And it could not be anything other than war poetry, this writing; because war was the zenith of competition, thriving at the absolute peak of its boom while everything else, every other "national capital" and every one of the millions of proletarians who were forced to fight for its "benefit", "rectified the borders" of hell so that they might better situate themselves in its centre. In spite of what Lenin and other theorists of "monopoly capital" might have had to say, World War I was the first global trademark of competition as the principle of capital worldwide, of capital in its repulsive, depersonified, universal aggregate.

§ § §

On 1 March, 2003, the share price of News Corp closed on $10.70. When stocks peaked four years later, in January 2007, shares closed on $23.25. Over the same period, shares in CNN parent-company Time Warner rose from $24.07 to $48.01. Time Warner's shares "spiked" from $23.07 to $30.02 on 1 April 2003. This is a list of prices. But what do these figures *represent*? What does it mean to say that they represent *anything* at all? How much pressure of attention do we bring to this concept? The subsidiaries of News Corp and Time Warner – we can name them: Fox News and CNN – both competed for viewers throughout the decade, just as each benefited from "global events", one of the effects of which was to encourage US television viewers to watch the news. In the right kind of "economic climate", which is to say, one where consumers might conceivably buy the commodities they *see*, increasing viewing figures translate in turn into increasing advertising revenue. The promise of sustained advertising income, high profits and "corporate ambition" influence a company's ability to access private capital in order to drive long-term expansion; while all of these "factors" find their distorted mirror-image in a statistic stating total market capitalisation, which provides the aggregate value of a company by multiplying the current value of one share by the total number in issue. At the time of writing News Corp possesses a market capitalisation of $49.33 billion, Time Warner of £35.36 billion.

The first answer to my questions is as follows. These are the capitalist *prices* of a triumphant capitalist culture: they are the representatives in bourgeois categories of capitalist control over real human labour. And yet do we know what it means (do we know the full psychology) of this specific weakness, of having no control over the labour by which we sculpt meaning in images and in language, when our enemies have control over so much? What kind of competition does this thought compel us to define? Marx wrote in *Wage Labour* and *Capital* that the effect of competition between capitals – the advancement of the division of labour – is that the worker "becomes transformed into a simple monotonous force of production, with neither physical nor mental elasticity." In consequence, Marx writes, work, reduced to the discharge of a partial function, "becomes accessible to all", if only in the limited and grimly typical sense that every member of the newly de-skilled pool of the "industrial reserve army" is forced to engage in internecine conflict over a *finite* number of jobs. What this means is that for anyone who has the relative fortune to be *in* work, "competitors press upon him from all sides."[19] In general, then, the result of capitalist competition is the intensification of competition between those who are subject to capital. What we discover when we shuffle into the "hidden abode" of production is that the second level of social reproduction – the reproduction of humans – repeats the behaviour of the first, of *value*. And so does this tell us what we need to know about how competition incarcerates itself in life, out of the frying pan of exclusively economic relations and into the monotonous forces of production of our present cultural industries? But if competition in the "field" of culture were to be *homologous* with competition within the system of capitalist exploitation and employment, merely a sub-Mayakovskian isomorph in trousers, swerving across the superstructure, then culture defined by its antagonism to capitalist social relations could hardly enter into competition with the culture which supports those relations. It could not do so because the terms of the homology would dictate that the primary interest of antagonistic culture is only the avoidance of *jostling* with whomever it deems to be its allies; and because the idea of leaping into the fray armed with one's skills in versification to *bring it* to News Corp (NSW) and its $49.33 billion market capitalisation is somewhat akin to imagining the struggle of David and Goliath after the surgical removal of David's limbs. And this will not do at all. But then how does triumph against the culture of the centre continue to be imagined, if it is imagined? And are the efforts of Lewis and Pound now revealed to us as merely delusion and megalomania, bad etiquette, intellectual corruption, the wild preludes to the political imbecility we already know to convict them of?

Here is one way of answering that question. The way we imagine a triumphant culture against capitalism is, first of all, by learning to build the exact image of what it means at present to be defeated, which is to say, to be isolated, unconvincing, speechless; or if not silent then to be impotently garrulous, screamingly marginalised into the straitjacket we wear to mark our entitlement to disquiet – and to be all of these in the face of a share value *in the business* of rising into ever new intensities of delight, ascending piously heavenward in joyful recognition of the enduring truths of human degradation and misery. To be precise about this has never been more urgent: this much we can assert willingly. This is one answer. But is it *right*? Can the effects of competition be maintained like this, folded into such a pristine semblance of negativity? What other desires for *inappropriate* competition continue to assert themselves? Can those desires be volatilised and not extinguished?

The rest of this article will reflect on a special issue of Keston Sutherland's magazine *Quid, Ira Quid* (2004), a collection of five poems almost all of which respond directly and undeniably to the images of torture in Abu Ghraib.[20] It will not comment substantially on another intervention into the public cultural discourse on Iraq, *The poetry is not in the pity*, a much more various compilation edited by Sean Bonney, Harry Gilonis, Frances Kruk and issued in 2009 in response to a reading by veterans of the wars in Afghanistan and Iraq at the Imperial War Museum.[21] *The poetry is not in the pity* does not offer its diversities in witless homage to the "variety" of human responses that the war might "provoke", in the language afforded to objects whose assigned *raison d'être* is to permit their spectator to reassure himself of his own capacities for sentimental benignancy. The collection is a violent reproof of that social ritual; its variety is calculated to advance the critique of a poetry that justifies again and again the regimentation of the imperialist state's standing army by insisting on the indefeasible persistence of the *inner life* of the troops who routinely kill for it. No doubt it was rightly despised its recipients, the elderly ladies and valetudinarian gentleman whose patronage for the museum is facilitated by their shareholdings in the companies profiting from the war that the museum promotes. (Shareholder hermeneutics are as circular as any other kind).

But it is in consequence of its relative consistency that the remainder of this article will focus on *Ira Quid*. It is (and it remains) the closest thing "contemporary UK poetry" has or had to a poetic *project* against the war; it remains so despite the fact that its writers committed to no common program or politics. But what is a general characterisation of this poetry? I might begin, antagonistically, with a burlesqued and generalised account. In the "curved mirror" of liberal complicity, moral responsibility is distorted into a false uniformity; capitalist imperialism is tapered into the "states" and "citizens" who inhabit it; the citizens of the imperialist nations are dressed in the one-size-fits-all pronoun "us" and lined up with the soldiers who beat, raped and murdered the Iraqis they imprisoned. Is this a just response to imperialism? Two months before the war in Iraq was officially declared, Keston Sutherland had written in a notice on the website Circulars that the war was "the effect of the suffering of a proletarianised population massed across Africa and Asia, [of] their suffering and daily submission to the capitalist work process and the value exploited from them by corporations and Western consumers alike."[22] Much of the same livid energy and disgust is shot through every line and snaps in every break of the poetry in *Ira Quid*, and later in *The poetry is not in the pity* too; but is it "massed" across it "alike", as Sutherland says when he writes that the proletariats of Africa and Asia are as if a single, "daily submissive", exploitable heap, as later the human pyramid at Abu Ghraib will be, before it is turned into "the collapsed pyramid of accountability and desire" in Andrea Brady's poem, the metaphors rising towards the heavens in a tower of hot, over-articulate despair, or just as "Kant and Fichte soared to Heavens blue" in the admiring opinion of the nineteen year-old Karl Marx; *is it really*; and are "Western consumers" really so adjustably fungible, so "alike" to the corporations in whose stock (perhaps) their pension funds invest? This is not, as it might appear, merely a quibble about the "ethics" of pronouns, since that vague and comfortably intractable problem scrambles the demands of political accuracy, the demands of accuracy which the digital images of Iraqi corpses with their eyeballs melted across their cheeks must surely place on us, if "questioning" is to prevent itself from blurring with lachrymose complacency into the tears of sanctimonious regret wept by state leaders. The tears are lost in a run-off into the mere sentiment whose purpose is to irrigate the brutality it regrets but does not oppose. J.H. Prynne in his "Refuse Collection" may also address "us" with an obliterating expansiveness, when he writes "Till they yelp and/ will rise up against us in a storm of justice", but whatever his attitude in theory towards the mechanics and the theological niceties of capitalist exploitation, Prynne has the speed of poetic thought to force "us" to stop, and his line continues jerkily "or/ let's pause to redefine that run up a treaty sell/ them into so-called paradigm", disadjusting the remote control so that the image of "who we are" can refract the ardour of self-negation, ardour which is not only imprecise but is actively complicit in the concealment of "class" by "nation". Prynne's line finally (and typically) will not disclose which element of his vision of "our" just and eschatological defeat he will "redefine", whether it is "us" or the false pleasure "we" might rake in visioning an eschatology whose historical abstraction reconcretises itself as the exotic emollient cataplasm for the pangs of the liberal psyche (and where better to apply it than in front of the television, the common denominator of every bad analysis of the indifferentism of commodity consumption?); and yet perhaps the most generous way to read "Refuse

Collection" is to recognise in that nested incertitude not the consolations of ambiguity (the euphemism of social cretinism) but instead a difficult straining in language to speak rightly in the face of what is – as Justin Katko says – *evil*, a writing that hates its failure restfully and intelligently enough not to pretend that it succeeds.[23]

Poets are not the unacknowledged legislators of the world: they may perhaps be the magistrates of one of its parishes. And though poetic language may strive to be *passionate* for justice, as Prynne once wrote to Edward Dorn to tell him that it must; and though it may self-abnegate with a cry of "fiat justitia, pereat mundeas", as earlier Heinrich Heine imagined it would when he fantasised his books being made into "cones" in which snuff would be delivered to old women, after the communist revolution had equitably obliterated the perquisites on which Heine the poet relied; – though poetry may strive with emphatic querulousness against all injustice, there is nothing unusual about the basic fact that poets are distant from the violence they most deplore.[24] When our poets "kick the door in" and enter the scene of cruelty, *flâneurs* of the imagination transacting in more brutal fields, they are not an avant-garde of faithful witnesses, relating to *le peuple* back home the experience of the war, as for example the poets who joined the International Brigades in '36 went as witnesses for an ethical culture ("I am your choice. Your decision", says Auden). "The people" today possess the same televisions or web browsers and read the same journalism. What is poetry to do?

Or what kind of arguments does *Ira Quid* have to make? What does it take its marginality to be? How does it relate itself to the concepts in which *imperialism* is typically characterised? One way to answer that question involves taking a step backward, to the magazine's first pages. The title page of *Ira Quid* shows a stick diagram faintly resembling the front cover of *Monthly Review*'s 1972 publication of Arighiri Emmanuel's *Unequal Exchange*.[25] Emmanuel's work, a great classic of a Marxian theory of international relations, whose central contention is that asymmetrical labour costs in commodities exchanged between rich and poor countries constitutes a kind of exploitation, is certainly a potential inspiration for the more raspingly aggressive formulation in Sutherland's "Short Critique". The cover of *Unequal Exchange* shows two coloured balls arranged on a crude line drawing of a pair of scales, one ball larger and outweighing the other, the uneven weights indicated by a diagonal line. The title page of Ira Quid shows two balls also, but with one ball now migrating underneath the scales and interning as its prop, while the other, stretched into an oval, and no longer met by a counterbalance, has sunk to the ground. An arrow at the end of the scale where the first ball *ought* to be indicates a downward force, so that the whole contraption has become a kind of dysfunctional see-saw or catapult, cantilevered into a subtle dispute with its archetype. In Iraq, even unequal exchange has gone wrong.

This is all well and good and thus one might well not choose to comment on it. But what is the relation of the poetry that follows this image in *Ira Quid* to the account in international trade economics of "what man has made of man", i.e., an arrangement of two balls in which one derives its hypertrophy from the emaciation of the other? Emmanuel's *Unequal Exchange* is a theory of prices, which is to say that it tells us only what ought to be obvious, that workers who receive low wages produce commodities whose cost for workers who receive high wages will be low (and vice versa). Perhaps the logic of the *détournement* is something like this: As the potlatch of talon missiles rained in on Iraq, playing out the most elemental logic of the military-industrial gift economy, with the full "economic" logos of the war not understood but as yet only implied, and taking as its emblem the image of an oil pipeline, which, telescoped across confused landscapes of antagonism and mediation, ascends into a horizon of indifferent and inscrutable rationality, it was not enough to defeat a "theory" (Ricardian "comparative advantage") whose sovereignty could not be defined by its cogency. Language must break apart at this its limit, of what we can tell ourselves that we "know", just as the dynamic of capitalist society breaks apart into the perplexity of its unsurpassable dissolution. The scales become a see-saw.

The more revolutionary-sounding proposals in *Ira Quid* are, correspondingly, metrically stunted, syntactically disempowered, coadjacent with the jargon of their etiolation (Brady: "at least/ these ones were resisting cocked in their mouths"; Calton: "insurmountable global risk of/ vivid just resistance"). We can go on imagining this now, in 2012, not in consequence of any placid popular "submission" before exploitation but because the insurgency against it is so diversely splintered, is shattered beyond the limits at which our most prominent theories of political organisation might imagine it can once again hold them in unity, under our guidance. But what then does this mean for the language of this poem; what happens when we move into that? Is there any more life in the veins it expropriates than there is in the *détourned* cartoon placed in the magazine's title page? Is its own language more fragmented or broken than this?

Some taxonomy may be in order. In *Ira Quid*, there are many kinds of broken language. There are ordinary disjunctures. Text splits apart or cracks into disunity; individual words are mutilated out of shape. In Calton's "Risk Douse", "rapine", or perhaps "rape" becomes "rap on", an aphasic or non-Anglophone distortion, as if language should become almost sluggish with trauma. Elsewhere words are hidden or splintered across phrases, as when in "Refuse Collection" the *rota* of capital, its circuit of accumulation, becomes the "apache rotor capital" of the US army attack helicopters whose fuselages Iraqis sometimes had the temerity to fire on, as they passed above what Ambassador Paul Bremer called their "sleepy farming compounds"; or then it becomes the "sweet rot adoring placid" of capital surveying its new domain. These breaks cleaving the interior of the line are of course multiplied at the line's end (every poem in *Ira Quid* is a poem versified), but the line break too is extended across an axis of additional enjambments whose existence is virtual or implied: in the poems in *Ira Quid*, virtual enjambment can set in one word after the real break or one word before it. The first kind of interruption is most often applied in Calton's poem, as when "hawkers" – lumpenproletarian street sellers or lumpenbourgeois politicians – "flash/ out string up, rain/ down". Here the sense is interrupted at the end of the first line and then again after the first word of the second line, its imposition traded off against the threat of the non-idiomatic phrase "out string" or "out string up". Enjambment, in this sense if in no other isomorphic with "The West", invades what it delineates. The other, second kind of interruption is most importantly worked in "Song of the Wanking Iraqi". When Sutherland writes "the temperature/ is right so the vapour won't evaporate it/ can be permethrin", the virtual break occurs one word before enjambment and the double break discloses itself as such only once the second line has been scanned. The second break is experienced *after* the enjambment but is textually localised *before* it: in this *ex post facto* verse technique, meaning is ruptured *retrospectively*, what we believed to be true is negated on condition of continuing. Or, more simply, the superaddition of grammatical elements in a line permits a new unit of sense to be produced only by retrospectively breaking an old one. What seemed to evade solecism must later be shattered. To what end? Does this experience of retrospective negation *allegorise* the more basic experience of information processing in a capitalist news industry, an industry whose continued profitability is equal to its schedule of oblivion? It would be very easy to say that it does, and that the language "critiques" this condition. But then why would it do that? Does the mere facticity of its analogy constitute a critique? And yet it remains to be established that this analogy is real and not just tendentious, since my experience of retrospective negation of sense, active while I read this poetry and constitutive of my account of *what it* is, does not feel to me while I undergo it as if it is much akin to (as if I can say it is *just like*) my experience of watching the news. Why would I then decide that it must be akin to it, just on the basis of the poetry's own irrefragable interest in the disinformation which the news industries commodify? Or (and here is the point *in nuce*): what is the purpose of these disjunctions, if it is not *unmediatedly* a political point?

When we read the lines "and a vapour fed in/through the pipe in short jets the temperature/ is right" we can create a "new" sentence beginning with "through" only on condition that we *reject* the sentence that grammatically continues itself by means of the enjambed adverbial phrase "*in/ through*". The experience of reading the poem, then, is not the *toleration* of compiled lexical, semantic or rhythmical ambiguities: it is, rather, the fluency of repudiation immanent to the act of readerly "choice". Repudiation and election are reproduced as structures of emphasis. *Ira Quid* cumulatively imagines a Theory of Reader Repudiation. And John Wilkinson's "Multistorey" also is full of breaks whose possibility only becomes livid for a reader when she has been trained to expect them. "Fair's fair storied is that number you'd first/ push against" is, *potentially*, a line of grammatical verse, straining towards solecism but not yet quite achieving it, and it takes a certain habit of perception to feel that the copula "is" is also insistently the *interrogative* "is", attacking its own ground. The significance of the potential break – the meaning of it but also its *importance*; since why after all *should I care?* – is altered by the meaning of the grammatical line "Fair's fair & storied is that number", whose *Kleinbürger* sententiousness reaches a veritable crescendo of flaccidity when it becomes apparent that the phrase "that number" is the *subject* and not the *object* of "Fair's fair & storied". The spectacle of a 24th-rate Popean imitator who inverts his pomposity and finds it good does then perhaps tell us why the eleventh syllable of this flummoxed pentameter begins to rebel against its surroundings: "first" rises up in a storm of justice to "push against" the language which owns it, organising a new first heave against language that "didn't hurt" and doesn't think it hurts not to.[26]

We are not hurt enough, we readers of this poetry; that may be so, and it may take language more sheerly bristling with incandescences and more distraught, more febrile or sensitively decomposed than the language we are inundated with, from day to day, by the experts of public speech, to snap us into a state of attention less martial than our present complacency. It will take more than that. For where in language does solidarity begin? Out of what dimension of competition with the forces of capital, including its cultural forces – all the means of its production of language and spectacle – could there arise a force in language that is capable of something more than the atomised anatomy of its present marginality, the marginality of any culture that is not, *de facto* and *de jure*, the reflection of capitalist relations of property, extended worldwide by exchanges of which we can say it hardly matters whether they are "equal" or not, in capitalist terms, because capitalist equality implies inequality *wherever it occurs*, and relies for its existence on the ceaseless and crippling reproduction of that inequality? Where do we turn? To dream of the realisation *within our experience of reading* of a language competent to assert itself and to rise up and to "enforce" our complicity is now uniquely foolish, it is the abuse of an ambition conducted in the whimsical search for a verb (what else can I say that this language *does?*), and it cuts off in reading like shrapnel through a limb the truer task of ascertaining what happens in writing whose premature allegorisation can only mock the political object it strains for. Because the language which makes up this poetry is not enforcing our complicity or anyone else's, and nor does it aspire, in a strange perversion of Walter Pater's formula, to the condition of *policing*; but at its very best it is work conducted in the name of competition: the final competition between a capitalist culture racinated in the soil with blood and the communist culture that must at last overcome it. To say that the work is defined by the creation and reproduction of *divisions* in language is not yet to decide that the poetry is adequate to its task (that it *enforces* its protocols); it is not adequate to the extent and qualitative complexity of division in language, just as no "politics" has yet been adequate to the task even of "knowing" the extent and qualitative complexity of divisions in social life.[27] The work is staggering for being so preliminary because we its performers remain so distant from the state where our art could carry the world before it, as capitalist culture now so definitely does. Not only do we not "know" what it would mean to create a true, which is to say a *global*, unity against capital, but we do not know the breadth of our disunity. The situation of the imperialist Aeneas might still be ours,

> He rose, the Coast and Country to survey.
> Anxious and eager to discover more:
> It look'd a wild uncultivated Shoar;
> But whether Human Kind, or Beasts alone
> Possess'd the new-found Region, was unknown.[28]

It has always been in the interests of conquerors to believe that the lands they arrive in are possessed by "Beasts", and in Dryden's translation Aeneas has begun to answer his own question before he claims its answer is "unknown", because throughout the history of empire whatever can be said to look "uncultivated" has not *yet* found its rightful owner, the person for whom the Region is "new-found". And Prynne concludes similarly: "Our land ours/ raw and forever", he says, to you, to "Shit-Boy" and the "broom handle" that can "go all night". Prynne's line traces out the defeat of collectivity in the resources it most owns: the second "our" is the phonetic surrogate of a *y* in the (uniquely) enforced glide from the plosive *d*, of *your* land, a collectivity abolished and resolved into *dour* acceptance. What happened at Abu Ghraib was of course the far limit of "our" ability to believe in our capacity for unity with the "exploited masses" of Iraq ("masses" who are themselves splintered beyond the far limits of the cognisance of any "non-speaker" of Iraqi Arabic), but it is specifically in the address to the presently unalterable truth of disunity, in the moment where we find language shimmering with its disarray, high on breaks and "anxious and eager to discover more" – it is precisely *then* that the competition which is the law of life under capital breaks down in virtuality. This is not a "plea for efficacity", as Simon Jarvis once wrote: what it is instead is the one way in which the *idea* of the full extent of the arrest of communist culture can be kept in the targets of communist cadences and vocatives.[29]

For Pound, the inventor of the first "first heave", England was an ersatz empire because its culture had not yet learnt to know its own breadth. The sheepish parochialism of English speech rhythm closes its borders against the wealth of cadences whose totality represents the true jewel of the imperium, the import it most needs to satiate the poet enthroned at its centre. If Pound's books of translations were the restitution of the *various* beauty proper to the language of an empire, *Ira Quid* provides the most extensive collection of *breaks* that English verse has yet known. The tremendous variety of these, of grammatical and prosodic and typographical breaks, of real implied and virtual breaks, shifting and converging like the "gigantic network of narrow streams" in Rosa Luxemburg's description of the mass strike, are the reflection in engaged verse technique of the increasing multiplication of divisions, of the class lines that divide, splinter and fragment those masses whose historical task is to destroy capital.[30] The breaks offer a vision of unity seared through the realisation of its opposite.

What is the meaning of "distance" in an anti-capitalist and anti-imperialist poetry in 2003? The poetry in *Ira Quid* is not written to restitute potency to the city or to the imperium, and "distance" is not conceived through the telescopes of Romantic aesthetics. Distance, in other words, is not *sublimity*, given its proper aristocratic dominion by William Hazlitt when he wrote that "passion is the Lord of Infinite Space"; for distance in language, capable always of being overcome, is the semblance of a *total* system of communications in which the possibility of absolutely free movement – the opposite of Ricardo and Emmanuel's "immobility of factors" – is intimated without the collapse of the total global architecture of social distinction, from the suburban grid-sprawl of Manchester, described so well in 1842 by Engels, to the system of biometric border policing now in global operation.[31] Distance in language must be made somehow insuperable. But is it possible? What resources are available for the realization of that end? *Ira Quid* is thick with resources throughout: the breaks in a language established beyond computation; the *élan vital* of repudiation; the allegorisation of vivid resistance in pauses and stutters, assembled on a line of bourgeois tongues whose existence is virtualised in pronominal forecasting, as crude as oil itself. And then contrariwise to this, tracking backwards, the signs of the world it arises out of: the evocation of a strand of Marxist politics faltering in the twilight of national liberation struggles; the high-tech discontents of a superpower attempting to "manage" with Talon missiles the "emergent complexity" of its declining competitiveness; the fullest effort in consumerist iconography to diminish the potential *agents* of class struggle into the *victims* of abuse, Stakhanov rotating with Shit Boy on a display turntable brought to you by CNN. And at last, above all these, the image of triumph.

It is difficult now to imagine what it would mean to triumph against bourgeois culture. The emergence into (what falsifies itself as) the "public domain" of the images of torture produced at Abu Ghraib must have established the maximum for our distance from it. The poetry in *Ira Quid* knows that to outwit bourgeois culture is not yet to defeat it, because wit is not the principle of bourgeois culture's dominion. Bourgeois culture dominates by its scale, which in the last instance (and perhaps elsewhere also) is the transubstantiation of capitalist control over social labour into the flesh and blood of marketable spectacle. It is difficult to imagine what it would mean to triumph against bourgeois culture, really at last to *triumph* against it, to triumph in equal measure against Renoir's pastel mystifications of the innocent sublimity of childhood imagination and against the National Gallery of Art Washington where that mystification appreciates value; but why is that so? It is, after all, so easy to know the *conditions* of its defeat. But then it is difficult, in part, because it is impossible to make writing glow alight into frenzy with an image of triumph grounded simply in the true acknowledgement of the basic circumstances in which it might compete with the culture industry, whose specialists in *the new* are forever on hand adjustably to absorb whatever admonitions its enemy cultures might devise for it. Dead effort, the totality of human performance controlled by the law of value, by the process of value exploitation under the rule of capital, invades language just as the burnt leaves in Book One of Dryden's *Aeneid* *invade* the sky, in columns of ashes, in an allegory that would be sickening (because it would be so demeaning) if it were not already our truth. Aeneas sacks Carthage. And then, somewhat later, poetry devises new resources of repudiation, it strains to make language more resourceful than any language that has ever preceded it, and the resources sit in our mouth and allegorise nothing except the implacable effortlessness of their performance. In the world we discover our mouths to be *implacably effortless*: the tongue idles on its floor; teeth develop clientelistic relationships with gums; the whole cavity teems with parasites; and this effortlessness cannot be placated, because it is not ours; our effort will not be effort and nor will it be ours for so long as the culture of the enemy commands more effort than we can know. And what we can know, I think, is a variety of pastoral, a strain of it radiant with triumphant calamity, the physical condition of bourgeois individuality as the instance of an allegory whose social truth can only be assured in the fact of its denial, down the dark corridors of a detention centre where triumph now is.

Notes

[1] Olson, *Selected Writings* (New York, NY: New Directions, 1966), p. 18.

[2] Bernard Shaw, *Common Sense About the War*, Special War Supplement to the *New Statesman*, November 14, 1914 (London: The Statesman Publishing Co., Ltd., 1914). Reprinted in *What I Really Said About the War* (London: Constable and Company, 1931), p. 46.

[3] Ibid., p. 83.

[4] The phrase belongs to the arch-reactionary Gustave le Bon's description of the influence of demagogues on "the masses". *The Crowd*, 1st ed 1895 (New York, NY: Transaction Publishers, 2009), p. 141.

[5] Shaw, *What I Really Said*, p. 110.

[6] Hulme's "Preface" is reprinted in the *Collected Writings*, ed. by Karen Sengeri (Oxford: Oxford University Press, 1994), p. 249.

[7] Eliot, Review of *Reflections on Violence*, by George Sorel, *Monist* (27 July 1917), p. 478.

[8] *BLAST: Review of the Great English Vortex*, 1 (London: John Lane, 1914); *BLAST: Review of the Great English Vortex*, 2 (London: John Lane, 1915). Both editions of *BLAST* are now accessible online from *The Modernist Journals Project*, though with some obtrusive copyright conditions. http://www.modjourn.org/render. php?id=1143209523824844&view=mjp_object [accessed 28/01/2012]

[9] *BLAST* 2, p. 25.

[10] This may well be why the shedding of duck tears is noticeably absent from Canto 16, where Pound's final poetic elegies to Gaudier-Brzeska and T.E. Hulme are located. "And ole T.E.H. he went to it,/ With a lot of books from the library,/ London Library, and a shell buried 'em in a dug-out,/ And the library expressed its annoyance." *The Cantos of Ezra Pound* (London: Faber and Faber, 1960), xvi, p. 75.

[11] Patricia Rae, *The Practical Muse: Pragmatist Poetics in Pound, Hulme, and Stevens* (Cranbury, NJ: Associated University Presses, 1997), p. 79.

[12] *BLAST* 1, p. 48.

[13] In fact it isn't too excessive to claim that Pound was seeking to get his unmentionables into print, unmolested by the thick black line of censorial emendation, since "contes" is an act of self-censorship which serves only to draw attention to the fact that the word which is emended shares its root – testere, to witness – with testicle.

[14] *Letters of Ezra Pound, 1907-1941*, ed. by D.D. Paige (London: Faber and Faber, no date), letter 103, p. 141.

[15] Ibid, p. 140.

[16] From a letter from Pound, in which he reports on Eliot's Holiday. Eliot "walked into his landlady's bedroom, 'quite by mistake', said he was looking for his wife. Landlady unconvinced." Cited in Humphrey Carpenter, *A Serious Character: The Life of Ezra Pound* (London: Faber, 1988), p. 264.

[17] Hobson, *Imperialism*, 1st ed. 1902 (Ann Arbor, MI: University of Michigan Press, 1965), p 157.

[18] Nietzsche's comments occur in the dedicatory Preface of his *The Birth of Tragedy*. "But perhaps such readers will find it offensive that an aesthetic problem should be taken so seriously – assuming they are unable to consider art more than a pleasant sideline, a readily dispensable tinkling of bells that accompanies the 'seriousness of life…'" *The Birth of Tragedy/The Case of Wagner*, trans. By Walter Kaufmann (New York. NY: Vintage, 1967), p. 16.

[19] Marx, *Wage Labour and Capital*, available at http://www.marxists.org/archive/marx/works/1847/wage-labour/index.htm. [accessed 13/03/2012].

[20] *Ira Quid, Quid 13* (Cambridge, 2005). *Ira Quid* is unpaginated. Most of the quotation in what follows will be from its pages, but though I will make it clear from which poet I am quoting, my intention is to provide a discussion of the issue as a whole, and as such references will typically forgo conventionalities such as poem titles, line numbers, etcetera.

[21] *The poetry is not in the pity* (London: yt communication, 2009).

[22] Sutherland, *A Short Critique of Pacifism*, http://www.arras.net/circulars/archives/000212.html [accessed 28/02/2012]

[23] Justin Katko, "On 'Song of the Wanking Iraqi'", *Cambridge Literary Review* (2, 2010). Katko's reading of Sutherland's poem is not only one of the most detailed yet to be written; it is one of the most detailed readings; an exceptionally ambitious attempt to determine just to what extent the meaning that a reading discloses is capable of being desired. It deserves a longer discussion than can be attempted here, and so this note must instead function merely as a homage.

[24] Prynne quoted in Keston Sutherland, "To The Honourable Ambassador Confer Blanck (On Poetry and Stupidity in General)", *Quid* 18 (2007). Heine, "Preface" to the French Edition of *Lutèce*, "The Future Belongs to the Communists" Available at http://www.marxists.org/reference/archive/heine/lutece/preface.htm [accessed 29/02/2012]

[25] The relevant edition is Arghiri Emmanuel, *Unequal Exchange* (New York, NY: Monthly Review Press, 1972).

[26] The idea that the "first heave" was made against the English pentameter is of course Pound's. It occurs in Canto 81. *The Cantos of Ezra Pound* (New York, NY: New Directions, 1975), p. 518.

[27] Or, as Sean Bonney writes: "But remember, most poetry is mimetic of what some square thinks is incomprehensible, rather than an engagement with it." *Four Letters Four Comments* (Scarborough, ME: Punch Press: 2011), unpaginated.

[28] *Virgil's* Aeneid *Translated by John Dryden*, ed. by F. M Keener (London: Penguin, 1997), Bk.I, ll. 424-27, p. 13.

[29] Jarvis, *The Unconditional* (Cambridge: Barque Press, 2004).

[30] Luxemburg, *The Mass Strike, the Political Party and the Trade Unions*, trans. by Patrick Levan, ch. 4, "The Interaction of the Political and the Economic Struggle",

available at http://www.marxists.org/archive/luxemburg/1906/mass-strike/ [accessed 29/02/2012]

[31] William Hazlitt, "Why Distant Objects Please" in *Table-Talk* 2 vols (London: 1824), vol 2, p. 220. Engels' chapter on "The Great Towns" of England is in *The Condition of the Working-Class in England* in Marx-Engels *Collected Works*, 50 vols (London: Lawrence and Wishart, 1975–2005), vol 4.

Alex Pestell

"All in for folly and mustard":
Pound, Zukofsky, and *Word is Born*

This is a brief study of *Word is Born* (2006), Michael Kindellan and Reitha Pattison's slim collection of translations of the troubadour poet Bertran de Born (c.1140–c.1215), preceded by a sketch of some of the possible precursors to its authors' approach to literary translation. Bertran de Born is perhaps best known to readers of contemporary poetry as one of the figures behind the histrionic self-fashioning of Ezra Pound's early personae (see Makin 42). In fact, Pound's direct poetic engagement with de Born is limited to five poems: "Na Audiart" (1908), a poem inspired by de Born's *canso* "dompna, puois de mi no·us cal", and a translation of this poem (1914); "Planh for the Young English King" (1909), a translation of a poem falsely attributed to de Born; "Sestina — Altaforte" (1909), an original poem drawing from de Born's oeuvre; and "Near Perigord" (1915), a Browningesque essay in historical reconstruction. They constitute only a minor contribution to Pound's vast collection of translations and versions from Occitan, Anglo Saxon, Chinese, Latin, Greek, German, French, and Italian. But phrases and cadences from Pound's versions of de Born echo through his work, and they donate to subsequent literary translation an abiding habit of thought—one in which the recreation of a historical *cors* (petrified by a historiographical tradition) is believed to be enabled by crafted music impassioned by a unique *cor*.[1] Crucial to his exercises, Pound always insisted, is the transmission of knowledge through a surfeit of sensuous detail. Accuracy is not prized highly in these translations. The obloquy heaped on "Homage to Sextus Propertius", for example, is now a treasured chapter in its history. James Laughlin is eager to point out some of Pound's "schoolboy boners": "sitiens" (thirsty)—"sitting"; "vota" (vows)—"vote"; "fugantes" (putting to flight)— "fleeing"; 'vela' (sails)— 'veil", followed by

the PRIZE, the *grand* prize!

"Cimbrorumque minas et benefacta Mari"

(roughly: "the threat of Cimbrian invasion and Marius' public service and the profit in defeating them")

"Welsh mines and the profit Marus had out of them"   (481)

Similar "boners" adorn "The Seafarer" (Pound translates "byrig" [towns] as "berries", "wrecan" [to make] as "reckon", and so on). The glee with which Laughlin acclaims Pound's mistranslation of Propertius is indicative of a more general distaste for pedantry deriving from Pound's criticism of the American academic system, the "beaneries" which favour specialisation over the holistic treatment of symptomatic historical and cultural vortices (a predisposition to self-education recurs in another American translator of Occitan, Paul Blackburn). Pound's homophonic transference of "minas" (which, admittedly, survives in the English "minatory") into "mines" recognises an ineliminable acoustic kinship whose embrace must be the initial *point de repère* for the non-specialist reader (see Sullivan 101). At the same time the line refuses pedantry a little too ostentatiously, like a public schoolboy's pun, a supercilious joke that hints at the "Cambrian" submerged in the movement from "Cimbrorum" to "Welsh". Mental gears shift with each word choice—sense is plundered from various regions of the experience of thinking, a *soissebutz* or borrowed meaning like de Born's "dompna soisseubuda" (as Pound calls her) in "dompna, puois de mi no' us cal".[2]

Perhaps the best-known work to have taken up the implications of Pound's creative mistranslations is Louis and Celia Zukofsky's *Catullus*. Zukofsky's approach to writing bottomed on a sense of language as rule-driven, and his *Catullus* is a game bound by particularly demanding laws: as Zukofsky put it in the Translator's Preface, his version "follows the sound, rhythm, and syntax of his Latin—tries, as is said, to breathe the 'literal' meaning with him" (243). Literally literal, for as Burton Hatlen points out, the approximation is not only of meaning but of the length, sound, and quantity of syllables in every line (349). The homophonic approach revivifies the syllables of the original text, and metastasises metaphors latent in the source: Hatlen's example, from song 32, shows how "I'm a bow", which translates "Amabo", overcomes its initial conceptual distance from the source word to emerge in the ithyphallic image at the end of Catullus' poem (Hatlen usefully reminds us that "[a]nyone who has ever seen an erect penis knows that it is a "bow" in at least three senses" [351]).

The results are sometimes close to the original sense. In song 12, "ioco atque uino" (Catullus 256) becomes, naturally enough, "joke or wine" (Zukofsky 251). In this case there is a legible relaxation of Zukofsky's prosodic obbligato, words in the translation slipping onto adjacent lines at the behest of the sense made by the original sentence, rather than of the acoustic properties of the Latin. At other times, though, the crush of syllables nudges immediate sense to one side. Catullus' "quodcumque agit", from song 39, is now "code come quack it", although "renidet" is permitted to retain its sense in "he grins it". Zukofsky's molossus drains the Latin of its semantic specificity, perhaps acknowledging the ease with which Latin words like *quidquid, ubicumque* and *quodcumque* acquire an uncanny sound life of their own, a code quacked by the language with little regard to meaning. The next words in the Latin ("hunc habet morbum" [Catullus 270]) are rendered as "Hunk, a bit more bum" (Zukofsky 263). Here it's possible to discern, on the high road from "habet morbum" to "a bit more bum", the opportunist on the *qui vive* for the puerile, a site where the classicist can ostentatiously disclose his impish spirit, the modernist his intimacy with the archaic history of intimate verse. Modern verse translation post-Zukofsky often registers this compaction of impulses—the recognition of the necessity to brush the dust of Melville's "sub-sub-librarian" from classics bowdlerised by bored familiarity, to pre-empt accusations of ink-pot lucubrations with the groan-worthy "hunc" / "Hunk", and to solicit judgements like Alan Brownjohn's "ultimately silly" as a marker of the ceremonious hierarchies of propriety operative in the production and reception of poetry.[3] But the approach also affords opportunities for innovation: unfolding unconscious implications, taking the ancient as springboard for reflection upon the contemporary, and upon the practice of verse translation itself.

Michael Kindellan and Reitha Pattison's *Word is Born* is a collection of parallel translations of eight poems by Bertran de Born. The originals are not present: instead Pattison's and Kindellan's translations of the same source poem occupy facing pages, inviting comparisons between their approaches and speculation as to the source that could inspire such divergent interpretations. The homophonic principle can be seen at work throughout *Word Is Born*, but is combined with feigned or unfeigned guesses, near misses, calques and distant excursions from the original. Often the transportation of meaning from the source to the destination text is legible on a line-by-line basis. Often, stanzas morph in the transition from de Born's to Kindellan and Pattison's verse forms, making avenues that now open on the Occitan original, now on some other, entirely new vista.

Take this, from de Born's "Un sirventes on motz non faill". I quote it first in parallel with Kindellan's translation.

Anz viu a guisa de coart,
    et es tant ples de nuailla
greu m'es qan l' autra gens se part,
    et el s'esten e badailla.
	What guise, then, and what heart. Nuance
	grooming the non plus is part-'n-parcel of
	estaminet babble. Vile knots belabour

	and by dint, a somnambular gargle is for the greater good.
Guillem de Gordon, fol bataill avetz mes dinz vostre sonaill – et eu am vos, si Dieus mi gart.[4]	("Songs Three", 6)

Kindellan extracts "guise" straightforwardly from its root "guisa": attire (with a range of connotation reaching from the necessary protection of the human body to the wilful artifice of self-fashioning) *and* a manner of living, a *modus operandi*. Homophony and sense coincide here, as they often must: part of the cunning of this method is the evidential plausibility of its guise. This permits the straightforward handshake of a *faux ami* in "coart", where schoolboy French hands over "coeur" even to the beaneried mind awake to such traps. The decision to retain or discard the proffered error is then, perhaps, contingent on the translator's taste for a language-use that thinks as much in acoustic anamnesis as according to a model of utilitarian communicability, each involving different kinds of "[n]uance". Nuance (in the sense of shades of meaning prized by ordinary language theorists, words as *oilettes* through which to target gradations of human behaviour) is ceremoniously trampled in the rendering of "nuailla". But nuance as musical modulation within a predetermined spectrum retains its relevance here, particularly in the ceremony of *Word is Born*, one part of which is to replace by hook or by crook with radically French vocabulary de Born's source vocables (so that, for instance, "s'esten e" becomes "estaminet"). Translation in this guise creates a lexical cloud (*nuance* from Old French *nue* deriving from Latin *nubes*) that dissolves to recreate phonetic and conceptual shades that vary in sharpness and hue. So "Guillem de Gordon" harshly becomes the opportunistic sophomore gag "Vile knots", any pretence to accuracy discarded in the refusal even to transfer an intact proper name. And later, "somnambular gargle"—which seems to derive from the two end-words "sonaill" and "gart"—affects with its guttural murmuration to encompass the (to the non-Occitan speaker) garbled and gargled monosyllables of the final line: "et eu am vos, si Dieus mi gart". Here a prismatic, approximate homophony takes us far from the source meaning, but simultaneously articulates an *ars poetica* which, in its evocation of good-humoured bodily exertion, keeps pace with the spirit of de Born's (and, the poem's dedication implies, Stephen Rodefer's) own poetic practice: "Vile knots belabour // and by dint, a somnambular gargle is / for the greater good".

Here is an overlapping passage, with Pattison's translation:

Guillem de Gordon, fol bataill	William, crazy pugilist
avetz mes dinz vostre sonaill –	with me at our last rout
et eu am vos, si Dieus mi gart.	we'll battle again, if God keeps me.
Pero per fol e per musart	Perowne, equally all in for folly and mustard,
vos tenon d'esta fermailla	how your mortise closed hard on
li dui vescomt' et es lor tart	The dewy viscount and that tart of a page
que siatz en lor batailla.[5]	who would sit on his old battle wound.

("Method Number One", 5)

This excerpt is characteristic of Pattison's approach in its more piebald patterning, which alternates fidelity, and homophonic supplements, to de Born's source. At times, an imaginable context is retained (as in the first three lines above, where loyalty in battle is a recognisable ethical commonplace in troubadour poetry) even if the translation apes Pound's plausible blunders. At others, as in the succeeding four lines, though Pattison cleaves closer to the original than Kindellan, convulsive excursions into the unfamiliar make of de Born's implicit morality a sticky uneven texture. "But" for "Pero" could well have been drawn from a knowledge of contemporary Spanish, but Pattison opts instead for the obscure "Perowne", perhaps the "square Base of stone or mettall, some fiue or six foot high, whereon" the *OED* records in a citation from Randle Cotgrave, *A dictionarie of the French and English tongues*, "in old time, Knights errant placed some discourse, challenge, or proofe, of an aduenture". De Born's perron, his challenge and proof of an adventure, is this poem, which, situated in the warm glow of a successful operation securing his property from his brother's depredations, boasts that not a word misses its target, and complains of the unceasing labour of battle (as Pattison puts it, "Every day contentious and over a barrel"). But in *Word is Born*, words miss targets, or hit rather different targets, all the time, driven by other principles than sculpt the metaphorical massy *perowne* according to solid Poundian precepts ("each block cut smooth and well fitting" [Pound, *Cantos* 229]). *This* perron is "equally all in for folly and mustard": game for the messy but accurate translation that adds the wagging "-ly" to "fol", and for the rejection of yet another (after *perowne*) possible display of erudition (the *OED* tells us that "musart" comes into English as "musard" thanks to Richard Coeur de Lion, otherwise known by de Born as "Sir Yes-and-no" [Pound, *Spirit* 45]) in favour of the homophonic "mustard", which we are positively invited to lick up after the volley of lateral consonants our tongues flick out for in "equa*lly* all ... fo*lly*". Similarly, accuracy and pungent error combine in the alchemical transformation of the two viscounts to "The dewy viscount and that tart of a page", where de Born's enmities are still in place but melted into a far more labile substance.

De Born's song "Nostre seingner somonis el mezeis"—translated in Pattison's "mon Archy" and Kindellan's "Songs Five"—occupies the aftermath of a struggle during which a multilateral alliance of Western powers (having struck a temporary truce) launched a third crusade against the sultanate of Saladin, who had captured "the True Cross... and the king" ("la vera cros, e·l reis").[6] Debatably this pair of translations contains, deliberately or not, the highest frequency of identical or near-identical misidentifications. De Born begins

> Nostre seingner somonis el mezeis
> totz los ardiz e·ls valens e·ls presatz[7]

In Pattison this becomes: "From the mezzanine / our evening's atonal crooner / summons his lost ardour / for the covalent present"; in Kindellan: "Its dour ownership drew up all the old mezzanine / cause of loss that ardour in equivalence went presto!" (9-10). In both, "mezeis" becomes "mezzanine": architecturally conceived of as hovering between two floors, our lord (traditionally identified as Henry II [see Kastner 197-8]) becomes a kind of muezzin in Pattison's translation, where a sense of regularity imbues "our evening's atonal crooner" with a ritual quality. In both, "los" is homophonically misidentified with "loss"/"lost", the definite article ("los") drowned in the transference from the adjectival noun "ardiz" to the floating "ardour". Both writers take "valens" and exchange it for words which borrow different shades from its Latin root, "covalent" insisting on the power in *valere*, "equivalence" emphasising a potential parity of worth or value. Comparison of power and value between two sundered parts (the double relation implied in co- and equi-) is central to these poems, and to their relation to de Born's original. Tim Morris observes that Pattison's poem "carefully splits its title into 'mon Archy'. This would seem to imply that where the suffix of government is ironised, the speaker's acceptance of the feudal status quo is suspended" (n.pag.). This split continues through the architecture of both poems, as a mezzanine splits floors, Christian kings become muezzins, definite articles are lost, and "valens" loses its valency. As Kindellan has it, at least one kind of equivalence goes "presto!" Another arrives, though, in the coincidence, already noted, of Pattison's and Kindellan's word choices in this poem. The lost equivalence both seem to be intent on is, arguably, that inherent in the signifying practices of the Church Militant. De Born warns

> e·l sepulcres a de secors fraitura
> don tuit crezem, ab leial fe segura,
> que lo sainz fuecs i deisen.

This is translated by Paden et al as: "and help is needed at the Sepulcher, where, as we all believe with true and certain faith, the holy fire descends". A note informs us that this alludes to "the belief that on Easter Day the tapers on the Holy Sepulchre were kindled by a fire from Heaven": an Eucharistic equivalence of spirit and matter (387). Fractures discerned in the monarchy and, by extension, the symbology of Christianity (the true cross) "no succour or strength / of deontic cream can suture", in Pattison's translation. A more hysterical rendering emerges from Kindellan:

Don't you think it crazy that I modelled the scream
of labial separation from one sanctified fuck, man?

"[C]rezem" (belief) becomes "crazy": not any belief, but the belief that the
pain of childbirth ("labial" taken cross-eyed from "ab leial")[8] stands in some
pattern of equivalence for an original sin, a sin which is only redeemed by the
conception of Christ by the Holy Spirit. The signifying practices that originate
in such concepts are now peculiarly void of efficacity—an "armless parade /
of semaphore"—but belong to a tradition to which we are still "beholden",
a "charade that we're locked and loathed and rooting for". Other polemical
points are legible in the mistranslations common to both translators. Most
obvious is Kindellan and Pattison's rendering of "no-bateiatz" ("unbaptized")
as "Non-Combatants" (in Pattison's version) and "non-combatants" (in
Kindellan's version). Kindellan's "Christian non-combatants" are "in the
dell / beholden of the armless parade / of semaphore": we in whose name
war is conducted "on several fronts" without our having to do much but
sit around "all puckered with empathy". Hovering between cynicism, anger
and obstreperous excitement, the poems' voices rattle across an irascible
spectrum of provocation and despair in the gutter between the two versions,
occasionally picking up the shadow of a critical perspective, as when, in
Pattison's poem, a contrast is almost implied between the "Christians and
Non-Combatants", suggesting the identification of the non-violent with
the invaded populace of the Middle East. Their political positions do not
admit of a unifying perspective—they're borrowed from the disorder of
our perception of the *cors* of de Born's history—a conjectured movement
from war-mongering youth to contemplative monastic maturity—filtered
through the *cor* of the authors' own compromised relations to the body
politic. Mock-cantabile lines such as Kindellan's "s'il vous plais, / put out the
fire in my car / sez me in the fez" confirm a bilious detachment chastising
itself for its "mellifluous aorta" (in Pattison's words) ("Songs Eight", "Le
Bateleur", 17-8).

Clarities and opacities in *Word is Born* constitute a scratched, crosshatched
lens that dulls, refracts and intensifies signals from de Born's poems. These
scrambled gleams of monarchy and anarchy emerge as tributary to the
original texts:

GOD DEPUNCTUATES HARD FISTS
MASQUES ARE PENNED IN ANARCHY
KISMET IS LABIAL; A COMMON SAP

so the messages went.

("Seven", 15)[9]

In lines such as these of Pattison's, the authority of Geoffrey II, Duke of Brittany's' lady is imbued with an uncanny oracular menace with which it's difficult not to associate the enduring yet attenuated voice of old texts in the ears of their translators. The borrowed poems contained in *Word is Born* emblematise the inaccessible processes through which thoughts prompted by long-dead authors coalesce into words in the here and now. In his essay on the collection, Ian Patterson notes how "the private or contingent associations or promptings that fill in the gaps between words or thoughts that spring up from translation or transformation won't usually turn up, so we have to track them through their distorted obverse in our own reading experiences" (350). These translations, following Zukofsky and Pound, almost thematise this distortion, making the private public in an oblique ceremony of lexical adjudication liberated from the codices of traditional literary translation. So, for example, we have a line such as "e·m fai de mos arbres issart" ("and cut my timber") (de Born 122-3), wherein de Born thunders against his plundering enemies, rendered by Kindellan (with hilarious understatement) as "Erm, you make the most of trees" ("Songs Three", 6).

Here the interpunct drops out of play and is replaced by our modern transliteration of a similarly subsemantic gargle; this "Erm" might be interpreted as a pantomimed *cheville*, a confessional vocable admitting ignorance, a grunt sounding the guesswork performed, at times, in Pound's translations. It stands for the private, cloudy processes by which a word in the source is transfigured into an entirely new word in the destination language (imagine that "Erm" stretched into a magnified, granular surface by turns obliterating and amplifying the source text).

> The ennui of a Homeric villanelle
> can be delivered in an amusing
> indistinguishable Walloon gabble
> or have the touch of Midas
> if called forth in the voluble
> Gasconian twang, or Bretton,
> some high-falutin argot.
> Despite my asthmatic Schwabian
> song, it's still more sonorous than
> the paucity of any soapy Lombardy
> vulgarisms. Limoges has a fine
> early slang : silica falling over Jaffa oranges.

("Seven", 15)

"It is mainly for the sake of the melopoeia that one investigates troubadour poetry" (Pound, *ABC* 52). These are not, finally, poetries of self-defilement, for all their self-conscious displays of wilful, delirious compromise. Their cadences display a microscopic syllabic focus suggesting extreme pleasure in the choices made available to the translator when freed from the literal as conventionally understood. It is a manumission which, however, still leaves the translator shackled to, and newly reminded of, the opportunities, the true and false friends, made available in her native tongue: "To me is my heart's achiral spec thus returned" ("Songs Four", 8).

Notes

[1] I borrow these terms from Jacques Roubaud's study of the troubadours, *La fleur inverse*, 243-4: "From the singer's heart the canso goes towards the lady's body. It flies from the *cor* to the *cors*. ...She is put into rags by gazes and desires, reconstituted as more beautiful by the rhymes".

[2] See Pound, *The Spirit of Romance*, 47, and Roubaud, *La fleur inverse*, 244: "Each real domna gives to the lady sung by the cansos a bit of her body to build the *soissebutz* body present in all the songs".

[3] Hatlen quotes Brownjohn's review of *Catullus* in the *New Statesman* 78 (Aug 1, 1969), 151: "knotted, clumsy, turgid and ultimately silly" (qtd. 349).

[4] "He lives like a coward, and he's so full of flab it pains me when he stretches and yawns while the others ride out. Guillem de Gordon, you've put a dead clapper in your bell, so I love you, God keep me." *The Poems of the Troubadour Bertran de Born*, 122-5.

[5] "Guillem de Gordon, you've put a dead clapper in your bell, so I love you, God keep me. But the two viscounts take you for a fool and a dolt because of your treaty, and they think it's high time for you to be in their army".

[6] "Nostre seingner somonis el mezeis", *Poems of the Troubadour Bertran de Born*, 386-7. See the editors' introduction to this song, 384-5.

[7] "Our lord himself summons all the spirited and the worthy and the noble".

[8] See Blackburn, *The Journals*, 129: "Overtones are constantly being lost. Let him [the translator] approach polysemia crosseyed, coin in hand".

[9] For the original see "seigner en coms, a blasmar", *Poems of the Troubadour Bertran de Born*, 226-9.

Works Cited

Blackburn, Paul. *The Journals*. Ed. Robert Kelly. Santa Barbara, CA: Black Sparrow Press, 1975.

———. *Proensa: An Anthology of Troubadour Poetry*. Ed. George Economou. Berkeley, CA: University of California Press, 1978.

Catullus, Gaius Valerius. *The Poems of Catullus: A Bilingual Edition*. Trans. Peter Whigham. Berkeley, CA: University of California Press, 1966.

de Born, Bertran. *The Poems of the Troubadour Bertran de Born*. Ed. William D. Paden, Jr., Tilde Sankovitch and Patricia H. Stäblein. Berkeley, CA: University of California Press, 1986.

Hatlen, Burton. "Zukofsky as Translator". *Louis Zukofsky: Man and Poet*. Ed. Carroll F. Terrell. Orono, ME: National Poetry Foundation, 1979. 345-64.

Kastner, L.E. "Notes on the Poems of Bertran de Born: V". *Modern Language Review* 32.2 (1937): 169-221.

Kindellan, Michael and Reitha Pattison. *Word is Born*. Cambridge: Arehouse, 2006.

Laughlin, James. "Ezra Pound's Propertius". *Sewanee Review* 46.4 (1938): 480-91.

Makin, Peter. *Provence and Pound*. Berkeley, CA: University of California Press, 1978.

Morris, Tim. "Counterstrokes". *Jacket* 31 (2006). Web. 13 November 2012.

Patterson, Ian. "Born Again, Born Better: Text Generation and Reading Strategies in Michael Kindellan and Reitha Pattison, *Word is Born*". *Complicities: British Poetry 1945-2007*. Ed. Robin Purves and Sam Ladkin. Prague: Litteraria Pragensia, 2007. 341-51.

Pound, Ezra. *The Spirit of Romance*. New York, NY: New Directions, 1952.

——. *ABC of Reading*. London: Faber, 1961.

——. *The Cantos*. New York, NY: New Directions, 1993.

Roubaud, Jacques. *La fleur inverse: Essai sur l'art informel des troubadours*. Paris: Ramsay, 1987.

Sullivan, J.P. *Ezra Pound and Sextus Propertius: A Study in Creative Translation*. London: Faber, 1964.

Zukofsky, Louis. *Complete Short Poetry*. Baltimore, MD and London: Johns Hopkins University Press, 1991.

Tim Atkins

Happiness / The Art of Poetry
— Being a translation of the 10 Buddhist
Ox-Herding Poems

My daughter, my daughter, what can I say
Of living?
I cannot judge it.
　　—George Oppen 'Of Being Numerous'

*

Because poetry &

　　thinking about it

Phrased in personal terms & based in cooperation　　collaboration　even

　　　　The building of a personal poetry empire　　　I reject utterly

he said

& with it the idea that a poem can be owned

Ted Berrigan sent back his MA with the note that he was the master of no art

It　　　closes　　　it　　　　　　the way that I encloses everything

The length of the thought is the distance between the thinker &
enlightenment

In itself an act of on-going revision & restatement

If reading a poem explains everything you have misread it

　　　　Only occasionally would he answer Allen

　In Venice　　When there was a drop in beard weight

　　　At the 6th International

　　　Concrete Poetry Karaoke Competition

**

In *Canto 1*   Duke Ellington goes in search of it

Coming across the Chinese with so many ear-rings & cigarettes that the poems
leak   In a letter to *The Times* of London

The ant covers more ground than the buffalo he said Given infinite time I
MIGHT be able to read a Chinese poem   he said

They have replaced Gaudier-Brzeska's studio in Fulham with a movie house

They have replaced poetry & the manifesto with the grant proposal & by-pass

                —For to write in such a manner shows conclusively that
the writer thinks from books

Convention &   Cliché   & not from life   he said

                                        & why not—   for this is a
manifestation of love—   also—he said

            What's left for me to do?   I want a poetry of immedi-
ate experience   open community & contradiction

                I seek refuge   with the mischief of created things

Pu Ling-En / Jesus   let me be clear in my opposition   to all forms
of kabbala

            It is necessary to any originality to have the courage to
be an amateur

Only Impalas & Koalas   Cannot—

                (IMPERATIVE)   Escape   Samsara

***

They found penicillin by fucking it up   in a dish   & this beautiful method

Red wet & chaotic   wildly in love with the processes of living   at the knee points & elbows   he said

The way to read a poem is to be it   he said   confusing & not caring   two poems for just one

Bullet point   ideological swatches   from   Many social sectors of his own society & an immense variety of other cultures

He did not fall in love   like Dr Foster   with 3 local odes from Poundland

He said   this complex   polyvocal   textuality   was the result of his search

Tooting you have given me nothing & now I am everything

Sexual repression   manifested as a series of pamphlets   & masquerading as political pronouncements

In *The Salo Cantos*   he says   before lapsing into silence   How is it possible to be upon this earth & not   Love   some or at least   one living   ant or warm daughter

Instead of losing both

 In a dictionary   he said

Everything she owns   I bought her   Everything   She knows I taught her

Fellow Poets—   Concerning modes of contemporary practice   —This is-CLEARLY

An Unsustainable Position

****

I have never read a political poetry that I could not manage   he said   But
I have stepped in some—in it

Issa wrote at the time the information in *The Cantos* was common
knowledge

It pleases the author & insects   attracted to surprise   & this heat   In at or
behind the state capitol

Beardless boys & tea   SKIPPING!   what you don't understand

I have never read a political poetry   he said   I could make Thomas
swallow

EMOTIONAL as well as intellectual acquaintance   & swooning at corners

You cannot read without glasses   he said   political means

Misreading "glasses" for "classes"

Because the heart is always open unless you hammer it

& this is also my understanding   political means

                    How   d.a.levy changed Cleveland   HOW

Osip Mandelstam

        Changed

Stalin

*****

Even now if I manage to get back into Guido's skin   he said

English poetry is a suburban sport which saves only itself when it crosses over a significant

Body of water   He said   to translate is to trade   & not to betray

He said one says   intelligence in poetry is as useful as large breasts in the bedroom   T.S.Eliot said

     & with the words scarcely uttered one ceases to be that thing

 It has fucked itself in the ass so many times that its children are   he said

Hobnobs sausages & steppers-in-buckets   repeatedly   rummaging in DUST   in the closet

In need of a season at the beach   in a book called *Personae* & not-being-Walt casting off   as it were   fear of women   the erasure of violence   the outlaw-ing of chaos & curiosity   —*A Woman's Poetry!*   —in which we are all lovers

Hate he said is the power to see the dissimilar in the similar   THENThe Invisible Man!   With his hair cut straight across his forehead

Where / Who / What

(I enter the pelt from a different angle)

The fuck IS Ralph Hawkins

The way to get famous is   two verbs at the end of this poem

     pound / & browning

******

The composition of a poem   he says   it says here

Koto I think you should   He continues

The thing that matters in art is

Koto I think   A force

Transfusing welding and unifying

    & its opposite   for   We who love

Cucumbers   Shortenings   cross-cuts   implications

The real poem contains

At this point the poet imagines a holy Swiss cheese

So Many Gaps   A Happy Language

That SALVATION   without the concept of sin

On the map of all futures

        he said either

Flies out   or   flies in

****

In his avoidance of the canon

In(sane)sects grow with the same rhythm as big organizations   I have driven away from   & towards them

For example the poem of the footnote   the poem of the cockroach chewing   the poem of the impossible   language

Interfering with cigars & cigarillos   in Rapallo   made out of image & sound   light—as—language

The pointy beard says something like   Sudden Liberation! & the other one   after   happiness

When the emotions illuminate the perceptive powers   THE TASK OF POETRY TODAY IS TO—   (sigh)

—*YOU DECIDE*—   (or—

As if he was collaging the whole of his knowledge into his translations

(a) A work of   unintentional   genius   misunderstanding & accident

(b) Aesthetically tainted   disingenuous   gauche / even —& therefore unworthy of discussion

(c) What?   I spit   on   & miss   your position

(d) Like a flower—inconsequential but amusing

 In Chinese poetry the fixed observer is removed

& everything has permission

****

Concerning the master-slave relationship

I am reminded of

A long weekend at Key West with Peter & John

Waking up   inside a couple of Miami Dolphins

To gain insight into   my 17th thesis*

Wanting to have his cake & eat it   which equals   the truest way to get
through it

A noun does not exist in nature   things are only the terminal points

Any vocabulary is a faux-vocabulary   You Klutz a flaming email does not
constitute direct action

Concerning the wave of recent disputes in Armenian poetry

I am bending over the stove of peace   it is large & inviting   & I
am happy

O! Pu Ling-En—

In your red silk chemise

All language is a dialect with tanks

I roll through the world   & it rolls over ~~thee~~ me

****

The way to liberate English poetry   he says   is   Koto   Victor Hugo says

You should not be allowed to write a book before you have read   1500 of

them   So Do So   Too

SO—

Abandon

All Stupid

Suburban

Prejudice   ///// he said ////// & I am off of *that* list—

///// Leaving philosophy & black eye-liner   FOR poetry

 Because

HAPPINESS   —*over 200 haiku on frogs)*

IS   —*& 50 on snails) —90 on cicada) —150 on mosquitos) — & 97 on fle*

as)   —I MEAN!!!!!!—

Is THE

Is The ONLY   happiness

HAPPINESS IS THE ONLY ECONOMY

****

Intellectuals are rebels, not revolutionaries
César Vallejo

Poetry, you know—well, of course
Marcel Proust

There is no enlightenment outside of daily life
Thich Nhat Hanh

Biographical Notes

Tim Atkins is the author of *Horace* (O Books), *1000 Sonnets* (if p then q), *Petrarch* (four volumes – Barque, Book Thug, and Crater Presses), *Folklore* (Salt Publishing), and *Honda Ode* (a Japanese translation of *On the Road*, published by Oystercatcher Press). Editor of the long-running online poetry journal *onedit*, he teaches at the University of East London and is London correspondent for *Lungful!* magazine.

Ryan Dobran is currently a Ph.D. candidate at the University of Cambridge, where he works on late twentieth-century British poetics. He co-edits *Glossator: Practice and Theory of the Commentary.* He has two collections of poetry forthcoming from Barque Press, and from Critical Documents.

Amy Evans is an Assistant Lecturer in English and Creative Writing at the University of Kent. She co-edited with Shamoon Zamir *The Unruly Garden: Robert Duncan and Eric Mottram, Letters and Essays* (Peter Lang, 2007). Her annotated transcription of Duncan's teaching bibliography for his classes on H.D. at the New College of California can be found in *The Journal of Cultural and Religious Theory* (10.2, Spring 2010). Her poetry publications include the chapbooks *Collecting Shells* (Oystercatcher Press, 2011) and *The Sea Quells* (Shearsman Books, 2013) and the multiply-authored collection with Nat Raha, Frances Kruk and Becky Cremin, *Viersome #1* (Veer, 2012). She is currently editing the letters of Robert Duncan and H.D.

Gareth Farmer is a poet and lecturer in English at the University of Bedfordshire. He specialises in modern and contemporary poetry and poetics and stylistics. His Ph.D., completed at the University of Sussex in 2011, was on the critical and creative writing of the poet Veronica Forrest-Thomson. He has published a number of articles on Forrest-Thomson and continues to work on a variety of projects involving her work. He is the senior academic consultant to the Veronica Forrest-Thomson Archive at Girton College, Cambridge. More broadly, Gareth is interested in theories of literary affect, particularly how these intersect with social and political identity formation. Most recently, Gareth contributed to a symposium on the poetry of F.T. Prince at the University of Southampton and published an essay on the Elizabethan novels of Anthony Burgess. Gareth's poetry has been widely published.

Allen Fisher is a poet, painter, publisher and art historian, and lives in Hereford. He is currently Emeritus Professor of Poetry & Art at Manchester Metropolitan University, where he was formerly Head of Contemporary Art. He has over 140 single-authored publications of poetry, graphics and art documentation to his name; most recently *PROPOSALS*, published in 2010. He contributed to performance work in the 1970s; exhibited in many shows from Fluxus Britannica,

Tate Britain, to his own retrospective at the King's Gallery, York. Examples of his work are in the Tate Collection, the Living Museum, Iceland and various international private collections. His last one-person show was in October 2013. Check out www.allenfisher.co.uk.

Harry Gilonis is a poet, editor, publisher, and critic who has been reading *The Cantos* in a pro-am capacity since the mid-'70s. Not wholly relevantly, he played the part of Pound, a speaking rôle, in an avant-garde musical in the early '80s. Publication of his paper on Pound and the "China" Cantos for the London Cantos Reading Group is looming. He has been at work for some years now on *North Hills*, a project of "faithless" recastings of classical Chinese poetry – which turns out to be the most avant-garde writing up until L=A=N=G=U=A=G=E writing. The poems from *North Hills* included herein are mostly derived from the same originals as some of the poems in *Cathay* (with a few other early pieces of Ezro-Chinoiserie thrown in for good measure). Selections from *North Hills* have appeared in pamphlets and anthologies, including *Acacia Feelings* from Richard Parker's Crater Press, and in a full-length book, *eye-blink*, from Veer Books in London; his paper at a recent London conference on "Poetry and Revolution", on the Chinese revolutionary/poet Ch'iu Chin, is a sort-of-offshoot (www.bbk.ac.uk/cprc/events/Harry_Gilonis_-_Poetry_and_Revolution_conference_paper.pdf).

Robert Hampson is Professor of Modern Literature at Royal Holloway, University of London, where (among other things) he teaches on the MA in Poetic Practice. He is best known for his work on Joseph Conrad, which includes three monographs – *Joseph Conrad: Betrayal and Identity* (1992); *Cross-Cultural Encounters in Joseph Conrad's Malay Fiction* (2000) and *Conrad's Secrets* (2012) – as well as four editions and numerous articles, but he has also been involved with contemporary British and North American poetry as critic, editor and practitioner since the early 1970s. His most recent works in this area are *Frank O'Hara Now* (2011 – co-edited with Will Montgomery), *an explanation of colours* (Veer, 2011), *out of sight* (Crater, 2012) and *reworked disasters* (Knives Forks and Spoons Press, 2012).

Danny Hayward is a writer living in London. His poetry and critical writings can be found in books and journals such as *Veer*, *Mute*, and *World Picture*.

Alexander Howard recently completed an AHRC-funded D.Phil in American Literature. Entitled, "The Life and Times of Charles Henri Ford, *Blues*, and the Belated Renovation of Modernism" (2011), his thesis focused on American Surrealism, Modernist Little Magazines, and Queer Aesthetics and Poetics. He has published on modernist poetry, periodical culture, and contemporary American fiction. His work has appeared in *U.S. Studies Online* (Spring 2011), *Transgression and its Limits* (Newcastle: Cambridge Scholars Publishing, 2012), the second volume of the *Oxford Critical and Cultural History of Modernist Magazines* (Oxford: Oxford University Press, 2012), and is forthcoming in the *Journal of*

Modern Periodical Studies (2013). He is currently working on two projects. The first is a monograph on the queer second-generation modernist editor and Surrealist poet Charles Henri Ford; the second focuses on the relationship between far-right political extremism and Ezra Pound's pedagogy in the 1950s.

Laura Kilbride lives and works in Cambridge, where she is preparing a thesis on the poetry of A.C. Swinburne. With Rosa Van Hensbergen she co-edits *The Paper Nautilus*, the second issue of which contained unpublished poems by Grace Lake/Anna Mendelssohn. Her first pamphlet publication, *Errata,* came out from tipped press in 2011.

Joshua Kotin teaches in the English department at Princeton University. He is currently completing a book entitled *Private Utopias: Autonomy after Walden*. From 2005 to 2008, he was Editor of *Chicago Review*.

Tony Lopez is best known for his book *False Memory* (The Figures, 1996; 2nd ed., Shearsman Books, 2012), which samples and satirizes the fragmented language of commodity culture in modern Britain. His most recent collection is *Only More So* (UNO Press, 2011; Shearsman Books, 2012) the latest of 25 books of poetry, criticism and fiction. He has received awards from the Wingate Foundation, the Society of Authors, the Arts and Humanities Research Council and Arts Council England. His poetry is featured in *The Art of the Sonnet* (Harvard), *Twentieth-Century British and Irish Poetry* (Oxford), *Vanishing Points* (Salt), *The Reality Street Book of Sonnets* (Reality Street), *Other: British and Irish Poetry since 1970* (Wesleyan University Press) and *Conductors of Chaos* (Picador). His critical writings are collected in *Meaning Performance: Essays on Poetry* (Salt Publishing, 2006) and *The Poetry of W.S. Graham* (Edinburgh University Press, 1989). He taught for many years at the University of Plymouth and was appointed the first Professor of Poetry there in 2000 and Emeritus Professor in 2009. He currently works by commission on public art incorporating text. http://tonylopez.org.uk

Eric Mottram (1924-1995) lectured at King's College London where he was the UK's first full-time Professor of American Literature. Mottram co-founded the Institute of United States Studies in 1963, and, with Bob Cobbing, the *Poetry Information* series at the Institute of Contemporary Arts. As Editor of *Poetry Review* (1971-1977), Mottram coined the term "The British Poetry Revival," a movement in which he was a central figure. Mottram wrote over thirty volumes of poetry alongside his pioneering critical works on American and British modernist and contemporary writing, most notably *William Burroughs: the algebra of need* (1971) and *Allen Ginsberg in the Sixties* (1972). His library and papers are held in the Eric Mottram Collection at King's College London.

Richard Parker is a lecturer in the Department of American Studies at Dokuz Eylül University in Izmir, Turkey. He has written papers on Ezra Pound, Louis Zukofsky and other recent poetries in the USA and Britain. He is the editor and printer of the Crater pamphlet series and has had various books of his own poetry published, including *from The Mountain of California…* (Openned), *China* (Knives, Forks and Spoons Press), *The Traveller and the Defence of Heaven* (Veer) and *49* (Oystercatcher Press).

Alex Pestell has a Ph.D. on the work of Geoffrey Hill from the University of Sussex, and is the editor of John Wilkinson's selected poems, *Schedule of Unrest* (Salt Publishing, 2014).

Sean Pryor teaches English at the University of New South Wales, and is the author of *W. B. Yeats, Ezra Pound and the Poetry of Paradise*. He is currently at work on a book on the impossibility of redemption for and through modernist poetry.

Mark Scroggins lives and teaches in south Florida. He is the author of three books of poetry: *Red Arcadia* (2012), *Torture Garden: Naked City Pastorelles* (2011), and *Anarchy* (2003); a biography: *The Poem of a Life: A Biography of Louis Zukofsky* (2007); a critical monograph: *Louis Zukofsky and the Poetry of Knowledge* (1998); and numerous essays and reviews.

Gavin Selerie was born in London, where he still lives. He taught at Birkbeck, University of London for many years. His books include *Azimuth* (1984), *Roxy* (1996) and *Le Fanu's Ghost* (2006) – all long sequences with linked units. A Selected Poems, *Music's Duel*, was published by Shearsman Books in 2009. His work has appeared in anthologies such as *The New British Poetry* (1988), *Other: British & Irish Poetry since 1970* (1999) and *The Reality Street Book of Sonnets* (2008). His poems generally involve a layering of voices through history and landscape.

Robert Sheppard's long work *Twentieth Century Blues* was published by Salt. Other poetry collections are published by Shearsman Books, including a volume of fictional translations, *A Translated Man*, and by Knives, Forks and Spoons Press, including his book of stories, *The Only Life*. Professor of Poetry and Poetics at Edge Hill University, he has published criticism on British poetry widely, including *The Poetry of Saying* (Liverpool University Press, 2005).

Keston Sutherland is a British poet, and Professor of Poetics at the University of Sussex. His books of poetry include *The Odes to TL61P* (Enitharmon Press, 2013), *The Stats on Infinity* (Crater, 2010), *Stress Position* (Barque Press, 2009), *Hot White Andy* (Barque Press, 2007) and *Neocosis* (Barque Press, 2005). His critical work on Marx and poetry, *Stupefaction: a radical anatomy of phantoms*, was published by Seagull Books in May 2011.

David Vichnar is an editor, publisher, translator and critic from Prague, Czech Republic. He is author of *Joyce Against Theory* (2010) and co-editor, most recently, of *Praharfeast: James Joyce in Prague* (2012). He co-edits *VLAK* magazine, co-organises the annual Prague Poetry Microfestival, and manages Equus Press. His reviews and articles on contemporary experimental writers (Christine Brooke-Rose, the Oulipo group, or the Situationists), as well as translations of contemporary experimental poets, both Czech and Anglophone, have appeared in a number of magazines. He currently resides in Paris where he is completing his Ph.D. on Joyce and the post-war European avant-garde movements.

Juha Virtanen teaches at the University of Kent, where he has recently completed a study of innovative poetry and performance between 1950 and 1980. He has written conference papers and articles on Allen Fisher, Allen Ginsberg, Bill Griffiths, Charles Olson and others.